D1669094

Vulnerability to Poverty

Also by Stephan Klasen

ABSOLUTE POVERTY AND GLOBAL JUSTICE (*edited with E. Mack, T. Pogge and M. Schramm*)

DETERMINANTS OF PRO-POOR GROWTH: Analytical Issues and Findings from Country Cases (*edited with M. Grimm and A. McKay*)

POVERTY, INEQUALITY AND MIGRATION IN LATIN AMERICA (*edited with F. Nowak-Lehmann*)

POVERTY, INEQUALITY, AND POLICY IN LATIN AMERICA (*edited with F. Nowak-Lehmann*)

Also by Hermann Waibel

VEGETABLE PRODUCTION AND MARKETING IN AFRICA: Socio-Economic Research (*edited with Dagmar Mithofer*)

INTERNATIONAL RESEARCH ON NATURAL RESOURCE MANAGEMENT: Advances in Impact Assessment (*edited with D. Zilberman*)

Vulnerability to Poverty

Theory, Measurement and Determinants, with Case Studies from Thailand and Vietnam

Edited by

Stephan Klasen

and

Hermann Waibel

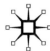

Editorial matter and selection © Stephan Klasen and Hermann Waibel 2013
Individual Chapters © Contributors 2013

All rights reserved. No reproduction, copy or transmission of this
publication may be made without written permission.

No portion of this publication may be reproduced, copied or transmitted
save with written permission or in accordance with the provisions of the
Copyright, Designs and Patents Act 1988, or under the terms of any licence
permitting limited copying issued by the Copyright Licensing Agency,
Saffron House, 6–10 Kirby Street, London EC1N 8TS.

Any person who does any unauthorized act in relation to this publication
may be liable to criminal prosecution and civil claims for damages.

The authors have asserted their rights to be identified as the authors of
this work in accordance with the Copyright, Designs and Patents Act 1988.

First published 2013 by
PALGRAVE MACMILLAN

Palgrave Macmillan in the UK is an imprint of Macmillan Publishers Limited,
registered in England, company number 785998, of Houndmills, Basingstoke,
Hampshire RG21 6XS.

Palgrave Macmillan in the US is a division of St Martin's Press LLC,
175 Fifth Avenue, New York, NY 10010.

Palgrave Macmillan is the global academic imprint of the above companies
and has companies and representatives throughout the world.

Palgrave® and Macmillan® are registered trademarks in the United States,
the United Kingdom, Europe and other countries.

ISBN: 978–0–230–24891–5

This book is printed on paper suitable for recycling and made from fully
managed and sustained forest sources. Logging, pulping and manufacturing
processes are expected to conform to the environmental regulations of the
country of origin.

A catalogue record for this book is available from the British Library.

A catalog record for this book is available from the Library of Congress.

10 9 8 7 6 5 4 3 2 1
22 21 20 19 18 17 16 15 14 13

Contents

Tables

Figures

Preface

While there is already a mature literature on poverty, its measurement and determinants in developing countries, from a policy perspective, it is at least as important to prevent future poverty as it is to combat existing poverty. But preventing poverty requires identifying households and individuals who are particularly prone to poverty, i.e. suffer from higher vulnerability to poverty. In recent years a theoretical literature has developed on how to conceptualize vulnerability to poverty, while empirical contributions have lagged behind. The contributions in this volume partly extend these conceptual questions, but primarily focus on empirical applications of the concept. In particular, we study the determinants of vulnerability, household coping strategies and possible policy responses to reduce vulnerability in Thailand and Vietnam. The findings of this volume are the results of a multi-year research programme on the 'Impact of Shocks on the Vulnerability to Poverty: Consequences for Development in Emerging Southeast Asian Economies', funded by the German Research Foundation (DFG). An important part of the research programme consisted of the generation and analysis of new and innovative data on vulnerability to poverty, using a panel household survey in six provinces of the two countries. Consequently, some of the contributions are also methodological, focusing on ways to measure and analyse vulnerability to poverty using survey data.

While some of the analysis and the messages are country-specific, we believe that the methodological, conceptual and empirical contributions in the volume will also be of interest to researchers and policy-makers who are concerned about vulnerability to poverty in other contexts.

Acknowledgements

As with many such research projects, this one has depended on the collaboration of many actors who have contributed to its success; this volume is the result of much effort by a large number of people who have contributed in one way or another.

First of all, we would like to thank the German Research Foundation (DFG) for generously funding the Research Group 756: 'Impact of Shocks on the Vulnerability to Poverty: Consequences for Development in Emerging Southeast Asian Economies' since 2006. We would like to particularly thank Dr. Patrizia Schmitz-Möller, who helped us all along the way from the pre-application in 2005 to the successful renewal application in 2009. We also would like to thank the DFG reviewers of the project, Professor Michael Kirk, Professor Elmar Kulke and Professor Martin Odening, who gave very helpful comments and suggestions.

Second, we would like to thank our partners in Thailand and Vietnam whose cooperation was critical to the implementation of this research programme. In particular we would like to thank our national coordinators for the data collection project, Dr. Suwanna Praneetvatakul from Kasetsart University in Thailand, as well as Drs. Dang Kim Son, Nguyen Do Anh Tuan and Phung Duc Tung from the Institute of Policy and Strategy for Agriculture and Rural Development (IPSARD). The heavy burden of data collection among the over 4000 households in some 400 villages rested on the shoulders of numerous provincial supervisors, team leaders and enumerators. All of them deserve tremendous thanks, but only some can be mentioned here. In Thailand these are Drs Piyatat Pananurak, Thanaporn Athipanyakun, Songporne Tongruksawattana and Ornsiri Rungruxsirivorn. Further, there are Theda Gödecke, Niratchara Kerdbanchan, Supanika Chanawirat, Pilaiwan Boonsin and Santichai Chevachaipimol. In Vietnam, we owe thanks to the following survey team leaders: Mai Cong Thanh, Nguyen Thi Thu Huong Nguyen Ba Trong, Nguyen Thi Thu Huong, Kieu Thi Nam, Vu Thi Kim Thu, Nguyen Hoai Nam and Tong Thanh Thinh.

The field teams were supported by Elena Groß, Iris Gönsch, Christina Grundstedt, Jens Krüger, Tobias Lechtenfeld, Felix Povel, Kai Mausch, Marc Völker and Vu Thi Hoa, who supported the survey work in both countries in a multitude of ways including developing the questionnaire, providing interviewer training or directly participating in the field work.

Data management and data cleaning was organized by Dr. Bernd Hardeweg, who deserves special thanks for all the programming work for the management of this huge amount of data. Mr. Jan Meier was instrumental in programming the data entry masks. Data cleaning was carried out by researchers and staff of the participating institutes in the research programme. Special thanks go here to Tobias Lechtenfeld, who worked particularly intensely on data cleaning and the construction of income and consumption aggregates.

We would like to thank colleagues and reviewers who provided informal comments at several of the project workshops as well as formal reports in the review stage of this edited volume. A word of thanks must also go to the editors' secretaries, Ms Renate Nause at Hannover and Ms Michaela Beckmann at Göttingen, who did much of the invisible work for this research programme.

Lastly, we would like to thank Katharina Trapp and Lea Strub for their excellent work in formatting the volume and dealing with all the complex logistical details of putting together such a book.

Contributors

Jürgen Brünjes is a research associate and lecturer at the Institute of Economic and Cultural Geography, Leibniz Universität Hannover, Germany. His research focuses on economic geography, rural labour markets and entrepreneurship in developing countries.

Bernd Hardeweg was involved in the research group as a post-doctoral research associate at Leibniz Universität Hannover, Germany. Equipped with country experience in Thailand and Vietnam, he was responsible for implementing data collection and management for three waves of the household survey. His research focuses on agricultural economics and rural development issues in Southeast Asia.

Vera Junge is a research associate at the Institute of Economic and Cultural Geography at Leibniz Universität Hannover. She studied Economic Geography at Leibniz Universität Hannover and Universidad Complutense de Madrid, and is completing her PhD on internal migration and regional development in Thailand and Vietnam.

Niels Kemper is a post-doctoral researcher at the University of Mannheim, Germany. He is affiliated with the DFG Collaborative Research Centre on the Political Economy of Reforms (Project: Robust Methods for the Evaluation of Policy Reforms). In the past he was affiliated with the DFG Research Group on Vulnerability to Poverty in Southeast Asia (Project: Financial Institutions). He also consulted for the GTZ and ILO. He studied at the Goethe University Frankfurt, Germany, and the New School University in New York, USA, and accomplished his doctoral studies at the Goethe University. His main research interests are methods of programme evaluation as well as credit and land markets in developing countries.

Carmen Kislat is a research fellow at the Institute of Money and International Finance at Leibniz Universität Hannover. She is an academic coordinator of the Research Training Group 'Globalization and Development'. Her research interests are development economics and in particular development finance in Southeast Asia.

Stephan Klasen is a professor of Development Economics and Coordinator of the Courant Research Centre 'Poverty, Equity, and

Growth in Developing and Transition Countries' at the University of Göttingen, Germany. He has also consulted for the World Bank, UNDP, UNESCO, the OECD and several other bilateral and multilateral development organizations. He holds a PhD from Harvard University, and has since held positions at the World Bank, King's College Cambridge, UK, and the University of Munich. His research focuses on issues of poverty, inequality and gender in developing countries.

Rainer Klump has been a professor of Economics, Economic Development and Economic Integration at Goethe University Frankfurt, Germany, since 2000. He is a principal investigator within the DFG Cluster of Excellence 'The Formation of Normative Orders'. Within the DFG Research Group on Vulnerability to Poverty in Southeast Asia, he is a co-director of the project on financial institutions. He has studied economics at the universities of Mainz, Paris I and Erlangen-Nuremberg, and has had academic appointments at the universities of Erlangen-Nuremberg, Freiburg, Würzburg and Ulm. His main research areas are theories, empirics and policy implications of economic growth and development.

Kai Mausch is an associate professional officer at the International Crops Research Institute for the Semi-Arid Tropics (ICRISAT), Hyderabad, India and is based in Malawi. He holds a PhD in Economics from Leibniz University Hannover, where his research focused on the contribution of the non-farm economy to rural poverty reduction in central Vietnam. His research focuses on global ex-ante and ex-post impact assessment from varietal technology dissemination in the context of an ICRISAT research programme.

Tobias Lechtenfeld is a research associate at the Development Economics Research Group at the University of Göttingen, Germany. He has extensive field experience from managing large-scale household surveys in East and West Africa, the Middle East and Southeast Asia. As part of these surveys, he has designed several vulnerability modules. In addition, he has worked as a consultant for public aid organizations in Germany, the Netherlands and the United Kingdom. His research focuses on social protection, health economics and impact evaluation of development programmes.

Ingo Liefner is a professor of Economic Geography at Justus Liebig University Giessen, Germany. He holds a doctorate degree from Leibniz Universität Hannover and has been teaching Economic Geography in Hannover and Giessen. His research focuses on networks and firm organization, knowledge generation and knowledge transfer, and regional economic development in developing and newly industrializing countries.

Lukas Menkhoff is a professor of Money and International Finance at Leibniz Universität Hannover. He is a speaker for the Research Training Group 'Globalization and Development', member of the Research Group 'Vulnerability in Southeast Asia' (both in cooperation with the University of Göttingen) and the former chairman of the German Development Economics Association. His research focuses on International Finance, in particular Foreign Exchange Markets and Development Finance.

Tung Duc Phung is a development economist. He is the chairman of the Indochina Research and Consulting Company (IRC) in Hanoi, Vietnam. He has been the lead sampling expert of General Statistics Office of Vietnam, and has been involved in the survey design of numerous international and national surveys in including the well-known Vietnam Household Living Standard Survey (VHLSS). He has worked with the Institute of Policy and Strategy for Agriculture and Rural Development under the Ministry of Agriculture in Vietnam. He holds a Master's Degree in Economic Policy from Suffolk University, Boston, USA, and a PhD in Economics from the School of Economics and Management, Leibniz Universität Hannover. Dr. Phung's expertise is in survey design and implementation as well as poverty analysis and vulnerability to poverty studies.

Felix Povel is now working for the German Development Bank (KfW). Furthermore, he was engaged in consultancies related to the achievement of the MDGs, regional integration in Southern Africa, capacity building in Zambia, private sector development and national poverty reduction strategies. He completed his PhD at the Development Economics Research Group at the University of Göttingen, Germany. His research focuses primarily on poverty dynamics, vulnerability and insurance in agriculture. Povel has field experience from research projects in Asia, Africa and Latin America. He has studied, conducted research and taught at universities in Germany, Spain, France, Ethiopia and the USA.

Suwanna Praneetvatakul is an associate professor of Agricultural and Resource Economics at the Department of Agricultural and Resource Economics, Faculty of Economics, Kasetsart University, Bangkok, Thailand. She is the Chair of the Faculty's Master Program on Natural

Resource Management. She is collaborating with several international research institutes on research in Thailand, including the DFG project 'Vulnerability to Poverty'. She has been country coordinator for the project's data collection activities in three provinces in Northeastern Thailand. Her publications are mainly in the field of agricultural development and natural resource management.

Javier Revilla Diez is a professor of Economic Geography at Leibniz Universität Hannover. After his PhD on the economic and regional transformation processes in Vietnam, he focused on knowledge-based regional development (especially regional innovation systems), labour markets and vulnerability research in Europe and Asia.

Ornsiri Rungruxsirivorn is a senior economist at the Ministry of Finance in Thailand. She studied at MIT and Northwestern University, USA, and worked as a research assistant at the NBER. Thereafter she joined the Fiscal Policy Office at the Thai Ministry of Finance before she accomplished her doctoral studies at Leibniz Universität Hannover. During her doctoral study, she was affiliated with the DFG Research Group on Vulnerability to Poverty in Southeast Asia.

Dominik Schmid is Junior Policy Advisor at the Gesellschaft für Internationale Zusammenarbeit (GIZ), Eschborn, Germany. He holds a PhD in Geography from Justus Liebig University Giessen, Germany, where his research has been about the rural non-farm economy in Thailand and Vietnam. His professional and research interests focus on rural development and transport policies in a developing country context.

Erich Schmidt was a professor of Agricultural Economics and director of the Institute of Market Analyses and Agricultural Policy at the School of Economics and Management at Leibniz Universität Hannover until his retirement in 2006. He has some 40 years' experience in agricultural market and policy research and some 15 years' experience in agricultural research in developing countries. He was Senior Economist at the Institute of Agricultural Market Research, Federal Research Centre of Agriculture (FAL), Braunschweig, Germany, Professor of Agricultural Economics at the Institute of Agricultural Economics at Georg-August-Universität, Göttingen, Germany and Professor of Agricultural Market Research at the Faculty of Horticulture, Leibniz Universität Hannover. He was Dean of the Faculty of Horticulture; Deputy Member of the Planning Committee, Leibniz Universität Hannover; and Member of the Scientific Advisory Board of the Federal Ministry for Food,

Agriculture and Forestry. He has worked on topics of EEC- and international agricultural markets, trade and policies as well as on environmental economics of agricultural systems in developing countries.

Songporne Tongruksawattana is now working for CIMMYT, the international Maize and Wheat Improvement Center in Nairobi, Kenya. She holds a PhD in Development and Agricultural Economics from Leibniz Universität Hannover. Her research focuses on rural farm households in Thailand and Vietnam with specific areas of shock-coping and risk-mitigation strategies within the context of vulnerability to poverty.

Marc Völker holds a position with the Statistical Office of the State Rhineland-Palatinate, Germany since late 2011. He was a research associate and PhD student at the Institute of Development and Agricultural Economics, School of Economics and Management at Leibniz Universität Hannover. He has worked in Vietnam in the context of the DFG-funded research unit FOR756 on Vulnerability to Poverty in Southeast Asia. He obtained his PhD in Economics in 2010.

Hermann Waibel is a professor of Agricultural Economics and the Director of the Institute of Development and Agricultural Economics, at the School of Economics and Management at Leibniz Universität Hannover. He is the Speaker of the Research Unit of the Deutsche Forschungsgemeinschaft (DFG) on the 'Impact of Risks and Shocks on Rural Households in Emerging Market Economies in South East Asia'. He has some 30 years' experience in research and development in Southeast Asia. He was an associate professor of Agricultural Systems at the Asian Institute of Technology (AIT) in Bangkok. He worked as a consultant for the World Bank, the Asian Development Bank (ADB), the EU Commission, the German Agency of International Development (GIZ), FAO and others. He has been on secondment as visiting scientist with the ADB. He has published on the topics of natural resources management, biotechnology, agriculture and environment in developing countries. His current research focus is on rural development in Asia.

1
Introduction and Key Messages

Stephan Klasen and Hermann Waibel

1.1 Motivation

In many ways, the last ten years have been rather good for developing countries. Average income growth rates have been quite high – in fact, substantially higher than in industrialized countries – and absolute income poverty has come down substantially (Chen and Ravallion, 2010). While much of this success in reducing poverty is related to particularly high growth rates in some populous Asian economies (including China, India, Indonesia, and Vietnam), substantial rates of per capita growth and associated poverty reduction has been experienced in the majority of countries from all regions. Even in Sub-Saharan Africa, growth has been higher than in rich countries, and poverty rates have started to come down, albeit only slowly and from a very high level (Bourguignon *et al.*, 2008).

At the same time, the last few years have been characterized by a very high level of volatility, with important repercussions for poverty in developing countries. This high volatility is, first, linked to sharply increasing and highly volatile commodity prices, including fuels, minerals, and food. While some developing countries have also benefited from these high commodity prices, many poor households have suffered, as they are net purchasers of food and are also negatively affected by rising energy prices; food and energy prices rose dramatically in 2007 and 2008, then fell and have recently risen again to very high levels (IMF, 2011). A second source of volatility has been high volatility in world output growth, with repercussions for developing countries which are deeply linked to the world economy. Most notably, the sharp downturn in 2009 as a result of the global financial crisis has affected developing countries substantially, although the effect has been heterogeneous and was more muted than anticipated due to strong policy responses in industrialized and some large developing countries (IMF, 2011). However, the continual uncertainty of the global financial markets caused by high levels of debt of countries in Europe and the USA poses threats for developing countries, as a renewed global economic downturn cannot be ruled out any more. Lastly, there are increasing dangers of global non-economic shocks that could affect developing countries. Among these are adverse developments resulting from climate change as well as global health scares such as SARS or avian flu.

These more macro-level sources of vulnerabilities come on top of persistent exposure to shocks to households in many developing countries. These shocks include demographic shocks such as illness and death of household members, economic shocks such as unemployment and adverse price or output developments, some of which are in turn related to flood, drought, pest outbreaks and other natural disasters. The susceptibility to shocks is particularly high in rural areas where the exposure to shocks – especially those related to adverse weather conditions, pests and diseases, as well as volatility in input and output prices – is large. At the same time, the ability of rural households to counteract these shocks is particularly limited due to imperfect credit and insurance markets. Some of these micro-level shocks are purely idiosyncratic, affecting only individual households; others affect entire villages and regions; and some, of course, are directly linked to the macro volatilities discussed above. As a result of these risks at different levels, it is not certain that many households whose average income is now above the poverty line have left poverty for good. Also, one might suspect that the movements in and out of poverty intensify due to the increasing volatilities just described.

In response to these developments, it is critical to assess to what extent households are affected by these risks, what impacts they have if they occur, and how households can shield themselves against the risks. These are precisely the questions that the research agenda on measuring vulnerability to poverty and analysing its determinants is trying to address. Starting with some initial work in the late 1990s (for example, World Bank, 2000), this research programme has defined vulnerability as an *ex-ante* concept that is trying to assess the propensity of households to be negatively affected by shocks. In contrast to the work on income poverty measurement, which determines actual poverty levels *ex post* and seeks to explain trends and determinants in poverty, vulnerability research tries to examine the *ex-ante* poverty risk of households. This is critical from a research as well as a policy perspective. From a research perspective, this approach thereby integrates shocks and risks into poverty research and combines both strands to make ex-ante assessments of future poverty risks and examines their drivers. From a policy perspective, it is clear that successful poverty reduction policies should target those people at risk of future poverty rather than simply try to help those who were identified as poor in the past.

Despite the importance of this issue, available research on vulnerability, its determinants and policy implications is still rather limited. While there has been a considerable amount of conceptual work on the measurement of vulnerability to poverty (see Chapter 2), there is a great lack of empirical work implementing these concepts, studying the determinants of vulnerability and deriving policy conclusions. This is largely related to the high demand on the specialized data required to analyse vulnerability, as well as the complexity of the task of assessing ex-ante risks.

This book aims to fill these gaps and thereby contribute to this forward-looking agenda on measuring vulnerability to poverty, assessing its determinants and deriving policy implications to reduce such vulnerability. More specifically, it is based on a joint inter-disciplinary research programme, funded by the German Research Foundation, on measuring and analysing the vulnerability to poverty in Thailand and Vietnam. These countries were chosen as prime examples because their average incomes have been rising rapidly in recent decades, leading to falling average income poverty rates. In spite of this success, vulnerability to poverty remains high, especially in rural areas, linked to high exposure to a wide variety of micro-level and macro-level shocks. The observed high regional disparity in welfare is caused by the limited ability of rural households in these countries to cope with shocks. However, there is likely to be considerable heterogeneity between the two countries and the regions within them. The study of this heterogeneity will be an important aspect of the analyses below.

Particular contributions of this book are to critically review and empirically apply advanced concepts in vulnerability research, to study the extent, distribution, and determinants of vulnerability to poverty in rural areas in Thailand and Vietnam using large household panel surveys that were specifically designed to measure and analyse vulnerability to poverty, and to analyse to what extent agriculture, non-farm employment, and financial markets are sources of risks and shocks, and/or offer opportunities for coping strategies to mitigate vulnerabilities to poverty. Unique features of the contributions in this volume are that they are all based on the same household survey data, that methodological issues in designing, implementing and analysing surveys to study vulnerability figure prominently, that a broad inter-disciplinary approach is taken to study the determinants of vulner-ability to poverty and that the contributions offer valuable lessons for research as well as policy. While many of the substantive conclusions of the essays are related to the particular context in Thailand and Vietnam, the contributions to the volume are also aimed to be broad enough to give a good overview of the state of the art in vulnerability research and to offer both substantive and methodological lessons to researchers and policy-makers interested in vulnerability issues in other parts of the developing world.

1.2 Conceptual and measurement issues in vulnerability research

This section summarizes the contributions of the book before highlight-ing the common themes and lessons for research and policy emerging from the analysis. Part I of the book focuses on the measurement of vulnerability and deals with conceptual and measurement issues, while Part II examines the empirical drivers of vulnerability to poverty in Thailand and Vietnam.

Chapter 2, by Klasen and Povel, reviews the state of art in vulner-ability research. The authors show how the concept developed from combining research on poverty dynamics and research on risks, shocks, insurance and coping mechanisms. Vulnerability research combines the two strands of the literature by trying to provide forward-looking measures of downside risk or poverty risk. The chapter then critically reviews existing measures of vulnerability that exist in the literature. Currently, there continue to be competing views on how best to measure vulnerability. Among the critical issues to consider are to what extent one should consider all types of downside risks, or only downside risks that place a household below the poverty line. Also, the concepts differ in the way they estimate the likelihood and severity of future adverse events, with some drawing on past experience of shocks and others on subjective assessments of households of future risks. In this context, the authors present an approach that uses subjective risk assessments of households to estimate the likelihood of adverse downside events. They apply this measure using the data from Thailand and Vietnam to illustrate the feasibility of the approach. The chapter concludes by emphasizing that there is still room for improvement as far as theo-retical concepts of vulnerability are concerned. But the writers stress that the bigger challenge is related to the empirical implementation of these concepts, as it requires high quality tailor-made household panel surveys, which are rarely available in developing countries.

Chapter 3, by Hardeweg, Klasen, and Waibel, presents the panel household survey used in Thailand and Vietnam and underlying the research presented in this book. The chapter first demonstrates that tailor-made panel data to study vulnerability is largely lacking in developing countries, while also placing this survey in the context of the literature. It also reviews the requirements of such tailor-made surveys. Among these are that they must have a panel dimension, be extremely detailed about risks, shocks, their impacts, and availability and use of coping strategies, and be large enough to capture relatively rare but potentially devastating events. The chapter then discusses sampling, choice of regions, and questionnaire issues for the panel household survey, which to date includes three waves and about 2200 households each in the two countries. Lastly, the chapter presents a range of descriptive analyses to demonstrate that the surveys match up on basic demographic and economic information with other available surveys, contain a good amount of high quality information on risks, shocks, and coping mechanism, and that the locations and sampling strategy chosen are appropriate for these types of analyses. The chapter also emphasizes the importance of carefully generating information about the many linkages between households (for example, via migration, informal networks, remittances, mutual support) as this critically affects the ability of households to manage vulnerability.

Chapter 4, by Klasen, Povel, and Lechtenfeld, focuses particularly on how to design survey questionnaires that allow an assessment of ex-ante vulnerability to poverty. They first show that standard household surveys that are readily available do not lend themselves to measuring vulnerability to poverty. This is particularly the case when only standard cross-section income or expenditure surveys are available which require strong and ultimately unrealistic assumptions to derive vulnerability assessments based on them. The authors then critically review the lessons learnt from trying to elicit in-depth information on risks, shocks and their impacts and coping strategies in the panel surveys undertaken in Thailand and Vietnam. After presenting the way in which these modules were designed, the authors show that these modules can generate comprehensive and consistent information on shocks and risks. In particular, it appears that households seem to have a reasonable sense of their risk perceptions, an issue that is also investigated in more detail in Ligon and Povel (2011). It is also possible to obtain reasonable estimates of shock intensity, although several biases can arise depending on the length of time of a shock and the way the questions about intensity are phrased. In addition, a range of measurement error issues arise when eliciting this type of information ranging from recall bias to enumerator effects, the interdependence of events and the difficulty of differentiating between the intensity of a shock and its net effect after several coping strategies have been applied. More generally, capturing ex-ante and ex-post behavioural responses to perceived risks is particularly challenging, and this is crucial unfinished business for future research on the measurement of vulnerability.

Chapter 5, by Lechtenfeld, extends an approach commonly used in poverty research – the merging of survey and census data to generate poverty maps for small geographic areas – to vulnerability research, and applies this to the case of Vietnam. In the household survey, a model is used that predicts vulnerability using variables that are also available in the census. That way, the vulnerability of small geographic areas such as districts or even sub-districts or villages can be assessed. This chapter implements this approach for Vietnam and compares its results to traditional poverty mapping. The key methodological conclusion is that it is entirely feasible to generate such vulnerability maps, which are of considerable policy interest for targeting policy interventions in developing countries that try to prevent poverty from occurring in the first place. When comparing poverty maps with vulnerability maps of Vietnam, the author shows that in some areas the two are highly correlated, but that in other areas there are significant differences. Among the biggest differences are that many households headed by younger males and coming from ethnic minorities are not found to be poor but are nonetheless identified as vulnerable. This shows that poverty and vulnerability mapping yield significantly different results with important consequences for the targeting of social programmes.

Chapter 6, by Mausch, Revilla Diez and Klump, is supplementary to the analysis in the chapters so far, as here the authors use secondary data from the Vietnam Household Living Standard Survey 2002 and 2004, and focus on analyses of poverty dynamics. It thereby identifies a range of methodological and substantive issues that will also be addressed in the chapters on the drivers of vulnerability in Part II. In particular, the chapter contributes to the debate whether, and to what extent, income diversification of rural households can be an enduring pathway out of poverty. The authors apply a poverty decomposition approach, concentrating on four basic household types, namely farm households, non-farm-households, mixed farm households and mixed non-farm households. Results confirm that on average non-farm income opportunities reduced poverty and have promoted pro-poor growth; an open question is whether they have also reduced vulnerability to poverty. The results point to the need to include more detailed information about droughts, floods and other shocks in the context of a longer panel, and in order to detect patterns of specialization and diversification as ways to reduce poverty and vulnerability, issues that are taken up presently.

1.3 Drivers of vulnerability, and household responses in Thailand and Vietnam

The chapters in Part II analyse particular determinants of vulnerability to poverty and the possibilities of reducing such vulnerabilities. The section first includes some chapters that assess the nature of risk and the opportunities for households to mitigate these risks, before turning to institutions and policies that might support households in reducing their vulnerabilities.

Chapter 7, by Völker, Tongruksawattana, Schmidt and Waibel, analyses the impact of the 2008 food price crisis on vulnerability to poverty of rural households in Thailand and Vietnam. The massive increases in food prices in 2007 and 2008 (and again in 2010/11) have placed great strain on poor households, and this chapter estimates the impacts in the two countries. The methodology is based on a mathematical risk programming approach that is applied to two typical agricultural households in Thailand and in Vietnam. The model compares the probability for household income to fall below the poverty line under two price scenarios for agricultural commodities and inputs, while simultaneously taking into account other, mostly weather-related, shocks. Results for the Thai household, which can be described as a commercial type of agricultural system, show that the agricultural price shocks of 2008 prompt such households to adjust their agricultural portfolio towards subsistence crops, and at the same time further engaging in off-farm employment. This strategy appears to be successful in keeping the likelihood of falling into poverty low. For the Vietnamese household – that is, households in remote locations with poor market access – the 2008 price shock led to an increase in vulnerability to poverty mainly because of such households' need to purchase higher-priced rice, and the limited ability of the household to adjust its agricultural portfolio. In both countries the degree of risk aversion has an effect on agricultural portfolio adjustment. Extreme risk aversion will increase the pressure on the Thai household to seek employment outside agriculture, the Vietnamese household extreme risk aversion would require either lowering average consumption or engaging more strongly in generating income from natural resources (such as illegal logging). Clearly, the food crisis has been a severe shock to some households in both countries. Also, the ability to cope with such shocks differs greatly, depending on location and the portfolio of options available.

Given the nature of shocks such as those analysed in Chapter 7, households have a range of ex-ante and ex-post strategies at their disposal to mitigate the impact of a shock or cope with its occurrence ex post. Chapter 8 by Praneetvatakul, Phung and Waibel examines to what extent households are able to reduce their exposure to shocks by ex-ante diversification strategies. Most households have several income sources, and diversification does indeed play an important role for the reduction of risk. These diversification strategies differ, however, considerably between countries. While in Vietnam diversification is taking place mostly within agriculture by planting a larger variety of crops to reduce the risk of failure of any one of them, in Thailand it is off-farm employment that constitutes the most important means of diversifying income sources. The chapter argues that the more limited approach to diversification taken in Vietnam is related to poor infrastructure and lower off-farm employment opportunities, particularly in remote rural areas, pointing to the need for policy to address these issues in order to increase the resilience of households.

Apart from ex-ante diversification, ex-post coping strategies are another option to reduce vulnerability. Chapter 9, by Tongruksawattana, Junge, Waibel, Revilla Diez and Schmidt, studies ex-post coping strategies by households in Thailand and Vietnam. The ability of a household to effectively cope with different types of shocks depends on a number of factors such as initial wealth status, asset levels and portfolios of income-generating activities, including agricultural as well as non-agricultural activities, either through self-employment or wage labour. Also, demographic and location factors will play important roles. This chapter analyses the nature and impact of (negative) shocks and associated ex-post coping strategies and their determinants for rural households in Thailand and Vietnam. Using a probit model, in both a univariate and a multivariate specification, the coping behaviour of rural households of six provinces in the two countries is analysed. The chapter shows that shocks occur frequently in both countries, but households resort to coping strategies more frequently in the case of demographic than in the case of agricultural shocks; coping strategies are less frequently used in Thailand, presumably due to higher incomes.

Borrowing emerges as the most important coping strategy. The chapter also shows that shocks, impacts, and coping strategies differ greatly between and within the two countries, so that policy-makers need to examine these location-specific factors when designing strategies to mitigate the impact of shocks.

One of the options for ex-post coping strategies is reliance on financial markets to smooth income fluctuations. Chapter 10, by Kemper, Klump, Menkhoff and Rungruxsirivorn, examines to what extent the chosen smoothing mechanism (for example, borrowing, selling assets, drawing down savings, mutual insurance or increases in labour supply) depends on the existence of credit constraints. While the literature is divided on the impact of credit constraints on smoothing mechanisms, the paper finds, using a multinominal logit framework, that empirically the response to shocks does not differ between households that are credit-constrained and those that are not; in contrast, the chosen smoothing mechanisms depend greatly on the nature of the shock. These findings suggest that credit constraints in the two countries are not as severe as one might have presumed, which is related to the strong intervention by governments and NGOs in this market.

One such public intervention in improving credit access in rural areas has been the village funds programme in Thailand, which provides a revolving loan fund to villages. This programme, now one of the largest microfinance programs in the world, is studied in Chapter 11 by Kislat and Menkhoff. Earlier studies indicate that the programme is successful in improving credit access to the poor. They extend this work to a panel setting, and find that village fund borrowers are consistently characterized by a lower economic status; accordingly, village fund loans are an important lifeline to those households, thus reaching the intended beneficiaries. However, the authors cannot identify any significant substitution between village fund loans and other loans, raising doubts about the long-term impact of the village fund programme. Eventually one would expect and hope that households use the village fund loans as a stimulus for investments, and thus continue financing in later periods via other sources of credit.

As already discussed in Chapters 8 and 9, another way to reduce vulnerability is to rely on off-farm employment as a way to diversify income and deal with shocks ex post. The last chapter of this volume, Chapter 12 by Brünjes, Schmid, Revilla Diez and Liefner, examines to what extent the rural non-farm economy is actually able to reduce poverty and vulnerability. Not every non-farm activity has the same potential to reduce the risk situation of rural households. This chapter analyses what types of regional non-farm wage jobs reduce a household's perceived risks, and studies the determinants of participation in such activities in Thailand and in Vietnam. It finds that households that engage in high-return permanent activities expect fewer shocks, and those that participate in low-return temporary activities expect more shocks to happen within the next five years. Participation in risk-reducing high-return permanent activities depends crucially on household assets like education and social capital, but also on the location and thus the physical access to these activities. At the moment, high-return permanent wage labour makes up only a small share of non-farm employment, especially in Vietnam. Hence, if the rural non-farm economy is to unleash its full potential in reducing the vulnerability of rural households, it will need to considerably broaden the access to high-return permanent activities, particularly to those faced by high levels of vulnerability.

1.4   Conclusions for research and policy

While the chapters sketched above provide rich and specific details on their particular area of investigation, it is possible to draw out some general lessons and policy messages from the contributions to this volume. They can be grouped into (i) methodological lessons and issues for vulnerability research, (ii) specific lessons on vulnerability and possible policy responses in Thailand and Vietnam, and (iii) some generalizable findings on the drivers and possible policy responses to vulnerability. We will deal with them in turn, before identifying remaining research gaps.

The book offers a range of methodological lessons for vulnerability research; we highlight four. First, it is possible to empirically estimate the vulnerability of households using the concepts discussed in the literature. While some simplifying assumptions are needed, sensible, consistent and reliable estimates can be provided if tailor-made panel surveys are used that specifically elicit critical information on shocks, risks and coping strategies. In such surveys, standard tools of poverty analysis, such as profiles and small-area mapping, can be used, which yield interesting and policy-relevant results. Second, relying on standard available household survey instruments will not be a fruitful way to study vulnerability; the limitations of these all-purpose surveys are simply too great to generate reliable measures of vulnerability. Instead, tailor-made panel surveys with substantial sample sizes are required. They also offer the advantage that a broad range of questions related to vulnerability to poverty can be addressed in such surveys, as we demonstrate with contributions in this book. Third, creating such tailor-made instruments requires considerable care; in particular, eliciting reliable information on shocks, their impacts, perceived risks and coping strategies requires detailed survey instruments, and it is critical to anticipate a range of potential biases and errors and to build in specific approaches to address them. Lastly, using data on ex-post shocks or ex-ante perceived risks will provide related but far from identical information. As both types of data are beset by different possible biases, eliciting information on both is particularly fruitful as this information can be used to address some of these biases.

Regarding Thailand and Vietnam, the contributions of this volume demonstrate first, that high levels of vulnerability constitute a persistent threat for many rural households in those two countries. In both countries, many households report a large number of shocks affecting their livelihood, although the impact appears to be smaller in Thailand than in Vietnam. But clearly one cannot assume that high growth and poverty reduction will necessarily spell an end to these vulnerabilities. For many households, household-specific, local, national and international shocks can continue to threaten livelihoods. At the same time, the chapters in Part I demonstrate, secondly, that vulnerability and poverty are distinct phenomena that require separate analysis, and will generate different approaches to policy responses and targeting. A third message is that households already engage in a range of activities to mitigate risk ex-ante or deal with shocks ex post. Here, some important differences emerge between the two countries. In Vietnam, households are much more restricted in their ability to use diversification to reduce the exposure to risk, and thus have to engage in more coping strategies ex post to mitigate their impact. In Thailand, however, households have more opportunities for diversification and as a result have less need for coping strategies, particularly in the case of economic shocks. Moreover, it is important to note that households use coping strategies more frequently in the case of demographic than economic shocks. Findings from both countries suggest that poorer households have less recourse to reliable diversification and coping strategies, particularly with regard to non-farm employment, and here is a clear role for governments; among the policies to be considered are improved infrastructure access in rural areas, and targeted support to promote off-farm employment opportunities. A fourth lesson is that credit constraints are not as important in these countries as might have been presumed. After years of massive expansion of microcredit by governments and NGOs, it indeed appears to be the case that households in Thailand and Vietnam have reasonably good access to credit; programmes such as the Village Fund programme in Thailand have played an important role. The challenge in this area is not so much further expansion of services as sustainability and transition from microcredit to more formal systems of credit.

Beyond Thailand and Vietnam, the book also offers a number of important lessons for researchers and policy-makers concerned with reducing vulnerability. First, vulnerability to poverty is not only, or even primarily, an issue affecting the poorest countries of the world. Particularly countries where even remote rural populations are directly affected by conditions in world markets may be subject to just as much or more vulnerability than countries whose linkages to world markets are much weaker. Global recessions, commodity booms and busts, climate change, and global health threats will strongly influence the fortunes of households, even in dynamically growing economies such as Thailand and Vietnam. Second, demographic shocks related to health and mortality are more important drivers of vulnerability of households than is commonly presumed. Promoting public health and reducing household spending on health care (through reductions in out-of-pocket spending or insurance mechanisms) can play an important role in mitigating these risks. Third, the analysis from Thailand and Vietnam suggest that maybe the policy emphasis on dealing with vulnerability should shift somewhat. In recent years, most of the emphasis has been on expanding access to microcredit and, more recently, micro insurance as predominant ways to deal with risk and vulnerability. The findings of this volume suggest that improving the ability of households, especially poor households, to better diversify their economic activities, and allowing them better access to off-farm employment opportunities, may be at least as important as microfinance interventions to reduce the vulnerability of households. This also requires the more serious addressing of the question of how structural change in agriculture can be facilitated in rural areas which are remote and have low potential for agricultural and non-farm enterprises. In addition, the rapid and continuing out-migration of younger household members in these emerging economies raises new problems for the demographic and social structure of remote rural areas.

While we hope that the contributions in this volume will advance the research and policy agenda on vulnerability, many open issues and questions for further research remain. Many emanate directly from the analyses of the chapters and are discussed there. Here we focus on a few issues that go beyond the individual contributions. On the methodological front, the validation of various conceptual and empirical approaches to vulnerability measurement remains largely an open issue. While we have shown that it is possible to estimate vulnerability to poverty with tailor-made surveys, the ability of these measures to accurately forecast poverty risk will require longer-running panel surveys. As these are increasingly being undertaken in developing countries (including further waves of our Thailand and Vietnam panel), this is an issue where we can expect results in coming years. Similarly, all of the empirical analyses of vulnerability that we know of treat the different risks as independent; in reality, however, they are likely to be interdependent, and modelling this interdependency will be critical to the generation of conceptually sound and empirically more accurate measures of vulnerability. Third, as vulnerability is affected in complex ways by perceptions as well as ex-ante and ex-post coping strategies, closer linkages between vulnerability research and the rapidly expanding field of behavioural economics is likely to prove particularly fruitful. In particular, understanding how households form expectations about risk, and adjust behaviour in the face of risk, should be high on such a joint research agenda.

On the substantive front, there is a great need to consolidate research approaches and place them in a more comparative setting. While the number of individual studies on shocks, risks, and coping are multiplying, they are often based on single specialized surveys, using different approaches and with different policy issues in mind. A more explicit comparative setting would prove helpful here. That way, it would be possible to address, for example, whether some of the key findings here (for example, on the importance of demographic and health shocks, the importance and inequality in diversification and coping opportunities, and the lesser importance of credit constraints) are generalizable to settings in South Asia, Africa or Latin America. This would then also help develop more clearly policy approaches that specifically address vulnerability to poverty. In this vein, closer linkages at the policy level to the large policy literature on social protection (for example, Grosh *et al.*, 2008; ERD, 2010) would ensure that the insights from these literatures are combined to provide more sound policy advice on the ability of various social protection instruments to combat vulnerability to poverty.

References

Bourguignon, F. A. Benassy-Quere, S. Dercon, A. Estache. J. Gunning, R. Kanbur, S. Klasen, S. Maxwell, J. Platteau and A. Spadaro (2008): "Millennium Development Goals at Midpoint: Where Do We Stand and Where Do We Need to Go?" Background Paper for European Report on Development. EU, Brussels.

Chen, S. and M. Ravallion (2010): "The Developing World Is Much Poorer Than We Thought, But No Less Successful in the Fight against Poverty", *Quarterly Journal of Economics*, 125(4): 1577–625.

ERD (2010): "European Report on Development: Promoting Social Protection in Sub Saharan Africa", European Commission, Brussels.

Grosh, M. C. del Ninno, E. Tesliuc and A. Ouerghi. (2008): *For Protection and Promotion: the Design and Implementation of Effective Safety Nets*, The World Bank, Washington DC.

IMF (2011): *World Economic Outlook*, September 2011, IMF, Washington DC.

Ligon, E. and F. Povel. (2011): "Eliciting Subjective Probabilities to Predict Shocks in Thailand and Vietnam," *mimeo*, University of Göttingen.

World Bank (2000): *World Development Report 2000/01: Attacking Poverty*, Oxford University Press, New York.

Part I

Conceptual and Measurement Issues in Vulnerability Research

2
Defining and Measuring Vulnerability: State of the Art and New Proposals

Stephan Klasen and Felix Povel

2.1 Introduction

Life in developing countries often is marked by poverty and risk. Prominent studies such as *Voices of the Poor: Crying Out for Change* (Narayan *et al.*, 2000) acquaint their readers with the daily struggle faced by poor households that try to escape their hardship in the face of recurring illness, natural disasters and other hazards. In the absence of well-functioning credit and insurance markets – a distressing reality in most developing countries –exposure to these adverse events renders households highly vulnerable. This can affect not only households who were poor to start with and who might face utter destitution as a result of adverse shocks, but also non-poor households who can fall back into poverty, and thus also need to be considered in an analysis of vulnerability to poverty.

But what is the exact meaning of being vulnerable? As we will see, the answer to this question is not as straightforward as it may seem at first glance. One of many interpretations of vulnerability is presented in the World Development Report 2000/2001 (World Bank, 2000) that states: "vulnerability measures the resilience against a shock – the likelihood that a shock will result in a decline in well-being". The report puts vulnerability in the spotlight of poverty research by presenting it as an important component of combating poverty.

The reason for assigning such a prominent position to this component, as well as for increased economists' interest in vulnerability, is threefold: first, vulnerability impacts negatively on the well-being of households. In other words, not only current conditions, such as levels of income and consumption, matter for actual welfare, but also the risks a household faces, as well as its (in)ability to prevent, mitigate, and cope with these. Of particular note is the fact that this vulnerability to poverty can remain a serious threat to well-being for households whose long-term income has for a long time surpassed the poverty line.

Second, vulnerability is not only a dimension but can also be a cause of long-term deprivation. For instance, vulnerable poor households facing a risky future are more likely to opt for stable, low-return sources of income than to invest in endeavours whose outcome is, on average, more lucrative but also more uncertain. Though a rational choice, this behaviour may trap households in poverty by rendering higher levels of income impossible. Therefore, combating vulnerability has the potential to reduce long-term poverty.

Third, vulnerability shifts the attention from ex-post poverty outcomes to ex-ante poverty risks by trying to identify the (types of) households with highest future poverty risks. This is critical for policymakers in order for them to design appropriate poverty reduction strategies that address these forward-looking poverty risks.

The aim of this chapter is to review current vulnerability research, present "state of the art" concepts, identify the most important shortcomings of these concepts, and propose approaches to deal with some of the problems. We intend to do so on the one hand by accepting the relevant benchmark for an assessment of vulnerability, that is, that vulnerability as such has to focus on the risk of negative future outcomes (Hoddinott and Quisumbing, 2003). Most commonly, "negative" in this context refers to a scenario in which a household is below the poverty line (Calvo and Dercon, 2005). We argue that the poverty line certainly has its merits as a relevant reference point, but also suffers from some shortcomings; for example, it categorically disregards all potential changes above the poverty line, and labels households progressing towards *upward* movements below it as still being vulnerable. These shortcomings can be addressed by choosing the current level of well-being as a relevant threshold, which in turn comes at the cost of other weaknesses. A combination of both benchmarks may be even more useful, as it ensures that only future states of the world in which a household is poor *and* worse off than today impact on vulnerability. On the other hand, we propose a new source of information which has the potential to improve present approaches to empirically assess the vulnerability of households. While current approaches typically rely on information of fluctuations from the past in order to model future vulnerabilities, thus are *backward*-looking, data on subjective risk perception of households is truly *forward*-looking. Therefore, the latter might be well suited for analyses of vulnerability.

The remainder of this chapter is structured as follows: Section 2.2 reviews the literature that has led to the emergence of vulnerability-related research, thus studies concerned with the impact of shocks on well-being, consumption and income smoothing, as well as transient and chronic poverty. Section 2.3 aims at clarifying the term "vulnerability" that has diverse meanings depending on the context in which it is used. Also, it outlines briefly which aspects a vulnerability measure should incorporate, as well as what sort of data it requires to be applied econometrically. Thereafter, in Section 2.4, the concepts and measures of vulnerability as uninsured exposure to risk, vulnerability as low expected utility, vulnerability as expected poverty, and vulnerability to poverty are critically scrutinized. In Section 2.5, weaknesses of these approaches to vulnerability are revealed and solutions proposed, before Section 2.6 illustrates how some of these shortcomings can be dealt with in practice. Finally, Section 2.7 concludes.

2.2   Antecedents to vulnerability research

In development economics, numerous different strands of literature tackle particular aspects relevant to vulnerability research. In fact, the emergence of clear-cut concepts and measures of vulnerability can be seen as a result of studies from different research areas concerned with the impact of shocks on well-being, consumption smoothing and risk sharing, income smoothing, and poverty dynamics respectively. Therefore, for a better understanding of vulnerability research, it is useful to quickly review these different literatures. Although they often cannot be disentangled – for example, the way shocks affect well-being depends on the ability to smooth consumption, and may then generate patterns of transitory and chronic poverty – in the remainder of this section the literature that precedes current vulnerability research is presented along these lines.

Adverse events referred to as shocks, and their consequences with respect to welfare outcomes such as consumption, health, and education, are widely investigated. Especially in developing countries, where households are frequently deprived of functioning credit and insurance markets (Besley, 1995), such shocks may cause hardship and destitution. Although theoretically all types of shocks are of interest to the researcher, in practice, the literature has particularly focused on health shocks as well as weather shocks affecting agricultural production.[1] Studies concerning the former include Dercon and Krishnan (2000), Gertler and Gruber (2002), Skoufias and Quisumbing (2005), Beegle *et al.* (2008), and Grimm (2009). Regarding the latter, the focus is often on droughts and floods, and includes studies such as Fafchamps *et al.* (1998), and Kazianga and Udry (2006).

As long as health shocks do not occur as a result of an epidemic, they belong to the group of *idiosyncratic* events; that is, they affect only (one person within) one household, and the probability of such events is uncorrelated across members of a community. Instead, natural disasters and weather events typically constitute *covariate* shocks, which are events that impact on the well-being of whole communities, provinces or even states. As is well known from the insurance literature, there is scope to provide mutual insurance against idiosyncratic shocks, while mutual insurance against covariate shocks is not possible. Thus villagers often can and do insure each other through informal mutual insurance against health and mortality shocks, while they cannot insure each other against weather risks. It is therefore critical to differentiate between these two types of shock.

While most of the shock literature focuses on the short-term impact of adverse events, it recently started to concentrate on their medium- to long-term consequences. For example, Alderman *et al.* (2006) show that pre-school malnutrition worsens health and educational outcomes of adults in rural Zimbabwe. Exploiting the same dataset, Elbers *et al.* (2007) quantify both the ex-ante and ex-post effects of risk on growth; they find that risk substantially reduces growth between 1980 and 2000. Beegle *et al.* (2008) predict an increase in child labour in Tanzania with shocks to crop production as well as rainfall variation, and examine the impact of that increase on education, employment choices, and marital status ten years later. Maccini and Yang (2009) use weather conditions around the time of birth to explain differences in health, education, and socioeconomic outcomes of Indonesian adults.

One general conclusion that can be drawn from the aforementioned literature is that the impact of adverse events crucially depends on the ability of households to insure against such shocks in order to smooth their consumption. Consumption can be smoothed via, for instance, the use of informal insurance networks, which means sharing risk (Townsend, 1994, and Morduch, 1999), asset depletion (Fafchamps *et al.*, 1998), and migration (Lambert, 1994). Literature related to consumption smoothing and risk sharing has proliferated in development economics. It is surveyed in, for example, Townsend (1995), Deaton (1997), Dercon (2002), and Morduch (2004). The overall finding of this literature is that households smooth their consumption to some extent but by no means entirely. As will be shown below, consumption smoothing and risk sharing can be interpreted as directly affecting vulnerability. In fact, each vulnerability measure that chooses consumption as its dimension of welfare and does not refer to a poverty line as benchmark is very closely related to consumption smoothing.[2]

Households that have limited capacities to smooth their consumption may additionally engage in income smoothing. Income can be smoothed, for instance, ex ante by diversifying income sources (Morduch, 1994 and 1995, as well as Ellis, 1998) and adopting low-risk and low-return crop and asset portfolios (Rosenzweig and Binswanger, 1993) or ex post by shifting labour allocation from farm to off-farm employment (Kochar, 1999).

Changing degrees of shock exposure, as well as of capacities to smooth consumption and income, suggest that the poverty status of households is not fixed but changes over time (Jalan and Ravallion, 1998). In other words, the poverty status of a household is dynamic, and a distinction between transient (or stochastic) and chronic (or structural) poverty can usefully be made. Numerous analyses find that large proportions of the population move into and out of poverty over time, which means that they suffer from transient poverty (examples include Ghaiha and Deolalikar, 1993, Jalan and Ravallion, 1998 and Baulch and Hoddinott, 2000). On the other hand, there is also a portion of the poor that is affected by chronic poverty (Chronic Poverty Research Centre, 2004 and 2008). Chronically poor households either are structurally poor in the sense that their (physical and human) asset base is so low that it does not enable them to escape poverty, or are put by a strong or persistent negative shock into a "poverty trap", which can be described by equilibrium levels of poverty where initial poverty forces households to adopt survival strategies that further entrench them in their poverty. Such poverty traps can persist for a long time unless positive changes enable households to escape this bad stalemate in poverty.[3] For instance, Lokshin and Ravallion (2005) investigate Indonesia's financial crisis of 1998 and find that in 2002 a large share of Indonesia's poor would not have suffered from this form of destitution without the 1998 crisis.

Chronic poverty can also exist in non-income dimensions. A study by Günther and Klasen (2008) conceptualizes chronic poverty in a non-monetary dimension. Using panel data from Vietnam from 1992 and 1997, they compare chronic income and non-income poverty, and show that their static correlation is rather low while trends in chronic income and non-income poverty are relatively similar.

Based on these literatures, the question arose as to which households are affected by such negative shocks, are unable to smooth consumption, and thus may move in and out of poverty. This is exactly the question about the "vulnerability to poverty" to which we turn now.

2.3   Some clarifications of the term "vulnerability"

Since the beginning of the new millennium, the term "vulnerability" has been used extensively in the literature. It refers to the concept of poverty combined with risk and the efforts and capacities to manage risk (Holzmann *et al.*, 2003). Also, it is an approach of thinking dynamically about poverty and switching from an ex-post to an ex-ante perspective. Although there is consensus on these elements as being essential to a concept of vulnerability, it is impossible to provide an agreed definition of vulnerability, since it "has become one of those slippery terms (like 'sustainability') that is now used to signify so many different things that it is in danger of losing any real meaning" (Cannon, 2008).

There are many possible sources of confusion regarding vulnerability. For example, it may be analysed at different levels: attempts to quantify vulnerability at the country level include Briguglio (1995 and 1997), Briguglio and Galea (2003) and Farrugia (2004). These studies try to measure a country's ability to cope with economic vulnerability by, for instance, constructing indices which include country characteristics like macroeconomic stability and dependence on exports and imports, as well as the degree of economic openness. Another important source of vulnerability at the country level are environmental shocks such as earthquakes, typhoons and hurricanes, droughts, floods, and so on (Guillaumont, 2009). Furthermore, vulnerability can be investigated at the regional level; for instance, Naudé *et al.* (2008) use a dataset on 354 magisterial districts from South Africa to create a local vulnerability index. The rationale behind vulnerability research at the regional level is that there exist regional factors – as opposed to national or household-specific factors – which affect households' well-being and may cause geographic poverty traps (Jalan and Ravallion, 2002). Such aggregate vulnerability assessments have also received a great deal of attention in discussions on the risks associated with climate change at the country or regional level (Tompkins *et al.*, 2005). The approach that is followed in this chapter, however, focuses on vulnerability at the *household* level. That is, it is concerned with households' current levels of well-being as well as with their exposure to adverse events and their capacity to cope with them.[4]

Another potentially confounding factor with regard to vulnerability is that different strands of related research focus only on particular types of hazards. For instance, there is the disaster management literature which defines vulnerability exclusively with respect to natural disasters.[5] Other literatures focus exclusively on health risks (such as HIV AIDS, SARS, malaria and so on) and their impact on household well-being (Gertler and Gruber, 2002).

Despite these differences, two issues seem to unite all the strands of vulnerability research. First, it is widely acknowledged that risk is the crucial ingredient of vulnerability research (Siegel *et al.*, 2003). It impacts on well-being and influences behaviour, as well as decision-making processes (Elbers *et al.*, 2007, and Dercon, 2009). Fortunately, the definition of risk is much less ambiguous than the one of vulnerability itself: it is defined by a probability distribution of events which, in turn, are characterized by their severity including their duration (Siegel *et al.*, 2003). Although technically risk does not have to have a negative connotation, such a meaning is commonly attached to it (Calvo and Dercon, 2005).[6]

Second, while it is difficult to determine precisely what vulnerability is, it is relatively easy to show what it is not. Thus, the concept of vulnerability is distinct from the concept of poverty:[7] as already indicated, poverty is usually a static, vulnerability a dynamic, concept (World Bank, 2000). And even if poverty analyses incorporate dynamics – as is the case with examinations of transient and chronic poverty – they differ from vulnerability in the sense that the latter, at least theoretically, is forward- as opposed to backward-looking (Dercon, 2005). Expressed less theoretically, currently poor households may be non-vulnerable, that is looking towards a bright future, whereas currently non-poor households suffer from vulnerability if they are confronted with a risky outlook, possibly pushing them below the poverty line. At the same time, static poverty and vulnerability tend to be highly correlated with each other; for example, poor households are likely to be more vulnerable because they live in locations which are more exposed to natural disasters (Sharma *et al.*, 2000). In addition, if vulnerability is defined as the future threat of poverty, the correlation between current poverty and vulnerability is obvious, as most currently poor households invariably face a higher risk of poverty than most currently non-poor households. Lastly, vulnerability is different from simply the variability of the welfare outcome of interest – although a prominent measure of vulnerability relies on this notion. For instance, a household may be exposed to serious threats but lucky enough to experience only little variation in its consumption; in this case focusing on the variability of actual welfare outcomes would understate the household's true vulnerability.

After these initial clarifications, it is useful to clarify desirable ingredients of vulnerability concepts. First of all, since vulnerability is a forward-looking concept that aims at quantifying something ex ante, a time horizon has to be fixed which determines whether vulnerability in the upcoming week, month or year and so on is measured. Secondly, the forward-looking character of vulnerability also implies that households' subjective time preference should be taken into account: the immediate threat of an illness may be more important for the current well-being and behaviour of a household than a potentially bad harvest next year. Thirdly – and arguably most importantly – a benchmark (such as the poverty line or the current level of well-being) must be set that allows one to measure the extent of vulnerability with respect to a particular loss. Moreover, it is crucial to find a method of quantifying the probabilities and degrees of deprivation of every possible state of the world which falls below this benchmark. As will be shown below, this will be one of the most important challenges when empirically applying vulnerability concepts. Among other factors, it implies knowledge of the households' risk profile, and it must also account for the households' capacities to prevent, mitigate and cope with risks.[8] Last but not least, risk attitudes have to be considered. Risk-neutral households behave in a different way than risk-averse ones do. Also, the welfare of different households is differently affected by risk. Most likely, households in developing countries are risk-averse (for example, Newbery and Stiglitz, 1981, as well as Binswanger, 1981). But even in this case it is of interest to reveal heterogeneous risk attitudes.[9]

Given these considerations, it is clear that the data requirements are particularly challenging.[10] Thus, not only the exposure to adverse events has to be captured, but also the extent to which households fear them, as well as the ways in which they deal with them. As aforementioned, we are interested in vulnerability at the *household* level, therefore household surveys constitute the primary data source within the context of vulnerability research. Furthermore, since vulnerability is a dynamic concept, panel data which captures inter-temporal variability in well-being is better suited to its analysis than is cross-sectional data. However, the latter may still be used when vulnerability as expected poverty is estimated (see below). Also, cross-sectional data may contain retrospective information on past shocks or be combined with time-series data on, for instance, rainfall patterns which would add an inter-temporal component to the otherwise "static" data. In addition to this vulnerability-specific data, information conventionally collected in household surveys is required to fully assess households' levels of vulnerability. This information includes, but is not limited to, determinants of households' risk management capacities such as their stock of assets, endowments of land, social networks, access to credit and insurance markets and so on.

2.4 Existing concepts and measures of vulnerability

Concepts and measures of vulnerability at the household level can broadly be grouped into vulnerability as uninsured exposure to risk, vulnerability as low expected utility, vulnerability as expected poverty, and vulnerability to poverty. With the exception of the latter this categorization is adapted from Hoddinott and Quisumbing (2003) who offer a thorough comparison of different concepts of vulnerability including their advantages and shortcomings. Another useful guide to the analysis of risk and vulnerability is provided by Hoogeveen *et al.* (2004). Also, insightful studies with respect to vulnerability as uninsured exposure to risk, vulnerability as low expected utility, and vulnerability as expected poverty are Ligon and Schechter (2004), as well as Gaiha and Imai (2009) who apply these concepts empirically to the same dataset and compare the results. Vulnerability to poverty is the most recent of the four concepts and is discussed in Calvo and Dercon (2005).

2.4.1 Vulnerability as uninsured exposure to risk

The concept of vulnerability as uninsured exposure to risk stems from the risk-sharing literature (for example Townsend, 1994, and Amin *et al.*, 2003). It simply measures whether income shocks translate into changes in consumption. If idiosyncratic income shocks did not significantly impact on consumption there would be "perfect" risk sharing within the group of interest (mostly the village). In this sense vulnerability as uninsured exposure to risk is closely related to the World Bank's definition of vulnerability according to which "vulnerability measures the resilience against a shock" (World Bank, 2000).

When applied econometrically, idiosyncratic and covariate shocks are usually measured using the growth rate of average household income (Δy_{htv}) and the growth rate of average village income ($\Delta(\overline{\ln y_{tv}})$), respectively, of household h in village v at time t as shown in Equation 2.1:

$$\Delta \ln c_{htv} = \alpha + \beta \ln \Delta y_{htv} + \gamma \Delta(\overline{\ln y_{tv}}) + \Delta \varepsilon_{htv} \tag{2.1}$$

where $\Delta \ln c_{htv}$ denotes the growth rate of consumption per capita between periods t and $t-1$, and $\Delta \varepsilon_{htv}$ reflects the change of the error term between these two periods. In empirical applications of the concept, Equation 2.1 is usually extended by including other explanatory variables such as household and fixed-time effects. Vulnerability as uninsured exposure to risk rises with an increasing β. Complete risk sharing is implied by $\beta = 0$. The coefficient γ captures the impact of (uninsurable) covariate shocks on consumption.

Besides the work by Townsend (1994) and Amin *et al.* (2003), empirical studies include, for instance, the study by Skoufias and Quisumbing (2005), who discuss the results of five IFPRI case studies which analysed vulnerability as uninsured exposure to risk of households in Bangladesh, Ethiopia, Mali, Mexico and Russia. They show that in none of these countries is there perfect risk sharing, and that food consumption is less affected by idiosyncratic shocks than non-food consumption.

From our point of view the concept of vulnerability as uninsured exposure to risk has great merits in the consumption smoothing and insurance literature but does not really advance the vulnerability concept for the following reasons: first, it is conceptually not forward-looking; also, the concept of vulnerability as uninsured exposure to risk implies that it is not levels that matter, but only changes of consumption – albeit changes with respect to the current level of consumption. Third the concept is not concerned with the likelihood of adverse idiosyncratic and covariate shocks, a key ingredient of a vulnerability concept. Finally, the risk attitude of households is not accounted for.

2.4.2 Vulnerability as low expected utility

The concept of vulnerability as low expected utility draws on the association of vulnerability with variability. More precisely, it scrutinizes the variance of consumption (or income) of households and interprets it as their vulnerability. The higher the variance, the more vulnerable a household is.

This approach was applied early by, for example, Glewwe and Hall (1998), Dercon (1999) and Coudouel and Hentschel (2000), all of whom label households that experienced a high variability of income (in the latter case) or consumption (in the former cases) in the past as vulnerable. However, Ligon and Schechter (2003) were the first to formally conceptualize vulnerability as low expected utility, putting "expected utility" at the core of vulnerability assessments. The concept sets the vulnerability of household h (VEU_h) equal to the difference between the household's utility derived from certainty-equivalent consumption

(z_{CE}) and the household's expected utility derived from its actual consumption (c_h):

$$VEU_h = U_h(z_{CE}) - EU_h(c_h) \qquad (2.2)$$

By assuming U_h to be a weakly concave, strictly increasing function, vulnerability as low expected utility accounts for risk preferences and is thus well suited for quantifying the welfare loss generated by shocks. Another very useful feature of this concept is that vulnerability can be decomposed into a poverty component, a covariate-risk component and an idiosyncratic-risk component, as shown in Equation 2.3:

$$VEU_h = U_h(z_{CE}) - U_h(Ec_h) \qquad \text{(poverty component)}$$

$$+ \{U_h(Ec_h) - EU_h[E(cy_h \mid X')]\} \qquad \text{(covariate-risk componet)} \qquad (2.3)$$

$$+ \{EU_h[E(c_h \mid X')] - EU_h(c_h)\} \qquad \text{(idiosyncratic-risk component)}$$

where $E(c_h \mid X')$ equals the expected value of consumption given a vector of covariant variables X'. Ligon and Schechter (2003) apply the measure of vulnerability as low expected utility to data from post-communist Bulgaria, and find that education and owning livestock reduce vulnerability whereas living in urban areas and larger households is associated with higher levels of vulnerability.

The big advantage of the concept and measure of vulnerability as low expected utility is that it assigns a prominent position to the risk attitudes of households. Also, it, in principle, considers all key ingredients of vulnerability concepts, including the role of the likelihood and severity of shocks on welfare. However, the advantage of risk sensitivity comes at the cost of allowing possible positive outcomes to compensate for the vulnerability-increasing effect of possible negative outcomes. Furthermore, negative shocks are not even weighted more than windfalls; a household might be labelled "non-vulnerable" although in at least one possible future state of the world it faces severe destitution, so such a property is not in fact desirable. Related to this, this approach takes as the benchmark current consumption, which suggests that very rich and very poor households may be just as vulnerable if they face the same risk profile and have the same risk attitudes. So it is not particularly focused on vulnerability to deprivation, and thus its link to the poverty literature cited above is somewhat tenuous.

In addition, while conceptually forward-looking, the empirical application of vulnerability as low expected utility is not actually forward-looking. By using past variation in consumption or income it implicitly and very stringently assumes that this variation is stationary over time and will be the same in future. Lastly, as already discussed above, from our point of view vulnerability is not equal to the variance of a welfare indicator around the mean of a certain indicator of well-being like consumption. If we have only a little information on past variations (for instance, very few waves of panel data), we may underestimate the actual risk a household faces, which is likely to be greater than the realized outcomes in a short span of time. Moreover, we may mistakenly assess the relative vulnerability of households. Even if two households face the same risk profile, one household might appear less vulnerable in this formulation if it had been lucky in the past and experienced fewer negative shocks than had another household.

2.4.3   Vulnerability as expected poverty

Having discussed two approaches of vulnerability which do not refer to the poverty line as a relevant threshold for their analysis, we now turn to concepts that explicitly consider this benchmark.[11] Measures of expected poverty were inspired by Ravallion (1988), and advanced by, for instance, Holzmann and Jorgensen (1999), who define vulnerability as "the risk of economic units (such as individuals, households, and communities) to fall below the poverty line (that is, having insufficient consumption and access to basic services) or, for those already below the poverty line, to remain in or to fall further into poverty". Other approaches to expected poverty include Pritchett *et al.* (2000) as well as Mansuri and Healy (2000). They interpret vulnerability as the probability that a household would experience at least one episode of poverty in the next few years.

The approach of vulnerability as expected poverty (*VEP*) formally conceptualizes this idea (Chaudhuri *et al.*, 2002). More precisely, it measures the probability that a household's future consumption ($c_{h,t+1}$) will be below a pre-determined poverty line z in future, and sets it equal to its actual degree of vulnerability:

$$VEP_{ht} = \mathrm{pr}(c_{h,t+1} \leq z) \tag{2.4}$$

That is, the concept is forward-looking although, for instance, the rate at which households discount the future is not considered. The poverty line serves as a clear-cut benchmark, and *VEP* is explicitly aimed at quantifying the probability of being below this reference point.

On the other hand, vulnerability as expected poverty as presented in Equation 2.4 does not account for risk sensitivity: Households are said to exhibit the same degree of vulnerability if they have the same expected outcome. However, uncertainty is likely to have a negative impact on well-being, therefore a household which will certainly receive the expected outcome should be less vulnerable than households facing different possible future outcomes. The severity of expected poverty is not considered, either. That is, a household with a 50 per cent probability of being a little below the poverty line has the same vulnerability as a household with a 50 per cent probability of being far below the poverty line.

These shortcomings can easily be addressed by combining vulnerability as expected poverty with the Foster–Greer–Thorbecke (1984) measures of poverty (Hoddinott and Quisumbing, 2003). Assuming that $\sum_{i=1}^{N_h} p_{hi}$ reflects the sum of probabilities of all possible future scenarios faced by household h, and that $I_{hi}(\cdot)$ represents an indicator which equals one if $c_{hi,t} \leq z$, and zero otherwise, Equation 2.4 can be transformed into:

$$VEP_{ht} = \sum_{i=1}^{N_h} p_{hi} * I_{hi}(c_{hi,t+1} \leq z) * \left(\frac{z - c_{hi,t+1}}{z} \right)^{\alpha} \qquad (2.5)$$

Here, α captures the depth of poverty and the type of poverty which is measured: $\alpha = 0$ provides the expected poverty headcount, $\alpha = 1$ the expected poverty gap, and $\alpha > 1$ the expected severity of poverty.

Nonetheless, the concept of vulnerability as expected poverty based on the Foster–Greer–Thorbecke measures of poverty integrates households' risk attitudes only imperfectly. This is due to the fact that $\alpha > 1$ also implies a measure of risk aversion (with $\alpha = 1$ implying risk neutrality). But this has problematic connotations in the context of vulnerability assessments. It actually implies that households have increasing absolute risk aversion. However, such a risk preference is contrary to empirical findings (Hoddinott and Quisumbing, 2003; Binswanger, 1981).[12] It also implies (if the higher risk now includes states of the world that are above the poverty line) the unfortunate connotation that in some circumstances increases in risk can reduce vulnerability (Hoddinott and Quisumbing, 2003). Empirical applications of vulnerability as expected poverty are numerous (for example, Suryahadi and Sumarto, 2003 and Kamanou and Morduch, 2004, as well as Christiaensen and Subbarao, 2004). Günther and Harttgen (2009) extend this method to account for the share of vulnerability to poverty accounted for by idiosyncratic and covariate shocks. Although as shown in the previous equation vulnerability of expected poverty can be combined with the Foster–Greer–Thorbecke measures of poverty, most of them focus on the probability of being poor, that is the expected headcount of poverty. Furthermore, these approaches estimate the expected distribution of future expenditures for households, which underlie the subsequent quantification of vulnerability, via methods that are not truly forward-looking and imply unsatisfactory assumptions. For example, Chaudhuri *et al.* (2002) use error term distributions from cross-sectional data, arguing that they reflect all possible future states of the world for each household in the sample. In this method it is implicitly assumed that (i) past distributions reflect future distributions, that is that the world is stationary, (ii) measurement error in consumption data does not exist (the error term is the idiosyncratic source of uncertainty which would be biased by such an error), and (iii) all sampled households are exposed to the same distribution of consumption changes, which means that their risk exposure is homogeneous. None of these assumptions is likely, however, to hold true in reality. An alternative approach is put forward by Kamanou and Morduch (2004) who use the bootstrap method to derive distributions of possible future expenditures from observed household characteristics and past fluctuations of consumption; again, strict assumptions are necessary, such as the homogeneity of households with respect to their risk exposure.

Finally, in the applications of vulnerability as expected poverty, an arbitrary probability threshold has to be established below which households are regarded as being vulnerable.[13] As Chaudhuri *et al.* (2002) point out, the choice of this benchmark is subjective. Most authors simply use 50 per cent; thus they consider as vulnerable those households which have a probability of 50 per cent or more of being poor in the future (Chaudhuri *et al.*, 2002). Alternatively, Rajadel (2002) sets the "vulnerability line" equal to the observed headcount ratio of poverty. Zhang and Wan (2008) compare both vulnerability lines and find that the former performs better with respect to predictive power of future poverty.

2.4.4   Vulnerability to poverty

Another concept that relies on the poverty line is the axiomatic approach of vulnerability to poverty advanced by Calvo and Dercon (2005). In their framework, vulnerability is a probability-weighted average of future states of the world-specific indices of deprivation. They calculate the vulnerability to poverty of household h as shown in Equation 2.6:

$$vulnerbility\ to\ Poverty_h = 1 - \left(\sum_{i=1}^{N_h} p_{hi} \times x_{hi}^{\alpha} \right) \qquad (2.6)$$

where α ranges between zero and one. N_h reflects the number of possible future scenarios, p_{hi} denotes the probability of the state of the world

i to occur and x_{hi} is a state-specific degree of deprivation which equals $\frac{\tilde{y}_{hi}}{z}$. $\tilde{y}_{hi}$ is a censored outcome measure; that is, all outcomes where y_{hi} is above the poverty line z are censored at z, and consequently do not change the vulnerability measure. The closer (further away) α moves to (from) one, the less (more) risk aversion is assumed. By not allowing α to rise beyond one, the possibility of risk proclivity is discarded. α is not only a parameter of risk aversion but also comparable to the α from the Foster–Greer–Thorbecke measures of poverty in the sense that it measures the severity of possible future poverty if it is below one.

Among the axioms proposed within the context of vulnerability to poverty, the following two are particularly important:[14] first, the axiom of risk sensitivity implies that while keeping the expected outcome constant an increase in uncertainty faced by a household should be reflected in a higher degree of vulnerability (that is, the measure of vulnerability to poverty accounts for risk attitudes). Second, the focus axiom is supposed to ensure that the vulnerability measure is exclusively sensitive to negative future states of the world. Instead, positive future outcomes must not be reflected in the measure.[15] In other words, this axiom guarantees that a household is not labelled "non-vulnerable" even though in a possible future scenario it faces destitution (as it could be, for example, in the case of vulnerability as low expected utility). Since Calvo and Dercon (2005) are concerned with vulnerability to poverty, they interpret the axiom as being adhered to if exclusively outcomes below the poverty line impact on a measure of vulnerability.

In a later work Calvo and Dercon (2007) introduce an aggregate measure of vulnerability to poverty which follows the axiomatic approach. Another application of the concept of vulnerability to poverty is, for example, de la Fuente (2010) who uses vulnerability to explain households' prospects for receiving support from others. More precisely, after estimating vulnerability to poverty the author instruments it by rainfall patterns and some interactions of rainfall with other explanatory variables in order to account for reverse causality. His results suggest that those who are vulnerable to poverty are not more likely to receive more remittances.

Calvo (2008) extends the measure of "vulnerability to poverty" to "vulnerability to *multidimensional* poverty". He shows that when combining the concept of vulnerability to poverty with multidimensional poverty, special attention should be paid not only to the correlation between different dimensions of well-being, but also to their correlation between different states of the world. Using household data from Peru, as well as consumption and leisure as dimensions of well-being, he illustrates the application of vulnerability to multidimensional poverty.

The concept and applications of vulnerability to (multidimensional) poverty build on a clear-cut threshold (the poverty line), assign probabilities and degrees of deprivation to each relevant state of the world, and account for risk aversion. However, as in the case of other concepts of vulnerability, the empirical applications are not truly forward-looking and are based on problematic assumptions about the relevance of past variability to future risks. For example, Calvo (2008) estimates past consumption for five periods and interprets the corresponding error terms as idiosyncratic shocks drawn from a "random" distribution. He assumes further that it is only these five events that can possibly occur in future and that they are equally likely, which he himself suggests is "oversimplified".

2.5 Approaches to address conceptual and empirical shortcomings of existing measures of vulnerability

Although the literature on concepts and measures of vulnerability is rich and rapidly evolving, each concept continues to have some shortcomings in its assumptions or empirical application. Two issues will be focused on here: the relevant benchmark and the basis for estimating future risks.

Conceptually, most recently from the work by Calvo and Dercon (2005) the poverty line has been established as the widely accepted benchmark against which vulnerability of households is assessed. However, there are at least two reasons to doubt that the poverty line as a pre-determined threshold is invariably the best choice as a (unique) reference point:

First, by using this benchmark, households are unequivocally labelled "non-vulnerable" as long as they do not face at least one future state of the world in which they will be poor. Thus, a household which is likely to fall from well above the poverty line to just above it is not considered to be vulnerable, whereas a household which is likely to fall much less far, namely from just above the poverty line to just below it, is defined as vulnerable. Although the former

> not only faces a future very similar to that of the latter (both households will be very close to the poverty line) the former – unlike the household expected to be just below the poverty line – faces a much higher loss of welfare; nevertheless, it is still said to be non-vulnerable. It should be noted, however, that this shortcoming is not peculiar to the quantification of vulnerability but applies to the measurement of poverty in general.

Second, the choice of the poverty line as the benchmark may not be consistent with the way households perceive shocks. There is a sizeable literature on habit-formation effects that suggests that the subjective well-being of households reacts particularly strongly to negative changes in (relative)

incomes, regardless of whether households are poor or not (for example, Easterlin, 2003). Thus, at least subjectively, current levels of well-being are quite an important benchmark for households. Conversely, households below the poverty line might find the prospect of a positive shock that would take them closer to the poverty line not so much a source of continued vulnerability as a positive prospect.

Certainly, for policy targeting the poverty line is an important, if not the crucial, benchmark. But also the direction of prospective movements below this threshold,

as well as shortfalls above it, matter, and therefore the introduction of the current level of well-being and the combination of both of these reference points have the potential to add value to ongoing vulnerability research.[16]

As an alternative, choosing the current level of well-being as the relevant benchmark may be useful, since households rely on their own *status quo* as reference point for any assessment of future outcomes. Such a benchmark

would require a re-interpretation of the focus axiom. More precisely, only *negative* changes from current well-being would be considered; that is, the measure would merely reflect *vulnerability to downside risk*.

In spite of the potential advantage of such an approach, its shortcomings are obvious, particularly from the point of view of a policy maker who aims at fighting poverty: first, any assessment of vulnerability that exclusively refers to the current level of well-being as benchmark suffers from the unsatisfactory characteristic that it does not place any special weight on poor households. In fact, very rich households may also be

considered vulnerable; for example, households whose wealth is tied up in the stock market may be labelled vulnerable to stock market fluctuations. In other words, in contrast to the use of the poverty line, where households expected to be just above as against just below the benchmark are classified very differently although they are threatened by a very similar future, here the problem is that households might be classified very similarly despite the fact that they face a very different future in terms of their expected levels of consumption. Second, a vulnerability measure which is based on the current level of well-being would not be affected by upward movements below the poverty line, which may certainly reflect the attitude of *chronically* poor households that do not feel vulnerable due to such movements. However, from the point of view of *transitorily* poor households, it may be desirable to incorporate even these sorts of changes into the measurement. To exemplify this, consider a usually non-poor household that is observed right after falling into poverty. For such a household, every state of the world which leaves it in deprivation would arguably contribute to its perceived vulnerability – at least as long as the reference point of this household is not its current but its accustomed level of well-being. Also, regardless of the subjective views of households, upward movements below the poverty line should increase recorded vulnerability if the ultimate goal of the measurement is to contribute accurately to the design of poverty-reducing policies.

Finally, as in the case of poverty measurement, the use of an absolute benchmark which is fixed and commonly accepted facilitates comparisons of vulnerability across different regions and countries.

When considering the arguments in favour of and against the two reference points, it emerges that a combination of both the poverty line and the current level of well-being as relevant benchmarks may add value to vulnerability research. Such an amalgamation would again require a modification of the focus axiom in the sense that it is exclusively states of the world that are considered in which a household is below the poverty line *and* facing downside risks to its current level of well-being. Consequently, only *downside* risks which put households (further) *below* the poverty line would be considered. In other words, there could be households that are threatened by poverty but are not vulnerable because their outlook is towards being *less* poor, and these would not be covered.[17]

With respect to the empirical analysis of vulnerability, a key weakness of current studies is that they equate past shocks with future risks. The disregard of the actual exposure to, as well as of the probability and potential severity of, risks leads Dercon (2009) to criticize the common focus of vulnerability literature on "fate" rather than on "fear" in households. Also Cafiero and Vakis (2006) stress that "none of … [the empirical approaches to vulnerability] is truly consistent with an ex-ante view of assessing the true consequences of risk exposure". The underlying assumption of these approaches, that shocks will evolve over time and space just as they did beforehand, is by no means likely. For example, a household which suffered from a drought in the past does not face a corresponding risk if meanwhile a reliable irrigation system has been built. Therefore, households' vulnerability is as dynamic as the concept itself. This point has already been made by Davies (1996), who argues that vulnerability is not a steady state, and Siegel *et al.* (2003) who point out that "levels of vulnerability themselves change over time".

The crucial question in this context is how data on the probability and characteristics of relevant future states of the world which are below the benchmark of interest can be generated. One possible answer to this question is surprisingly straightforward: households have to be asked directly about their risk perception.[18] This way of data gathering not only avoids retrospective information and has the potential to reveal perceived probabilities and severities of future risks but also has other advantages. To follow this argument, recall that vulnerability matters, among other factors, because of two aspects: its negative effect on current well-being as well as its impact on economic behaviour and, consequently, on future well-being (for example Ligon and Schechter, 2004, Elbers *et al.*, 2007 and Dercon, 2009). Well-being is obviously subjective. Imagine a household fears, that is perceives the risk of, a drought. Even if researchers "objectively" estimate a very low probability for the drought to occur the household might still harbour this fear – with all its negative implications for current well-being. In addition, these subjective risks may drive actual behaviour, such as investments in risk-mitigation strategies. Finally, when asking households directly, the researcher can easily determine the time horizon of his or her vulnerability assessment by explicitly referring to the period of interest (the upcoming week, month, year, and so on).

In spite of these advantages, the use of data on perceived risks certainly comes at the cost of other stringent assumptions and new problematic issues which are thoroughly discussed in Chapter 4 of this book. Among others, there are the so-called heuristics of probabilities which suggest that individuals are not well equipped to "objectively" assess risks they face (Kahneman *et al.*, 1982). For example, the heuristic of availability provokes a person to consider past experiences when assigning probabilities to possible future events.[19] Consequently, a survey respondent is more likely to expect an illness to take place with a high probability if his or her household has been prone to this kind of shock in the past.[20] In an extreme scenario the respondent may rely entirely on past shocks when forming expectations. In this case the elicitation of subjective probabilities would not add more value to the quantification of vulnerability than would the elicitation of past shocks.

2.6   A measure of perceived vulnerability to downside risk

Based on the considerations above, Povel (2009) develops a measure of perceived vulnerability to downside risk which chooses a household's current level of well-being instead of a pre-determined threshold such as the poverty line as reference point. This subsection is to illustrate the feasibility of such an approach. The empirical analysis is based on risks perceived by a sample of rural Thai and Vietnamese households.

More precisely, Povel (2009) presents a measure of vulnerability that assigns an index of deprivation d_{hi} – with zero implying no deprivation and one implying the highest possible deprivation – to every future state of the world i that a household h can possibly experience. Each of these states is weighted with its probability of occurrence p_{hi} before all of the weighted deprivation indices are added up. Thus, for N_h possible future states of the world, the vulnerability of household h (V_h) is given by Equation 2.7:[21]

$$V_h = \sum_{i=1}^{N_h} p_{hi} \times d_{hi}{}^{\alpha}, \quad \text{with} \quad 0 \le d_{hi} \le 1 \quad \text{and} \quad \sum_{i=1}^{N_h} p_{hi} = 1. \tag{2.7}$$

α is a parameter measuring risk attitudes. If $\alpha > 1$ risk aversion is assumed, if $0 < \alpha < 1$ a kind of "risk-loving loss aversion" is implied, and if $\alpha = 1$ households are said to be risk neutral.

The measure of perceived vulnerability to downside risk is applied to data from the second wave of a household survey conducted within the context of the research project on "Vulnerability in South-East Asia" in 2008.[22] The empirical application relies primarily on information provided by the risk section of the survey's questionnaire, which is discussed in greater detail in Chapter 4. This section was designed to shed light on, *inter alia*, the probability of downside risks a household faces during the upcoming five years, as well as the severity of the impact of those risks on income. Since the data originates from the present (t) and reflects expectations concerning the time after t, it is well suited to an ex-ante assessment of vulnerability.

Concerning the perceived impact on income of a future event, the respondents had to state whether it would have "high", "moderate", "low", or "no" impact if it occurred within the next twelve months. The respective answers were transformed into numerical values such that the worst possible state-specific index of deprivation from Equation

2.7 equals one. Perceived probabilities were obtained by asking the respondents about the expected frequency of occurrence of a certain event within the next five years. To a frequency of zero (one, two, three, four, five or more) a probability of 0 per cent (20 per cent, 40 per cent, 60 per cent, 80 per cent, 100 per cent) was assigned. The probability of a certain future state of the world was then calculated by multiplying the probabilities of the risks expected to take place in this state by each other, as well as by the probabilities that all other possible risks would not occur.

Assuming equally risk-averse households, that is setting α from Equation 2.7 equal to 2, Povel (2009) uses this information to quantify the vulnerability of 2070 Thai and 1805 Vietnamese households to 11 downside risks.[23] As Table 2.1 shows, households in Vietnam are more vulnerable to perceived downside risks than households in Thailand. The average of the vulnerability indices of the former (0.0529) is about 75 per cent higher than that of the latter (0.0302). In addition, the lower bound of the 95 per cent-confidence interval of Vietnam's aggregate vulnerability (0.0499) is considerably above the upper bound of Thailand's corresponding interval (0.0319). Another finding is that households are much more heterogeneous in terms of vulnerability in Vietnam than in Thailand: perceived vulnerability values in the former country range between 0 and 0.4298 (with a standard deviation of 0.0654) whereas they range between 0 and 0.3301 (with a standard deviation of 0.0388) in the latter country.

The results of a multivariate analysis of the determinants of vulnerability to downside risk in Thailand and Vietnam are presented in Table 2.2. In both countries the share of household members employed

Table 2.1 Perceived vulnerability to downside risk in Thailand and Vietnam ($\alpha = 2$)

	min	median	mean	max	standard deviation	95% confidence interval
Vietnam (n = 1805)	0	0.0305	0.0529	0.4298	0.0654	0.0499 0.0559
Thailand (n = 2070)	0	0.0166	0.0302	0.3301	0.0388	0.0286 0.0319
Total (n = 3875)	0	0.0223	0.0408	0.4298	0.0540	0.0391 0.0425

Source: Povel (2009).

Table 2.2 Determinants of vulnerability to downside risk in Thailand and Vietnam, dependent variable: vulnerability to downside risk ($\alpha = 2$)

independent variables	Thailand	Vietnam
# of household members	0.0022***	0.0008
	(–0.0005)	(–0.0011)
share of household members with off-farm employment	0.0042	–0.0208***
	(–0.0037)	(–0.0078)
share of self-employed household members	–0.0047	–0.0279**
	(–0.0063)	(–0.0123)
share of household members employed in own agriculture	0.0278***	0.0374***
	(–0.0036)	(–0.0074)
age of household head	–0.0011**	0.0009
	(–0.0005)	(–0.0008)
squared age of household head	0.0000**	0.0000
	(0.0000)	(0.0000)
sex of household head (1 = female, 0 = male)	–0.0021	0.0016
	(–0.0021)	(–0.0046)
household head belongs to ethnic minority (1 = yes, 0 = no)	0.0010	0.0127**
	(–0.0042)	(–0.0050)
years of school enrolment of household head	0.0014	0.0023*
	(–0.0010)	(–0.0012)
squared years of school enrolment of household head	–0.0001	–0.0001
	(–0.0001)	(–0.0001)
lagged household income	–0.0013*	–0.0045***
	(–0.0008)	(–0.0014)
land of household (in ha)	0.0012*	–0.0024
	(–0.0007)	(–0.0020)
Squared land of household	–0.0001*	0.0001
	(0.0000)	(–0.0001)
Constant	0.0372**	0.0417*
	(–0.0165)	(–0.0227)
Observations	2008	1704

Note: Both regressions are Tobit estimations; standard errors in parentheses; asterisks denote significance at the 1%- (***); 5%- (**); 10%- (*) level; dummy variables at the province level are included but not reported.
Source: Povel (2009).

in agriculture has a strongly significant (at the 1 per cent level) and positive impact on vulnerability. Given the adverse events underlying the dependent variable, namely, *inter alia*, two agricultural and four weather-related risks, this result is not surprising. The fact that the shares of household members with off-farm or self-employment do not impact significantly on vulnerability in Thailand implies that non-agricultural income sources are certainly not as risky as agricultural sources but do not have a vulnerability-decreasing effect, either. In contrast, Vietnamese households which diversify their income sources and engage in off-farm or self employment do not just escape the threat of future harm associated with agricultural employment but even decrease their degree of vulnerab ility. In the case of off-farm employment this relation is significant at the 1 per cent level, regarding self-employment at the 5 per cent level.

In Vietnam the income-richer a household, the less it suffers from perceived vulnerability. This correlation is significant at the 1 per cent level, whereas in Thailand this relation is statistically significant at the 10 per cent level. This result was to be expected since higher income levels enable households to, among other things, access credit and insurance markets more easily and therefore to be able to manage risk more efficiently by, for example, contracting insurances.

Both countries also differ in terms of the impact of land holdings on vulnerability. Similarly to income, land holdings are expected to decrease vulnerability because they facilitate the households' access to credit markets when used as collateral. On the other hand, more land leads to a higher degree of perceived vulnerability to downside risk if it increases the risk exposure of households. In Thailand the vulnerability of households increases – significantly at the 10 per cent level – with each additional hectare of land holdings. That is, the latter effect seems to outweigh the former. By contrast, in Vietnam there is no statistically significant relationship between vulnerability and the size of land holdings.

The age of the household head is negatively correlated with vulnerability and statistically significant at the 5 per cent level. However, this relation is not linear since the head's squared age impacts significantly negative on perceived vulnerability. While the Thai case is plausible – increasing age is likely to be associated with increasing (risk management) capacities, employment opportunities and income – it is not apparent why the situation is not similar in Vietnam, where the correlation is not distinguishable from zero. The same applies to household size: in Thailand more household members are associated with higher levels of vulnerability, probably because bigger households are more prone to risks like illness or job loss, whereas in Vietnam this correlation is again not statistically significant. By contrast, in Vietnam the ethnic minority dummy is significantly correlated with vulnerability, whereas in Thailand it is not. In other words, in Vietnam households headed by a member of an ethnic minority tend to be more exposed to risks than households in the ethnic majority.

Surprisingly, the "sex of household head"-dummy and years of school enrolment do not show a significant, or only a very weak, correlation with perceived vulnerability. The fact that female-headed households are not more vulnerable than their male-headed counterparts can possibly be explained by remittances; these improve households' risk-management capacities because they stem from an income source subject to risks other than the ones "at home" and may vary in scale depending on the households' needs to cope with adverse events. In both countries female-headed households receive more remittances per household member than their male-headed counterparts (on average about 55 per cent more in Vietnam and 17 per cent more in Thailand).

The lack of predictive power of the proxy for education might be caused by two contrary effects: on the one hand, households with better educated household heads perceive themselves as less threatened by risks because they can deal with them more efficiently. On the other hand, better educated individuals probably assess future risks more adequately in terms of their probability and severity than less educated ones, therefore their risk perception may seem to be relatively pronounced. In fact, the latter argument would explain the significantly positive coefficient (at the 10 per cent level) in the Vietnamese specification. Since in both countries the squared years of school enrolment are not differentiable from zero there is no statistical evidence for a non-linear relationship between vulnerability and education.

This application shows that it is feasible to study vulnerability using ex-ante risk information and that the results generate new insights into perceived vulnerability of households. At the same time, the quantification of the risks, their probabilities and their severity is clearly an issue that deserves further attention as currently rather crude methods of quantification were used based on the available data.

2.7   Summary and directions for future research

Vulnerability research constitutes a relatively recent and rapidly evolving part of development economics, with important implications for development policy. While the conceptual discussion is quite advanced, it appears that all existing concepts continue to suffer from conceptual or empirical shortcomings. Perhaps the most serious relates to the fact that all of these concepts effectively use past data on shocks and their impact in order to assess future vulnerability. Also, there are some questions about the exclusive use of the poverty line as the relevant benchmark.

The approach of perceived vulnerability to downside risk proposed by Povel (2009) suggests ways to tackle these issues: first, it takes a household's current status of well-being as reference point. Second, it is applied to the forward-looking, subjective risk perception of households, in this case rural households in Thailand and Vietnam. It showed that both levels and determinants of perceived vulnerability to downside risk differ considerably between the two countries.

Clearly, more research is needed on this important issue. Among the critical issues to consider are: further conceptual work on combining different benchmarks, possible biases of subjective risk perceptions, the ability to better capture the impact of past shocks and future risks, and comparative assessment of different conceptual and empirical approaches which includes the comparison of the performance of different benchmarks in empirical applications. Much progress will also depend on the generation of suitable panel data on well-being, shocks and risks, an issue that is currently being pursued within the context of this research program.

Notes

1. Note that more recently civil war as another type of shock increasingly receives attention (see, for instance, Bundervoet *et al.*, 2009).
2. Note that also vulnerability measures that consider the poverty line to be their relevant benchmark are related to consumption smoothing. However, in these cases unsuccessful consumption smoothing does not impact on vulnerability as long as consumption levels stay above the poverty line.
3. Such poverty traps can exist at the household or regional level. See Jalan and Ravallion (2002) for further discussion.
4. Despite these different levels of analysis, vulnerability research at these different levels of aggregation is concerned with very similar aspects at the country, regional, and household level. Thus, in all three cases it deals with the risk of experiencing negative events that have the potential to decrease the wellbeing of individuals and the abilities to deal with them.
5. More precisely, in this context vulnerability is understood as the potential damage from natural disasters that can materialize at any level of analysis (Kreimer and Arnold, 2000). This damage depends on people's capacities to anticipate, cope with, and recover from natural disasters (Blackie et. al., 1994).

6. As will be discussed below, only concepts which interpret vulnerability as variability do not exclusively rely on downside risks.
7. Note that the discussion in this paragraph focuses on poverty in a single (usually monetary) dimension. If poverty is seen as a multidimensional concept, vulnerability could be interpreted as another dimension of it (World Bank, 2000).
8. Risk management strategies include the consumption and income-smoothing strategies mentioned above. For a detailed discussion of them see, for example, Holzmann and Jorgensen (1999).
9. Note that all of the empirical applications in the field of vulnerability research that are presented below do not tackle at least one of the points raised here – for example, to our knowledge there exists no study which explicitly considers discount factors within the context of vulnerability – and the applications are very vague regarding at least one of the other points.
10. For an extensive discussion of data requirements see Chapters 3 and 4.
11. Another approach which is not presented here aims at merging the concepts of poverty and vulnerability such that the poverty line is augmented by a vulnerability component (Cafiero and Vakis, 2006).
12. In the case of Foster-Greer-Thorbecke measures of poverty, the absolute risk aversion is given by $(\alpha -1)*$(poverty line)/(poverty line – household consumption) (Hoddinott and Quisumbing, 2003).
13. Note that this is done in addition to an arguably arbitrary poverty line.
14. The axioms which are not elaborated are: (i) axiom of symmetry over states, (ii) axiom of continuity and differentiability, (iii) axiom of scale invariance, (iv) axiom of normalization, (v) axiom of the probability-dependent effect of outcomes, (vi) axiom of probability transfer, and (vii) axiom of constant relative or absolute risk sensitivity. For an in-depth discussion of them, see Calvo and Dercon (2005).
15. Note that in the context of vulnerability research the focus axiom had already been implicitly put forward by authors such as Siegel *et al.* (2003). Calvo and Dercon (2005) offer the following example to illustrate the need for the focus axiom: "let us imagine that the poor buy each week a state lottery ticket – they spend a very small sum of money, but 'you never know', and there is a 0.001 per cent chance of winning the top prize of $10,000. The following 'policy' measure would make these households less vulnerable [if the focus axiom was not applied] …: increase the top prize to $10 million!"
16. Note that the idea of using the current level of well-being as relevant threshold in the context of vulnerability research is not new. For example, in its World Development Report from 2000/2001 the World Bank (2000) states that "vulnerability [is] the resulting possibility of a decline in well-being". Also, the concept of vulnerability as uninsured exposure to risk implicitly draws on this benchmark.
17. This formulation only considers downside risks facing poor people. An alternative approach could be to also consider upside risks for poor people as long as they are still below the poverty line, but put a much smaller weight on the risks. This would also account for the perception of transitorily poor households that feel more vulnerable due to the prospect of less deprivation (see above).
18. For an in-depth discussion of subjective risk perception and its measurement see Chapter 4.

19. Kahneman *et al.* (1982) analyse two other heuristics: first, the heuristic of representativeness implies that a person regards a certain sequence of events as being more likely than another although both sequences have the same probability. For example, when playing roulette in a casino people tend to bet on red if black won several previous times. However, the probability of red and black remains equal and unchanged all the time. Second, the heuristic of adjustment (or anchoring) provokes the respondent to stick to any value which he or she may have had in mind beforehand. Thus, if a certain value is suggested to the respondent during an on-the-spot interview, he or she may succumb to the heuristic of adjustment and then state this value disproportionally often.

20. In this case, examinations of past shocks and subjective risks will suffer from the same problem; that is they will overestimate the risk of an illness for a household that recently experienced such a shock.

21. Note that this measure belongs to "the class of measures where vulnerability is a probability weighted average of state-specific 'deprivation indices'" (Calvo and Dercon, 2005).

22. For more information regarding the survey see Chapters 3 and 4.

23. Appendix 2.A.1 provides summary statistics from the three demographic, four weather-related, two agricultural and two economic risks included in the measure.

References

Alderman, H., J. Hoddinott and B. Kinsey (2006): "Long-Term Consequences of Early Childhood Malnutrition", *Oxford Economic Papers*, 58(3): 450–74.

Amin, S., A. Rai and G. Topa (2003): "Does Microcredit Reach the Poor and Vulnerable? Evidence from Northern Bangladesh", *Journal of Development Economics*, 70(1): 59–82.

Baulch, B. and J. Hoddinott (2000): "Economic Mobility and Poverty Dynamics in Developing Countries", *Journal of Development Studies*, 36(6): 1–24.

Beegle, K., R. H. Dehejia, R. Gatti and S. Krutikova (2008): "The Consequences of Child Labor: Evidence from Longitudinal Data in Rural Tanzania", *Policy Research Working Paper 4677*, World Bank, Washington DC.

Besley, T. (1995): "Nonmarket Institutions for Credit and Risk Sharing in Low-Income Countries", *Journal of Economic Perspectives*, 9(3): 115–27.

Binswanger, H. P. (1981): "Attitudes toward Risk: Theoretical Implications of an Experiment in Rural India", *Economic Journal*, 91(364): 867–90.

Blackie, P., T. Cannon, I. Davis and B. Wisner (1994): *At Risk: Natural Hazards, People's Vulnerability, and Disasters*, Routledge, New York.

Briguglio, L. (1995): "Small Island Developing States and their Economic Vulnerabilities", *World Development*, 23(9): 1615–32.

Briguglio, L. (1997): "Alternative Economic Vulnerability Indices for Developing Countries", *mimeo*, Report prepared for the Expert Group on the Vulnerability Index, UNDESA, New York.

Briguglio, L. and W. Galea (2003): "Updating the Economic Vulnerability Index", *Occasional Papers on Islands and Small States*, Islands and Small States Institute, University of Malta, Valletta.

Bundervoet, T., P. Verwimp and R. Akresh (2009): "Health and Civil War in Rural Burundi", *Journal of Human Resources*, 44(2): 536–63.

Cafiero, C. and R. Vakis (2006): "Risk and Vulnerability Considerations in Poverty Analysis: Recent Advances and Future Directions", *Social Protection Discussion Paper 0610*, World Bank, Washington DC.

Calvo, C. (2008): "Vulnerability to Multidimensional Poverty: Peru 1998–2002", *World Development*, 36(6): 1011–20.

Calvo, C. and S. Dercon (2005): "Measuring Individual Vulnerability", *Department of Economics Discussion Paper Series*, 229, Oxford University, Oxford.

Calvo, C. and S. Dercon (2007): "Chronic Poverty and All That: The Measurement of Poverty over Time", *CSAE Working Paper Series*, WPS/2007–04, Oxford University, Oxford.

Cannon, T. (2008): "Reducing People's Vulnerability to Natural Hazards – Communities and Resilience", *WIDER Research Paper 2008/34*, UNU-WIDER, Helsinki.

Chaudhuri, S., J. Jalan and A. Suryahadi (2002): "Assessing Household Vulnerability to Poverty from Cross-sectional Data: A Methodology and Estimates from Indonesia", *Discussion Papers 0102–52*, Columbia University, New York.

Christiaensen, L. and K. Subbarao (2004): "Toward an Understanding of Household Vulnerability in Rural Kenya", *Journal of African Economies*, 14(4): 520–58.

Chronic Poverty Research Centre (2004): *The Chronic Poverty Report 2004/05*, Institute for Development Policy and Management, University of Manchester, Manchester.

Chronic Poverty Research Centre (2008): *The Chronic Poverty Report 2008/09 – Escaping Poverty Traps*, Institute for Development Policy and Management, University of Manchester, Manchester.

Coudouel, A. and J. Hentschel (2000): "Poverty Data and Measurement", Draft for the Sourcebook on Poverty Reduction Strategies, World Bank, Washington DC.

Davies, S. (1996): *Adaptable Livelihoods: Coping with Food Insecurity in the Malian Sahel*, St. Martin's Press, New York.

Deaton, A. (1997): *The Analysis of Household Surveys: A Microeconomic Approach*, Johns Hopkins University Press, Baltimore.

de la Fuente, A. (2010): "Remittances and Vulnerability to Poverty in Rural Mexico", *World Development*, 38(6): 828–39.

Dercon, S. (1999): "Income Risk, Coping Strategies and Safety Nets", *mimeo*, prepared for the 2000/1 World Development Report, Katholieke Universiteit Leuven, Leuven.

Dercon, S. (2002): "Income Risk, Coping Strategies and Safety Nets", *World Bank Research Observer*, 17: 141–66.

Dercon, S. (2005): "Vulnerability: a Micro Perspective", *mimeo*, paper first presented at the ABCDE for Europe World Bank conference, May, Amsterdam.

Dercon, S. (2009): "Fate and Fear: Risk and Its Consequences in Africa", *Journal of African Economies*, 17(2): 97–127.

Dercon, S. and P. Krishnan (2000): "Vulnerability, Seasonality and Poverty in Ethiopia", *Journal of Development Studies*, 36(6): 25–53.

Easterlin, R. (2003): "Explaining Happiness", *Proceedings of the National Academy of Sciences*, 100(19): 11176–83.

Elbers, C., J. W. Gunning and B. Kinsey (2007): "Growth and Risk: Methodology and Micro Evidence", *World Bank Economic Review*, 21(1): 1–20.

Ellis, F. (1998): "Household Strategies and Rural Livelihood Diversification", *Journal of Development Studies*, 35(1): 1–38.

Fafchamps, M., C. Udry and K. Czukas (1998): "Drought and Saving in West Africa: Are Livestock a Buffer Stock?" *Journal of Development Economics*, 55(2): 273–305.

Farrugia, N. (2004): *Economic Vulnerability: Developing a New Conceptual Framework and Empirically Assessing Its Relationship with Economic Growth*, PhD dissertation, University of Malta, Msida.

Foster, J. E., J. Greer and E. Thorbecke (1984): "A Class of Decomposable Poverty Indices", *Econometrica*, 52: 761–6.

Gaiha, R. and K. Imai (2009): "Measuring Vulnerability and Poverty: Estimates for Rural India", ch. 2 in: W. Naudé, A. Santos-Paulino and M. McGillivray (eds), *Vulnerability in Developing Countries*, United Nations University Press, Helsinki.

Gertler, P. and J. Gruber (2002): "Insuring Consumption Against Illness", *American Economic Review*, 92(1): 51–76.

Ghaiha, R. and A. Deolalikar (1993): "Persistent, Expected and Innate Poverty: Estimates for Semi-arid Rural South India 1975–1984", *Cambridge Journal of Economics*, 17: 409–21.

Glewwe, P. and G. Hall (1998): "Are Some Groups More Vulnerable to Macroeconomic Shocks than Others? Hypothesis Tests Based on Panel Data from Peru", *Journal of Development Economics*, 56: 181–206.

Grimm, M. (2009): "Mortality Shocks and Survivors' Consumption Growth", *Oxford Bulletin of Economics and Statistics*, 72(2): 146–71.

Guillaumont, P. (2009): "An Economic Vulnerability Index: Its Design and Use for International Development Policy", *Oxford Development Studies*, 37(3): 193–228.

Günther, I. and K. Harttgen (2009): "Estimating Households' Vulnerability to Idiosyncratic and Covariate Shocks: a Novel Method Applied in Madagascar", *World Development*, 37(7): 1222–34.

Günther, I. and S. Klasen (2008): "Measuring Chronic Non-Income Poverty", in: A. Addison, D. Hulme and R. Kanbur (eds), *Poverty Dynamics: Interdisciplinary Perspectives*, Oxford University Press, New York.

Hoddinott, J. and A. Quisumbing (2003): "Methods for Microeconometric Risk and Vulnerability Assessments", *Social Protection Discussion Paper 0324*, World Bank, Washington DC.

Holzmann, R. and S. Jorgensen (1999): "Social Protection as Social Risk Management: Conceptual Underpinnings for Social Protection Sector Strategy Paper", *Social Protection Discussion Paper No. 9904*, World Bank, Washington DC.

Holzmann R., L. Sherburne-Benz and E. Tesliuc (2003): *Social Risk Management: The World Bank's Approach to Social Protection in a Globalizing World*, Social Protection Department, World Bank, Washington DC.

Hoogeveen, J., E. Tesliuc, R. Vakis and S. Dercon (2004): "A Guide to the Analysis of Risk, Vulnerability and Vulnerable Groups", *Policy Research Working Paper*, World Bank, Washington DC.

Jalan, J. and M. Ravallion (1998): "Transient Poverty in Postreform China", *Journal of Comparative Economics*, 26: 338–57.

Jalan, J. and M. Ravallion (2002): "Geographic Poverty Traps? A Micro Model of Consumption Growth in Rural China", *Journal of Applied Econometrics*, 17: 329–46.

Kahneman, D., P. Slovic and A. Tversky (eds) (1982): *Judgment Under Uncertainty: Heuristics and Biases*, Cambridge University Press, New York.

Kamanou, G. and J. Morduch (2004): "Measuring Vulnerability to Poverty", in S. Dercon (ed.), *Insurance against Poverty*, Oxford University Press, New York.

Kazianga, H. and C. Udry (2006): "Consumption Smoothing? Livestock, Insurance and Drought in Rural Burkina Faso", *Journal of Development Economics*, 79(2): 413–46.

Kochar, A. (1999): "Smoothing Consumption by Smoothing Income: Hours-of-Work Responses to Idiosyncratic Agricultural Shocks in Rural India", *Review of Economics and Statistics*, 81(1): 50–61.

Kreimer, A. and M. Arnold, eds (2000): *Managing Disaster Risk in Emerging Economies*, World Bank, Washington DC.

Lambert, S. (1994): "La migration comme instrument de diversification intrafamiliale des risques. Application au cas de la Côte d'Ivoire", *Revue d'économie du développement*, 2: 3–38.

Ligon E. and S. Schechter (2003): "Measuring Vulnerability", *Economic Journal*, 113: 95–102.

Ligon E. and S. Schechter (2004): "Evaluating Different Approaches to Estimating Vulnerability", *Social Protection Discussion Paper 0410*, World Bank, Washington DC.

Lokshin, M. and M. Ravallion, (2005): "Lasting Local Impacts of an Economy-Wide Crisis", mimeo, World Bank, Washington DC.

Maccini, S. and D. Yang (2009): "Under the Weather: Health, Schooling, and Economic Consequences of Early-Life Rainfall", *American Economic Review*, 99(3): 1006–26.

Mansuri, G. and A. Healy (2000): "Assessing Vulnerability: An Ex-ante Measure and Its Application Using Data from Rural Pakistan", *mimeo*, Development Research Group, World Bank, Washington DC.

Morduch, J. (1994): "Poverty and Vulnerability", *American Economic Review*, 84(2): 221–5.

Morduch, J. (1995): "Income Smoothing and Consumption Smoothing", *Journal of Economic Perspectives*, 9(3): 103–14.

Morduch, J. (1999): "Between the State and the Market: Can Informal Insurance Patch the Safety Net?" *The World Bank Research Observer*, 14(2): 187–207.

Morduch, J. (2004): "Consumption Smoothing Across Space", in Dercon, S. (ed.), *Insurance against Poverty*, Oxford University Press, New York.

Narayan, D., R. Chambers, M. K. Shah and P. Petesch (2000): *Voices of the Poor – Crying Out for Change*, World Bank and Oxford University Press, New York.

Naudé, W., M. McGillivray, and S. Rossouw (2008): "Measuring the Vulnerability of Subnational Regions", *Research Paper No. 2008/54*, UNU-WIDER, Helsinki.

Newbery, D. and J. Stiglitz, (1981): *The Theory of Commodity Price Stabilization*, Oxford University Press, New York.

Povel, F. (2009): "Perceived Vulnerability to Downside Risk", *mimeo*, University of Göttingen, Göttingen.

Pritchett L., A. Suryahadi and S. Sumarto (2000): "Quantifying Vulnerability to Poverty: A Proposed Measure, with Application to Indonesia", *Social Monitoring and Early Response Unit Working Paper*, World Bank, Washington DC.

Rajadel, T. (2002): "Vulnerability and Participation to the Non-Agricultural Sector in Rural Pakistan", *TEAM Working Paper*, Université Paris, Paris.

Ravallion, M. (1988): "Expected Poverty under Risk-Induced Welfare Variability", *Economic Journal*, 98(393): 1171–82.

Rosenzweig, M. and H. Binswanger (1993): "Wealth, Weather Risk and the Composition and Profitability of Agricultural Investments", *Economic Journal*, 103(416): 56–78.

Sharma, M., I. Burton, M. van Aalst, M. Dilley and G. Acharya (2000): "Reducing Vulnerability to Environmental Variability: Background Paper for the Bank's Environmental Strategy", World Bank, Washington DC.

Siegel, P., J. Alwang and S. Jorgensen (2003): "Rediscovering Vulnerability through a Risk Chain: Views from Different Disciplines", *Quarterly Journal of International Agriculture*, 42(3): 351–70.

Skoufias, E. and A. R. Quisumbing (2005): "Consumption Insurance and Vulnerability to Poverty: A Synthesis of the Evidence from Bangladesh, Ethiopia, Mali, Mexico and Russia", *European Journal of Development Research*, 17(1): 24–58.

Suryahadi, A., and S. Sumarto (2003): "Poverty and Vulnerability in Indonesia Before and After the Economic Crisis", *Asian Economic Journal*, 17(1): 45–64.

Tompkins, E., S. A. Nicholson-Cole, L. Hurlston, E. Boyd, G. Brooks Hodge, J. Clarke, G. Gray, N. Trotz and L. Varlack (2005): *Surviving Climate Change in Small Islands: A Guidebook*, Tyndall Centre for Climate Change Research, Norwich, UK.

Townsend, R. M. (1994): "Risk and Insurance in Village India", *Econometrica*, 62(3): 539–91.

Townsend, R. M. (1995): "Consumption Insurance: An Evaluation of Risk-Bearing Systems in Low-Income Economies", *Journal of Economic Perspectives*, 9: 83–102.

World Bank (2000): *World Development Report 2000/2001 – Attacking Poverty*, Oxford University Press, New York.

Zhang, Y. and G. Wan (2008): "Can We Predict Vulnerability to Poverty?" *Research Paper No. 2008/82*, UNU-WIDER, Helsinki.

Appendix 2.A.1: Downside risks included in the vulnerability to downside risk measure applied by Povel (2009)

Risk		Stated by number (%) of households		Mean probability (including all households)		Mean severity (including all households)		Mean probability (excluding households which do not expect respective risk to occur)		Mean severity (excluding households which do not expect respective risk to occur)	
		Thailand (n=2070)	Vietnam (n=1805)	Thailand	Vietnam	Thailand	Vietnam	Thailand	Vietnam	Thailand	Vietnam
demographic	illness	1583 (76.5)	1278 (70.8)	0.4766	0.4722	0.5286	0.4867	0.6232	0.6670	0.6912	0.6874
	person leaves the household	402 (19.4)	423 (23.4)	0.047	0.0655	0.0643	0.1119	0.2418	0.2794	0.3313	0.4774
	person joins the household	351 (16.9)	369 (20.4)	0.0431	0.0517	0.0626	0.0952	0.2541	0.2531	0.3689	0.4658

weather	flooding	462 (22.3)	948 (52.5)	0.1453	0.4104	0.169	0.4253	0.6511	0.7814	0.7572	0.8097
	drought	1180 (57.0)	932 (51.6)	0.3611	0.3317	0.4459	0.3952	0.6334	0.6425	0.7822	0.7655
	unusually heavy rainfall	381 (18.4)	607 (33.7)	0.1015	0.2275	0.1025	0.2429	0.5517	0.6764	0.5566	0.7222
agricultural	storm	549 (26.5)	1030 (57.1)	0.1495	0.4608	0.157	0.4143	0.5636	0.8076	0.5921	0.7260
	crop pests	758 (36.6)	1179 (65.3)	0.2769	0.5175	0.2395	0.4985	0.7562	0.7922	0.6541	0.7632
	livestock disease	281 (13.7)	864 (47.8)	0.0866	0.291	0.0789	0.3467	0.6377	0.6079	0.5810	0.7243
economic	strong increase in interest rate on loans	257 (12.5)	287 (15.9)	0.0653	0.068	0.09	0.1261	0.5261	0.4279	0.7252	0.7934
	strong increase of prices for input	1196 (57.8)	654 (36.2)	0.5056	0.2372	0.4906	0.2697	0.8751	0.6547	0.8490	0.7443

Note: Values for probability and severity of a risk range between 0 (lowest) and 1 (highest).
Source: Povel (2009).

3
Establishing a Database for Vulnerability Assessment

Bernd Hardeweg, Stephan Klasen and Hermann Waibel

3.1 Introduction

Until today there have been few databases that satisfy the theoretical requirements for studying vulnerability to poverty, as indicated in Chapter 2. Among existing datasets the Ethiopian Rural Household Survey used, for example, by Dercon *et al.* (2002; 2005) is prominent and provides a panel dataset well suited to vulnerability analysis. The first wave of data collection was carried out in 1989 in six farming villages in central and southern Ethiopia, with a focus on the crisis and recovery in the 1980s. An expansion of the survey to 15 villages across the country in early 1994 yielded a sample of 1477 households. Additional rounds of the survey were carried out in late 1994, 1995, 1997, 1999, and 2004. In the 1995 wave, a general shock module was implemented, which was further improved in later rounds (Dercon *et al.*, 2005).

In Thailand, the "Townsend Thai project" started in 1997 with a cross-sectional survey in four provinces of Thailand, namely two in the Central region (Lopburi and Chachoengsao) and two in the Northeast (Sisaket and Buriram). This comprehensive database of a total of 2800 households in 198 villages includes a 5-year household and business panel from 1997 to 2001. The focus of the project is on financial institutions including risks and the effects of household- and firm-specific shocks (Townsend, 2004).

In Vietnam, the Vietnam Household Living Standards Survey (VHLSS) is an ongoing survey of the Vietnamese population started in 1992 with funding provided by World Bank (WB), the Swedish International Development Cooperation Agency (SIDA) and the United Nations Development Program (UNDP); some of the waves have a panel dimension. It now includes some 30,000 households and information on income, expenditures, economic activity and education, and has also more recently included modules on health, education and risks, among others.

While these datasets constitute important advances, there is still a lack of comprehensive panel data that covers a longer time span and includes information on the shocks and risks which rural households in particular are facing. In this chapter we report on the design and use of a survey instrument suitable to collect data for compiling a database specifically for the purpose of assessing vulnerability in two emerging market economies in Southeast Asian countries, namely Thailand and Vietnam.

The dataset described in this chapter comprises some 4400 households in 440 villages in six provinces in Thailand and Vietnam, collected in 2007 and 2008. Additional waves were conducted in 2010 and in 2011 in two out of six provinces. The provinces included in the survey are Buriram, Nakhon Phanom and Ubon Ratchathani in Northeast Thailand, and Dak Lak, Ha Tinh and Thua Thien Hue in the Central Highlands of Vietnam. The provinces are predominantly rural and are located in peripheral areas bordering Laos and/or Cambodia. The choice of locations allows researchers to effectively study vulnerability to poverty, as households and individuals in rural and geographically remote regions are expected to be more vulnerable to poverty than populations of urban and central regions.

The chapter is laid out as follows: in the next section we discuss the issues critical to the collection of data for measuring vulnerability to poverty. In Section 3.3 we report the survey implementation, including survey design and sampling procedure. In Section 3.4 we present some descriptive results that show some features of the target population and demonstrate why empirical research on vulnerability is promising with the dataset at hand. In the last section we conclude and look at the prospects of expanding the current panel data.

3.2   Data requirements for vulnerability assessment

Three issues are particularly important when collecting household-level data for vulnerability studies, namely: (i) household definition, (ii) coverage of data items and (iii) time span.

As regards the first issue, one of the shortcomings of many household surveys in developing countries is that they use a rather narrow definition of a household in order to avoid ambiguities during interviews, thereby obtaining complete enumerations and avoiding double-counting. Thus a household is usually defined as those persons who are linked through sharing a common dwelling and generally eating their meals together ("sitting at the same table") (Grosh and Munoz, 1996: 213). While it is desirable to have a clear-cut *a priori* definition of household membership, there is a disadvantage if household definition is exclusively based on locality, as it may not capture the reality of rural households in rapidly developing economies. A narrow household definition tends to ignore important interpersonal, social and economic relations and links with persons otherwise regarded as outsiders to the household; for example, in rural households many younger members have migrated to urban industrial centres but nevertheless maintain close ties with their natal households, perhaps with the intention to return later, thereby leading to the establishment of multi-locational households (Wiggins and Proctor, 2001; Gödecke and Waibel, 2011; and for African cases see Schmidt-Kallert and Kreibich, 2004). Whereas static poverty measurements might be unaffected by looking only at the rural part of the household, ignoring the risk associated with migration and urban job security might well bias the vulnerability assessment of the rural household. In addition, household composition is likely to change over time – also in response to shocks or as a measure of ex-ante risk management, which has implications for vulnerability (for example, Klasen and Woolard, 2009). To capture these realities, a wider household definition has been adopted in this survey whereby all persons were included as judged by the household head.

The second issue is that vulnerability assessment requires coverage of items that go beyond the LSMS survey types covered in Grosh and Glewwe (2000).[1] A key requirement for any vulnerability-oriented survey is the inclusion of a module on past shock experience detailing the type of shock, timing, indicators of severity, coping actions and – where appropriate – attributing further consequences to the adverse events. Even though this type of data involves a number of pitfalls, such as unclear attribution of consequences to events, differences in perception of the same adverse event among different respondents and others (Hoddinott and Quisumbing, 2008), the information is required in order to relate outcomes to their causes. Other studies have used new types of data (for example including shock modules) to study poverty in a dynamic context, such as for example the Burkina Faso risk and vulnerability assessment by the World Bank, which has experimented with new measurement methods to better identify the most vulnerable among the poor (World Bank, 2004; Kozel *et al.*, 2008). These issues are discussed also in more detail in Chapter 4, which focuses on how to design modules to adequately capture shocks and risks, including our experiences in Thailand and Vietnam.

The third issue is the time dimension of the dataset. In the past, most empirical vulnerability research has resorted to existing survey databases – sometimes augmented by aggregate data from other sources (Hoddinott and Quisumbing, 2003). Single cross-sections of households, often patterned on Living Standards Measurement Studies (Grosh and Glewwe, 2000), can provide useful information on sociodemographic household characteristics, measures of household wellbeing, livelihood strategies and coping activities, even if not set up specifically for risk and vulnerability analyses. However, their main disadvantage is the absence of temporal variability. In order to calculate vulnerability to poverty using these survey instruments, the rigid assumption has to be made that cross-sectional variance approximates intertemporal variance, as in the method proposed by Chowdhury et al. (2002) discussed in Chapter 2. This assumption however will not hold where intertemporal and aggregate shocks occur (Hoddinott and Quisumbing, 2008), for example as in the case of the food price crisis in 2007/08 and the financial and economic crisis that followed.

To some extent the creation of pseudo-panels of cohorts can be used to incorporate the time dimension if a sufficiently large sample size is available (Hoddinott and Quisumbing, 2008). However as pointed out by Dercon (2002) for theoretically sound vulnerability assessments panel data are required, because they cover levels and changes at the most disaggregated *individual* level over time whereas cohort data will average out these different individual experiences within a cohort. In addition, past events are reported more accurately for the shorter recall periods in panels. Another advantage from an analytical perspective is the feasibility of fixed-effects models, allowing for controlling for unobserved time-invariant characteristics (Hoddinott and Quisumbing, 2008). However, a meaningful number of panel data waves and the length of the time period covered are crucial since, as Dercon (2008) stresses, risk often has long-term consequences for the livelihoods and well-being of affected individuals, an issue that has been ignored in much of the empirical work so far.

Elbers and Gunning (2003) find that certain measures of vulnerability are strongly sensitive to the time horizon considered in the analysis. Concluding from results of stochastic models of household decision making, they question the accuracy of regression-based vulnerability measures. Dealing with structural economic mobility – a concept relevant for aggregate vulnerability studies – Naschold and Barrett (2011) compare the effect of different spell lengths on the estimates of total economic mobility. They find that with increasing spell length, the dispersion of the percentage changes in log real per capita income decreases. They conclude that the shorter the time intervals of the panel considered, the higher the apparent transitory poverty and total economic mobility estimates. Hence, estimates for the transitory share of poverty derived from short panel lengths have to be interpreted with caution (Naschold and Barrett, 2011). They suggest that longer panels are warranted.

Such panel data can still be complemented by items as suggested by Hoddinott and Quisumbing (2003). They pointed out that in addition to household data, locality information from different sources, such as community questionnaires, market surveys and focus group interviews, can provide important insights about the household's environment. Also, designated surveys on vulnerability can apply contextual methods that examine sensitive issues which are hard to capture through standard household surveys such as individual risk perceptions. Consequently, the use of standard household survey data has ensured that perceptions of risk by households have rarely been taken into account in empirical work, which has led to a focus on fate instead of fear as the effects of shocks on economic behaviour have been conflated with the consequences of living in a risky environment (Dercon, 2008). Furthermore, few studies have estimated the magnitude and nature of risk aversion, which is commonly assumed for farm households in developing countries (Yesuf and Bluffstone, 2009).

Our panel survey on vulnerability in Thailand and Vietnam, which by now has completed three waves and already completed field work for a further wave in 2011, tries to address these shortcomings by providing a panel dataset that has been specifically designed to capture the measurement and determinants of vulnerability to poverty, as we will describe in more detail in the next sections.

3.3 Household panel survey implementation

In this section we introduce the survey instrument for the village and household survey used in Thailand and Vietnam. In Section 3.3.2, we explain the sampling strategy applied in the two countries reflecting the heterogeneity of local conditions. In Section 3.3.3 we report some survey experience which may provide useful insights for other researchers planning to undertake similar projects.

3.3.1 Survey instruments

In order to meet the objectives of the research project, a questionnaire was designed with the aim of capturing the multiple components of vulnerability and applying different approaches to the vulnerability concept. The household survey used two separate questionnaires: a concise village questionnaire for characterizing conditions at the village level, and a comprehensive household questionnaire.

The former questionnaire has a size of three pages and collects information on the village location, economy, access to public infrastructure and social problems through interviewing the village head. The household survey instrument contains ten sections (see Table 3.1), and provides 420 and 502 variables in the first and second wave questionnaires, respectively. First, spatial and general information in section 2 variables are measured, which allow definition of size and boundary of the household. In section 3 the data on shocks and risks are elaborated that can identify some of the causes of vulnerability including the impact of a shock in terms of income and asset loss and the coping mechanism used by the households. Sections 4 to 6 encompass the income-generating activities such as income from agriculture, including crop and livestock, income generated from natural resources such as fishing, hunting, collecting and logging, income from off-farm employment, and income from micro and small-scale enterprises such as cottage industries or transport business. Section 7 deals with borrowing, lending, and receipt of public and other transfer payments as well as receipts from insurance contracts. Section 8 is on household consumption expenditures, differentiating between food and non-food items for a one-year recall period; and section 9 covers assets, including the house as a major item of household wealth.

The different sections include modules or sets of questions which were developed by different disciplines in accordance with the theme of their research, for example, either to measure the components of vulnerability or to capture those factors that can explain variation in vulnerability to poverty. In Table 3.1 the main criteria and indicators for the vulnerability measurement in the household questionnaire are summarized. The different sections of the questionnaire generate variables that can make contributions to different aspects of vulnerability research; for example, the village questionnaire and section 1 of the household questionnaire contain information on infrastructure and location factors that can provide information for vulnerability mapping.

In summary, the questionnaire for vulnerability research in emerging Asian market economies is a well balanced combination of elaborating facts elicited from the respondent on a recall basis and his or her perceptions on future events, influenced by his or her experience and individual judgements. Generally a trade-off had to be made between the

Table 3.1 Modules of questionnaire and variables to measure vulnerability

Module/Content section	Main variables	Contribution to vulnerability research
0 Community/ village level information	Location, distance to cities or markets, access to public services, sources of employment, community infrastructure, management of community resources	Spatial variation in vulnerability
1* General survey information	Address, household headship	Household type
2 Household characteristics	Size, composition and dynamics, education, health	Possible determinants of household vulnerability
3 Shocks experienced during past five years and perceived risks for the next five years	Type, timing, duration, scope, severity, financial consequence, ex-post coping measures, covariance, subjective assessment of risk and well-being; type, frequency, severity, consequence of expected risks and ex-ante mitigation measures	Vulnerability measurement, causes of vulnerability, coping and mitigation strategies
4 Land, agriculture and natural resources	Land size and ownership status, land value, crop and livestock technology and production, self-consumption, productivity, costs, returns, timing and extent of natural resource extraction	Source of income, causes of vulnerability
5 Off-farm employment including wage labour	Type, contractual arrangements, location, travel costs, job acquisition costs, duration of work, wage and fringe benefits	Source of income, causes of vulnerability
6 Non-farm self employment including cottage industries	Type, investment, costs and returns	Source of income, causes of vulnerability
7 Borrowing, lending, public and other transfers and insurance	Type, sources, contractual arrangements, conditions amounts, payment frequencies	Source of income, causes of vulnerability, coping capacity

Continued

Table 3.1 Continued

Module/Content section	Main variables	Contribution to vulnerability research
8 Household consumption	Food and non-food items, other expenditures	Consumption levels
9 Assets including house	Purchase value, depreciation and service life	Coping capacity

* Village head questionnaire and section 1 of the household questionnaire.

degree of detail on measuring the household's activities (such as agricultural technologies) and comprehensiveness, for example by including a detailed shock and risk module.

Questions that require long recall periods or contain complex phraseology can lead to misinterpretation of questions. Many of these problems were overcome by proper testing, interviewer training and close survey supervision.

3.3.2 Sampling strategy

In line with the overall objective of the project, the target population consists of rural households whose per capita income is likely to be near the poverty line and whose conditions suggest that they could be poor in the future even if they are above the poverty line today. Since no prior information on the vulnerability status of these households existed, study areas were selected where it could be assumed vulernability would be an issue. In a first sampling stage, provinces were therefore purposively chosen that met the following conditions: low average per capita income, high dependence on agriculture, existence of special risk factors such as remoteness and peripheral location along the country's border, and poor infrastructure especially in irrigation and drainage facilities resulting in high-risk crop production. As a result, three peripheral provinces in Northeast Thailand, namely Buri Ram, Ubon Ratchathani and Nakhon Phanom, were selected, and in Vietnam three provinces from the Northern Central Coast and Northwestern highlands, namely Ha Tinh, Thua Thien Hue and Dak Lak, were purposively selected (see Figure 3.1). While the six provinces selected have in common their peripheral location along the border to Laos and Cambodia, they differ with regard to agro-ecological conditions, infrastructure and

Figure 3.1 Map of selected study provinces

Source: Own presentation based on ESRI Inc., ArcWorld supplement.

development potential. Comparing the provinces allows conclusions to be drawn for regional development issues, and may also facilitate a comparison between the two countries.

The sample was designed in such a way that it is representative of the target population and would allow the drawing of conclusions for the vulnerability of rural households in the selected provinces and areas with similar conditions. The sampling procedure consists of a three-stage cluster sampling design. The total sample size is 4400 households for the six provinces. The ultimate cluster size of ten households in a village was chosen based on organizational aspects of the survey. For Vietnam this is also in line with recommendations and with prior information that homogeneity within villages is rather high (Pettersson, 2003), and this can also be assumed for Thailand. Due to differences in available prior information a different sampling approach was undertaken in the two countries. In Thailand, assuming homogeneity within a province, the primary sampling unit (PSU)[2] was the sub-district. In Vietnam, provinces are more heterogeneous in terms of agro-ecological conditions, and therefore stratification was undertaken resulting in an imbalanced sample of the rural population of the three provinces.

Table 3.2 shows the different sampling stages for Thailand. In the selected provinces in Thailand, sub-districts were chosen with approximately proportional allocation. Urban sub-districts were not included in the survey, while the remaining population of the province was stratified in more densely populated (that is, peri-urban) and less densely populated (that is, rural) sub-districts. In order to ensure proportional coverage of the rural population, systematic random sampling based on a list ordered by population density was applied. Sampling frames were obtained from two databases maintained by the Department of Community Development, a village-level database (NRC2D) which provided the measure of size at the sub-district and village levels as of 2005, and a household database (BMN) of 2006 which was used as a listing frame for rural households.

At the second stage, two villages per sub-district were sampled with a probability proportional to size of population from each of the sampled sub-districts. The selection probability p_{rsv} for village v in sub-district s and stratum r is given by Equation 3.1:

$$p_{rsv} = \frac{a_r \cdot b \cdot m_{rsv}}{\sum_s m_{rs}},$$
(3.1)

Table 3.2   Overview of sample design in Thailand

Stage	Sampling unit	Selection criterion	Sampling probability
Target population	Province	Purposive selection: border provinces in Northeastern Thailand, low income, significant dependence on agricultural income and assumed risky environment	–
1st	Sub-district	Provinces are divided into strata with approximately proportional sample size a_r PPS systematic random sample with implicit stratification by population density	$\dfrac{a_r \cdot m_{rs}}{\sum_s m_{rs}}$
2nd	Village	Simple random PPS sample of two villages from each sampled sub-district	$\dfrac{b \cdot m_{rsv}}{\sum_v m_{rsv}}$, $b = 2$
3rd	Household	EPS systematic random sample with implicit stratification by household size	$\dfrac{c}{m'_{rsv}}$, $c = 10$

where a_r is the PSU sample size in stratum r, b is the number of villages sampled in each sub-district, m_{rs} and m_{rsv} is the population size of sub-district and village, respectively.

At the third stage a fixed size sample c of 10 households has been selected systematically from a list of households ordered by household size with equal probability of selection (EPS). The selection probability for households as shown by Equation 3.2 leads to a constant probability of selection for all households if a_r is determined proportionally to stratum size:

$$p_{rvh} = \frac{c}{m'_{rsv}} \cdot p_{rsv} = \frac{a_r \cdot b \cdot c}{\sum_s m_{rs}} \cdot \frac{m_{rsv}}{m'_{rsv}} \tag{3.2}$$

where m'_{rsv} is the number of households from the household listing frame.

As secondary data for sampling in Thailand was available at the village level, and population density and agro-ecological conditions were assumed to be sufficiently homogeneous within the province, the sample is self-weighting by design.

Following this scheme, the sampling ratios achieved for the three provinces in Thailand were well above the biannual socioeconomic surveys (NSO 2008) and are comparable to the one obtained by the Thai Townsend project (Binford *et al.*, 2004).

In Vietnam, the three selected provinces are rather diverse in terms of natural conditions. While Dak Lak province is part of the landlocked Central Highland bordering Cambodia to the west, Thua Thien-Hue and Ha Tinh extend from the coast to the mountainous border with Laos. In order to take into account this heterogeneity, agro-ecological zones were defined. As shown in Table 3.3, these strata differ significantly in size. Thus a proportional allocation of 2200 samples would have led to insufficient absolute sample sizes in some of the strata. In order to allow meaningful inferences for these entities, the ultimate absolute sample size was fixed at a minimum of 160 households per stratum. For the first-stage sampling units (communes)[3] no measure of size was available at the time of sampling. Instead the population share of the respective district d was used for weighting commune selection. The selection probability of a commune is thus defined by the first fraction on the right side of Equation 3.3.

$$p_{rdsvh} = \frac{a_r \cdot m_{rd}^*}{N_{rd} \sum_d m_{rd}^*} \cdot \frac{2 \cdot m_{rdsv}^*}{\sum_v m_{rdsv}^*} \cdot \frac{10}{m_{rdsv}} \tag{3.3}$$

At the second stage, villages were sampled with probability proportional to size based on population m^*_{rdsv} (see Equation 3.3). The third stage was again a systematic random sample with equal probability from household lists ordered by household size. This is the strategy recommended for the last stage in clustered sampling in order to capture a maximum of variation within the cluster. Data for the local administrative units and household sample frames were taken from the Agricultural and Rural Census 2006, which covers all rural households and was conducted by the Vietnam General Statistical Office.

The stratification applied in Vietnam included the specification of agro-ecological zones as analytical domains. Setting a lower bound to absolute stratum sample size for the sparsely inhabited strata leads, however, to varying selection probabilities for the Vietnam sample in the range from 0.147 to 5.85 per cent (Table 3.3). As a consequence, analysis of the survey data aimed at generating information about the provincial situation, such as provincial vulnerability profiles, require a weighting procedure. The sampling ratios for the provinces are almost twice those obtained in the Vietnam Household Living Standard Survey (VHLSS).

3.3.3   Survey experience

The conduct of the survey among 4400 households in Thailand and Vietnam revealed that it is possible to collect information on variables required to assess vulnerability to poverty. In particular, respondents

Table 3.3 Basic data for the target population and household sample in Vietnam

Province/Strata	Rural population	Population density (1/km²)	Pop. share (%) total	Pop. share (%) province	Sample allocation absolute	Sample allocation %	Selection probability range (%)
Dak Lak	1,335,193	102	41		760	35	
Rice plain	452,982	64		34	260	34	0.165–0.603
Mountainous area	882,211	145		66	500	66	0.164–1.766
Thua Thien – Hue	788,763	156	24		720	33	
Coastal area	376,693	322		48	240	33	0.224–1.074
Rice plain	357,612	179		45	240	33	0.175–0.575
Mountainous area	54,458	29		7	240	33	0.624–5.85
Ha Tinh	1,147,693	191	35		720	33	
Coastal area	567,609	246		49	360	50	0.196–0.783
Rice plain	338,781	489		30	200	28	0.171–0.536
Mountainous area	241,304	80		21	160	22	0.147–0.724
Total	3,271,649				2200		

Source: Provincial Statistical Year Books 2005, General Statistics Office, Hanoi; authors' calculations.

generally were willing to report shocks they had experienced in the past and to assess future risks. Interviews usually lasted between two and three hours. The interviewers were well trained, and a strict supervision procedure, including real-time editing of questionnaires and occasional follow-up contacts sometimes by phone (in Thailand), was implemented. Close to 100 per cent of the questionnaires were completed, and the share of ineligible samples, i.e. households that were dropped because of incomplete or obviously incorrect information was below 5 per cent in all provinces.

As one indicator of data quality, the resulting income and consumption aggregates which are valid can be considered. Table 3.4 shows that in Thailand little over 2 per cent of income or consumption data were missing or had implausible values, while in Vietnam these values were even lower, yet with more variation across the three provinces. Also, overall attrition between the survey waves was extremely low. Only 0.23 per cent of households could not be interviewed in the second wave, so that the issue of non-random selection in that wave is quantitatively hardly relevant.

One problem with the implementation of large surveys such as those in this project is that the prior information necessary to design the

Table 3.4   Number of observations with complete data by survey year

	2007		2008		
	Income and consumption	Total	Income and consumption	Total	Loss due to missings
Total	4,284	4,381	4,274	4,279	2.33%
Thailand	2,143	2,186	2,128	2,136	2.29%
Buriram	808	819	795	799	2.44%
Ubon Ratchathani	944	970	947	949	2.16%
Nakhon Phanom	391	397	385	387	2.52%
Vietnam	2,141	2,195	2,146	2,148	2.14%
Ha Tinh	692	720	713	713	0.97%
Thua Thien-Hue	710	718	694	696	3.06%
Dak Lak	739	757	735	735	2.91%

Source: DFG FOR756 Household survey 2007 and 2008.

sample is often incomplete and may sometimes be unreliable. For example, even though almost up-to-date listing frames were available, sampled households could not always be interviewed because of change in household structure, partial migration or household dissolution. Hence, the replacement rate varied between 18 and 22 per cent in Thailand and 17 and 23 per cent in Vietnam. These figures are a good indication of the dynamics of rural households in these two countries. Temporary migration and commuting in response to changing economic conditions is a common strategy of households in emerging market economies. These issues are part of the results and can generate lessons on a number of questions in relation to the derivation of static and dynamic poverty measures. These will be dealt with in the context of this research project, for example by looking at the implications of household definition and household size, as well as household formation and dissolution processes.

3.4   Testing data for vulnerability assessments

The purpose of this section is to undertake some testing of data for several selected variables in order to obtain some initial indication as to whether the assumptions made at the outset of the research project can be confirmed and whether the data bear the potential to answer the research questions formulated by the project. The descriptive statistics presented here aim to provide an overview of the socioeconomic conditions of the households in our sample. Furthermore, the comparisons between provinces and countries will suggest possible differences in the factors that could be responsible for differences in vulnerability to poverty. In addition, the descriptive analysis of the data can give first indications for changes in demographic and economic conditions including household welfare and thus can provide information for regional planning, for example on structural change in agriculture.

The following selection of variables is believed to be important for the measurement of vulnerability and causes thereof. These factors include household characteristics, like age composition and education, as well as indicators of household wealth, like income and its composition and consumption relative to respective poverty lines. Other important variables are household debt and the frequency of shocks, as well as the risks expected.

3.4.1   Household characteristics

Data on household characteristics reveal a great deal of evidence on the organization of households and families in the rural areas of emerging market economies.

Household sizes in emerging Asian economies tend to be much smaller than, for example, those in poor African countries. Hence the model of a traditional, mostly labour-driven, subsistence farm household (for example Ellis, 1998) no longer applies. In the three provinces in Thailand, average nuclear members per household[4] range from only 3.91 to 4.03, and between 3.84 and 4.62 in Vietnam. In Thailand especially, rural households are characterized by migration, with strong implications for the age structure and dependency ratio. In Figure 3.2 the age structure of the rural population for one of the three provinces in Thailand (Buri Ram) is shown.

This illustrates a gap in the age group from 18 to about 34 years, and therefore shows a quite different pattern from the typical population pyramid in a developing country, where the majority of people are young. This can be seen when comparing the rural population between the province of Buri Ram and the whole of Thailand. Figure 3.2 also shows the gender difference. A typical characterization for a household in a rural area in Thailand is that the grandparents in the village take care of the grandchildren while their own children work outside and often far away from the village.

The organizational pattern of rural households has several implications for vulnerability assessment. First, the well-being and the threats for these households are linked to the job security of the absent household

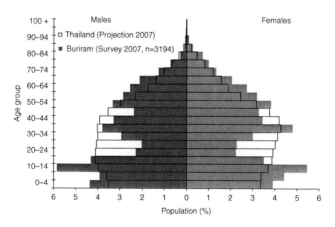

Figure 3.2 Age structure of rural household members in Buriram province

Sources: DFG FOR756 Household survey 2007. Thailand projection: Institute for Population and Social Research (2003). Note that the gaps between the age structure between the national data and the data for rural Buriram Province points to the relevance of migration in particular.

members. This was shown during the Asian financial crisis, when thousands of casual labourers lost their job and returned to their villages (Bresciani *et al.*, 2002). Second, the organization of agriculture is tailored to the reduced labour capacity with children at school; the elder household members are likely to avoid labour-intensive and technology-intensive farm enterprises and thus may not adopt high-return agricultural products such as poultry and vegetables on a commercial scale. Third, the absence of the "parents" in a village may impair the social structure, leading to an increase in social problems such as alcohol or drug use among the youth who receive remittances but lack educational guidance from their parents.

For Vietnam this pattern may not yet be so strong in those areas (such as Ha Tinh) where subsistence agriculture is still playing a major role, but it is emerging in the more diversified and more rapidly developing province of Thua Thien-Hue (see Figure 3.3).

Education is expected to be a major variable, explaining differences in poverty and vulnerability. Households with low levels of educational status may be less likely to use improved technologies in agriculture and are generally less able to diversify outside agriculture. As a consequence they may have to remain in low-return or high-risk income-generating activities. A view on the overall level of educational attainment of household members older than 15 years[5] in the six provinces is shown in Figure 3.4.

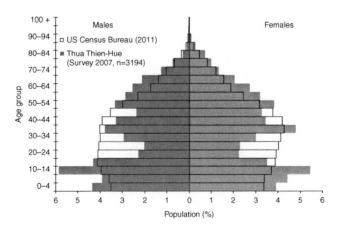

Figure 3.3   Age structure of rural household members in Thua Thien-Hue

Sources: DFG FOR756 Household survey 2007 and US Census Bureau (2011) for Vietnam population.

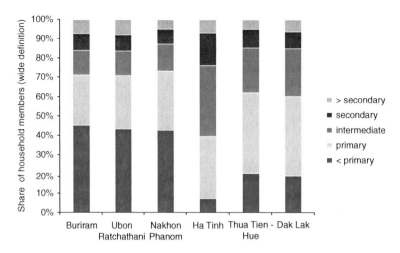

Figure 3.4 Educational attainment of household (wide definition)
Source: DFG FOR756 Household survey 2007.

Over half of the members of the households in the sample in the three provinces in Thailand had not finished primary education, and around 80 per cent had no intermediate or secondary education. Dropout from elementary school after Grade 4 can be the result of the need for agricultural labour or the taking up of opportunities for unskilled wage labour, thus contributing to household income instead of completing school. The situation appears to be a bit better in the Vietnamese provinces where in Ha Tinh, the least developed province, 23 per cent of household members older than 15 years had finished intermediate education. In the two remaining provinces the situation is still slightly better than in Thailand; around 65 per cent have had no secondary education. Persons who completed secondary education are few, in the range of 5 to 15 per cent, while household members with higher than secondary education in all the provinces does not even reach 5 per cent. While a more detailed analysis is required, these indicative results suggest that education could be a major source of vulnerability in the study areas.

3.4.2 Consumption and income

Since the aim of the project is to study vulnerability to poverty, the survey is supposed to capture households whose income or consumption level is somewhere near the poverty line. Generally, the sample should provide a sufficient number of households whose total wealth, assets, income and consumption is low. Also we expect that consumption and income poverty rates in the study provinces will be higher than the national average, with differences between the two countries.

Average monthly per capita income and consumption is shown in Table 3.5. In all six provinces the average household is well above the international line of absolute poverty ($1.25 a day in purchasing power parity adjusted terms) and also above the $2-a-day line which is sometimes called moderate poverty (Bauer *et al.*, 2008).

Table 3.5 shows mean and standard error of income and consumption in the selected provinces. At a first glance there are two messages: (a) in all provinces, mean income and consumption are well above any standard poverty line and (b) in two provinces, consumption exceeds income, suggesting that consumption smoothing through sales of assets or borrowing is a strategy.

The standard error is mostly below 10 per cent, but varies across the provinces and tends to be higher in Thailand. Considering the higher sampling rates at the province level, this suggests that our survey attains higher accuracy than national scale surveys such as the Thai SES and the VHLSS, and is therefore suited to the purposes of the research group.

In Figure 3.5 per capita income up to a level of PPP US$10 per day is plotted as a cumulative distribution curve against two poverty lines, that is the line of absolute poverty of $1.25 and the $2 line for moderate

Table 3.5   Average per capita income and consumption

	Per capita income per month (PPP US$ 2005)				Per capita consumption per month (PPP US$ 2005)			
	2007		2008		2007		2008	
	Mean	SE	Mean	SE	Mean	SE	Mean	SE
Buriram	139.5	8.4	156.4	12.2	126.4	4.1	135.4	4.5
Ubon Ratchathani	175.3	13.3	159.5	10.7	132.1	4.9	124.5	4.7
Nakhon Phanom	121.8	7.4	115.7	7.9	126.2	5.4	102.9	3.4
Ha Tinh	81.7	8.0	109.0	7.3	81.6	3.3	87.8	3.0
Thua Thien-Hue	88.3	5.8	84.1	5.0	93.7	3.4	92.6	4.1
Dak Lak	117.7	8.9	139.7	10.8	101.3	6.2	96.1	4.7

Source: DFG FOR756 Household panel survey.

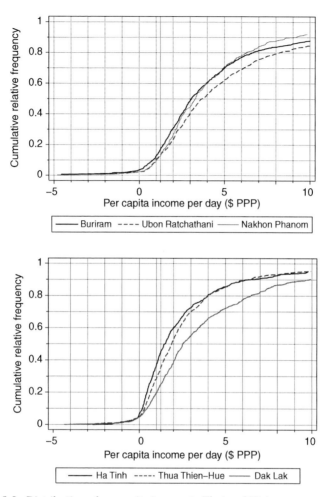

Figure 3.5   Distribution of per capita income in Thai and Vietnamese provinces

Source: DFG FOR756 Household survey 2007. The top figure shows the three Thai provinces, the bottom figure the three Vietnamese provinces.

poverty. The graph reveals clear differences between the two countries, bigger than the difference among the provinces. It is also interesting to note the effect of the shift in poverty line. If we loosely define this difference as the vulnerable part of the population, the effect is clearly larger in Vietnam.

Table 3.6 shows the shares of income generated by different sources and an index of income diversity. One of the problems here was that in some cases negative net income components were obtained. Hence, in Table 3.6 only non-negative income data were included. Except in Dak Lak, where agricultural income dominates, in the remaining provinces off-farm employment is the biggest contributor to household income.

Income from agriculture and livestock in most cases ranks second, followed by remittances from family members or other persons who support the household. Income from natural resource extraction generally plays a minor role not exceeding 5 per cent, and is highest in Nakhon Phanom. However this income could be important in case of shocks affecting agriculture and in areas where other income sources are less accessible as, for example, in the mountain areas of Thua Thien-Hue province. Income from non-farm business is generally higher in Vietnam than Thailand. It is highest in Thua Thien-Hue, the most commercialized of the six provinces. Income shares are influenced by the imputed value for the house, which was set at 8 per cent of market value of the house, and thus accounts for around 20 per cent of the total income. Calculating the Simpson index for the diversity of income sources shows that overall there is a high level of diversification which is higher in Thailand compared to the provinces in Vietnam. The lowest index is in

Table 3.6   Income sources (share of total income in %)

Income source	BR	UR	NP	HT	TH	DL
N (households)	808	944	391	692	710	739
Remittances	16.9	13.6	19.8	14.6	8.7	1.6
Use value of house	21.3	19.4	18.1	19.7	21.8	17.2
Agriculture and livestock	17.2	16.9	13.5	24.5	15.2	42.6
Natural resource extraction	1.0	2.7	5.2	4.2	3.6	0.8
Off-farm employment	26.9	27.2	27.3	15.4	21.7	22.7
Non-farm self-employment	12.2	17.4	12.0	18.5	26.9	13.0
Capital and transfer income	4.4	2.8	4.0	3.1	2.2	2.1
Simpson Index (positive income components)	49.3	51.2	52.7	42.6	48.6	40.1

Source: DFG FOR756 Household survey 2007.

Dak Lak, where coffee production dominates as income source. It can be concluded that diversification plays a role as a coping strategy, which suggests that in-depth studies on this issue will be important to better understand vulnerability in these provinces.

3.4.3 Poverty

Headcount ratios for income and consumption show the expected differences between Thailand and Vietnam (see Table 3.7). Also, in all provinces consumption poverty is lower than income poverty, but the two do not always correspond. For example, in Hue province close to 30

Table 3.7 Poverty (headcount ratio) based on income/consumption and different poverty lines

Province	Income poverty		Consumption poverty		Official poverty rate
	2007	2008	2007	2008	TH: 2007, VN: 2008
PPP US$1.25 (2005)					
Buriram	19.9	25.4	3.1	3.5	–
Ubon Ratchathani	15.2	17.8	2.9	4.0	–
Nakhon Phanom	13.9	22.2	3.1	7.5	–
Ha Tinh	48.0	20.5	10.7	7.6	–
Thua Thien-Hue	27.4	25.8	5.7	7.8	–
Dak Lak	27.5	24.9	12.5	7.9	–
PPP US$2.00 (2005)					
Buriram	34.1	40.0	15.0	16.0	23.8
Ubon Ratchathani	25.8	32.3	14.5	19.1	13.7
Nakhon Phanom	28.2	40.3	17.6	30.3	17.9
Ha Tinh	63.2	41.9	39.3	33.6	26.5
Thua Thien-Hue	48.8	46.6	28.9	27.7	13.7
Dak Lak	41.9	41.3	34.0	30.6	21.3

Source: DFG FOR756 Household survey 2007 and 2008. Official poverty data for Thailand refer to 2007 using provincial poverty lines ranging from PPP US$2.48 to 2.55. *Source*: NESDB (2008); official poverty data for Vietnam refer to 2008 using different poverty lines for urban (PPP US$2.20) and rural areas (PPP US$1.73) throughout all provinces; GSO (2011).

per cent are income-poor but only 5.7 per cent were consumption-poor in 2007. Hence, consumption smoothing through dis-saving occurs frequently, suggesting that vulnerability may exist. Comparing the results for the two poverty lines reveals some interesting differences. For example, the province of Nakhon Phanom in Thailand shows the lowest headcount ratio for income poverty at the $1.25 line, but this ratio more than doubles when applying the $2 line.

This may be taken as an indicator that the probability of falling below the line of absolute poverty in Nakhon Phanom could be higher than in the other provinces. Conversely, in Ha Tinh the headcount ratio is highest for the $1.25 line with almost half the households below the threshold, which goes up to over 60 per cent if the $2 line is applied. Thus in relative terms, Ha Tinh has the lowest increase in poverty on lifting the benchmark, suggesting that chronic poverty may persist in addition to vulnerability. The latter is also a function of the poverty line, in addition to risk attributable to households' activities and their coping capacity.

This clearly shows the sensitivity of measured vulnerability to the location of the poverty line, which would support the use of several poverty lines to study the robustness of vulnerability assessments.

It is also interesting to compare the headcount ratio found in the sample of households in the Thai and Vietnamese provinces with the official provincial headcount ratios. The latter combine rural and urban populations, and therefore we find consistently higher headcount ratios for the rural population in our six provinces. Note also that poverty rates differ markedly between the two years. In Thailand they go up and in Vietanm they go down largely because in Thailand most hosueholds are food deficit households who suffered from the sharp increase in food proces in 2008.

3.4.4   Household wealth and debt

Long-term poverty and vulnerability is also greatly affected by assets, wealth and debt, a subject to which we now turn. First, looking at per capita wealth (that is, value of livestock, and owned land, value of owned house and household assets, and financial assets) measured in 2005, PPP US$ shows that there is considerable variation between the provinces, which however is higher in Vietnam than Thailand. Table 3.8 shows average wealth holdings by quintile for the six provinces.

Looking at the lowest and the highest quintile shows differences and similarities between the two countries. For example, the province of Dak Lak in Vietnam is close to Nakhon Phanom, which is the least wealthy

Table 3.8 Per capita wealth by quintiles, 2007 (PPP US$)

Quintiles	1st	2nd	3rd	4th	5th
Buriram	1,982	4,669	8,195	14,617	41,788
Ubon Ratchathani	2,492	5,772	9,984	17,192	53,294
Nakhon Phanom	2,295	4,620	7,652	13,253	34,506
Ha Tinh	861	1,593	2,575	4,095	12,068
Thua Thien-Hue	1,029	2,050	3,052	5,369	14,507
Dak Lak	1,164	2,814	5,667	10,707	33,423

Source: DFG FOR756 Household survey 2007.

province of the three in Thailand. Particularly large is the gap between the income groups in the province of Ubon Ratchathani, where the wealth of the upper group is over PPP US$50,000, while in the lowest quintile it is less than PPP US$3000. In comparison, in the province of Ha Tinh 60 per cent of the households are below a per capita wealth of PPP US$3000, with just over 12,000 in the highest quintile.

Overall the data show that the distribution of wealth is rather uneven in all provinces. The relative distance between the quintiles amounts to a factor of 2–3, but it is increasing in the upper two quintiles. This variation suggests that the sample contains three types of household, namely those who are unlikely to be vulnerable, those who may be in permanent poverty, and a large group which is potentially vulnerable to poverty in the case of shocks.

Household indebtedness can be the result of failed investment due to bad decisions or bad luck. High levels of debt can limit the household's ability to take up gainful opportunities in the future, thus trapping the household in poverty and making it more vulnerable. To measure the impact of debt on the household's well-being, the debt per capita or the net wealth can be used as indicators. The latter is calculated by deducting debt from total wealth. Another possibility is to calculate the debt–income ratio, which was found to be in the order of 2.5 in Thailand based on official statistics (NSO 2008).

Obtaining data about debt is problematic, as repayment schedules are highly variable, making it difficult to estimate remaining debts at a certain point in time.

Debt per capita in the six provinces ranges between less than $300 and $1300. It is about three times higher in Thailand than Vietnam, which indicates more advanced integration of poor households in Thailand's financial systems and perhaps higher levels of investment.

Annual net income plus annual interest paid can be used as a measure for the household's ability to repay debt, and this can be related to household debt (see Table 3.9). This ratio is similar to the one determined by the National Statistical Office in Thailand from the 2007 Household Socio-Economic Survey. As shown in the table below, in Thailand the ratio is well above two and in Ha Tinh it is around one. Assuming a debt service to income ratio of 20 per cent, it would take households over 10 years to repay their debt.

3.4.5   Shocks and risks

While in later chapters of this book a detailed analysis on the role of shocks and risks is presented, a brief introduction will be given here, as such data are crucial in the analysis of vulnerability.

The overview of the data collected in the first wave, which reports the households' shock experiences from 2002 to 2007, shows that households in the six provinces had on average experienced 1.18 shocks in the previous five years.

Regarding the type of shocks, those related to agriculture, such as flood, drought, bad weather, pests and diseases, are dominant in all provinces, which underlines the likelihood that a considerable share of households in our database could be vulnerable to poverty (see Figure 3.6). Quite reasonably, agricultural shocks are more pronounced in Vietnam than

Table 3.9   Debt–income ratio for the 2007 survey

Province	2007
Buriram	2.44
Ubon Ratchathani	2.17
Nakhon Phanom	2.50
Ha Tinh	1.39
Thua Thien-Hue	1.05
Dak Lak	0.98

Source: DFG FOR756 Household survey 2007

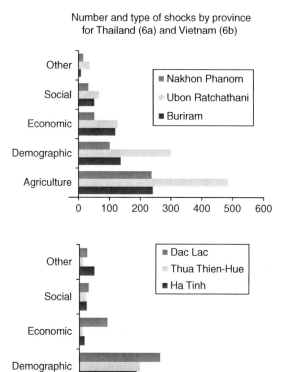

Number and type of shocks by province
for Thailand (6a) and Vietnam (6b)

Figure 3.6 (a) Type of shocks by province for Thailand, (b) Type of shocks by province for Vietnam

Source: DFG FOR756 Household survey 2007.

Note: The 2007 survey asked for shock occurrence during the past five years. The absolute numbers reported here are not suited for inter-province comparisons, especially in Thailand where sample sizes vary from 480–980 among provinces.

Thailand. Most of these shocks are covariate, affecting a larger part of the village or district.

However demographic (such as illness or death of household member, departure or arrival if household members have left home) and economic (business failure, job loss, price changes) shocks play a role too. Social shocks include conflicts with neighbours, and have been found to be less frequent than demographic and economic shocks.

The information on expected risks shown in Figure 3.7 provides another important variable for vulnerability models. The information derived from the panel survey of the 4400 households can provide the probabilities of future events and can help to explain households' strategies for ex-ante coping. As shown in Figure 3.7, households expect between almost two and over four shocks to occur during the next five years. On an ordinal scale ranging from "no impact" to "high impact", about half are expected to have a high impact if they occur in the following year. Again, differences between countries and provinces will stimulate analysis regarding causes of risks and strategies to minimize their impact.

3.5   Concluding remarks

The intention of this chapter was to provide an overview of the data available and at the same time arrive at some initial judgements regarding the adequacy of the approach chosen and the quality of data which were collected from six provinces in Thailand and Vietnam.

With this overview we can draw some preliminary conclusions, some of which will be verified in later chapters of the book. First, the provinces, which were purposively selected, are adequate for the purpose of the project to advance the vulnerability concept and undertake

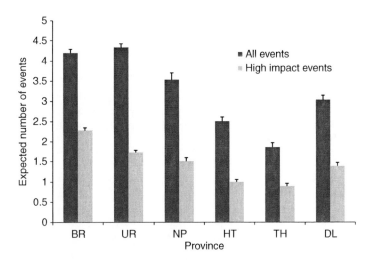

Figure 3.7   Expected number of adverse events
Source: DFG FOR756 Household survey 2007.

empirical testing of various vulnerability concepts. The sampling procedure which we have applied is sufficient to provide the data that can be used to answer the research questions. The areas selected offer a rich blend of conditions that provide a fertile ground to study theoretical and empirical issues of poverty from both a micro and meso perspective; for example, the pattern of shocks is similar in all the six provinces but there is likely to be considerable variation in the coping capacity of households, both ex ante and ex post. The distributions in household wealth, income and consumption suggest that we have observations that greatly facilitate the study of the various components of vulnerability.

Second, we can demonstrate that the quality of the data collected is adequate to carry out the crosscutting and sector analysis geared towards testing existing vulnerability definitions, and to identify factors that can explain the welfare status of rural households from a dynamic perspective. The three-stage cluster sampling approach has been effective in controlling the cost of survey operations and limiting the number of influencing factors while at the same time generating sufficiently large group sizes for various types of comparisons. Looking at some simple data quality parameters such as the completeness of the answers in the questionnaires, sample attrition, the number of missing cases, and the number of complete aggregates after data cleaning was performed, we see that these potential data problems are rather minor, suggesting high-quality data. The standard errors of the means for many of the variables are at a level that implies that the sample size is adequate.

Third, on the basis of the available and expected research results, there are good prospects for additional data collection through which a significant scientific contribution towards a better understanding of dynamic poverty in emerging market economies can be made. For example, the dynamic changes that take place in these two countries make it necessary to view poverty reduction in a wider geographic context. This implies that the measurement unit for vulnerability, which is the rural household, becomes an endogenous variable. For example, the high degree of fluctuation and the large mobility of household members in migrating back and forth between their village home base and the urban centres question the classic concept of a household as a consumption community. Hence, one of the challenges is to capture the dynamics of various types of "virtual households", and to collect information from resident and absent household members in order to assess the risk associated with off-farm employment in addition to the risk of agricultural enterprises. This has been carried out in the 2010 survey, the results of which will be presented in future papers.

Notes

1. The core modules include metadata, consumption, household roster, education, health, employment, anthropometry, transfers and other non-labour income, and housing as well as community and price data. Additional modules on environmental data, fertility, migration, household enterprises, agriculture, savings, credit and time use have been proposed by Grosh and Glewwe (2000).
2. The district level was ignored because districts are administrative units with no expected impact on vulnerability differences.
3. Communes in Vietnam are similar to sub-districts in Thailand.
4. Nucleus members have been defined as persons living in the household for at least 180 days of the reference period, and newborns younger than 180 days.
5. These can be expected to have completed schooling – not taking into account, however, informal adult education programmes, which are prominent in Thailand.

References

Bauer, A., R. Hasan, R. Magsombol and Guanghua Wan (2008): "The World Bank's New Poverty Data: Implications for the Asian Development Bank", *Working Paper Asian Development Bank*, 2008(2).

Binford, M., T. Lee and R. Townsend (2004): "Sampling Design for An Integrated Socioeconomic and Ecological Survey by Using Satellite Remote Sensing and Ordination", *Proceedings of the National Academy of Sciences of the United States of America*, 101(31): 11517–22.

Bresciani, F., G. Feder, Gershon, D. Gilligan, H. Jacoby, T. Onchan and J. Quizon, (2002): "Weathering the Storm: The Impact of the East Asian Crisis on Farm Households in Indonesia and Thailand", *World Bank Research Observer*, 17(1): 1–20.

Chaudhuri, S., J. Jalan and A. Suryahadi (2002): "Assessing Household Vulnerability to Poverty from Cross-Sectional Data: A Methodology and Estimates from Indonesia", Discussion Paper 0102-52, Columbia University, New York.

Dercon, S. (2002): "Income Risk, Coping Strategies, and Safety Nets", *World Bank Research Observer*, 17(2): 141–66.

Dercon, S. (2008): "Fate and Fear: Risk and Its Consequences in Africa", *Journal of African Economies*, 17(2): 97–127.

Dercon, S., J. Hoddinott and T. Woldehanna (2005): "Shocks and Consumption in 15 Ethiopian Villages, 1999–2004", *Journal of African Economies*, 14(4): 559–85.

Elbers, C. and J. W. Gunning (2003): *Vulnerability in a Stochastic Dynamic Model*, Tinbergen Institute, http://papers.ssrn.com/sol3/papers.cfm?abstract_id=446405

Ellis, F. (1998): "Household Strategies and Rural Livelihood Diversification", *Journal of Development Studies*, 35(1): 1–38.

General Statistics Office (GSO) (2011): *Summary Results of the Vietnam Household Living Standard Survey 2010*, General Statistics Office, Hanoi, Vietnam, http://www.gso.gov.vn/default_en.aspx?tabid=483&idmid =4&ItemID=11148

Gödecke, T. and H. Waibel (2011): "Rural–Urban Transformation and Village Economy in Emerging Market Economies during Economic Crisis: Empirical Evidence from Thailand", *Cambridge Journal of Regions, Economy and Society*, 4: 205–19.

Grosh, M. and P. Glewwe (2000): *Designing Household Survey Questionnaires for Developing Countries : Lessons from 15 Years of the Living Standards Measurement Study*, Volume 3, World Bank.

Grosh, M. and J. Munoz (1996): "A Manual for Planning and Implementing the Living Standards Measurement Study Survey", *LSMS Working Paper*, No. 126.

Hoddinott, J. and A. Quisumbing (2003): "Data Sources for Microeconometric Risk and Vulnerability Assessments", *Social Protection Discussion Paper Series*, No. 0323, World Bank.

Hoddinott, J. and A. R. Quisumbing (2008): *Methods for Microeconometric Risk and Vulnerability Assessments*, SSRN eLibrary.

Institute for Population and Social Research (2003): *Population projection for Thailand 2000–2025*, Mahidol University, http://www.ipsr.mahidol.ac.th/content/home/PDF/ Pub_Population%20Projector2543_2568.pdf

Klasen, S. and I. Woolard (2009): "Surviving Unemployment Without State Support: Unemployment and Household Formation in South Africa", *Journal of African Economies*, 18(1): 1–51.

Kozel, V., P. Fallavier and R. Badiani (2008): "Risk and Vulnerability Analysis in World Bank Analytic Work – FY2000–FY2007", *World Bank Discussion Paper*, No. 0812.

Naschold, F. and C. B. Barrett (2011): *Do Short-Term Observed Income Changes Overstate Structural Economic Mobility? Oxford Bulletin of Economics and Statistics* 73(5): 705–17.

National Economic and Social Development Board (NESDB) (2008): *Thailand Poverty Indicators 1988–2007*, National Economic and Social Development Board, Bangkok.

National Statistical Office (NSO) (2008): *The 2007 Household Socio-Economic Survey – Whole Kingdom*, http://service.nso.go.th/nso/nsopublish/service/survey/socioRep_50.pdf, Bangkok.

Pettersson, H. (2003): *Mission Report: Recommendations Regarding the Sample Design of the Vietnam Household Living Standard Survey*, Mission Report Statistics Sweden.

Schmidt-Kallert, E. and V. Kreibich (2004): "Split households", *Magazine for Development and Cooperation*, 12.

Townsend, R. M. (2004): *Townsend Project Overview*, http://cier.uchicago.edu/

US Census Bureau (2011): *International Data Base*, http://www.census.gov/population/international/data/idb/informationGateway.php

Wiggins, S. and S. Proctor (2001): "How Special Are Rural Areas? The Economic Implications of Location for Rural Development", *Development Policy Review*, 19(4): 427–36.

World Bank (2004): *Burkina Faso – Risk and Vulnerability Assessment*, World Bank, Washington, DC.

Yesuf, M. and R. A. Bluffstone (2009): "Poverty, Risk Aversion, and Path Dependence in Low-Income Countries: Experimental Evidence from Ethiopia", *American Journal of Agricultural Economics*, 91(4): 1022–37.

4
Using Household Surveys to Capture Vulnerability: Issues and Challenges

Stephan Klasen, Tobias Lechtenfeld and Felix Povel

4.1 Introduction

While the conceptual work on vulnerability reviewed in Chapter 2 is already quite advanced, the actual measurement of vulnerability to poverty of households is lagging behind. In fact, most empirical assessments of vulnerability have used very simplified methods to assess vulnerability to poverty, such as basing them on a single cross-section or vulnerability scores, or related short-cut procedures. Often these assessments are based on rather crude assessments of shocks experienced and risks faced by households. This is not due to the lack of dedication to the task or the fieldwork or econometric skills of the researchers involved. As will be discussed in more detail below, this is largely due to the fact that the measurement of vulnerability to poverty is extremely demanding as far as data needs are concerned. In particular, adequately capturing shocks and risks and their impact on vulnerability is very challenging.

This chapter focuses on the design and implementation of household survey instruments for vulnerability research, and it discusses the strengths and weaknesses of existing ones. It highlights difficulties in questionnaire design for capturing the intensity and duration of shocks, the ex-ante reaction of households to such shocks, and different attitudes towards risk. It critically highlights to what extent existing surveys (including the Thailand/Vietnam surveys) have been able to address these issues, and points out improvements in instrument design that can greatly reduce response bias during data collection.

The adequate design of survey instruments to study the problem at hand is central to the quality of data and analysis, to avoid measurement error and biased estimates (see for example Bound, Brown and Mathiowetz, 2004; Carroll *et al.*, 2006; Hyslop and Imbens, 2001). While measuring poverty through income and consumption is already quite challenging (for an overview see Meyer and Sullivan, 2003), measuring probability distributions of risk and shocks or quantifying the impact of shocks over time requires advanced instruments. Nevertheless, "if enough care is devoted to the design of questionnaires, it is possible to elicit high quality information about the probability distribution of future variables that are important for economic welfare and are relevant to determine economic choices" (Attanasio, 2009). Keeping this hopeful quote in mind, this chapter will provide a constructive review of survey instruments that are particularly suitable for measuring vulnerability to poverty.

The chapter is structured in three main parts: Section 4.2 provides an overview of current practice in vulnerability research; Section 4.3 presents useful ideas for cross-sectional studies and lessons learned from our large household panel survey in Thailand and Vietnam; Section 4.4 discusses a number of remaining issues and potential remedies. Section 4.5 concludes.

4.2 Current practice: survey measurement of vulnerability

When vulnerability became a research focus about a decade ago (see for example World Bank, 2000), empirical researchers had to realize that it was quite difficult to measure different vulnerability concepts with existing household data. In effect, some of the underlying postulations were not tested but rather assumed as given; for example, the dichotomy of idiosyncratic and covariate shocks is typically used to justify the use of non-specialized data sources, yet without proving the existence of any such clear distinction between idiosyncratic and covariate shocks. According to this approach, rainfall and other climate-related events are used as proxies for large covariate shocks, while illnesses of household members, as available from household surveys, indicate idiosyncratic shocks.

Clearly, the distinction between idiosyncratic and covariate events is more difficult. Typhoons regularly hit coastlines in Southeast Asia, can and often do have devastating effects on families living in simple houses while neighbours with improved housing are able to weather heavy storms. In effect, even the experience of covariate shocks has an idiosyncratic character that is conditional on the household characteristics.

Similarly, assumptions about the distribution of idiosyncratic shocks are difficult to test. Some communicable diseases (for example influenza) or pandemics (for example cholera) often have a covariate character and may be correlated to other covariate events (for example malaria). When testing for consumption smoothing of health shocks, it remains unclear whether households were actually capable of smoothing, or whether events were widely covariate and affected neighbouring households as well.

Ideally, measures of vulnerability based on household surveys would include the frequency, intensity and scope of events affecting a broad spectrum of household characteristics. From a theoretical perspective, vulnerability analysis requires information on predictable – and especially unpredictable – events (for example climate, health, agricultural, macro-economic), a series of control variables describing household members, their dwellings and activities (for example demographics, housing conditions and income sources), their set of possible behavioural responses (for example asset stocks, social networks, family ties, access to financial services, migration of household members), and learning responses and mitigation behaviour (for example history of investments, income diversification).

In the absence of long-running longitudinal household data (such as the long-running household panel surveys available in a number of developed countries, including the Panel Study of Income Dynamics in the USA, or the German Socioeconomic Panel), a majority of studies on vulnerability make do with micro-data which was either collected with a focus on other policy issues – for example Demographic and Health Surveys (DHS) rainfall data – or is based on a multi-purpose questionnaire covering poverty aspects and basic demographics – for example Living Standards Measurement Surveys, (LSMS) – often lacking a panel structure that would be needed to track poverty dynamics. In addition, few panel studies exist that allow the (limited) tracking of household poverty dynamics.

In practice, two types of data use can be distinguished: The first wave of studies has used data that was collected when vulnerability was not yet established as a notion in poverty research; these papers are often based on cross-sectional surveys, but some also make use of existing (short) panel surveys. A second wave of papers has been using data from vulnerability modules, which are nevertheless constrained to narrow aspects, or lack important aspects of dynamic poverty analysis. Examples of each are discussed below.

4.2.1   Studies using existing household surveys

Many studies using existing household surveys make use of cross-section surveys. A large group uses a single cross-section combined with a data-driven strategy to measure vulnerability. The work by Chaudhuri (2002) and extensions by Harttgen and Günther (2009) fall into this type. The impact of shocks is identified in the data as the difference between actual and predicted incomes, the latter being based on a standard income regression.[1] A second group uses available shorter- or longer-term panel data to study the impact of shocks and risks on the trajectories of consumption of households over time. These include the studies by Dercon and Krishnan (2000), using a three-wave panel, and Dercon (2004) on Ethiopia, with data from 1989 to 1997. The work by Elbers *et al.* (2007) is the only long-term panel so far, which follows Zimbabwean farmers over 30 years. The data is unfortunately very limited due to many changes in the survey tools, resulting in very few control variables and only a single asset that is employed to simultaneously proxy for changes in consumption and asset stock.

4.2.2 Vulnerability modules

More recently, vulnerability modules have been combined with a standard household survey instrument to overcome the inherent limitations of the above approaches. Here we review some prominent examples.

The Townsend project uses shock modules in the panel survey in Thailand. While shocks are measured, no data is obtained on household responses, leaving household behaviour in a black box (Kinnan, 2009; Paulson and Townsend, 2004). In addition, several World Bank-led LSMS surveys contain modules on shocks and vulnerability to varying extents. These include the recent LSMS rounds in Kenya, Vietnam and East Timor. While these modules appear very well designed, they are limited in scope; for example, the module on Vietnam is restricted to primarily female health shocks. While this is clearly an important source of income variation, it may not be sufficient to test household responses to the large mix of idiosyncratic and covariate risks faced by households in poor countries.

4.2.3 Shocks versus risks

All of the survey instruments discussed above have tended to focus on capturing the role of shocks on household consumption paths. But past shocks do not necessarily reflect adequately the future risk profile of household consumption. Thus it may be very useful to additionally capture household risk perception. Data on risk perception contributes to vulnerability research in several ways: first, it provides truly forward-looking information which is vital for the ex-ante measurement of vulnerability. Second, a household's current level of well-being is determined not only by its current status in terms of, for instance, income, consumption, education and health, but also by the risks it perceives (Ligon and

Schechter, 2003). Third, risk perception influences behaviour and the decision-making processes (Dercon, 2009). People exposed to risk may apply risk management strategies which – in the absence of functioning credit and insurance markets – possibly result in high and persistent poverty rates (Elbers *et al.*, 2007).

Although there is still some scepticism regarding the measurement of subjective expectations among economists (Manski, 2004), in recent years, more and more surveys have emerged that elicit such information.[2] Some of them are explicitly concerned with expected risks (for example Hill, 2009), that is with information relevant to vulnerability, while others intend to elicit, for example, expected future earnings (for example Jensen, 2006).

Advocates of asking people directly about their future expectations are, for example, Attanasio (2009), Delavande *et al.* (2009) and De Weerdt (2005). Also, Dercon (2009) points out that in many ways the fears of households as opposed to their actual fate is of interest to the researcher. This development is underlined by the growing understanding that people's expectations revealed by survey interviews do not have to be rational but rather have to genuinely describe their perceptions (Manski, 2004).

There is considerable evidence suggesting that collecting high quality data on risk perception is possible (Delavande *et al.*, 2009). In developed countries the elicitation of subjective expectations is well advanced. For example, in the USA the so-called Survey of Economic Expectation is conducted regularly; it aims at revealing respondents' perceptions regarding, among others, economic insecurity. Examples for empirical work with subjective expectation data in developed countries include Dominitz and Manski (1997 and 2004), as well as Gan *et al.* (2003).

The elicitation and the use of data on risk perception in developing countries is less extensive, but "can and should be promoted" (Attanasio, 2009).[3] Work by, among others, Delavande and Kohler (2008), Attanasio *et al.* (2005), Lybbert *et al.* (2007) and Luseno *et al.* (2003) shows that respondents in developing countries understand the concept of probability and are able to provide high quality data on subjective expectations. On the other hand, there are also examples indicating that respondents may have difficulties in stating their risk perception appropriately (Mahajan *et al.*, 2008). This mixed evidence points to the fact that the design of the questionnaires, as well as the quality of the enumerators, is crucial for successfully eliciting subjective expectations.

In questionnaires in developed as well as developing countries, the most common way of asking for perceptions about the future is using simple expectation questions. For instance, in a developing countries context, Nguyen (2008) and Jensen (2006) present different scenarios to students and ask "How much do you think you will earn?" under these given circumstances (Delavande *et al.*, 2009). The aforementioned Survey of Economic Expectation uses questions such as "What do you think is the per cent chance that you will lose your job during the next 12 months?" However, there is evidence suggesting that respondents are more capable of assessing probabilities in terms of frequencies than in terms of objective likelihood estimates (Bless *et al.*, 1992). That is, subjective probabilities tend to be more accurately elicited by asking, for example, "In how many out of 100 cases do you think that ...?" instead of "What is the per cent chance that ...?"

The cognitive task of providing probability estimates, which is required to assign probabilities to the risks identified, may be eased by narrowing down the possible answers. For example, one could ask "Do you think that in 0, 20, 40, 60, 80, or 100 out of 100 cases ...?" instead of "In how many out of 100 cases do you think that ...?" Interestingly, this reduction of answer categories is not likely to lead to a substantial loss of information. According to Tourangeau *et al.* (2000), respondents simplify the task of estimating the probabilities anyway: when being asked for probabilities on a scale ranging from 0 to 100 their answers tend to be lumped at multiples of 10 and the value 5. Bruine de Bruin and Fischhoff (2000) argue that the answer categories should not comprise 50 out of 100 or 50 per cent. They point out that when being asked about probabilities, respondents often confuse the actual probability of 50 per cent with their inability to provide an estimate. Therefore, it is not certain whether a stated likelihood of 50 per cent really indicates a probability or rather a "don't know".

A more advanced way of measuring expectations focuses on distributions as opposed to point estimates. For example, Dominitz and Manski (1997) use a per cent chance formulation in order to reveal a cumulative distribution function for future income in developed countries. They first ask respondents for the highest and lowest amount the latter could possibly earn. They then define four threshold levels within this range, and ask for the per cent chance that the respondents' income will be below the first, second, third and fourth of these benchmarks.

Also in the context of developing countries, methods for eliciting distributions of subjective expectations are increasingly applied. Thus, De Mel *et al.* (2008) ask Sri Lankan microenterprises about their expected profits two months into the future. They then ask the respondents to think about 20 hypothetical businesses which are exactly like their own, as well as about all possible positive and negative risks, and to assess how many of these businesses will end up in each of some pre-defined profit intervals.

A popular practice to elicit subjective expectations in developing countries is the use of visual aids. For example, Delavande and Kohler (2008) provide respondents with ten stones which they assign to different events (for example the subjective expectation of being infected with HIV or the likelihood of death in the next year or next five years) in order to indicate their probability assessment. Attanasio *et al.* (2005) and Attanasio (2009) make use of a ruler which is graded from 0 to 100. During on-the-spot interviews, respondents state their perception of probabilities by pointing to this ruler. Other studies using visual aids such as balls and stones include Hill (2009), who elicits Ugandan farmers' expectations about future coffee prices, and Giné *et al.* (2008), who reveal respondents' expectations regarding the onset of the monsoon.

While these are all innovative ways to elicit risk perceptions and expectations, there are clearly some weaknesses, including systematic overestimates of rare events and the inability to assess the likelihood and impact of extremely rare events. Thus while it can properly be claimed that it is possible to elicit reliable information on perceived vulnerability, it is unclear how closely this perceived vulnerability correlates with actual vulnerability.[4]

To conclude, this survey of the literature generates several interesting findings. First, many of the empirical approaches measuring vulnerability are essentially short-cut methods to make the best use of available data. While methods and available data clearly lead to differences in the quality of the resulting vulnerability estimates, it appears that all of the empirical implementations are quite a way off a completely satisfactory approach. Clearly, more custom-made data is required for more progress in the field of vulnerability measurement. Second, it is useful and possible to elicit seemingly reliable information on ex-ante risk perceptions of households.

4.3 Lessons learnt from vulnerability surveys in Southeast Asia

Having reviewed current practices of eliciting vulnerability related information, this section deals with the insights gained by two waves of a vulnerability survey conducted in Southeast Asia. The first wave was implemented in 2007, the second in 2008; further waves have been implemented (2010 and 2012). The first two waves both used a comprehensive questionnaire in on-the-spot interviews especially designed to reveal the shock and risk exposure of households. As already discussed, in the previous chapter, data on (i) household member characteristics such as demographics, education and health; (ii) shocks and risks; (iii) agriculture; (iv) off-farm and self-employment; (v) borrowing, lending, public transfers and insurance; (vi) expenditures; (vii) assets; and (viii) housing conditions was collected from some 4000 households in rural and peri-urban areas or predominantly rural provinces in Thailand and Vietnam.[5] To ensure that respondents would correctly understand the questions posed to them, special attention was given to an extensive pilot survey whose results helped the questionnaires to be devised.

Particularly the shock and risk sections, which are provided in Appendix 4.A.1, allow the thorough study of household vulnerability. Both of them cover exclusively negative events which are the essence of any vulnerability measure (see Calvo and Dercon, 2005, 2008).[6] Also, the combination of questions about shocks experienced in the past and risks expected to occur in future sheds light on the accuracy of elicited expectations (Delavande *et al.*, 2009).

The first questionnaire's shock section is designed as follows: at the start, respondents are asked for the three major shocks that have affected their household during the past five years. Here, no specific types of shock are suggested, therefore the respondent can think independently about any adverse event he or she considers worth mentioning. Thereafter, specific shocks are read out to the respondent, who is supposed to state whether his or her household had such experiences (see Table 4.1).

Concerning shocks which are mentioned either directly or in response to enquiry by the respondent, a range of additional questions is posed: first, it is asked when the event took place. Second, three questions aim at eliciting the shock's severity by letting the respondent estimate (i) whether the impact on the household was high, medium, low, or non-existent (these answer categories are read out to the respondent); (ii) how much income his or her household lost due to the event; and (iii) the monetary value of lost assets. Third, the idiosyncratic or covariate nature of the shock is revealed by asking who else was affected by the event. Fourth, respondents are supposed to state the three most important strategies they applied in order to cope with the shock. Fifth, by asking whether despite the coping strategies implemented the household still had to reduce household consumption, the household's (in)ability to smooth consumption is elicited. Lastly, in order to gather

Table 4.1   Adverse events covered by the vulnerability survey in Southeast Asia

Adverse events included in wave 1	Modifications in wave 2
1. Illness of household member 2. Death of household member 3. Household member left the household 4. Person joined the household 5. Money spent for ceremony in the household 6. Household damage 7. Theft 8. Conflict with neighbours in village 9. Relatives/friends stopped sending money (remittances) 10. Flooding 11. Drought 12. Unusually heavy rainfall 13. Crop pests 14. Storage pests (including rats) 15. Livestock disease 16. Landslide, erosion 17. Job loss 18. Collapse of business 19. Unable to pay back loan 20. Strong increase of interest rate on loans 21. Strong decrease of prices for output 22. Strong increase of prices for input 23. Change in market regulations	New events: 1. Accident 2. Law suit 3. Storm 4. Was cheated 5. Snow/ice rain (only in Vietnam) Dropped events: 1. Death of household member 2. Unable to pay back loan Modified events: 1. Job loss split into agricultural and non-agricultural job loss

information about the persistence of shocks, it is asked how long it took to recover from the event.

The shock section is complemented by questions regarding household trends in subjective wellbeing ("Do you think you are better off than last year?" and "Do you think you are better off than five years ago?"). In addition, it is asked whether, and to what degree, the household's income fluctuates. This question is then combined with subjective wellbeing ("What is the impact of income fluctuations on the wellbeing of members of your household?") which again provides insights into the shock-management capacities of the household.

The risk section is designed to shed light on, *inter alia*, the probability, as well as the severity, of the impact on income of downside risks a household faces during the upcoming five years. Respondents are confronted with the same list of adverse events as in the shock section and asked whether they think that any of these events will occur in the next five years. Respondents who report expecting a certain risk to take place are then asked additional questions about that risk's perceived probability and severity. With regard to its severity, enumerators ask for the estimated impact of the event on the household's income if it were to occur next year. As in the shock section, respondents are provided with the possible answer categories: high, medium, low, or none. The probability of a risk is revealed via frequencies: respondents are asked how often they perceive the risk in question to occur during the next five years. To the stated frequencies of 0, 1, 2, 3, 4, 5 or more, probabilities that the event will take place during the upcoming 12 months of 0%, 20%, 40%, 60%, 80%, or 100% can be assigned.

The eliciting of the respondents' risk perception using simple expectation questions was done for three reasons: first, the results of the pilot survey suggested that respondents were able and willing to provide high-quality answers to this type of question. Second, it poses little challenge to the enumerators. Third, it is the least time- and cost-intensive approach to reveal subjective expectations. Moreover, it was aimed at facilitating the cognitive task for respondents by building on some of the information provided in Section 4.2: probabilities are revealed by asking for natural frequencies as opposed to per cent chances, and respondents are given a few predefined answer categories. Also, the possible problem of confusing a chance of 50 per cent with epistemic uncertainty is avoided by not providing an answer category which represents a probability of 50 per cent.

Besides questions about risk perception, the risk section inquires about hypothetical coping strategies that a household would apply if it suddenly needed a small (5000 Thai baht or 1.5 million Vietnamese dong, respectively) or large (60,000 Thai baht or 15 million Vietnamese dong, respectively) amount of money.[7] In addition, respondents are asked to state whom they would ask first for a loan and how long it would take them to get the required money. The section is completed by a forward-looking question about subjective wellbeing ("Subjective wellbeing: Do you think you will be better off in the next five years?").

In general, the results obtained by all waves suggest that the vulnerability surveys implemented in Southeast Asia are valid instruments to elicit vulnerability-related information. They accomplish the collection of information about a household's shock history combined with its forward-looking expectations concerning adverse events without burdening the respondents with overchallenging questions. This is indicated, for example, by the fact that in less than 0.1 per cent of all cases in Thailand and Vietnam respondents provided "no answer" to the question as to whether they expect a certain risk to take place during the next five years.

Furthermore, when comparing the shock experience of households with their risk perception, significant and robust correlations are found: Table 4.2 shows OLS regression results from the Thai sub-sample which indicate that households are more likely to expect a drought if they had experienced it during a five-year period prior to the interview (Column 1).

Also, households expecting a drought in Wave 1 are more likely to experience it during the one-year period between Waves 1 and 2 (Column 3). These correlations remain significantly different from zero if controls are included (Columns 2 and 4).

The results are in line with other studies. For example, Delavande and Kohler (2008), as well as Attanasio and di Maro (2008) find past experiences of individuals or households to be correlated with their expectations about future outcomes.

However, lessons have also been learnt from the first wave of the vulnerability survey, which led to changes to the shock and risk sections in the second wave. In order to avoid the trade-off stemming from improving a given questionnaire on the one hand, and keeping up its panel structure on the other, almost all these changes are extensions of the respective sections instead of modifications to existing questions. In the remainder of this paragraph, these changes are discussed in greater detail:

First, in both the shock and risk sections, the list of adverse events covered by the questionnaire was updated with the insights gained during the first wave. As Table 4.1 above indicates, five new types of shocks and risks were added to the list. These events were frequently mentioned by respondents in the first wave under the answer category "Other; Specify". Meanwhile, the events "death of household member" and "unable to pay back loan" were excluded from the second wave; in Thailand in particular, the former was seen as an inappropriate question by respondents, so it was discarded by enumerators early on in the first wave. The latter ("unable to pay back loan") was excluded because it became clear that it is more the result of a shock than a shock itself. It could also be argued that events such as "money spent for ceremony in the household" are neither shocks nor risks because they do not strike unexpectedly but rather are planned by the household. However, they are still included in the second wave of the survey, due to the immense costs they may entail. Finally, the event "job loss" was split into agricultural and non-agricultural job loss in order to gain more information about the risks associated with the diversification of income sources.

Table 4.2 Correlation between risks and shocks

	(1)	(2)	(3)	(4)
	Drought expectation, t = 0		Drought experience, t = 1	
Drought experience, t = 0	0.206*** (0.012)	0.179*** (0.013)		
Drought expectation, t = 0			0.156*** (0.019)	0.082*** (0.020)
Controls	no	yes	no	yes
Observations	2136	2035	2136	2035
adj R-squared	0.057	0.123	0.019	0.066

Note: Table contains OLS estimates for Thailand; robust standard errors in parentheses; asterisks denote significance at the 1%- (***); 5%- (**); 10%-(*) level; "drought expectation" and "drought experience" are dummy variables equalling 1 if a drought is/was expected/experienced and 0 otherwise; controls include: (i) province dummies, (ii) log of household income, (iii) size of land holdings, (iv) household size, share of household members with (v) off farm employment, (vi) self employment, and (vii) employment in own agriculture, (viii) sex, (ix) ethnicity, (x) age and (xi) age squared, (xii) years enrolled and (xiii) years enrolled squared of household head.

The need to update the adverse events, which is explicitly asked about in the survey, suggests that even an extensive pilot exercise may miss important characteristics of the shock and risk exposure as well as cultural peculiarities of the households in the targeted area. Therefore, it is important not just to try to recover all this information during the pilot but also to allow the questionnaire's design to be flexible enough to be modified after the first wave.

Second, in the second wave, no code was available for the "don't know" response to any of the questions, to encourage prompting by the interviewer. In any case, any "don't know" responses were recorded as "no answer". Clearly, the restriction was intended to improve the quality of the information obtained. However, it seems that at least in part, "don't knows" from the first wave have been substituted by "no answers" in the second. For example, in the first wave about 10 per cent of Vietnamese respondents stated that they did not know whether a certain risk would occur during the coming five years. The corresponding "no answer" share was near zero, whereas in the second wave, the "no answer" code was elicited for about 3.5 per cent of the questioned events.

This outcome points to a tradeoff between prompting the respondent to give insightful answers on the one hand, and overburdening him or her with overly difficult questions. Since a "don't know" provides more information for imputation than "no answer", it may be preferable to retain the former option, that is allowing respondents to express uncertainty with respect to future events.[8]

Third, since the first wave did not provide any information regarding the covariance between different shocks experienced by one household, in the second wave the shock section was extended by questions which aimed at shedding light on this matter. In order to achieve this, the enumerators asked whether any of the shocks mentioned by a respondent led to or were the consequence of any of the other stated shocks. Respondents in both Thailand and Vietnam stated that only a small proportion of adverse events was causally interlinked, namely 5 per cent in the former country and 2.6 per cent in the latter. This result may indicate that there is little covariance between different shocks – or, more likely, that these questions are extremely, if not too, challenging for respondents.

Fourth, it turned out that the time horizon of five years for experienced shocks led to recall errors on the part of the respondents. More precisely, households seem to remember more recent events better than shocks which occurred several years ago (see Figure 4.1). Only the most extreme events seem to persist in memory. For example, the average income loss due to shocks in Vietnam (Thailand) was reported to be 2.7 (1.5) times higher in 2002 than in 2006.

The problem of recall errors was addressed in the second wave, which asked for shocks that affected households during the 12-month period that had elapsed between the two waves. As Figure 4.2 indicates, there is no apparent error related to recall-length in the second wave. These findings support the claim that surveys using retrospective questions improve the precision of the information they gather by reducing the time horizon they are asking for.

Fifth, the shock section was amplified by further questions which were intended to elicit additional information of interest: when a shock did not affect more than one person, it was asked who this person actually was. In total, 1692 of the 5480 recorded shocks (30.9 per cent) can be assigned to specific household members. Out of these, 722 (45.6 per cent) struck household heads. Such information is useful, for example, to differentiate better between the effects of idiosyncratic shocks that strike economically important household members such as household heads, and the consequences of events experienced by other members.

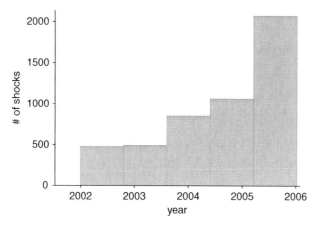

Figure 4.1 Total number of shocks recorded in 1st wave, by year

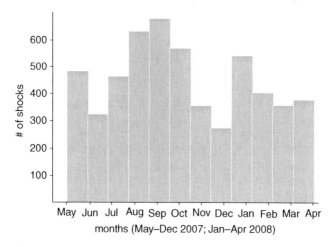

Figure 4.2 Total number of shocks recorded in 2nd wave, by month

Also, in addition to the existing questions regarding the impact of a shock (see above), the respondents were asked in the second wave to estimate the total extra expenditure due to this event. Thus, the intention was to complete the information about the severity of any given shock. On average, extra expenditure constitutes 30.4 per cent of the total loss incurred by a shock, whereas lost income accounts for 58.6 per cent and the monetary value of lost assets 11.0 per cent. Therefore, in order to capture the full extent of an adverse event, it is recommended that researchers ask about income, assets, and expenditures when eliciting the severity of a shock. Finally, shocks mentioned by respondents in the first wave from which they had not yet recovered when the interview took place were incorporated in the second wave. More precisely, it was asked how long it had taken to recover from these events in the second reference period, whether the household (still) had to reduce consumption due to them, and whether it had implemented any further coping strategies.

Sixth, the risk section was extended by an enquiry about risk prevention and mitigation strategies applied by households. The underlying intention was to elicit information concerning the otherwise unobserved costs of ex-ante risk-management strategies. With regard to each adverse event listed in the section, it was asked whether the households had done anything to prevent it from happening or to mitigate its impact. If respondents answered yes, questions about the type of risk management and its costs were posed. Enumerators were explicitly instructed not to double-count any of these expenditures. With respect to 5 per cent (10 per cent) of all expected risks, Thai (Vietnamese) respondents started to implement ex-ante risk management strategies. Similarly to the questions about the covariance between different shocks, this finding suggests that either only a few prevention and mitigation strategies are applied or that this type of enquiry is cognitively too challenging for respondents.

Seventh, two questions concerning the risk attitude of respondents were added in order to merge information about risk aversion with subjective expectations. This combination of questions helps to solve the "identification problem" (Manski, 2004) of determining whether ex-post realizations are due to preferences or to expectations. For example, a household may grow drought-resistant but low-return crops even though it does not perceive a drought occurring but rather because it is very risk-averse. Instead, a risk-neutral or risk-loving household may do so because it expects a drought to take place in the near future. The first question asked respondents to indicate their risk attitude on a scale ranging from 0 (unwilling to take any risk) to 10 (fully prepared to take risk). The second question presented the following scenario to the (Thai) respondents: "Imagine you had just won 100,000 baht in a lottery and you can invest this money in a business. You are not sure if the business goes well or not. If it goes well you can double the amount invested after one year. If it does not go well you will lose half the amount you invested. What fraction of the 100,000 baht would you invest in the business?"[9] Generally, respondents seem to have been able to answer these questions: the share of missing values or "no answers" is close to zero. However, answers are lumped at certain points. For example, when assessing their risk attitude on a scale from 0 to 10, 16 per cent (27 per cent) of the Thai (Vietnamese) respondents chose 0, and 38 per cent (15 per cent) chose 5. While the high proportion of completely risk-averse people seems to be plausible in the context of rural areas in developing countries, the overrepresentation of the focal response 5 suggests that there may be more effective ways of eliciting risk attitudes.

The modifications of the questionnaire between first and second wave were intended to improve the quality and quantity of vulnerability-relevant information gathered by the survey. However, as indicated above there are still unresolved issues in the design of vulnerability surveys, which will be discussed in the following section.

4.4 Remaining issues in the design of vulnerability surveys

As is the case with any other survey, the quality of vulnerability surveys depends on the quality of answers provided by the respondents. As Tourangeau *et al.* (2000) point out, data quality is determined by "the level of effort needed, specifically for recall-and-count; motivation; accessibility of episodic information; [and] task conditions, including question wording". In addition, during the course of interviews, questions are frequently misunderstood or misinterpreted, and respondents may devise answers to correspond to perceived judgment or to minimize effort (McFadden *et al.*, 2005).[10] While these issues are not new and remedies exist (see for example Deaton 1997; Ravallion 2003; UN, 2005), this section focuses on issues particular to vulnerability surveys with a focus on measurement error and implications for instrument designs. In particular we focus on several unresolved conceptual problems which are structured into three subfields: (4.4.1) measurement errors, (4.4.2) measurement of shocks and vulnerability, and (4.4.3) behavioural responses.

4.4.1 Measurement errors

Recall error

Recall error is a common problem in any household survey. When households are asked to estimate levels and trends report of the past, responses might be biased in all sorts of directions. On the aggregate level, this might be acceptable as long as there is good reason to believe that bias is normally distributed.

When looking at vulnerability and event data, recall has two channels through which recorded data can become biased. First, with increasing recall periods, the number of reported shocks decreases (see Figure 4.1 above). Second, reported severity is likely to be biased, since respondents will mainly recall harmful events from the more distant past and possibly remember the effect on assets, expenditures and income inaccurately.

The problem of recall error is serious, yet difficult to address. Ideally, recall periods should be short (or equally long) between survey waves, where data from years before the survey should be treated with caution. But until very long panel surveys are in place in developing countries where corresponding recall periods can be short (to just cover the period between the waves), the problem of recall bias in relatively long recall periods is difficult to avoid. However, if respective secondary data is available, researchers may approximate the degree of recall error by comparing subjective shock reports with, for example, objective weather or commodity price data.

Recall overload

Another issue is the tradeoff between revealing as much information as possible and overburdening the respondent with questions that are cognitively too challenging. This is particularly relevant in the context of surveys that include questions about perceived probabilities which according to Attanasio (2009) "are typically the most difficult to ask". The accuracy of such expectations depends, among others, on the events being judged, on the exact nature of the judgement task, and on the respondents' familiarity with these events, as well as with the concept of probability (Tourangeau *et al.*, 2000). The latter in particular renders difficult the elicitation of probabilities in developing countries, where many of the respondents do not know the concept of probability (Attanasio, 2009). For instance, it remains unclear how it can best be avoided that respondents lump their answers at certain focal points. Even in the first wave of the vulnerability survey from Southeast Asia, in which probabilities were asked for in terms of frequencies and only a few answers were possible, respondents from both countries perceived that almost 40 per cent of all expected risks would occur with a probability of 100 per cent. Instead, a probability of 80 per cent, that is the closest answer to 100 per cent, was named in only 2 per cent of the Thai and 3 per cent of the Vietnamese cases. Moreover, the probability of rare events tends to be overestimated by respondents (Delavande *et al.*, 2009, and Tourangeau *et al.*, 2000). This phenomenon is also present in our data from Southeast

Asia: For example, in the first wave almost none of the Thai respondents states that his or her household was affected by one of the three economic shocks: "strong increase of interest rate on loans", "strong decrease of prices for output", "strong increase of prices for input". However, these events are perceived to occur in future by 45 per cent, 60 per cent and 82 per cent of the Thai respondents, respectively.[11]

With respect to the elicitation of risk attitudes of households, again the problem of lumped answers may exist. As mentioned in the previous section, an implausibly high share of respondents of the Southeast Asian survey tended to choose 5 on a scale ranging from 0 (highest risk aversion) to 10 (lowest risk aversion). At the same time, the results of this survey clarify the fact that risk attitudes can be very heterogeneous, which is at odds with empirical applications that in general use one common parameter of risk aversion for every household (for example, Ligon and Schechter, 2003). Therefore, it remains an important task for future research to explore more effective ways of revealing risk attitudes in large scale household surveys.

Enumeration bias

Another concern that is not related to the design of vulnerability surveys but is very important for the quality of vulnerability related data is the possibility of enumerator bias. For instance, the risk data for the Vietnamese province of Dak Lak shows a relatively high level of risk perception. Breaking down the data by enumerator shows that for six out of nine enumerators, risk perception among the households interviewed was above average. This suggests that these interviewers had prompted questions differently. In contrast, one of the remaining interviewers did not record a single risk for any of their respondents.

This suggestive evidence for enumerator bias is substantiated by results from probit regressions which show that dummy variables for enumerators impact significantly on the likelihood of perceiving a risk to occur in future.[12] This outcome is in line with findings from Delavande *et al.* (2009) who find a significant correlation between enumerator dummies and subjective expectations. In light of such enumerator bias, it seems to be even more important to train the interviewers properly on the one hand, and to gather more information about them on the other. For example, it may be useful to analyse whether enumerator bias varies with the "match" between respondent and interviewer, that is whether both have the same sex, stem from the same ethnic root, and so on. During analysis, the inclusion of enumerator dummies and interaction terms is recommendable.

4.4.2   Measurement of shocks and vulnerability

Analysis of vulnerability often requires accounts of severity of events and household behaviour. Simple count data of shocks will not suffice, as it does not allow heterogeneity in household expectation, preferences or behavioural responses.

Shocks intensity

The ability to measure the impact of shocks is limited in household surveys, since surveys are typically carried out at a single point of time, and record recall data. This snapshot perspective of household surveys allows a precise ex-post measurement of the frequency of events during the previous period. For short recall periods over a year or two, frequency counts will be fairly accurate. While a count variable is very helpful, many applications would benefit from a more precise measurement of the shock impact. For instance, tests of consumption smoothing analyse whether households are able to maintain household consumption levels despite income shocks. Pooling similar events (say health shocks) with different intensity (low- and high-cost illnesses) will bias the results in favour of consumption smoothing, since the variation of shock intensity is lacking.

Measuring shock intensity, however, has its own caveats. Shock impact is evaluated at the moment of the interview, while the total cost of shocks occurs over a longer period of time. For example, assets may be lost during a flood (instant loss), but the repair of a dwelling after the flood leads to additional shock-related expenditures over an extended period. If the survey takes place before the entire cost of the shock has been incurred, the shock intensity will be underestimated. In the extreme cases where income losses (for example due to injury) are permanent, shock intensity will be understated.

Figure 4.3 below shows the value of reported agricultural shocks (defined as the sum of income loss, shock-related expenditures and asset loss) which occurred 1 to 12 months previous to the interview. Measurement thus takes place retrospectively, with time equalling 12. Clearly, shock value is higher from an event experienced 12 months ago. The measured value of the shock thus appears to depend on the moment of measurement, since a large share of the total cost occurs over time during the coping process. Failing to account for the entire decay function of shocks may lead to an erroneous conclusion about households regarding total impact and consumption smoothing. Especially in surveys with short recall periods of one to two years, it is important to control for the time since the event took place.

Breaking down the total effect into possible channels such as asset loss and destruction, additional expenditure and forgone income can

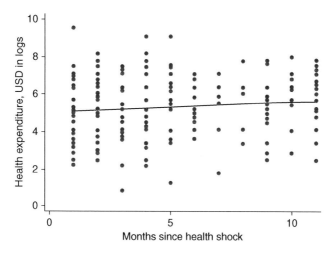

Figure 4.3   Decay of health shock impact over time (Thailand)
Source: Authors' calculations.

help to reduce the measurement bias, since assets are typically affected first. It might also be useful to prompt for the initial loss, which will correspond to the statistical mode in the figure below. The overall shock-related cost, which is represented by the area under the solid line, may be largely underreported when the measurement occurs directly after the event took place. This is, because over time households are better able to develop coping mechanisms and alter their activities to minimize the long-term effect of the event.

Pooling reported shock value that occurred 1 to12 months before the interview introduces a bias which decreases the mean value of the shock, since shocks develop their full value only over an extended period of time.

In brief, even when events are evenly distributed over time, the average impact of the event will be measured with error, since a decayed impact is measured as the total effect for all shocks but the most recent ones. Such measurement error of the effect of shocks might be circumvented by collecting the calendar month of each event using a calendarium often used to measure labour market events in panel surveys in developed countries. This would allow the estimation of the decay function and subsequent deflation of the reported event. Especially for short recall periods of one to two years, this approach would seem reasonable.

A third problem related to the measurement of shock severity also concerns the periodic nature of events and their impacts. When events are not evenly distributed over time, it becomes difficult to assign a possible bias. Consider seasonal events, such as heavy storms which tend to be clustered around the monsoon season. The month of data collection is then correlated with the reported effect.

A shock-diary approach can be used to address the measurement error associated with covariate event impact. Diaries have been successfully used in India, Bangladesh and South Africa to establish the economics of the poor in great detail (Collins *et al.*, 2009). Diaries are also used in Household Budget Surveys, which are conducted in many developing countries to supplement LSMS data with seasonally adjusted prices and expenditures.

Independence of events

When measuring events over the course of a year, several shocks can strike a given household. This plurality poses particular challenges to vulnerability research as well as to the measurement of vulnerability. First, on the measurement side it becomes problematic to properly capture the response to shocks correctly. Consider an unlucky family which is struck by a series of events; households may be able to borrow from family or friends for a while, but there are certainly limits to the availability of funds.

Second, social networks can simply break down. They may lose their function as an insurance substitute as soon as a covariate shock occurs, where each household will need to draw on its own savings and reduce its scope to lend to others. Thus, the effectiveness of an insurance substitute would depend on the recent occurrence of a covariate event.

Third, risk pooling can be very difficult to establish when idiosyncratic shocks occur with high frequency and effectively become covariate in their nature. That can be the case when nearly all households are struck by idiosyncratic shocks within a given period. Even if never more than 5 per cent of a village is sick, when all villagers have been sick over a year on average it becomes difficult to imagine how informal risk pooling would work. Formal products would certainly rely on re-insurance mechanisms that pool on a more aggregate level, but that is by definition not available to informal agreements.

Fourth, even without risk pooling, it is difficult to evaluate the effectiveness of coping mechanisms if households and communities experience several shocks. When events can be mitigated with money, households would use their most effective coping strategy on the first shock. For the second shock they would then use their second most efficient strategy, and so on. Of course, different responses are more effective for certain events; nevertheless, will the portfolio of available responses be constrained by the choice of reaction to previous events?

Capturing the available portfolio of responses when shocks occur might reduce the problem of unobserved conditionality. Simply pooling responses (by type or by event) as current practice can bias the estimates of effectiveness towards zero, since the history of events and coping responses is ignored.

Interpersonal comparability

Finally, the design of household surveys in general and vulnerability surveys in particular should facilitate an investigation of the interpersonal comparability of data on subjective judgments. As Delavande *et al.* (2009) argue, respondents' characteristics such as optimism or education may cause interpersonal incomparability. In a prominent illustration, McFadden *et al.* (2005) show that 62 per cent of Danish men and 14 per cent of Frenchmen regard their health status as being excellent. However, the life expectancy of the latter is in fact two years higher than that of the former. An example for facilitating the analysis of interpersonal comparability is given by the vulnerability survey from Southeast Asia: respondents are asked to indicate the severity of an experienced shock by stating whether its impact was high, medium, low or non-existent. Whether this assessment is interpersonally comparable can be analysed by comparing the income and/or the monetary value of assets different respondents claim to have lost due to this event. A more advanced approach in this context is the use of "anchoring vignettes" (for example, King and Wand, 2007, and King *et al.*, 2004): after respondents have indicated their subjective judgement, they are asked to assess hypothetical situations of a similar kind. The latter are then used to test the interpersonal comparability.

4.4.3 Behavioural responses

Motivated by the constant need to obtain nutrition, the notion of consumption smoothing theorizes that households strive to maintain a constant consumption stream despite any income volatility. Due to credit market imperfections, however, households may be unable to address volatility of income and expenditure unless they have access to informal arrangements that can serve as insurance substitutes (Ligon, 1998). Making use of such informal arrangements is thus a response to the risk of unexpected events. The need to obtain a smooth flow of consumption relates to nutritional needs and is thus particularly important to the population of the lowest income deciles that spends a relatively large share of income on food. When informal arrangements work well, there is in principle little need for introducing additional measures.

The concept of consumption smoothing has been repeatedly tested empirically, with very mixed results; see for example Ligon *et al.* (2000), Morduch (1995), Rosenzweig (1988), Suri (2005), Townsend (1994; 1995) and Udry (1994). The conflicting findings of these studies might be explained by the choices taken when households are repeatedly affected by adverse events. Learning effects from previous shocks play an important role in how coping is achieved. Households with previous shock experience are likely to be more effective in coping and – depending on their risk aversion – will be better prepared through insurance arrangements and other mitigation instruments.

Choice of coping

Few theoretical models for coping behaviour exist. In principle, coping is achieved through three main channels, which are (1) de-saving, (2) asset sales, and (3) borrowing.

Savings are often very limited in developing countries, where formal banks are rare and social norms prevent family members from saving. Assets may be available, but these can be very bulky (vehicles) or an essential part of household income (ploughs). Other assets may have low resale values (mattress) or be affected by the shock (animals during drought). All these factors reduce the ability of the household to turn assets into food.

As a result, household choices appear limited when they refer to borrowing in an attempt to reduce consumption volatility. However, economic theory suggests that agents will only take out loans for productive investments with high expected returns. In emergency situations, however, borrowing might become the coping mechanism of choice, even if no positive returns can be expected.

Choice of mitigation

A similar problem is related to the choice of ex-ante behavioural changes. Households might reduce capital investments if they are expecting high out-of-pocket expenditure during the year. Even if shocks occur at random, experience might show households that it is in their interest to keep some funds in reserve. This creates several challenges for data collection and analysis.

First, shock incidence and impact will differ between households due to differential preparedness, and not only due to the stochastic nature of the event itself. This introduces self-selection problems into the data and analysis. Shock data will contain random event data, reduced by non-random prevention strategies. In addition, severity estimates will be biased since they already contain the degree to which households were prepared for the event. But not appropriately controlling for mitigation will most certainly introduce bias into any estimates.

Second, timing and length of the main survey recall period do matter. In a multi-period setting, this year's mitigation behaviour might be a coping response to last year's event. Improving hygiene practices during health problems in the family can be such a case, possibly seen as prevention while also being a reaction.

Third, the length of the overall survey period strongly affects the effects. Elbers, Gunning and Kinsey (2007) show for Zimbabwe – applying a three-decade-long panel – that mitigation behaviour strongly reduces capital investments in favour of mitigation behaviour. In effect, growth at the household level is reduced by over 60 per cent.

While in-depth questions on mitigation behaviour and its motivation appear important, it is not clear how to resolve the problem of endogeneity in short-term studies when unable to control for the causes of individual mitigation.

In this section, several unresolved problems have been presented with their potential effects on data quality and estimates. It appears that more needs to be done to establish theoretically sound and empirically valid approaches to vulnerability measurement, as well as to identify its behavioural impact. In an attempt to do so, qualitative and laboratory techniques might yield substantial gains. For example, the use of behavioural games by Liu (2008) is an interesting approach to gain more insight into decision making under risk. Problems of covariance of shocks might rather be tested using a combination of secondary data on covariate events, census data and detailed vulnerability data similar to poverty mapping (Felkner *et al.*, 2009).

4.5 Conclusion

This chapter has highlighted a number of important issues that need to be borne in mind when measuring vulnerability through household surveys. By distinguishing between cross-sectional and longitudinal designs, it aims to provide the reader with insight and practical solutions into some key ingredients for promising approaches to capture vulnerability, including risks and shocks, and household behaviour. The chapter also points to a list of unresolved methodological questions which require particular attention during the questionnaire design, as they can quickly introduce measurement error into vulnerability estimates.

When no best-practice instrument exists, researchers are well advised to approach a problem from multiple angles. These can be qualitative or quantitative, and contain recent advances from network analysis, experimental studies or poverty mapping. Moreover, those working with secondary data on incomes, shocks and risks should carefully interpret the results in light of the possible problems described in this chapter. Our own results from Thailand and Vietnam suggest that progress can be made in accurately estimating shocks, perceived risks and associated vulnerability measures. But much work remains to be done.

Notes

1. Harttgen and Günther (2009) extend this method by dividing this difference into an idiosyncratic and a covariate component.
2. For more information about problems that may arise when people are asked for their expectations see, for example, McFadden *et al.* (2005).
3. Note that the use of subjective data in developing countries is not bound to expectations. Another popular field of application is poverty research, where subjective poverty assessments are conducted (compare, for instance, Ravallion and Lokshin (2001, 2002)). A common finding of these studies is that households are able to assess their poverty status quite accurately (Lokshin *et al.*, 2004).
4. See also Chapter 1 for a further discussion of these issues.
5. For a detailed description of the questionnaire's design, the sampling strategy, and fieldwork, see Chapter 3.
6. Note that at least two of the adverse events included in the shock and risk sections may also have a positive impact on the economic well-being of a household. Thus, the events "person leaves the household" and "person joins the household" may reflect migration and the exploitation of new income sources elsewhere in the former case, as well as the joining of a new household member who may contribute to the household's income in the latter.
7. Roughly 16 Thai baht and 4700 Vietnamese dong equal 1 purchasing power parity adjusted US dollar (PPP US$1).
8. See also Dominitz (1998) regarding this matter.
9. Roughly 16 Thai baht equal 1 purchasing power parity adjusted US$ (PPP US$1).
10. Regarding erroneous responses in surveys, the interested reader may turn to, for instance, Schwarz (2003), Gardiner and Richardson-Klavehn (2000), and Tourangeau *et al.* (2000).
11. Overall shock exposure and risk perception are nonetheless highly correlated with each other.
12. Detailed results are not presented here but are available upon request.

References

Attanasio, O. (2009): "Expectations and Perceptions in Developing Countries: Their Measurement and Their Use", *American Economic Review: Papers & Proceedings 2009*, 99(2): 87–92.

Attanasio, O. and V. di Maro (2008): "Income Expectations in Rural Mexico: Measurement and Models", *mimeo*.

Attanasio, O., C. Meghir and M. Vera-Hernández (2005): "Elicitation, Validation, and Use of Probability Distributions of Future Income in Developing Countries", *mimeo*, Paper presented at the 2005 Econometric Society Meeting.

Bless, H., D. M. Mackie and N. Schwarz (1992): "Mood Effects on Encoding and Judgmental Processes in Persuasion", *Journal of Personality and Social Psychology*, 63: 585–95.

Bound, J., C. Brown and N. Mathiowetz (2004): "Measurement Error in Survey Data", in: *Handbook of Econometrics*, Chapter 59, Volume 5, 2001: 3705–843.

Bruine de Bruin, W. and B. Fischhoff (2000): "Verbal and Numerical Expressions of Probability: It's a Fifty-Fifty Chance", *Organizational Behaviour and Human Decision Processes*, 81(1): 115–31.

Calvo, C. and S. Dercon (2005): "Measuring Individual Vulnerability", *Department of Economics Discussion Paper Series*, 229, Oxford University, Oxford.

Carroll, R. J., D. Ruppert, L. A. Stefanski and C. Crainiceanu (2006): *Measurement Error in Nonlinear Models: A Modern Perspective*, Second Edition. Boca Raton, Chapman & Hall/CRC, FL.

Collins, D. (2005): "Financial Instruments of the Poor: Initial Findings from the Financial Diaries Study", *Development Southern Africa*, 22(5): 735–46.

Collins, D., J. Morduch, S. Rutherford and O. Ruthven (2009): *Portfolios of the Poor: How the World's Poor Live on $2 a Day*, Princeton University Press, Princeton, NJ.

De Mel, S., D. McKenzie and C. Woodruff (2008): "Returns to Capital: Results from a Randomized Experiment", *Quarterly Journal of Economics*, 123(4): 1329–72.

De Weerdt, J. (2005): "Measuring Risk Perceptions: Why and How", *SP Discussion Paper*, 0533, World Bank, Washington DC.

Deaton, A. (1997): *The Analysis of Household Surveys: A Microeconometric Approach to Development Policy*, World Bank, Washington DC.

Delavande, A. and H.-P. Kohler (2008): "Subjective Expectations in the Context of HIV/AIDS in Malawi", *mimeo*, Working Paper, University of Pennsylvania.

Delavande, A., Giné, X. and D. McKenzie (2009): "Measuring Subjective Expectations in Developing Countries – A Critical Review and New Evidence", *Policy Research Working Paper*, 4824, World Bank, Washington DC.

Dercon, S. (2004): "Growth and Shocks: Evidence from Rural Ethiopia", *Journal of Development Economics*, 74: 309–29.

Dercon, S. (2009): "Fate and Fear: Risk and Its Consequences in Africa", *Journal of African Economies*, 17(2): 97–127.

Dercon, S. and P. Krishnan (2000): "Vulnerability, Seasonality and Poverty in Ethiopia", *Journal of Development Studies*, Volume 36(6): 25–53.

Dominitz, J. (1998): "Earnings Expectations, Revisions, and Realizations", *Review of Economics and Statistics*, 80: 374–88.

Dominitz, J. and C. F. Manski (1997): "Using Expectations Data to Study Subjective Income Expectations," *Journal of the American Statistical Association*, 92(439): 855–67.

Dominitz, J. and C. F. Manski (2004): "How Should We Measure Consumer Confidence?" *Journal of Economic Perspectives*, 18(2): 51–66.

Elbers, C., J. W. Gunning and B. Kinsey (2007): "Growth and Risk: Methodology and Micro Evidence", *World Bank Economic Review*, 21(1): 1–20.

Felkner, J., K. Tazhibayeva and R. Townsend (2009): "Impact of Climate Change on Rice Production in Thailand", *American Economic Review*, 99(2): 205–10.

Gan, L., M. Hurd and D. McFadden (2003): "Individual Subjective Survival Curves", *NBER Working Paper*, No. 9480, Cambridge, MA.

Gardiner, J. M. and A. Richardson-Klavehn (2000): "Remembering and Knowing", in: E. Tulving and F. I. M. Craik (eds), *Handbook of Memory*, Oxford University Press, New York: 229–44.

Giné, X., R. Townsend and J. Vickery (2008): "Rational Expectations? Evidence from Planting Decisions in Semi-Arid India", *mimeo*, World Bank.

Harttgen, K. and I. Günther (2009): "Estimating Households' Vulnerability to Idiosyncratic and Covariate Shocks: a Novel Method Applied in Madagascar", *World Development*, 37(7): 1222–34.

Hill, R. V. (2009): "Using Stated Preferences and Beliefs to Identify the Impact of Risk on Poor Households", *Journal of Development Studies*, 45(2): 151–71.

Hyslop, D. R. and G. W. Imbens (2001): "Bias From Classical and Other Forms Of Measurement Error", *Journal of Business and Economic Statistics*, 19: 475–81.

Jensen, R. (2006): "The Perceived Returns to Education and the Demand for Schooling", *mimeo*, Brown University.

Kinnan, C. (2009): "Distinguishing Barriers to Insurance in Thai Villages", *MIT Working Paper*.

King, G. and J. Wand (2007): "Comparing Incomparable Survey Responses: New Tools for Anchoring Vignettes", *Political Analysis*, 15(1): 46–66.

King, G., C. J. L. Murray, J. A. Salomon and A. Tandon (2004): "Enhancing the Validity and Cross-cultural Comparability of Measurement in Survey Research", *American Political Science Review*, 98(1): 191–207.

Ligon, E. (1998): "Risk Sharing and Information in Village Economies", *Review of Economic Studies*, 65: 847–64.

Ligon, E. and S. Schechter (2003): "Measuring Vulnerability", *Economic Journal*, 113: 95–102.

Ligon, E., J. P. Thomas and T. Worrall (2000): "Mutual Insurance, Individual Savings, and Limited Commitment", *Review of Economic Dynamics*, 3: 216–46.

Liu, E. (2008): "Time to Change What to Sow: Risk Preferences and Technology Adoption Decisions of Cotton Farmers in China", *Princeton University Working Paper*, 526.

Lokshin, M., N. Umapathi and S. Paternostro (2004): "Robustness of Subjective Welfare Analysis in a Poor Developing Country: Madagascar 2001", *World Bank Policy Research Working Paper*, 3191, Washington DC.

Luseno, W., J. G. McPEak, C. B. Barrett, G. Gebru and P. D. Little (2003): "The Value of Climate Forecast Information for Pastoralists: Evidence from Southern Ethiopia and Northern Kenya", *World Development*, 31(9): 1477–94.

Lybbert, T. J., C. B. Barrett, J. G. McPEak and W. Luseno (2007): "Bayesian Herders: Asymmetric Updating of Rainfall Beliefs in Response to External Forecasts", *World Development*, 35(3): 480–97.

Mahajan, A., A. Tarozzi, J. Yoong and B. Blackburn (2008): "Bednets, Information, and Malaria in Orissa", *mimeo*, Stanford University.

Manski, C. F. (2004): "Measuring Expectations", *Econometrica*, 72(5): 1329–76.

McFadden, D. L., A. C. Bemmaor, F. G. Caro, J. Dominitz, B. Jun, A. Lewbel, R. L. Matzkin, F. Molinari, N. Schwarz, R. J. Willis and J. K. Winter (2005): "Statistical Analysis of Choice Experiments and Surveys", *Marketing Letters*, 16(3/4): 183–96.

Meyer, B. D. and J. X. Sullivan (2003): "Measuring the Well-Being of the Poor Using Income and Consumption", *Journal of Human Resources*, 38, Special Issue on Income Volatility and Implications for Food Assistance Programs: 1180–220.

Morduch, J. (1995): "Income Smoothing and Consumption Smoothing", *Journal of Economic Perspecttives*, 9: 103–14.

Nguyen, T. (2008): "Information, Role Models and Perceived Returns to Education: Experimental Evidence from Madagascar", *mimeo*, MIT.

Paulson, A. and R. Townsend (2004): "Entrepreneurship and Financial Constraints in Thailand", *Journal of Corporate Finance*, 10(2): 229–62.

Ravallion, M. (2003): "Measuring Aggregate Welfare in Developing Countries: How Well Do National Accounts and Surveys Agree?" *Review of Economics and Statistics*, 85(3): 645–52.

Ravallion, M. and M. Lokshin (2001): "Identifying Welfare Effects Using Subjective Questions", *Economica*, 68(271): 335–57.

Ravallion, M. and M. Lokshin (2002): "Self-Rated Economic Welfare in Russia", *European Economic Review*, 46: 1453–73.

Rosenzweig, M. (1988): "Risk, Implicit Contracts and the Family in Rural Areas of Low-Income Countries", *Economic Journal*, 98: 1148–70.

Schwarz, N. (2003): "Self-reports in Consumer Research: The Challenge of Comparing Cohorts and Cultures", *Journal of Consumer Research*, 29(4): 588–94.

Suri, T. (2005): "Spillovers in Village Consumption: Testing the Extent of Partial Insurance", Working Paper.

Tourangeau, R., L. J. Rips and K. Rasinski (2000): *The Psychology of Survey Response*, Cambridge University Press, New York and Cambridge, UK.

Townsend, R. M. (1994): "Risk and Insurance in Village India", *Econometrica*, 62: 539–91.

Townsend, R. M. (1995): "Financial Systems in Northern Thai Villages", *Quarterly Journal of Economics*, 110: 1011–46.

Udry, C. (1994): "Risk and Insurance in a Rural Credit Market: An Empirical Investigation in Northern Nigeria", *Review of Economic Studies*, 61: 495–526.

UN (2005): "Household Sample Surveys in Developing and Transition Countries", *Studies in Methods Series*, No. 96, New York.

World Bank (2000): *World Development Report 2000/2001 – Attacking Poverty*, Oxford University Press, New York.

Appendix 4.A.1   Questionnaire

When considering the past 5 years, has there been any event causing a big problem (shock) affecting the household? Please think of any problems related to your family, farm, house or job.

a. What were the three major shocks that affected your household in the past 5 years?

	1	2	3	4	5	6	7	8	9
Event ID	Type of event	When did the event occur?	Estimated severity of the event on your household?	Estimated loss of income due to the event in the year of occurrence?	Estimated loss of assets due to the event in the year of occurrence?	Aside from your HH who else was affected by the event?	What was your major coping activity to deal with the event?	2nd coping activity
	A	97 if not known	Interv.: Read code B 1–4	(local currency)	THB/1000 VND	C	D	D
1								
2								
3								

b. Was your household affected by any of the following events in the past 5 years?
(Info: Read out Code A and note all those events, for which the respondent says yes.
Skip those already noted in Question a.))

4	
5	
6	
7	

Capital letters in shock and risk section indicate type of codes. Lists of respective codes are provided on pages 105 [or 106/7 if tables are not merged; see subsequent comment] and 108 [or 110 if tables are not merged], respectively.

10	11	12	13	14	15	16	17	18
3rd coping activity	Did the household still have to reduce household consumption expenditures because of the event?	How many years did it take to recover from the event?	Do you think you are better off than last year?	Do you think you are better off than 5 years ago?	Does your income fluctuate a lot?	What is the impact of income fluctuations on the wellbeing of members of your household?	What was the best year for your household in the past 5 years?	What was the worst year for your household in the past 5 years?
D	E	F	G	G	H if code = 1, go to Q17	B	97 = don't know	97 = don't know

First wave's questionnaire: codes for shock section

Code A
1 Illness of household member
2 Death of household member
3 Household member left the household
4 Person joined the household
5 Money spent for ceremony in the household
6 House damage
7 Theft
8 Conflict with neighbours in the village
9 Relatives/Friends stopped sending remittances
10 Flooding of agricultural land
11 Drought
12 Unusually heavy Rainfall
13 Crop pests
14 Storage pests (including rats)
15 Livestock Disease
16 Landslide, Erosion
17 Job loss
18 Collapse of business
19 Unable to pay back loan
20 Strong increase of interest rate on loans
21 Strong decrease of prices for Output
22 Strong increase of prices for Input
23 Change in market regulations
90 Other, specify
97 Don't know
98 no answer
99 Does not apply
21 Strong decrease of prices for Output
21 Strong decrease of prices for Output

Code B
1 High
2 Medium
3 Low
4 No impact
90 Other, specify
97 Don't know

98 no answer
99 Does not apply

Code C
1 no other HH
2 some other HH
3 most HH in village
4 most HH in district
5 most HH in country
6 most HH in province
90 Other, specify
97 Don't know
98 no answer
99 Does not apply

Code D
1 Did nothing
2 Took up additional occupation
3 Diversify agricultural portfolio
4 Substitute crops
5 Reduced production inputs
6 Took children out of school
7 Sent children to relatives/friends
8 Adult migrated to look for job
9 Adult migrated to live with Relatives/friends
10 Adult migrated to marry
11 Sold livestock
12 Sold land
13 Sold storage (e.g. rice)
14 Sold other assets
15 Used savings
16 Used insurance
17 Borrowed from relatives
20 Borrowed from informal moneylender
21 Borrowed from village funds
22 Borrowed from commercial bank
23 TH: Borrowed from BAAC/Coop. Bank
24 TH: Borrowed from Gov't Savings Bank
26 VN: Borrowed from VBSP
27 VN: Borrowed from VBARD
28 Help from government
29 Help from NGOs

Code D cont.
30 Help from relatives
31 Help from friends/neighbours
90 Other, specify
97 Don't know
98 no answer
99 Does not apply
90 Other, specify

Code E
1 yes
2 no
97 Don't know
98 no answer

Code F
0 less than 1 year
1 1 year
2 more than 1 year, but now recovered
3 not yet recovered
90 Other, specify
97 Don't know
98 no answer

Code G
1 Much richer
2 Richer
3 The same
4 Poorer
5 Much poorer
90 Other, specify
97 Don't know
98 no answer
99 does not apply

Code H
1 Not at all
2 Yes, a bit
3 Yes, a lot
90 Other, specify
97 Don't know
98 no answer
99 does not apply

First wave's questionnaire: Risk section

Now, please consider the following possible future events

1	2	3	4
Type of event	Do you think that any of the following events will occur in the next 5 years?	What would be the impact on your household's income if it occurred next year?	How often, do you think, will any of the following events occur in next 5 years? do not ask if Q2 = no
	A	B	C
1 Illness of household member			
2 Death of household member			
3 Household member left the household			
4 Person joined the household			
5 Money spent for ceremony in the household			
6 House damage			
7 Theft			
8 Conflict with neighbours in the village			
9 Relatives/Friends stopped sending remittances			
10 Flooding of agricultural land			
11 Drought			
12 Unusually heavy Rainfall			
13 Crop pests			
14 Storage pests (including rats)			
15 Livestock Disease			
16 Landslide, Erosion			
17 Job loss			
18 Collapse of business			
19 Unable to pay back loan			
20 Strong increase of interest rate on loans			
21 Strong decrease of prices for Output			
22 Strong increase of prices for Input			
23 Change in market regulations			

First wave's questionnaire: Risk section – *continued*

	Code E	
5 Suppose you would suddenly need 5,000 THB/1.5 Mill VND. Would you do any of the following things? Info: Read out list in Code E and note all that apply.		a
		b
		c
		d
		e
6 In case of applying for a loan: Whom would you ask first?		D
7 How many days would it take to get this amount?		
8 Suppose you would suddenly need 60,000 THB/15 Mill. VND. Would you need and try to apply for a loan?		A
9 In case of applying for a loan: Whom would you ask first?		D
10 How many days would it take to get this amount?		
11 Suppose you would suddenly need 60,000 THB/15 Mill VND. Would you do any of the following things? Info: Read out list in Code E and note all that apply.		a
		b
		c
		d
		e
12 Do you think you will be better off in the next 5 years?		F

First wave's questionnaire: Codes for risk section

Code A
1 yes
2 no
97 Don't know
98 no answer

Code B
1 High
2 Medium
3 Low
4 No impact
90 Other, specify
97 Don't know
98 no answer
99 Does not apply

Code C
1 1 in 5 years
2 2 in 5 years
3 3 in 5 years
4 4 in 5 years
5 5 in 5 years
90 Other, specify
97 Don't know
98 no answer
99 Does not apply

Code D
1 Borrow from relatives
2 Borrow from friends
   /neighbours
3 Borrow from pawnshop
4 Borrow from informal
   money-lender
5 Borrow from village funds
6 Borrow from commercial bank
7 Borrow from government bank
90 Other, specify
97 Don't know
98 no answer
99 does not apply

Code F
1 Much richer
2 Richer
3 The same

4 Poorer
5 Much poorer
90 Other, specify
97 Don't know
98 No answer
99 Does not apply

Code E
1 Did nothing
2 Took up additional occupation
3 Diversify agricultural portfolio
4 Substitute crops
5 Reduced production inputs
6 Took children out of school
7 Sent children to relatives/friends
8 Adult migrated to look for job
9 Adult migrated to live with
   relatives/friends
10 Adult migrated to marry
11 Sold livestock
12 Sold land
13 Sold storage (e.g. rice)
14 Sold other assets
15 Used savings
16 Used insurance
17 Borrowed from relatives
18 Borrowed from friends/
   neighbours
19 Borrowed from pawnshop
20 Borrowed from informal
   money-lender
21 Borrowed from village funds
22 Borrowed from commercial bank
23 TH: Borrowed from BAAC/Coop.
   Bank
24 TH: Borrowed from Govt. Savings
   Bank
25 TH: Borrowed from Village bank
26 VN: Borrowed from VBSP
27 VN: Borrowed from VBARD
28 Help from government
29 Help from NGOs
30 Help from relatives
31 Help from friends/neighbours
90 Other, specify
97 Don't know
98 no answer
99 Does not apply

5
Mapping Vulnerability: Extending Static Poverty Maps for Vietnam

Tobias Lechtenfeld

5.1 Introduction

In recent years, poverty mapping has gained popularity among researchers and policy makers as a powerful tool for identifying pockets of poverty and providing detailed information on regional differences in well-being (Demombynes *et al*, 2004; Elbers *et al*, 2007). Poverty mapping has the advantage of combining detailed household data from relatively small surveys that are not representative at the local level with census data which contains only a few key variables but provides complete coverage of households (Elbers *et al.*, 2003). Such maps can be very informative for researchers and policy makers, since they provide poverty estimates at a local level.

Mapping can be applied to address a wide range of questions relevant to informed policy making, including policy evaluation (Nguyen Viet *et al.*, 2010), urban crime analysis (Demombynes and Oezler, 2005) and planning infrastructure projects (Hentschel and Lanjouw, 1998). Most importantly, poverty maps are increasingly used for policy targeting. Governments are currently using spatial targeting to provide free health care for the poor (Sparrow, 2008) or to roll out cash-transfer programs and food-for-work programs (Elbers *et al.*, 2007; Fujii, 2007).

However, poverty maps are static in the sense that they are based on cross-sectional data. Maps show only a snapshot of the past, covering the survey reference period, typically twelve months prior to the interview with the household. They lack information about households moving in and out of poverty over time. When poverty maps are used for policy targeting this limitation can directly affect targeting performance. Previously non-poor households that have suffered from a shock and have fallen back into poverty would therefore not be eligible for benefits. This problem is particularly important when covariate shocks pull entire villages or districts below the program eligibility threshold.

This chapter proposes mapping ex-ante vulnerability instead of ex-post expenditure poverty, to better account for income and expenditure volatility over time. For this illustration, vulnerability as expected poverty is used. As also discussed in Chapter 2, vulnerability as expected poverty reflects the probability that families will find themselves below the poverty line in the coming year. Alternative vulnerability indicators might be useful for certain policy purposes and are discussed in the method section. Overall, the analysis shows that using vulnerability for geographic targeting has the potential to substantially improve targeting performance. In comparison, poverty estimates would miss about 20 per cent of households considered vulnerable.

This chapter is organized as follows. Section 5.2 presents the potential and limitations of poverty mapping, using a series of applied studies from Vietnam. Section 5.3 provides a brief background on the rural population in the three Vietnamese provinces that were used for this illustration. Section 5.4 presents key aspects of the mapping methodology and discusses potential challenges when mapping risk and vulnerability. In Section 5.5, the mapping result from poverty and vulnerability are compared in terms of targeting performance. Section 5.6 concludes.

5.2 Literature review

Spatial targeting of poverty in Vietnam started very recently (Minot 2000). Combining survey data from 1993 with the agricultural census from 1994, the study provides the first spatial disaggregation of rural poverty and inequality during Vietnam's transition process. He finds a striking difference between coastal and inland districts within the same province, and rightly points out that province-level poverty rates are seriously misleading as a basis for policy. The calculation of confidence intervals of the district estimates is, however, somewhat ad hoc, making it difficult to compare the measured differences. Nevertheless, the differences between level estimates appear fairly large and are estimated in a way similar to that which is considered best practice today.

In 1999, a full population census was conducted in Vietnam which can be combined with the 1998 Vietnam Living Standard Survey (VLSS) collected together with the World Bank. The resulting analysis points to location as a key determinant of poverty – far more so than individual characteristics including age or education (Minot *et al.*, 2003). Market access and agro-climatic factors explain about three quarters of the variation of poverty in rural areas. These factors also include rainfall, slope of land and soil quality, and underline the usefulness of geographical targeting for social programs. The poverty results are very different from previously used official poverty levels which were based on self-reporting by village heads. In fact, official and estimated poverty figures do not correlate much, indicating that the official poverty counts may be prone to political influence and seem to systematically miss pockets of poverty among minority groups in remote mountainous areas. Lastly, the authors conclude that urban poverty is more complex and driven by many unobserved covariates, since agro-climatic factors are not found to be directly responsible for urban poverty.

Nguyen Viet *et al.* (2007) develop an urban poverty profile of Vietnam's largest city and main commercial hub, Ho Chi Minh City, which according to official accounts has no poor. The authors, however, detect an average poverty headcount of around 10 per cent with some city districts experiencing poverty at over 30 per cent. For the update of the initial study, Nguyen Viet (2009) combines survey data from 2004 and 2006 with the 2004 census to compare poverty trends over time. Despite the 10 per cent annual GDP growth during the period, more than 20 per cent of the city districts have become poorer in 2006. This is explained by selection effects among arriving migrants, who tend to be asset poor. Since Ho Chi Minh City remains the principal destination of domestic migrants, rural poverty estimates are also likely to be affected by rural–urban migration.

Another paper looking at changes of household expenditure over time is the work by Baulch, Pham and Reilly (2011) using standard survey techniques. The authors are particularly concerned about the more than 50 ethnic minority groups in the country; the gap in income between them and the ethnic majority groups increased by 14.6 per cent between 1995 and 2004. Various possible explanations for the widening of the gap are tested, including differences in education, asset stock and other endowments, household demographics and agro-climatic factors. They conclude that while endowments are much smaller among ethnic minority households, these households also reap lower returns from existing endowments, driving more than half of the change in the income gap. Clearly, economic opportunities differ between ethnic groups. While kinship has been found earlier to facilitate commerce, the authors raise concerns that government authorities are giving preferential treatment to ethnic majority groups. Since ethnic minorities are concentrated in remote areas, this might explain why some of these districts are particularly disadvantaged.

Several impact evaluations exist for policies in Vietnam. A particularly interesting study combines macro- and micro-simulation methods. In their attempt to quantify the poverty reduction of a macro-economic policy change, Fujii and Roland-Holst (2008) use income, work and production data in a computable general equilibrium (CGE) model to estimate Vietnam's hypothetical poverty counts had the country not joined the World Trade Organization (WTO). By combining micro-simulation with CGE methods, the authors are able to map their counterfactuals, showing that some of the already poor districts in Northwestern Vietnam are not benefitting much from the opportunities created by trade. As a result, inter-district inequality increases.

To sum up, existing studies for Vietnam show that poverty analysis should be conducted separately between rural and urban areas, even though they are closely linked through migration, remittances and food markets. The key factors determining rural poverty seem to be location characteristics, such as agro-climatic factors. Household characteristics including the demographic composition, education, asset stock and other endowments only play a secondary role in determining poverty. Ethnicity appears to be of vital importance when it comes to securing income opportunities. In addition, micro–macro modelling has shown that the volatility of farm and non-farm income sources is systematically different. Consequently, location characteristics and ethnicity will be the key variables during poverty mapping. Since this chapter is concerned with covariate and household-specific risks, it will also use factors that might drive such events. In the following section the data sources and the distribution of covariates are presented.

5.3   Econometrics of vulnerability mapping

This section first presents the econometric methods and assumptions for standard poverty mapping. The section then discusses particular methodological challenges that can arise when applying these methods to vulnerability estimates.

5.3.1   Poverty mapping

Poverty mapping requires the combining of survey and census data (Elbers *at al.*, 2003). Based on very detailed survey data, a measure of household consumption is calculated from food and non-food expenditures of each household. Next, a GLS consumption regression is used to identify the predictors of low consumption,

$$\ln y_{ch} = x'_{ch}\beta + u_{ch}, \tag{5.1}$$

where the left-hand side is the log function of consumption y of household h living in location c. The vector x'_{ch} contains the covariates used to predict consumption. The error term u_{ch} can be decomposed,

$$u_{ch} = \eta_c + \varepsilon_{ch}, \tag{5.2}$$

into a location component η_c and a household component ε_{ch} allowing for spatial autocorrelation and heteroscedasticity. Some applications also include geographical and climate data to reduce the influence of unobserved location characteristics which might increase spatial autocorrelation through η_c. Once a good fit of the consumption regression is found, an out-of-sample prediction is carried out for the logged household consumption on the census using the estimates of the regression, resulting in

$$\hat{\ln} y_{ch} = x'_{ch} \hat{\beta} + \hat{\eta}_c + \hat{\varepsilon}_{ch}, \tag{5.3}$$

with $\hat{\ln} y_{ch}$ being predicted log expenditure and $\hat{\beta}$ being the estimated coefficient of the right-hand side variables. $\hat{\eta}_c$ is the mean of the household specific residuals within locality c, and $\hat{\varepsilon}_{ch}$ is the demeaned residual.

Using the resulting household specific consumption levels, the aggregate poverty and inequality can be calculated for small areas c, such as provinces or districts. The only requirement is that all variables used for the regression also exist in the census data.

While it is relatively straightforward to run the predictions of household consumption, the calculation of the correct standard error for those predictions is a central challenge in poverty mapping. Elbers *et al.* (2002, 2003) propose the use of Monte Carlo simulations. The idea in repeatedly running the predictions and aggregations is to obtain the correct standard errors $\tilde{\eta}_c^r$ and $\tilde{\varepsilon}_{ch}^r$, which are then used to simulate the log expenditure $\hat{\ln} y_{ch}^r$ and the coefficients $\hat{\beta}^r$.[1]

$$\hat{\ln} y_{ch}^r = x'_{ch} \tilde{\beta}^r + \tilde{\eta}_c^r + \tilde{\varepsilon}_{ch}^r \tag{5.4}$$

The debate on the calculation of predicted standard errors for household estimates is far from conclusive. The analysis here uses default settings provided by the poverty mapping program made available by the World Bank (based on Elbers *et al.* 2002, 2003) to calculate the standard errors, which tend to provide fair approximations. In any case, standard error issues are unlikely to play an important role in the final maps, since household estimates are aggregates at sub-district level.

5.3.2   Vulnerability mapping

The empirical strategy that is used for poverty maps can also be applied for vulnerability indicators. First, a vulnerability indicator needs to be constructed for each household in the survey data. Second, a model is specified that predicts vulnerability from the survey data, but only used variables that exist in both, the survey and the census data. Third, the model estimates are used for an out-of-sample prediction using the census data. Fourth, the vulnerability predicted for each household in the census is aggregated to a mean vulnerability level for each small area (such as a sub-district). Fifth, using a vulnerability threshold, all areas with high vulnerability are classified as vulnerable.

The first step – construction of a household level vulnerability indicator – is crucial for the results. At least three advanced vulnerability concepts have been proposed, each with their own advantages and assumptions (see Dercon *et al.* 2004 for a practical guide to vulnerability analysis). The main approaches are (a) vulnerability as expected poverty (Calvo and Dercon, 2005; Chaudhuri *et al.* 2002; Christiaensen and Subbarao, 2001; Pritchett *et al.* 2002), (b) vulnerability as uninsured exposure to risk (Tesliuc and Lindert, 2004) and (c) vulnerability as low expected utility (Ligon and Schechter, 2003, 2004, see also Chapter 2).

In principle, any of the three approaches can be used for mapping. Because of its conceptual similarity to poverty and usefulness for policy targeting, concept (a), vulnerability as expected poverty, is used for the illustrating vulnerability mapping. For the analysis, two indicators are calculated following the works of Calvo and Dercon (2005) and Chaudhuri *et al.* (2002), with minor adaptations to the available data.

Vulnerability by Calvo and Dercon

Calvo and Dercon (2005) propose a measure that defines vulnerability as the probability-weighted average of future states of the world with regard to expenditure poverty. Vulnerability increases with the indicator as it ranges from zero to one. While this measure is axiomatically well founded, it is virtually impossible, however, to measure the value and probability of all possible shocks which would be needed to calculate the future states of the world.

The survey data used for this illustration contains information on over 30 different shocks related to climate (storms, floods, droughts, hail), agriculture (pests, sudden increases in the prices of seeds and fertilizers, sudden price decreases of produced crops and livestock), markets (price increases, taxes and regulations), health (illness, birth, death), and family (violence, divorce, crime). Based on the distributions and cost of past shocks it is possible to create a vulnerability measure which includes the most important events. Through the design of the measure, rare events have virtually no influence on the vulnerability status even when associated with high losses. That is because a low probability of occurrence wipes out the influence of any associated economic loss, since occurrence probability and loss are multiplied when composing the measure. This feature makes it possible to calculate an accurate Calvo–Dercon measure of vulnerability from surveys that collect data from regularly recurring shocks.

When aggregating vulnerability, Calvo and Dercon (2007) propose a series of measures where idiosyncratic and covariate shocks have different welfare implications. While these should be considered for policies addressing covariate events, the authors acknowledge that the level of aggregate vulnerability can be conveniently measured as a combination of individual levels in line with Calvo and Dercon (2005), Chaudhuri et al. (2002) and Ligon and Schechter (2004), as has been done here.

Vulnerability by Chaudhuri et al.

The starting point of Chaudhuri *et al.* (2002) is the lack of panel data that includes information on shocks and losses for most developing countries. Instead, Chaudhuri *et al.* explore the possibilities of exploiting cross-sectional expenditure regressions that can be implemented from any household survey with a consumption module (for example, the LSMS World Bank surveys are available for most countries).

The Chaudhuri measure is based on the idea that when an expenditure regression is correctly specified, the residual is due to past shocks. In principle, those shocks can be idiosyncratic or covariate by nature, although using location fixed-effects in the expenditure regression would remove the effect of covariate shocks from the residual. In an evaluation of different vulnerability measures, Ligon and Schechter (2004) find the Chaudhuri approach performs better than the other measures as long as the environment is stationary and household expenditure is measured without error. It should be noted, however, that such conditions are rarely found, and other limitations exist which are well discussed in Günther and Harttgen (2009).

The resulting indicator is regression based using a three-stage FGLS method to obtain correct standard errors of the residual. To avoid endogeneity during poverty mapping, a different set of covariates should be used for the estimation of the Chaudhuri type of vulnerability and the mapping model used for the census predictions. Otherwise there would be endogeneity, because the same variables would be used for both the dependent and the independent terms of the mapping mode. The Chaudhuri measure used here is calculated using variables (location, crop choice) that help to explain differences in consumption, and the level of consumption (education, gender of head, marital status of head, dependency ratio). Except for the age of the household head, these covariates are not used for the poverty-mapping exercise.

5.4   Descriptive analysis

The data used for this analysis comes from the household panel of the Vulnerability in Southeast Asia project2 described in detail in Chapter 3, and the Vietnam Rural, Agriculture and Fishery Census from 2006. The survey data contains detailed information on risks and shocks and their consequences, but also covers standard modules on income, consumption and wealth. The farm census covers all the rural households in the three survey provinces. The survey data covers virtually the same period, from May 2006 to May 2007. It allows the construction of different vulnerability indicators at the household level. For this study, the two vulnerability indicators discussed above are used.

Covariates

The association of survey and census data is based on covariates that can be found in both datasets. The challenging part is to identify variables in census and survey that are identically defined and distributed, and hold sufficient explanatory power for predicting vulnerability. Table 5.1 shows the mean and standard deviation for the covariates available in the census and the survey used in the final model. Ideally, all covariates should have equal mean and distribution. The difference in means is only marginal for most variables. Given the large sample size of the census it is not surprising that the test of difference is nevertheless significant in many cases.

However, a few differences exist between survey and census in the key demographics. Household heads in the survey are 2.3 years older, and the dependency ratio of the survey households is slightly smaller. At the same time, the number of ethnic minority households in the census is only 14 per cent compared to 21 per cent in the survey. The number of self-employed households is about 4 percentage points lower in the survey, while wage employment is the same. In addition, households reporting their primary income source to be agriculture are 10 percentage points more common in the census. The remaining differences (education, livestock) are only marginal.

The larger land holdings found in the survey indicate that the random sampling process of the survey identified too many large farms.

Table 5.1 Descriptives of covariates in survey and census data

| | | (1) | | (2) | | (3) | |
| | | Survey | | Census | | Survey-Census | |
Variable	Unit	Mean	SD	Mean	SD	Difference	p-value
Age of head	Years	47.7	13.9	45.4	14.2	2.3	0.000
Male head	Share	0.83	0.38	0.83	0.38	0.00	0.864
Household size	Members	4.34	1.74	4.37	1.84	−0.02	0.555
Dependency ratio	Share	0.38	0.26	0.48	0.25	−0.10	0.000
Ethnic minority	Share	0.21	0.41	0.14	0.35	0.07	0.000
Vocational training	Share	0.01	0.09	0.03	0.16	−0.02	0.000
Junior college	Share	0.12	0.33	0.03	0.18	0.09	0.000
College	Share	0.01	0.10	0.01	0.09	0.00	0.285
University	Share	0.01	0.11	0.01	0.10	0.00	0.567
Self-employed	Share	0.77	0.42	0.81	0.39	−0.04	0.000
Employee	Share	0.13	0.34	0.13	0.34	0.00	0.828
Agriculture	Share	0.73	0.45	0.76	0.43	−0.03	0.001
Land holdings	m2 (ln)	5.38	2.31	4.61	3.76	0.77	0.000
Buffalos	Units	0.24	0.71	0.23	0.81	0.00	0.851
Chicken	Units	10.39	37.94	9.50	33.76	0.89	0.216
Cows	Units	0.66	2.86	0.61	1.80	0.05	0.185
Ducks	Units	3.30	39.03	2.04	38.53	1.26	0.127
Goats/sheep	Units	0.14	1.37	0.14	1.43	0.00	0.942
Pigs	Units	2.11	38.48	1.53	3.92	0.58	0.000
Observations		2,195		752,239			

To investigate the scale of this potential problem, the poverty and vulnerability predictions below are implemented using models with and without land holdings as independent variables. The difference in mean land size makes little difference, since households with large farms tend to have higher income and are neither poor nor vulnerable to poverty. This implies that any policy targeting for the provinces used here would not be misled by the difference in average land size as measured in the survey and the census. Consequently, land holdings can be included in the final model specifications.

To account for differences in education, tertiary training is used. Tertiary training includes obtaining degrees from vocational training, junior colleges, regular colleges and universities. The census does not ask questions about years of schooling, completed primary education, or reading and writing skills, meaning that differences in basic education cannot be controlled for. However, this may not be a serious problem, since primary enrolment rates are very high in Vietnam. A variable on primary education would most likely suffer from low variation across households, and in such event would probably hold little explanatory power.

While income and consumption are not available in the census, it does have information about the current employment status (wage-employed, self-employed or without work) and the economic sector (agriculture versus non-agriculture). About 10 per cent of household heads are not working, due to either age or lack of work. Out-of-work heads serves as the reference category for employment status; non-agricultural activity is the reference category for the economic sector.

5.5   Results

This section compares the poverty and vulnerability from the 2007 survey and census data. The chapter highlights where vulnerability maps are able to outperform poverty maps in terms of spatial targeting.

5.5.1   Regression model

The first step in creating poverty maps is finding a good model specification to predict poverty (or vulnerability) in the survey data; as the goal is prediction, the coefficients should not be interpreted causally but as useful correlates to predict poverty. Table 5.2 shows the regression results for household expenditure (in logged PPP US$) and the two vulnerability indicators. The observations are slightly lower in the vulnerability regressions, since not all households responded to the questions required to calculate the measures; the Calvo–Dercon measure in particular suffers from missing data. Nevertheless, overall model fit is very good. The models perform slightly less well for the vulnerability indicators than for the expenditure regression. Since few census variables are directly related to risks and shocks this is to be expected.

Table 5.2 Correlates of expenditure and vulnerability

		(1)	(2)	(3)
	Outcome	Consumption	Vulnerability	
		Total in logs	Calvo–Dercon	Chaudhuri
	Year	2007	2007	2007
Household and headship	Age of head	0.017**	−0.002**	−0.020***
		(0.006)	(0.001)	(0.003)
	(Age of head) square	−0.000***	0.000**	0.000***
		(0.000)	(0.000)	(0.000)
	Male head	0.089*	−0.003	−0.016
		(0.048)	(0.005)	(0.021)
	Household size	−0.107***	0.008***	0.075***
		(0.011)	(0.002)	(0.005)
	Dependency ratio	−0.387***	0.014**	0.118***
		(0.040)	(0.006)	(0.024)
	Ethnic minority	−0.421***	0.034**	0.139***
		(0.051)	(0.013)	(0.025)
Education of head	Vocational training	0.324***	−0.019	−0.135
		(0.114)	(0.022)	(0.086)
	Junior college	0.122**	−0.005	−0.105***
		(0.047)	(0.005)	(0.020)
	College	0.340***	−0.017***	−0.207***
		(0.083)	(0.006)	(0.036)
	University	0.349***	−0.004	−0.073**
		(0.093)	(0.007)	(0.032)
Sector and employment	Self-employed	0.112	−0.004	−0.226***
		(0.085)	(0.007)	(0.032)
	Employee	0.040	−0.008	−0.145***
		(0.074)	(0.008)	(0.037)
	Agriculture	−0.252***	0.010**	0.215***
		(0.031)	(0.004)	(0.018)

Continued

Table 5.2 Continued

		(1)	(2)	(3)
	Outcome	Consumption	Vulnerability	
		Total in logs	Calvo–Dercon	Chaudhuri
	Year	2007	2007	2007
Animals and land	Land holdings (ln)	-0.161***	0.015**	0.115**
		(0.048)	(0.006)	(0.044)
	(Land holdings) square	0.020***	-0.002***	-0.015***
		(0.005)	(0.001)	(0.004)
	Number of buffalos	-0.023	-0.002	0.010
		(0.023)	(0.002)	(0.009)
	Number of chicken	0.001*	-0.000*	0.000
		(0.000)	(0.000)	(0.000)
	Number of cows	-0.002	0.000	-0.002
		(0.008)	(0.001)	(0.003)
	Number of ducks	0.000**	-0.000**	-0.000*
		(0.000)	(0.000)	(0.000)
	Number of goats or sheep	0.008	-0.001**	-0.005**
		(0.007)	(0.000)	(0.002)
	Number of pigs	-0.000	0.000***	0.000
		(0.000)	(0.000)	(0.000)
	Observations	1,907	1,628	1,903
	Adjusted R2	0.331	0.287	0.498
	District FE	YES	YES	YES

Note: Robust standard errors in parentheses. Significance *** $p<0.01$, ** $p<0.05$, * $p<0.1$. Reference categories are for no tertiary education; no animals; unemployed, non-Agriculture. Constant suppressed; all district dummies included; district dummies not reported.

Future research might benefit from adding spatial information on rainfall, temperature and distance to rivers and coastline in order to obtain more precise estimates for vulnerability maps.

The results for expenditure are largely as expected. Age of head is associated with increased per capita consumption, with decreasing marginal returns. Families with male heads have more resources to spend. Household size and a higher dependency ratio decrease per capita consumption. Households from ethnic minorities have substantially fewer resources to spend. All the binary indicators for tertiary education of the household head show a correlation with higher expenditure. Interestingly, the returns to university education have a magnitude similar to that of vocational training, which is not too surprising given the rural farm setting. Employment seems to be correlated with higher expenditure, although the coefficient is not significant.

Families engaged in agriculture as their main income source consume less per capita than families, gaining most of their income from a non-farm income source. This points to the growing opportunities held by the non-farm sector for rural communities. Similarly, relationship between the (logged) size of land holdings and per capita consumption is U-shaped. This result points to heterogeneous effects, where farmers holding up to a certain size of land tend to have difficulties making ends meet. In contrast, the ownership of livestock seems to increase per capita consumption.

For the vulnerability indicators, the coefficients are slightly less significant. Since the vulnerability indicators increase with higher expected poverty, the correlations are opposite to the consumption regression. Nearly all covariates seem to hold some predictive power. Interestingly, female household heads are not exposed to greater vulnerability, which indicates that women are able to compensate for the lower financial resources (found in Column 1) by other means (see Klasen *et al.*, 2010).

5.5.2 Mapping predictions

Table 5.3 shows the correlation between predicted per capita consumption (ln) and vulnerability to poverty. While the two vulnerability measures are closely correlated, the correlation coefficients between expenditure and vulnerability are relatively low, indicating a possible mismatch between past consumption and vulnerability to future poverty which might seriously affect the targeting performance.

On mapping the results, some interesting patterns become visible. As an example, Figure 5.1 shows expenditure and vulnerability estimates on sub-district level for Ha Tinh province. The province is located in the North Central Coast region, in the narrowest part of Vietnam. It stretches from the coast in the east to the Lao border in the west, and is home to 1.2 million people. The province is regularly affected by typhoons, excessive rainfall and flooding.

Table 5.3   Correlations between expenditures and vulnerability

	Expenditure	Vulnerability	
	in logs	Calvo–Dercon	Chaudhuri
Expenditure in logs	1.000		
Vulnerability Calvo–Dercon	−0.411	1.000	
Vulnerability Chaudhuri	−0.287	0.815	1.000
N	752,239	752,239	752,239

Note: All correlations are significant at 1% level.

Sub-districts with darker colours are wealthier, indicating that average consumption is higher and vulnerability is lower. Policymakers would be mostly concerned about very light sub-districts. The shades reflect population deciles, which makes it easy to interpret the maps. Roughly 10 per cent of the province population is covered by each shade, which allows a direct ranking of sub-districts of different shades.

The three maps share a similar pattern of poverty and vulnerability, and are in line with the literature review. Households towards the (more developed) coastline (east) and towards the south tend to be better off. At the same time, households towards the Lao border (west) tend to have lower expenditure and are prone to higher vulnerability.

However, some important differences in shading exist between the expenditure map (Figure 5.1) and the vulnerability estimates (Figures 5.2 and 5.3). Several sub-districts with expenditure in the middle quintiles are highly vulnerable. This is particularly true for households living in the south-west of the province, which is among the most vulnerable areas. There is a fair degree of overlap between poverty and vulnerability estimates. However, for several sub-districts differences are found which might directly affect targeting performance.

Table 5.4 shows the relative targeting performance on a household level. To ensure comparability, the share of households marked as poor and vulnerable is the same. For this illustration, the poverty line is set at US$2 per day, resulting in almost 40 per cent poor households in the census estimates. The vulnerability threshold is also defined so that 40 per cent of all households are considered vulnerable.

The table directly compares targeting performance of household expenditure against the two vulnerability indicators in Columns 1 and

Poverty Mapping Vietnam: Ha Tinh Province (North Central Coast)
Indicator: Consumption per capita, 2007

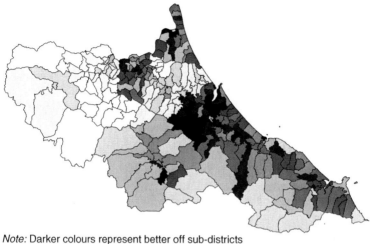

Note: Darker colours represent better off sub-districts

Vulnerability Mapping Vietnam: Ha Tinh Province (North Central Coast)
Indicator: Vulnerability, Calvo-Dercon (alpha=2), 2007

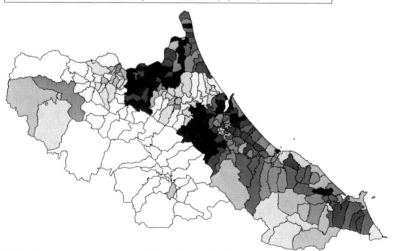

Note: Darker colours represent better off sub-districts

Figures 5.1–5.3 Mapping expenditure and vulnerability on sub-district level

Vulnerability Mapping Vietnam: Ha Tinh Province (North Central Coast)
Indicator: Vulnerability, Chaudhuri, 2007

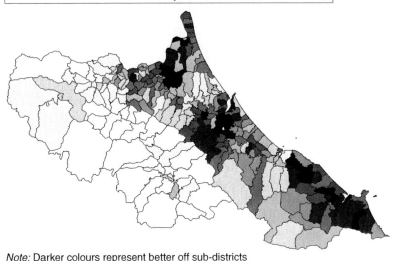

Note: Darker colours represent better off sub-districts

Figures 5.1–5.3   Continued

2. The first row shows for the Calvo–Dercon vulnerability measure that 78.4 per cent of all vulnerable households are also considered poor. Column 2 shows that 21.6 per cent of all households are classified as vulnerable while not poor. This figure presents the potential improvement when changing from expenditure-based policy targeting to vulnerability.

The mismatch in Column 2 is slightly larger when the Chaudhuri indicator is used for predicting vulnerability (23.8 per cent). Note, however, that the choice of vulnerability indicator is also quite important and should be tailor-made for the planned policy intervention. As Column 4 shows, the two vulnerability indicators have a mismatch of 27.2 per cent.

Besides looking at targeting performance, it is also quite important to understand which sort of households belong to each group. Table 5.5 shows the characteristics of the localities identified as (1) poor and vulnerable, (2) poor and not vulnerable, (3) vulnerable and not poor, and (4) neither poor nor vulnerable. The columns can be read in terms of poverty dynamics: households in Group 1 lay below the poverty line in

Table 5.4 Targeting performance between expenditure and vulnerability

		(1)	(2)	(3)	(4)	(5)	(6)
			Expenditure			Vulnerability Calvo–Dercon	
		poor	non-poor	total	vulnerable	non-vulnerable	total
Vulnerability Calvo–Dercon	vulnerable	78.4	21.6	100.0			
	non-vulnerable	9.2	90.8	100.0			
Vulnerability Chaudhuri	vulnerable	76.2	23.8	100.0	72.8	27.2	100.0
	non-vulnerable	10.2	89.8	100.0	11.7	88.3	100.0
Sample size		752239					

Note: Percentage points add up to 100 sideways within each column variable.

Table 5.5   Characteristics of targeting groups

Variable	Unit	(1) Vulnerable Poor	(2) Vulnerable Not Poor	(3) Not Vulnerable Poor	(4) Not Vulnerable Not Poor
Age of head	Years	42.3	39.2	51.2	46.5
Male head	Share	0.86	0.89	0.77	0.81
Household size	Members	5.48	4.32	4.78	3.92
Dependency ratio	Share	0.54	0.43	0.60	0.45
Ethnic minority	Share	0.39	0.34	0.02	0.04
Vocational training	Share	0.00	0.01	0.01	0.04
Junior college	Share	0.01	0.03	0.02	0.05
College	Share	0.00	0.00	0.00	0.01
University	Share	0.00	0.01	0.00	0.02
Self-employed	Share	0.94	0.91	0.88	0.74
Employee	Share	0.05	0.07	0.07	0.17
Agriculture	Share	0.96	0.86	0.89	0.66
Land holdings	m2 (ln)	6.35	5.29	6.15	3.74
Buffalos	Units	0.29	0.12	0.77	0.17
Chicken	Units	10.30	10.17	10.94	8.99
Cows	Units	1.01	0.77	0.58	0.45
Ducks	Units	1.10	1.59	1.57	2.48
Goats/sheep	Units	0.13	0.18	0.08	0.15
Pigs	Units	1.45	1.81	1.54	1.53
Observations		176,999	48,673	48,673	477,894

Source: Census data.

the past, and are expected to stay there in the future. Group 2 lay above the poverty line in the past, but is expected to fall below it in the future. Group 3 was poor in the past, but is expected to rise above the poverty line in the future. Group 4 is always above the poverty line. Comparison of these different groups throws up a few noteworthy differences. In terms of age, heads of vulnerable households are several years younger, possibly because they have access to fewer coping strategies such as lifetime savings or retirement transfers. In terms of gender, female-headed households are surprisingly common in Group 3, which is expected to rise out of poverty in the future. Household size is largest in Group 1, without much prospect of moving out of poverty. The dependency ratio is relatively higher among poor households, regardless of their vulnerability status. Ethnic minority households are particularly vulnerable, meaning that development policies targeting minorities are addressing a potentially important problem.

Tertiary education is also most common among households affected by neither poverty nor vulnerability (Group 4). The same group also has the most wage employment, which would imply lower income volatility. They also work the least in agriculture, and consequently have the smallest land holdings. The possession of livestock does not, however, have any clear effects.

Overall, the mapping results indicate that using vulnerability for geographic targeting has the potential to improve targeting policies to the populations most in need of support.

5.6 Conclusion

This chapter is concerned with the performance of vulnerability indicators for policy targeting. Following a recent trend among policy makers using small area estimates to identify locations that are eligible for healthcare and other interventions, the chapter proposes the use of vulnerability estimates. This seems particularly well suited to projects trying to improve resilience. Various indicators for vulnerability exist, reflecting uninsured exposure to risk, expected poverty or low expected utility, many of which can be specified to reflect the target population.

For illustration purposes, two indicators from the family of Vulnerability as Expected Poverty are used to compare their targeting performance to a classic expenditure-based measure. Data from a recent vulnerability survey covering three Vietnamese provinces is combined with farm census information. The results indicate that poverty estimates are generally closely related to vulnerability estimates. However, about 20 per cent of households estimated as eligible would not be considered poor. In terms of targeting, vulnerability seems to outperform poverty maps for such purposes.

A few open questions remain. A priori it is not clear which vulnerability indicator is best suited to mapping purposes. Given the limited number of surveys that collect information on risks and shocks, the Calvo–Dercon measure used here seems promising. However, the construction of the indicator requires a substantial amount of detailed data and is based on several assumptions whose impact on the estimates needs to be thoroughly checked when using it for policy guidance.

Notes

1. See Demombynes *et al.* (2008) for a more detailed description of the simulation procedure.
2. See www.vulnerability-asia.uni-hannover.de

References

Baulch, B., H. T. Pham and B. Reilly (2011): "Decomposing the Ethnic Gap Standards in Rural Vietnam: 1993 to 2004", Forthcoming in *Oxford Development Studies*.

Calvo, C. and S. Dercon (2005): "Measuring Individual Vulnerability", *Department of Economics Discussion Paper No. 229*, Oxford University.

Calvo, C. and S. Dercon (2007): "Chronic Poverty and All That: The Measurement of Poverty over Time", *The Centre for the Study of African Economies, Working Paper No. 2007–04*, Oxford University.

Chaudhuri, S., J. Jalan and A. Suryahadi (2002): "Assessing Household Vulnerability to Poverty: A Methodology and Estimates for Indonesia", *Columbia University Department of Economics Discussion Paper No. 0102–52*, Columbia University, New York.

Christiaensen, L. and K. Subbarao (2001): "Towards an Understanding of Vulnerability in Rural Kenya", *mimeo*, World Bank, Washington DC.

Demombynes, G. and B. Özler (2005): "Crime and Local Inequality in South Africa", *Journal of Development Economics*, 76(2): 265–92.

Demombynes, G., Chris Elbers, Jean O. Lanjouw, Peter Lanjouw, Johann Mistiaen and Berk Özler (2004): "Producing an Improved Geographic Profile of Poverty: Methodology and Evidence from Three Developing Countries", in: R. van der Hoeven and A. Shorrocks (eds), *Growth, Inequality, and Poverty*, Oxford University Press, New York: 154–76.

Dercon, S., J. Hoogeveen, E. Tesliuc and R. Vakis (2004): "A Guide to the Analysis of Risk, Vulnerability and Vulnerable Groups", Social Protection Unit, World Bank, Washington DC.

Elbers, C., J. O. Lanjouw and P. Lanjouw (2003): "Micro-Level Estimation of Poverty and Inequality", *Econometrica*, 71(1): 355–64.

Elbers, C., T. Fujii, P. Lanjouw, B. Özler and W. Yin. (2007): "Poverty Alleviation through Geographic Targeting: How Much Does Disaggregation Help?" *Journal of Development Economics*, 83(1): 198–213.

Fujii, T. (2007): "To Use or Not to Use? Poverty Mapping in Cambodia", in: Bedi, T., A. Coudouel and K. Simler (eds), *More Than a Pretty Picture: Using Poverty Maps to Design Better Policies and Interventions*, World Bank, Washington DC.

Fujii, T. and R. Holst (2008): "How Does Vietnam's Accession to the World Trade Organization Change the Spatial Incidence of Poverty?" *World Bank Policy Research Working Paper No. 4521*, World Bank, Washington DC.

Günther, I. and K. Harttgen (2009): "Estimating Households Vulnerability to Idiosyncratic and Covariate Shocks: A Novel Method Applied in Madagascar", *World Development*, 37(7): 1222–34.

Hentschel, J. and P. Lanjouw (1998): "Using Disaggregated Poverty Maps to Plan Sectoral Investments", *PREM Notes 5*, World Bank, Washington DC.

Klasen, S., T. Lechtenfeld and F. Povel (2010): "What about the Women? Female Headship, Poverty and Vulnerability in Thailand and Vietnam", *Courant Working Paper*, University of Göttingen.

Ligon, E. and L. Schechter (2003): "Measuring Vulnerability", *Economic Journal*, 113(486): C95–C102.

Ligon, E. and L. Schechter (2004): "Evaluating Different Approaches to Estimating Vulnerability", *Social Protection Discussion Paper No. 0410*, World Bank, Washington DC.

Minot, N. (2000): "Generating Disaggregated Poverty Maps: An Application to Vietnam", *World Development*, 28(2): 319–31.

Minot, N., B. Baulch and M. Epprecht (2003): "Poverty and Inequality in Vietnam: Spatial Patterns and Geographic Determinants", *IFPRI Research Reports No. 148*, International Food Policy Research Institute, Washington DC.

Nguyen, V. C. (2009): "Updating Poverty Maps for Ho Chi Minh City of Vietnam using a Small Area Estimation Method", *Economics Bulletin*, 29(3): 1971–80.

Nguyen, V. C., N. T. Tran and R. van der Weide (2010): "Poverty and Inequality Maps for Rural Vietnam – An Application of Small Area Estimation", *Policy Research Working Paper 5443*, World Bank, Washington DC.

Nguyen, V. C., R. van der Weide, H. Le and N. T. Tran (2007): "Construction of Poverty Map for the HCM City in Vietnam Using the 2004 VHLSS and the 2004 HCM Mid-Census", *mimeo*.

Pritchett, L., A. Suryahadi and S. Sumarto (2000): "Quantifying Vulnerability to Poverty: A Proposed Measure, Applied to Indonesia", *Policy Research Working Paper 2437*, World Bank, Washington DC.

Sparrow, R. (2008): "Targeting the Poor in Times of Crisis: the Indonesian Health Card", *Health Policy and Planning*, 23(3): 188–99.

Tesliuc, E. D. and K. Lindert (2004): "Risk and Vulnerability in Guatemala: A Quantitative and Qualitative Assessment", *Social Protection Discussion Paper 0404*, World Bank, Washington DC.

6
Rural–Rural Differences in Vietnamese Pro-Poor Growth: Does Households' Income Composition Make a Difference?

Kai Mausch, Javier Revilla Diez and Rainer Klump

6.1 Introduction

In Vietnam, the fight against extreme poverty has been very successful in the past decade, with overall poverty incidence falling to 12.9 per cent, food poverty reduced by more than half since 1993, and the share of people living with less than PPP US1 per day reduced to 2 per cent (Table 6.1). Nonetheless, recent research has produced some doubts as to whether this trend will continue, with fears that it might slow down or even reverse (Gaiha *et al.*, 2007). Furthermore, some groups were not able to benefit from the recent boom.

Dividing the poverty rate and the poverty gap into the rural and urban populations and the ethnic minorities, one can see that the rural population is lagging behind with the latest poverty rate (headcount ratio[1]) figure of 27.5 per cent, while the poverty rate among ethnic minorities was as high as 69.3 per cent in 2002.

Additionally, after a decade of constant decline, the food poverty rate rose again from 2004 to 2005, and the Gini coefficient rose continuously from 0.34 in 1993 to 0.37 in 2005 suggesting a pro-rich/anti-poor growth rather than a pro-poor growth (United Nations, 2005b: 3). As shown in Figure 6.1, regional disparities are also very large, with much lower poverty incidence in the boom regions surrounding Hanoi and Ho Chi Minh City, the highest rates being in the northern regions and the Central Highlands.

The massive poverty reduction can also be seen from Figure 6.1, where poverty rates are far lower for Figure 6.1(b) compared to Figure 6.1(a). Generally, despite impressive poverty reduction achievements, the ethnic and spatial poverty trends persist, leaving ethnic minorities and remote households falling behind the overall positive trend (Gaiha *et al.*, 2007).

Table 6.1   Poverty indicators of Vietnam

Indicator	Unit	1993	1998	2002	2004	2005
Poverty[a]	%	58.1	37.4	28.9	24.1	12.9
Urban	%	25.1	9.2	6.6	10.8	n.a.
Rural	%	66.4	45.5	35.6	27.5	n.a.
Ethnic minorities	%	86.4	75.2	69.3	n.a.	n.a.
Food poverty	%	24.9	15.0	9.9	7.8	10.9
Living on less than 1 $[a] day	%	39.9	16.4	13.6	10.6	2.2
Gini coefficient		0.34	0.35	0.37	0.37	n.a.

[a] Here the national poverty line is referred to.
Source: Own presentation based on United Nations (2005b: 3).

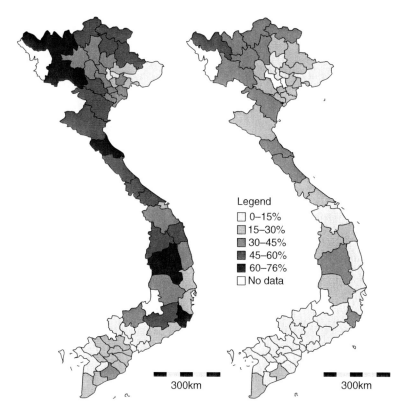

Figure 6.1   Poverty rates in rural Vietnam
Note: Map using ADePT Maps 2.0 (2009).
Source: Mausch (2010), p. 15 based on GSO (2002; 2004) data.

One widely discussed path out of poverty is income diversification of rural farmers into the rural non-farm economy (RNFE) (Collier, 2007). The connection between the poverty status of households and their participation in the RNFE has been the subject of multiple theoretical and empirical studies over the last decade, which mainly concluded that participation in the non-farm economy contributes to poverty reduction in developing countries. Furthermore, the promotion of wage employment in remote and low-income areas is a successful strategy to overcome income inequalities within a country (Schupp, 2002). Ideally, off-farm work yields both a more stable and a higher income than farm work (Dercon, 2002). It is less dependent on environmental conditions and fluctuating crop prices. In addition, as remuneration for off-farm-work is mostly monetary, it enables local residents to build up financial reserves.

Especially in the context of the recent debate around vulnerability to poverty, short-term setbacks are a major factor contributing to not only transitory but also chronic poverty. The question arises as to whether non-farm employment is able to mitigate potential agricultural shocks, or whether non-farm jobs are even more prone to external shocks based on fluctuations in demand. Here we focus on rural areas where poverty rates are still very high and less industry is found, and thus where the recent Vietnamese boom has not yet reached the vast majority of the people.

The objective here is not only to investigate the differences in the pro-poor growth performance across provinces, but also to extend this analysis by taking the income portfolio of households into account. Thereby, we will enrich and supplement the work of Bonschab and Klump (2007) and Klump (2007). In particular, the short-term fluctuations of pro-poor growth will be analysed with a narrower focus on households and their income portfolio. We will shed light on the differences in the pro-poorness of farming, off-farm employment[2] and a mixture of these two.

We show that especially the provision of opportunities for occupational choice is an important factor in poverty reduction as especially households that have been able to adjust their income portfolio do perform better in terms of pro-poor growth and poverty reduction. Flexibility of rural households' income-generating activities should be encouraged and enabled through the promotion of the non-farm economy so that the households are able to choose their income sources based on profitability, risks and the skills of the household members rather than their access to such opportunities. To start with, Section 6.2 provides an overview on pro-poor growth between 1993 and 2002. Section 6.3 takes a more comprehensive look into the dynamics and determinants of pro-poor growth on a regional level between 2002 and 2004. Section 6.4 summarizes the main results.

The data used in the analysis are the Vietnam Household Living Standard Survey (VHLSS) 2002 and 2004 compiled by the GSO. Based on a sample of about 30,000 households in 2002 and 9,200 households in 2004, the rotating sample design leads to an available panel of 3,991 households in total, and 3,132 in rural areas, covering 61 of the 63 Vietnamese provinces.[3] Analogously to McCaig (2009), the panel construction was adjusted to account for several matching errors occurring when using the original household identifier.[4]

6.2 Patterns of pro-poor growth in Vietnam until 2002

Pro-poor growth examines the distributional pattern of the growth process, examining to what extent the poor have benefitted from it.

The pro-poor growth measures applied in this study are shown by the growth incidence curve based on percentile growth rate of the poor (Ravallion and Chen, 2003). This measure makes it possible to see whether growth led to income increments for the poor, and how the rate of pro-poor growth (the average growth rates of the poor percentiles) fares relative to the overall growth rate, which allows an assessment of changes in income distribution in the growth process.

The huge successes in overall pro-poor growth were spatially biased (Table 6.2) analogously to the poverty reduction successes (Table 6.1).

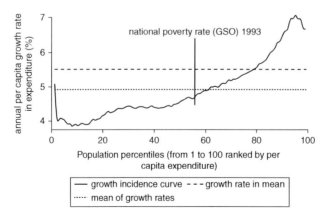

Figure 6.2   Vietnam's growth incidence curve, 1993–2002
Source: Bonschab and Klump (2005).

Table 6.2   Rates of pro-poor growth, 1993–2002 by sub-regions

Region	1993–1998	1998–2002	1993–2002
National	5.7	2.2	4.1
Urban	8.9	1.6	5.9
Rural	5.3	2.2	3.9
Northwest	4.5	–1.6	n.a.
Northeast	4.5	4.4	n.a.
Red River Delta	8.1	1.4	n.a.
North Central Coast	6.2	0.5	n.a.
South Central Coast	4.9	4.6	n.a.
Central Highlands	4.6	5.0	n.a.
Mekong River Delta	4.4	2.6	n.a.

Note: n.a. = not available.
Source: Bonschab and Klump (2005).

While for the 1993–1998 period the rate of pro-poor growth was higher in urban areas (8.9 per cent versus 5.3 per cent), the rate in urban areas fell even more than in rural areas for the period from 1998 to 2002 (1.6 per cent versus 2.2 per cent). However, the inequality became more pronounced for rural areas in the second period, indicating an even higher growth rate for the non-poor population (Bonschab and Klump, 2007).

The expenditure-based Gini coefficients for rural and urban areas have been fairly stable for many years, suggesting that the rising inequality is mainly based on rural–urban differences in overall growth rather than within each of these areas. This is intensified by a migration pattern in which the economically more active population migrates proportionately more from rural to urban areas (Klump, 2007). The pro-poor growth rates in the Central Highlands, unlike the rest of Vietnam, grew for the second period). Improved property rights on land played a major role in this process, and contributed strongly to the pro-poorness of growth. This policy improved the predictability of businesses and boosted longer-term investments, for example in perennial industrial and fruit crops, and therefore enabled income diversification (Bonschab and Klump, 2007).

With this background in mind, it is now important to assess how pro-poor growth developed between 2002 and 2004 for households with different income portfolios.

6.3 Pro-poor growth in rural Vietnam, 2002–2004

6.3.1 Short-term poverty dynamics and household income portfolio

To shed more light on the dynamics and the determinants of successful pro-poor strategies, the following section will decompose the pro-poor growth into the following five household income[5] types. First, a "farm" household does not participate in the labor market and solely derives its livelihoods from self-employed farming. Second, a "non-farm" household refers to a household that does not have any crop, livestock or aquaculture production. Third and fourth, two types of mixed-income households refer to the ones that derive income from both farm and off-/non-farm activities. These two mixed groups are divided, one group including households with farm income exceeding non-farm income ("mixed farm households"), and vice versa for the "mixed non-farm households". Fifth, the households referred to as "others" are households that have none of those income sources and rely on transfer payments or renting activities. Furthermore, the sample is reduced to rural areas, as Klump (2005) already found that the poverty in urban areas is now very low, while poverty remains high in rural areas.

Based on the results that poverty and pro-poor growth is spatially biased in Vietnam, the poverty incidence as well as the distribution of the household types across the 61 Vietnamese provinces covered is given in Figure 6.3. The poverty headcount ratios by province, subdivided by the four major household types, are depicted in Figure 6.3(e) – Figure 6.3(h). Furthermore, the share of the household types across the provinces is indicated in Figure 6.3(a) – Figure 6.3(d).

As indicated by the total shares of the household types in the sample, the non-farm households have very low shares, mostly below 15 per cent in all provinces with some exceptions in the Mekong Delta. Furthermore, farm households are greatly in the majority in the mountainous Northwestern region, the poorest in Vietnam. An interesting distribution of the two mixed types is prevalent in the central provinces, where the mixed non-farm households are the major group in the coastal provinces, while the mixed farm households are especially prevalent in the mountainous provinces along the Cambodian border in the south and the Lao border in the North Central Coast region.

Concerning poverty rates, in most provinces poverty is most widespread in the farm households group, while it is lowest for the non-farm households group. The non-farm households group is the smallest, with only 263 households, leading to some provinces in the Northwestern

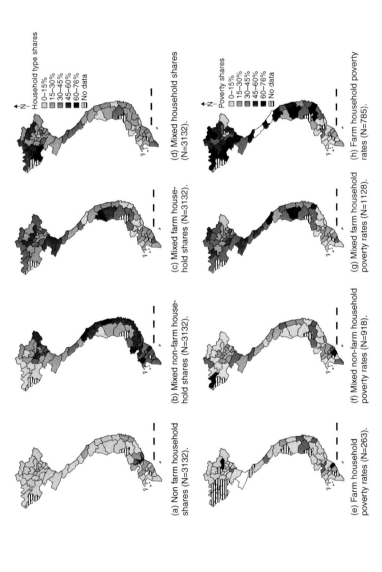

Figure 6.3 Household type shares by province, 2002 and poverty rates by household type and province, 2002

Note: Map using ADePT Maps 2.0 (2009).

Source: Mausch (2010), p.53 based on GSO (2002;2004) data.

and Central Highlands regions having no households at all in this group.

Of the two mixed types, those that rely more heavily on farm income are more often poor. On the one hand, poverty headcount ratios decline with the increasing importance of non-farm income for the households; on the other hand, the majority (62 per cent) of households – farm households and mixed farm households – still rely on farm income as their most important income source.

Based on the extreme differences in poverty rates across the household types, the question is whether households in the groups that are faced with higher poverty will change their income portfolio towards a more promising combination even in the short term. This will allow a first assessment of the households' decision making as well as further insight into the households' income dynamics. Using the types for the two survey years, many households do substantially or gradually change their income portfolio leading to different categorization for the two years. These "switched types" as well as the non-switched types and their shares are given in Figure 6.4. The left-hand numbers give the share of the respective group that changed their portfolio to the extent that they have been re-categorized into another group, while the right-

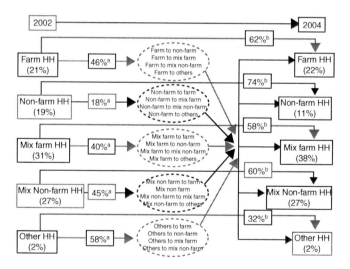

Figure 6.4   Income composition changes

Notes: [a]Share of group in 2002; [b]Share of 2004 group

Source: Mausch (2010), p. 55 based on GSO (2002; 2004) data.

hand numbers give the shares of the 2004 group that was in the same group in 2002.

While the shares of the groups remained rather stable across the years (with only small gains for the mixed farm households and losses for the non-farm households), it is obvious that between 2002 and 2004 there were major shifts. with up to 58 per cent of the households within one group changing to other groups. Among the four major types, the group of farm households is subject to the highest fluctuations, with 46 per cent of the households shifting from pure farming to other income structures. The most stable group on the other hand is the non-farm households, with only 18 per cent changing to other income sources and 74 per cent of the 2004 group remaining in the same group as in 2002. This might be based on the fact that one needs farm land in order to pursue any farm activity, but only 11 per cent within the non-farm households group have no land available at all. In order to account for these major shifts among the groups, the following analysis will be based on the nine major switched types rather than the original household categories.

Assuming rational behaviour of the households, the switched types should perform better in terms of growth and poverty reduction, as otherwise they would have been better off if they had stuck to their existing portfolio. On the other hand, the opposite outcome could occur when the switching takes place due to outside influences that force households to change. These could be shocks like job loss that makes some income sources unavailable or less lucrative. Based on the effects of the changes, one can gain at least some evidence of which scenario is more likely.

Table 6.3 gives some poverty/inequality indicators decomposed by the nine household types introduced. Remarkably, there is no group that during this period faced an increase in poverty due to the very high overall poverty reduction. Although the distribution became slightly more unequal, indicated by the increase of 0.01 points in the Gini coefficient, this increase does not constitute a major change in the income distribution.

Generally, the poverty headcount ratio was significantly higher for the group of households that did switch group between 2002 and 2004 in both years, suggesting that households were pushed into changing their income portfolio based on insufficient income from their existing sources.

The highest poverty headcount ratio and poverty gap is found in the 2002 group of farm households that switched to mixed farm

Table 6.3 Poverty by household type

Household type	Head-count ratio (%) 2002	Change in head-count ratio[a] (%)	Normalized poverty gap (%) 2002	Normalized poverty gap (%) 2004	Gini coefficient 2002	Change in Gini[a]	N
Total	35	−17	10	4	0.36	0.01	3132
Switched	38	−23	11	4	0.36	0.02	1317
Non-switched	33	−19	9	3	0.36	0.02	1815
Farm HH	44	−18	14	8	0.39	0.00	426
Mixed farm	39	−22	11	5	0.31	0.03	685
Mixed non-farm	22	−14	5	2	0.36	−0.04	499
Non-farm	12	−4	2	1	0.34	0.06	182
Farm to mixed farm	57	−29	17	7	0.34	0.03	270
Mixed non-farm to mixed farm	29	−16	8	4	0.31	0.06	222
Mixed farm to farm	46	−19	13	7	0.39	0.00	183
Mixed farm to mixed non-farm	37	−27	10	3	0.33	−0.02	227
Mixed non-farm to non-farm	30	−15	8	3	0.35	0.05	128

[a] Changes between years 2002 and 2004 in percentage points for the headcount ratio and absolute numbers for the Gini coefficient.
Source: Authors' calculations based on GSO (2002; 2004).

households in 2004. This group also realized the highest reduction in these indicators, with the headcount ratio having dropped from 57 per cent to about 28 per cent and the poverty gap having dropped from 17 per cent to 7 per cent. The smallest reduction in poverty took place in the group of non-farm households that did not change their income portfolio; but this group had a very low poverty level and poverty gap beforehand, which makes huge reductions unlikely.

Generally, the difference between switched types and non-switched types was bigger in 2002 in all indicators but became significantly smaller for 2004. This indicates some catching-up effects for the switchers. Nevertheless, the Gini coefficients remain similar in both periods.

The group that performs best of all groups in terms of reduction of poverty and inequality is the group of mixed non-farm households that already had the second lowest poverty headcount ratio in the first period; in the second period, this dropped to the lowest. The poverty gap went down by 3 per cent and the Gini coefficient by 0.04 points, which was the highest reduction. Similar movements took place in the group of mixed farm households that extended their non-farm engagement and are now considered mixed non-farm households; the poverty headcount went down from the above-average rate of 37 per cent to only 10 per cent, which is exactly the average for the second period. The poverty gap that was 10 per cent went down to 3 per cent, and the Gini went down as well; this happened for only two groups.

The switched households did encounter higher poverty incidence in both periods, but also realized higher poverty reductions in the poverty headcount ratio as well as the poverty gap. Therefore, based on these indicators, the change in income composition seems to pay off for the households and do reflect better their potential to generate income. Now, the question is whether the observed poverty changes are based on the shift of population from one group to another or whether the poverty reduction occurred within the groups. Table 6.4 provides a decomposition of the poverty changes along the household income types, deducting the population shift effects emerging from households which change their income portfolio. The decomposition proposed by Ravallion and Datt (1996) breaks the national growth down by the contributions of the primary, secondary and tertiary sector contributions to GDP. Here the income of the household groups is used instead. Due to the mixed types this decomposition cannot be interpreted with respect to any sectoral growth impact, since the sectors are not completely separated due to the classification of the mixed types. Nevertheless, this approach offers more insight into the differences of the four income

Table 6.4   Poverty decomposition by household type, 2002[a]

Household type	Absolute change	Percentage change
Change in poverty (HC)	−17.77	100
Total intra-sectoral effect	−17.62	99.14
Population-shift effect	−0.54	3.01
Interaction effect	0.38	−2.16
Intra-sectoral effects:		
Farm HH	−5.22	29.39
Non-farm HH	−0.3	1.68
Mixed farm HH	−7.45	41.90
Mixed non-farm HH	−4.51	25.37
Other HH	−0.14	0.80

[a] Decomposition according to Ravallion and Huppi (1991).
Source: Authors' calculations based on GSO (2002; 2004).

compositions than does the assigning of the most important sector to each household.

The high share attributed to the "intra-sectoral" effects shows that most of the poverty reduction observed in the data is attributed to increases in incomes within the household groups and not to population shifts across these groups.[6]

The highest contribution (41.9 per cent) to overall poverty reduction is attributed to the poverty reduction within the mixed farm household group. This is not only based on the very high poverty reduction itself but also on the group size. The group of mixed farm households accounts for almost 40 per cent of the households in both periods, and therefore has major impact on this decomposition. The same holds for all the other groups that were able to reduce poverty to different extents. The groups of non-farm and other households had only small reductions, and also, being low in number, had a combined impact of less than 3 per cent although constituting 10 and 13 per cent of all households in 2002 and 2004 respectively.

To summarize, based on the differences in poverty changes, the switched households do perform better than the non-switched households. But the poverty measures have been higher in 2002 and are higher still in 2004, though some catching up does take place.

6.3.2   Short-term fluctuations in pro-poor growth across household types

Based on the poverty decomposition across the household types, we now turn to the analysis of income growth from 2002 to 2004, generating further insights into the short-term intertemporal dynamics within the groups.

First of all, the growth-redistribution decompositions[7] generate insights into the distinction between the growth component of poverty reduction and the effect of redistribution. For all households, the growth component does exceed the redistribution component. Roughly 11 per cent of the 18 per cent total poverty reduction can be attributed to growth in mean incomes. The additional 7 per cent of poverty reduction can be ascribed to redistribution of incomes from households above the poverty line to households below the poverty line that enabled them to increase their income to a level above the poverty line.[8]

Table 6.5   Growth redistribution decomposition by household type[a]

Change household types	Change in poverty rate	Growth component	Redistribution component	N
Total	−17.92	−10.95	−6.97	3132
Switched	−22.6	−16.54	−6.07	1317
Non-switched	−19.42	−12.89	−6.53	1815
Farm HH	−15.77	−8.24	−7.53	426
Mixed farm	−21.59	−15.65	−5.94	685
Mixed non-farm	−14.51	−4.32	−10.19	499
Non-farm	−5.8	−4.96	−0.84	182
Mixed farm to farm	−18.98	−10.86	−8.13	183
Farm to mixed farm	−28.1	−20.33	−7.78	270
Mixed farm to mixed non-farm	−28.99	−16.66	−12.33	227
Mixed non-farm to non-farm	−15.73	−13.62	−2.11	128
Mixed non-farm to mixed farm	−14.48	−13.62	−0.86	222

[a] Decomposition according to Datt and Ravallion (1992).
Source: Authors' calculations based on GSO (2002; 2004) using ADePT 4.0 Poverty (2009).

Subdividing the effect to the switched and non-switched households, the same picture holds, with the switched types realizing higher poverty reduction than the non-switched types.

Splitting the whole sample into subsamples of the major change household types enables further examination of the differences across the household types with respect to the growth and redistribution components of the different poverty reduction performances. Within the group of households that did not change their income portfolio, poverty reduction in all groups – except the mixed non-farm household – is attributed mainly to growth rather than to redistribution. Within the group of mixed non-farm households, the poverty reduction of 15 per cent is attributed mainly to redistribution rather than to mean income growth.

The opposite trend in terms of growth versus redistribution components holds true for the mixed non-farm to mixed farm as well as non-farm households: the Gini coefficient did rise in these groups, and the observed poverty reduction is almost entirely attributed to growth rather than redistribution. Recalling the findings of Klump and Bonschab (2004: 20), who found the redistribution component to be positive for Vietnam, the same effects take place here, with the redistribution and growth components working in the same direction. Additionally, the growth component still dominates the redistribution effect, leading to poverty reduction over all groups.

Three groups, that is farm, mixed farm to farm and mixed farm to mixed non-farm households, do have fairly equal growth and redistribution components. The Gini coefficients for these groups have been stable (except from the mixed farm to mixed non-farm households, for within this group the Gini coefficient did decline slightly). For the rest of the groups, the growth component is considerably higher than the redistribution component. But a significant share of redistribution in favour of the poor did happen within these groups, although the Gini coefficient did rise. Again the switched households did perform much better, which gives additional support to the assumption that households do switch due to rational arguments for increased income opportunities.

A sizable share of households (42 per cent) did change their income portfolio, which might well be connected to their insufficient income as those households are significantly more often considered as poor. But the poverty reduction among the households that did switch was higher (23 per cent) than that of those who did not change (17 per cent). Finally, the mean growth components / redistribution component ratio is 2.8 times higher for the switched-type households than the non-switched households, which suggests switching is a successful strategy. Furthermore, the switch of income portfolio led to considerably higher growth within the group of switched households (11.5 versus 8.7 per cent).[9] All in all, the growth component is the most important across all groups except the mixed non-farm households. This indicates that a growth-based poverty reduction strategy would be more efficient than a redistribution policy. Therefore, a more detailed analysis of the growth that did happen is useful in order to facilitate adequate policy to target poverty reduction and to investigate whether the realized growth was pro-poor or whether the poverty reduction was based on mere growth in mean incomes over the whole population.

Turning to the pro-poor growth realized across the groups, the growth incidence curve (GIC) and the mean percentile growth rate of the poor (Ravallion and Chen, 2003) is utilized. Exemplarily, the GIC for rural Vietnam in total, as well as four selected household types, are illustrated in Figures 6.5 and Figure 6.6.

It is obvious that the rates of pro-poor growth do vary by more than 10 per cent across the household types, with the non-farm households group performing worst (0.53 per cent) and the mixed farm to farm households group performing best (11.63 per cent).

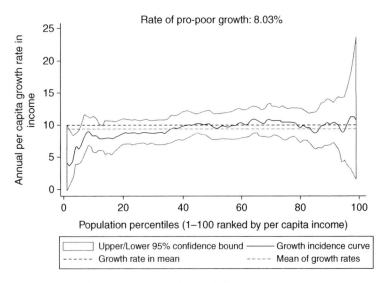

Figure 6.5   Growth incidence curve for rural Vietnam

Source: Mausch (2010), p. 62 based on GSO (2002; 2004) data.

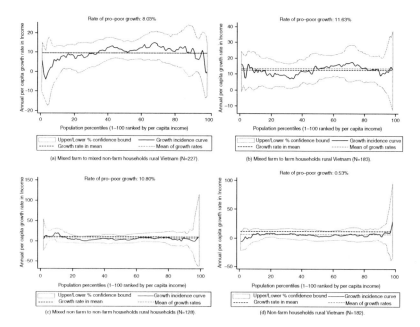

Figure 6.6 Exemplary growth incidence curves

Note: For the other groups, see Figure 6.8.

Source: Mausch (2010), p. 64 based on GSO (2002; 2004) data.

Taking the GIC for all rural households in the sample first, visual inspection leads to some basic insights into the implications of the different definitions. First of all, apart from some fluctuations, a general upward trend is visible from the graph, which implies that the growth rate of the bottom income percentiles was lower than that of the top income percentiles. Furthermore, the curve does run below the growth rate in mean curve up to approximately the 40th percentile but throughout all percentiles above zero. This again suggests that the poorest 40 percentiles realized a below-average growth rate.

Differentiating the GIC by household types, several differences emerge. For Figure 6.6(a), the trend of the bottom 30 to 40 percentiles to have a growth rate below the mean growth rate still holds, but in contrast to the population as a whole, almost all of the upper 10 percentiles are also realizing a lower growth rate. Nevertheless, the rate of pro-poor growth is exactly the same for this group, whereas for the other three subgroups the trends are not that clear, and judgement based on the graphs is not particularly easy. A downward slope is detectable, if anywhere, in Figure 6.6 for the mixed non-farm to non-farm households. These households had previously generated some additional income from agriculture, but by 2004this income source has dropped, and they are now focusing on non-farm income as their only income source. This group seems to have realized narrower pro-poor growth, even in terms of the second definition, as the poor achieved above-average growth rates. A final assessment is not possible, as only the lowest 15 percentiles realized above-average growth while for the 15th to 60th percentiles the growth rates are below average.

What can be accurately compared, however, are the rates of pro-poor growth that differ across the groups. The non-farm households realized the lowest rate of all groups, with only 0.53 per cent, while the mixed farm to farm and mixed non-farm to non-farm households achieved closely clustered above-average rates of more than 10 per cent. For easier comparison, Table 6.6 gives several measures related to pro-poor growth. These are the mean of growth rates, the rate of pro-poor growth according to Ravallion and Chen (2003) and finally the Ravallion and Chen (2003) rate of pro-poor growth adjusted by deducting the mean growth rates from the pro-poor growth rate.

First of all, as a basis for one of the measures of pro-poor growth, the mean growth rates do differ across the household types, from the lowest growth rate of 6.2 per cent to the highest of 12.4 per cent. The households that changed their income portfolio did realize slightly higher growth rates (1.6 per cent) as compared to the households that remained in the same group. Although poverty reduction was higher, poverty headcount was and remains higher (recalling Table 6.3: 39 versus 33 per cent for 2002, and 19 versus 17 per cent for 2004). The group realizing the lowest mean percentile growth rate is the group of non-farm households, while the mixed farm to farm households achieved the highest growth of 12.4 per cent.

Almost all subgroups among the switched household types did realize higher growth rates as compared to all other subgroups in the category of non-switched types. This indicates (like most other measures so far) that the income composition switches have been very successful for the households and that they pay off in terms of higher income gains.

Based on the pro-poor growth measure, which is calculated by deducting the mean of growth rates from the rate of pro-poor growth, this results in an overall negative pro-poor growth measure for all types except the mixed non-farm to non-farm households that realized a 3.3 per cent higher pro-poor growth rate as compared to the mean of growth rates. Therefore, according to this definition pro-poor growth

Table 6.6 Household typology changes and pro-poor growth rates

Change household types	Unit	Mean of growth rates	Rate of PPG[a]	Rate of PPG – mean of growth rates
Total	%	9.4	8	−1.4
Switched	%	10.3	9.5	−0.9
Non-switched	%	8.7	6.9	−1.9
Farm HH	%	8.3	6.6	−1.7
Mixed farm	%	9.7	7.6	−2.2
Mixed non-farm	%	9	7.4	−1.6
Non-farm	%	6.2	0.5	−5.7
Farm to mixed farm	%	11.8	9.6	−2.3
Mixed non-farm to mixed farm	%	9	5.9	−3.1
Mixed farm to farm	%	12.4	11.6	−0.8
Mixed farm to mixed non-farm	%	9.4	8	−1.4
Mixed non-farm to non-farm	%	7.5	10.8	3.3

[a] Rate of PPG according to Ravallion and Chen (2003).
Source: Authors' calculations based on GSO (2002; 2004).

can be found only in this group, while in all other household types mean growth was higher than the rate of pro-poor growth, indicating rising inequality.

Besides the differences that do exist between the groups, the regional differences found by Klump (2007) as well as Bonschab and Klump (2007) still persist. Figure 6.7 shows the pro-poor growth rates across the Vietnamese provinces based on the two different definitions. Clearly, the highest pro-poor growth rates can be found around the growth poles, especially in the Mekong Delta around Ho Chi Minh City but also around the Red River delta in the Hanoi region. Nevertheless, some places in less prosperous regions of Vietnam do also perform above average in terms of pro-poor growth, such as Da Nang province in Middle Vietnam or Bac Kan province in the Northeastern region.

What can also be seen from Figure 6.7(b) is that, according to def II, most regions face a negative pro-poor growth rate, meaning that growth

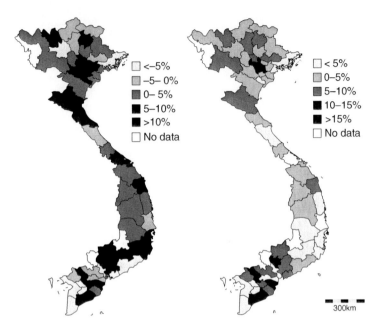

Figure 6.7(a) and 6.7(b)   Pro-Poor Growth (2002–2004) for definitions I and II across provinces

Note: Map using ADePT Maps 2.0 (2009).

Source: Mausch (2010), p. 67 based on GSO (2002; 2004) data.

actually was anti-poor and that the gap between the poor and the non-poor was widening from 2002 to 2004. There were even some places close to Ho Chi Minh City that realized pro-poor growth rates ranging from –10 per cent to –15 per cent.

6.4   Summary and conclusions

Besides the differences in poverty rates across the provinces, the income composition of households has a major impact on poverty prevalence. Furthermore, the income portfolio is less static than one would usually expect, even in a developing country like Vietnam. Even seemingly specialized households that derive income only from either farming or non-farming activities do (to a major extent) integrate other sources, based either on opportunities or on necessity, and therefore switch to different sectors. The steadiest group was the non-farm group, with more than 80 per cent remaining in the same group, while the most volatile group (apart from the other households) was found to be the farm households. Assuming these households are also more often impacted by shocks, especially flooding or droughts, this suggests some degree of necessity involved in the decision to change. For the group of non-farm households, shocks like job loss might be involved as well, but (even though casual labour is still very common) job losses are less common than flooding; Vietnam was hit by several typhoons in recent years, and farmers frequently lost their harvest as a result.

Besides showing mixed results in term of poverty and poverty reduction, the switched household types do generally perform better than the non-switched types, but also have higher poverty rates in 2002 (Table 6.7).

Table 6.7 Poverty and pro-poorness – summary

			PPG Definition[a]		
			I	II	
Change household types	Poverty rate below average in 2002	Poverty reduction above average	growth of the poor > 0	growth of the poor > mean growth	Rate of PPG above average[b]
Total			+	–	
Switched	–	+	+	–	+
Non-switched	+	–	+	–	–
Farm HH	–	+	+	–	–
Mixed farm	–	+	+	–	–
Mixed non-farm	+	–	+	–	–
Non-farm	+	–	+	–	–
Farm to mixed farm	–	+	+	–	+
Mixed non-farm to mixed farm	+	–	+	–	–
Mixed farm to farm	–	+	+	–	+
Mixed farm to mixed non-farm	–	+	+	–	0
Mixed non-farm to non-farm	+	–	+	+	+

[a] Categories based on Grosse *et al.* (2008).
[b] Here the Ravallion and Chen (2003) rate of PPG is referred to.
Source: Authors' calculations based on GSO (2002; 2004).

Furthermore, recalling the findings of Klump and Bonschab (2004: 20), who found the redistribution component to be positive for Vietnam, the same effects take place here, the redistribution and growth components working together. Additionally, the growth component still dominates the redistribution effect, leading to poverty reduction over all groups.

Similar results are shown in growth and pro-poor growth. Apart from the mixed results across the groups, most of the switched households did perform better. The seemingly very poor performance of the non-farm households, in particular, is based mainly on the very low level of poverty beforehand, and the remaining households seem to be facing markedly adverse conditions.

Nonetheless, those groups should not be allowed to drop out of sight. Although the incidences of poverty are low, it seems that the remainder are trapped in a low-income–low-growth scenario out of which they might not be able to extract themselves. Though mostly showing a similar pattern, the growth incidence curves do differ across the household types. Lower growth rates in lower income percentiles persist across almost all types, with only the mixed non-farm to non-farm households showing some kind of downward slope or at least an equally fluctuating pattern of overall percentiles.

Based on the above average pro-poor growth (and poverty reduction) rate of switched households and the below average pro-poor growth (and poverty reduction) rate of the non-switched households, a trend towards a catching-up effect can be concluded. This would, if enduring, reduce inequalities between these groups and will assist the group that suffers higher poverty incidence. Therefore, the flexibility of rural households should be encouraged and enabled through the promotion of the non-farm economy so that the households are able to choose their income sources based on profitability rather than availability. Additionally, it might be beneficial to support households in finding "their" portfolio, and encourage change where necessary. In this context, information for rural households concerning opportunities and possibilities of markets, either for employment or for self-employment, might also optimize their current portfolio. This will reduce entry barriers to new opportunities but will also improve current setups.

Neither specialization nor diversification seems to have clear poverty or pro-poor growth impacts. Though the effect of diversification is only based on a single group, one that used to do farming only and took up a non-farm income source for the second period, the effects are not clear even for this group, as similar poverty and growth patterns are found for the converse group, mixed farm to farm households. Therefore, judgement of these effects is not possible from the data at hand. To gain further insight into these effects would require a longer panel and several period to period inspections to detect patterns of specialization and diversification, for example as a possible development path, from farm to mixed farm to mixed non-farm to non-farm. Furthermore, a year-to-year panel including detailed information about droughts, floods and other shocks would enable a judgement on the necessity of switching income sources based on external influences like shocks, an issue covered in other chapters of this book.

All in all, due to the positive performance in terms of poverty reduction and pro-poor growth of the switched households, the recommendation to generate non-farm jobs in order to promote development and to serve the needs of the poor (Collier, 2007) holds also for rural Vietnam. Although – even within the favoured group of non-farm households that seemed to have managed the transition from farming to "modern" economic activities – some groups did remain poor, a certain degree of occupational choice will enable many households to improve their income portfolio and climb out of poverty.

Notes

1. The absolute number of poor divided by the total population size. Here, the terms headcount ratio and poverty rate are used analogue.
2. The definition of non-farm is wider. Wage employment, even in agriculture, will reduce risks for the household, and agricultural shocks like crop pests will not affect all households. Thus the income source will still be available. Therefore in the following, we will use the term "rural non-farm employment/economy" to include all activities that are not self-employed farming/livestock keeping/aquaculture.
3. Details on the sample design and data processing can be obtained from Tung and Phong (n.a.).
4. We want to thank Brian McCaig, School of Economics and Research School of Social Sciences, Australian National University, for sharing the information required to correct these errors.
5. All incomes converted to PPP US$ – based on ICP (2008) – in 2000 prices. Furthermore, all incomes are adjusted according to regional income comparison factors (rcpi) given in GSO (2002, 2004).
6. Major shifts across the groups have been shown above but these have been almost equal for all groups leaving the group sizes almost constant.
7. Decomposition of poverty reduction from growth in mean income versus poverty reduction due to changes in the distribution.
8. The fact that the Gini coefficient went up (see Table 3.6.1) during the same period is based on the differences in the measurement. The Gini coefficient referred to is based on the national poverty line which was adjusted during

the period. As here the comparison between households was focused on this fact does not affect the analysis and was therefore not accounted for.
9. Figures given are based on own calculation from GSO (2002, 2004).

References

ADePT 4.0 Poverty (2009): *Poverty Analysis Tool Developed in Development Economics Research Group*, World Bank, http://econ.worldbank.org/programs/poverty/adept

ADePT Maps 2.0 (2009): *Poverty Analysis Tool Developed in Development Economics Research Group*, World Bank, http://go.worldbank.org/UDTL02A390

Association of German Banks (2008): *Online Tool – Currency Converter*, http://www.bankenverband.de/html/reisekasse/waehrungsrechner.asp

Bonschab, T. and R. Klump (2005): "Operationalizing Pro-Poor Growth: Country Case Study Vietnam", Working Paper, Deutsche Gesellschaft für Technische Zusammenarbeit.

Bonschab, T. and R. Klump (2007): "Pro-Poor Growth in Vietnam: Explaining the Spatial Differences", in: Grimm, M., S. Klasen and A. McKay (eds), *Determinants of Pro-Poor Growth*, Palgrave Macmillan: 81–112.

Collier, P. (2007): *The Bottom Billion*, Oxford University Press.

Datt, G. and M. Ravallion (1992): "Growth and Redistribution Components of Changes in Poverty Measures – A Decomposition with Applications to Brazil and India in 1980s", *Journal of Development Economics*, 38: 275–95.

Dercon, S. (2002): "Income Risk, Coping Strategies and Safety Nets, Background paper for World Development Report 2000/2001", *World Bank Research Observer*, 17(2): 141–66.

Gaiha, R., K. Imai and W. Kang (2007): *Vulnerability and Poverty Dynamics in Vietnam*, Economics Discussion Paper, EDP-0708, University of Manchester.

Grosse, M., K. Harttgen and S. Klasen (2008): "Measuring Pro-Poor Growth in Non-Income Dimensions", *World Development*, 36: 1021–47.

GSO (2002; 2004): *Vietnam Living Standard Survey Data 2002 and 2004*, General Statistics Office of Vietnam.

ICP (2008): *2005 International Comparison Program (ICP) – Tables of final results*, http://www.worldbank.org/

Klump, R. (2005): *People, Places and Sub-National Growth: Country Case Study Vietnam*, Department of International Political Economy, Johann Wolfgang Goethe University of Frankfurt.

Klump, R. (2007): "Pro-Poor Growth in Vietnam: Miracle or Model?" in: Besley, T. and L. J. Cord (eds), *Delivering on the Promise of Pro-Poor Growth – Insights and Lessons from Country Experience*, Palgrave Macmillan and World Bank, 119–46.

Klump, R. and T. Bonschab (2004): *Operationalizing Pro-Poor Growth – A Country Case Study on Vietnam*, http://siteresources.worldbank.org/ INTPGI/Resources/342674-1115051237044/oppgvietnam

Kraay, A. (2006): "When Is Growth Pro-Poor? Evidence from a Panel of Countries", *Journal of Development Economics*, 80: 198–227.

Mausch (2010): *Poverty, Inequality and the Non-farm Economy: The Case of Rural Vietnam*, Logos Publishing House, Berlin.

McCaig, B. (2009): *Summary of 2002–2004 VHLSS Household Panel Construction,* http://www.cbe.anu.edu.au/staff/info/mccaig/McCaig_2002_2004_VHLSS_ household_panel.pdf

Ravallion, M. and S. Chen (2003): "Measuring Pro-Poor Growth", *Economics Letters,* 78: 93–9.

Ravallion, M. and G. Datt (1996): "How Important to India's Poor Is the Sectoral Composition of Economic Growth?" *World Bank Economic Review,* 10(1): 1–25.

Ravallion, M. and M. Huppi (1991): "Measuring changes in Poverty: A Methodological Case Study of Indonesia During Adjustment Period", *World Bank Economic Review,* 5: 57–84.

Schupp, F. (2002): "Growth and Inequality in South Africa", *Journal of Economic Dynamics and Control,* 26: 1699–720.

Tung, P. and N. Phong (n.a.): *Vietnam Household Living Standard Survey (VHLSS), 2002 and 2004 – Basic Information,* http://go.worldbank.org/DK46HUHUY0

United Nations (2005): *The Millennium Development Goals and Viet Nam's Socio Economic Development Plan 2006–2010,* http://www.un.org.vn/undp/undp/ docs/2005/sedp/ mdgsedpe.pdf

Part II

Drivers of Vulnerability, and Household Responses in Thailand and Vietnam

7
Impact of Food Price Shocks on Vulnerability to Poverty: A Mathematical Programming Approach

Marc Völker, Songporne Tongruksawattana, Erich Schmidt and Hermann Waibel

7.1 Introduction

The 2008 price crisis in the world markets for fuel, chemical fertilizer and agricultural commodities came as a shock to both producers and consumers. For farmers in Thailand and in Vietnam, this situation generated opportunities and risks. For agricultural households with a food surplus, higher commodity prices will lead to higher incomes provided price expectations hold and the price ratio of factor to commodity price remains favourable. For food deficit households, however, rising prices reduce their real income and tend to increase the risk of falling into poverty.

To analyse the effect of external price shocks on the response behaviour of farm households is challenging, because the uniqueness of such events limits the use of positive models to assess the reaction of households. Recent papers (for example Valero-Gil, 2008; World Bank, 2008; Tung and Waibel, 2010) used decomposition analysis to evaluate the effect of price shocks on poverty. While such studies are especially important for food insecure countries, there is much to learn from emerging market economies where the spatial pattern of poverty is heterogeneous. This is also true for Thailand and Vietnam, where large areas with rapid economic development coexist with regions where "pockets of poverty" remain. For Thailand this applies to households in the Northeastern region, while for Vietnam it is especially in the highland or mountainous areas where poverty has remained high or frequently reemerges as a result of shocks. The food price crisis of 2008 is a good example of such a shock that allows assessment of the impacts of this event to be made at household level. To capture the heterogeneity of the rural areas in the two countries, a methodology is needed that can provide insights into the ability of different types of rural households to react to such changes. While for aggregate analysis, positive (econometric) methods are preferable as they reflect actual behaviour of individuals, these are arguably less suitable to the obtaining of an in-depth understanding of adjustment processes at the micro level; mathematical programming (MP) can, however be a useful complementary methodological analytical tool that can facilitate the analysis of typical rural households as a case study. An advantage of such models is that they are robust and less demanding concerning the availability of aggregate data than are econometric models (Berger, 2001).

Interactions between resource endowments and constraints and activities concerning production, on-farm and off-farm labour allocation and consumption of home-produced as well as purchased goods can be made explicit, and risk can be taken into account (Taylor and Adelman, 2003). This case study model approach allows vulnerability to poverty of smaller geographical units to be assessed, and can therefore be a useful tool to design better targeting of poverty reduction and social protection policies.

In this chapter, the impact of the 2008 price shock on vulnerability to poverty, taking into account other multiple risks, is measured for agricultural households in Thailand and Vietnam. The objectives of the study are: (i) to develop and test additional methodologies to measure vulnerability to poverty of specific household types, (ii) to analyse the impact of the price shocks in 2007/2008 on agricultural households, taking into account other multiple risks, (iii) to compare the ability of rural households to respond to agricultural price shocks.

The data for these two case studies are derived from large-scale panel surveys in six provinces in Thailand and Vietnam collected within the scope of the DFG project (see Chapter 2). Data were collected in 2007, thus prior to the price hike, and in 2008, which refers to the peak of the price increase in major commodities such as rice (see Appendix 7.A.1).

7.2 Methodology and data

MP models allow rural households to be described as a vector of decision variables which reflect a set of income-generating activities of a typical rural household such that an objective function is maximized subject to specified resource and behavioural constraints. The flexibility of constructing typical households provides a direct way to calculate individual vulnerability measures for subsets of household types.

In this way, conclusions can be drawn for poverty reduction policies of smaller administrative units which would be more difficult to perform with econometric methods due to the problem of small sample size. As pointed out by Brooks *et al.* (2008), farm household modelling is a suitable approach to assess micro-level impacts of exogenous conditions on household behaviour recognizing their dual role as producer and consumer of food. On the other hand, there are some limitations of an MP model applied to poverty analysis. First, such models have the tendency to generate optimal portfolios with over-specialization, since not all real world constraints can be captured. Secondly, transaction and information costs, as well as the spatial dimension, are ignored. Such weaknesses can be overcome by developing a multi-agent model using a cellular automata (CA) framework. In agriculture the use of such models was pioneered by Balmann (1997). While multi-agent models are a useful advancement of sector level MP, especially for predicting diffusion of innovations or assessing the consequences of changes in natural resource use, for example, they are less appropriate for assessing the impact of exogenous price changes on poverty for specific types of households. Hence, MP models representing certain household types can be a practical alternative to more complex econometric household models that require rigid assumptions on own- and cross-price elasticities.

To apply such MP for poverty analysis of rural households in developing countries requires adequate reflection of the utility functions of the poor. Risk-averse behaviour is an important component of the household's decision-making process, adequately reflecting the conditions of people vulnerable to poverty. Various techniques for incorporating risk into mathematical models are available, such as quadratic programming (Markowitz, 1952; Freund, 1956), Hazell's (1971) minimization of total absolute deviation (MOTAD), and discrete stochastic and chance-constrained programming (Hazell and Norton, 1986). In this study, the "Target MOTAD" approach is used (Tauer, 1983), whereby the deviation from a defined minimum level of income (for example the poverty line) is minimized subject to the household's degree of risk aversion (McCarl and Spreen, 1996).

The Target MOTAD model can be specified as follows:

$$\max \sum_j \bar{c}_j X_j$$

Such that:

$$Y_0 - \sum_j c_{jt} X_j - Z_{\bar{t}} \leq 0, \quad \text{for all } t$$

$$\sum_t p_t Z_{\bar{t}} \leq \lambda$$

$$\sum_j a_{ij} X_j \leq b_i, \text{ for all } i$$

$$X_j, Z_{\bar{t}} \leq 0, \text{ for all } j, t$$

where $\bar{c}_j$ is the expected mean gross margin per unit of the j_{th} household activity across all states of shock occurrence, X_j is the level of the j_{th} household activity, Y_0 is the target income to be achieved (for example the minimum required income for the farm household to survive), c_{jt} is the expected gross margin per unit of the j_{th} activity in the t_{th} state of shock occurrence, $Z_{\bar{t}}$ is the negative income deviation from the expected mean gross margin in the t_{th} state of shock occurrence, p_t is the probability of occurrence of state of shock occurrence t, λ is the maximum average shortfall of income which still enables a satisfactory level of compliance with the target income, a_{ij} is the technical coefficient of the j_{th} resource required to achieve X_j, and b_i is the resource constraint level of i_{th} resource. By parameterizing λ, a set of efficient farm plans with the maximum possible value of household income for any specified level of allowable shortfall from the target income is obtained. Households with the highest risk aversion may choose the farm plan related to the smallest possible level of compliance with the target income. Less risk-averse farm households might prefer farm plans promising higher levels of expected income but also higher levels of compliance with the target income, providing that the absolute level of compliance with the target income remains sufficiently small.

The model developed in this study represents a one-year time period and includes the main income-generating activities of two households defined as typical for location-specific conditions in Thailand and Vietnam. The models were developed for two sets of agricultural prices, namely with and without the 2008 price shock. Other risks were incorporated in the model as a probability for each state of shock occurrence, assuming zero correlation among the individual shock events.

Model output yields the optimal activity portfolios of the two agricultural households, corresponding expected means and variances of total household income, for the situation with and without food price crisis reflecting the conditions in the years 2007 and 2008. Results can be presented as a cumulative distribution function (CDF) of total household income, formally written as:

$$F(x) = P(i \leq x) \tag{7.1}$$

where i is a random variable of the discrete type, representing total household income, with probability density function:

$$F(x) = P(i = x), \; x \in \Re \tag{7.2}$$

The value of the CDF at each level x of total household income i indicates the probability that total household income is smaller than or equal to x. If $x = PL$ and PL is specified as the poverty line, then the value of the CDF at PL gives the probability of the household to be poor. Following the concept of vulnerability as expected poverty (Chaudhuri *et al.*, 2002; Christiansen and Subbarao, 2001) and assuming that i is constructed based on another standard normal random variable, the expected mean of total household income, and the expected variance of total household income, this gives the vulnerability V_t of the household at time t, which can be formally specified as:

$$V_t = P(i_{t+1} \leq PL) \tag{7.3}$$

where i_{t+1} is the household's level of income at time $t + 1$, and PL is the income poverty line. The impact of price changes between 2007 and 2008 on household vulnerability to poverty can be seen by plotting the CDF of each year.

The data to establish the two typical households are derived from the provincial databases of 2007 of the DFG project, namely Ubon Ratchathani in Northeastern Thailand (Tongruksawattana *et al.*, 2008) and Thua Thien Hue in Vietnam (Völker *et al.*, 2008). For the latter case the sample was restricted to households located in the mountainous areas. In addition to the initial household survey in 2007 (see Chapter 3) an agricultural survey of a smaller sample was carried out in May 2008 and January 2009 in order to obtain more detailed information on agricultural technologies, specific resources, and behavioural constraints. Following the concept of typical farm models (Hemme, 2000; Mausch *et al.*, 2009), a four-step procedure was applied (see Figure 7.1). Hereby the provincial sample (Ubon) or sub sample (Hue) haswas used to identify a set of key indicators suitable to establish a typology of the rural households. In the first step, an income threshold of twice the rural poverty line was set to identify poor and vulnerable households.[1] Second, selected households were defined as farm households engaged in own agricultural production. Third, only households that had experienced at least one medium severe shock during the past five years were included. Fourth, the selected typical households reflect the most

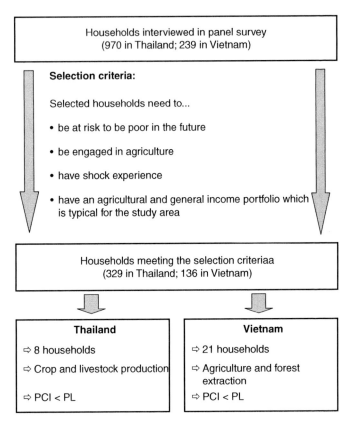

Figure 7.1 Selection of typical households
Source: Own illustration.

frequent composition of the respective household income portfolio. In Thailand, agricultural occupation was used as a proxy for income. In Vietnam, land allocation to cropping and remittances was used to define agricultural households.

The sub-sample for choosing households suitable to deliver information on typical households was 329 in Ubon and 136 in Thua Thien Hue. From this selection, 64 households in Thailand and 60 in Vietnam were randomly selected for in-depth data collection. From these sub-samples, eight households in Thailand and 21 households in Vietnam were defined as reasonably homogenous groups to formulate one typical household per country.

7.3 Model assumptions

Table 7.1 presents the basic parameters (for example per capita income, household size and so on) of the two typical households defined for the model. The figures are median values drawn from the underlying samples. For minimum annual household target income in Vietnam, labour capacity and rice consumption imputed values are used, while shock experience is defined as the average frequencies of each shock type observed in the respective country samples. It becomes clear from Table 7.1 that the households differ between the two countries. The typical agricultural household in Thailand has about half of its income-generating members working outside agriculture, while in Vietnam almost all income-generating household members are engaged in agriculture. Household income is higher in Thailand, and so is the regional poverty line. The latter value is used as minimum annual target income in the model households; that is PPP US$4411.65 in Thailand (National Statistical Office/National Economic and Social Development Board 2007) and PPP US$1750 in Vietnam (General Statistics Office Vietnam 1998 & 2008[2]). Land endowment per household is much larger in Vietnam[3] but agricultural land overall is of similar size in the two countries. Both households typically suffer several shocks. The average number of all shocks is higher in Thailand, and although idiosyncratic shocks are more prominent in that country, climate-related shocks are relatively more important in Vietnam.

Labour capacity in total person days per year was calculated in view of weather restrictions, social obligation, illness, housework activities, schooltime and leisure requirement considering differences among household members,[4,5] also differentiating between more demanding (for example ploughing) and less demanding (for example weeding) labour, and allowing for substitution of the different types of labour.

In the Thai model, the vast majority of the land is allocated for rice and cassava. An annual household requirement for glutinous rice was defined in order to account for local consumption preferences (Isvilananda and Kongrith, 2008), and a corresponding minimum requirement for consumption goods other than rice was defined.

In the Vietnam model arable agricultural land endowment is smaller, as the household represents a remote mountainous area with degraded forestland, shrubs and bare hills. Annual rice consumption requirements were based on FAOSTAT[6] in the absence of regional-specific information. Consumption of purchased goods (see Table 7.1) was derived as median value from the sample of the same shocks experienced; these were mainly weather and human health shocks.

Table 7.1   Characteristics of the model household

Characteristics	Unit	Thailand	Vietnam
Monthly per capita income	PPP$	67.2	34.9
Minimum annual household target income[a]	PPP$	4411.7	1750.0
Household size	persons	5.0	4.5
Agricultural member ratio	%	56.5	100.0
Annual family labour capacity			
Hard labour	person days	360.0	500.0
Light labour	person days	615.0	150.0
Land endowment			
Total land	ha	4.3	1.7
Crop land	ha	3.6	0.2
Annual consumption requirement			
Rice	kg		1012.0
Jasmine rice	kg	0.0	
Glutinous rice	kg	1122.5	
Vegetable	kg	234.4	
Cassava	ka	0.0	
Non-rice purchased consumption	PPP$	607.7	606.2
Shock incidents (2002–8)			
All shocks	number	4.2	3.5
Illness of household member	number	0.7	0.3
Flooding	number	1.0	0.2
Unusually heavy rainfall	number		0.3
Storm	number		0.9
Unusually cold weather	number		0.4
Crop pests	number	0.4	
Drought	number	0.7	
Death of household member	number	0.2	

[a]Annual target household income is set equal to regional poverty line. N = 8 (Thailand); N = 22 (Vietnam).

Source: DFGFR756 base survey and in-depth survey Ubon Ratchathani and Thua Thien Hue provinces.

In Table 7.2 the major crop portfolios and production technologies of the two households are presented that form the technical coefficients in the models. In Thailand, yield levels for jasmine and glutinous rice are slightly lower than the provincial average of 1971.25 kg/ha (OAE, 2010). The vegetable yield, which primarily represents backyard production for home consumption, is an aggregation of several vegetable types and harvesting cycles over a one-year period. The cassava produced, on the other hand, is for sale to industrial processing. The model allows complete substitution between jasmine and glutinous rice, but is limited to rice cassava substitution because of land quality differences. The household also produces livestock farming, including buffalo, cattle, and chickens. Animal manure from cattle and buffalo husbandry is available as organic fertilizer and can be a substitute for chemical fertilizers.[7] In addition, households apply other organic fertilizers, including chicken manure and compost purchased at the market. Input intensity is generally low, but external inputs (chemical fertilizers) are used. Production processes are partly mechanized (for example ploughing) but weeding and harvesting is dependent on labour with vegetable as the most labour intensive crop.

In Vietnam, the crop portfolio includes spring rice, autumn rice, cassava, corn, and banana. Yield levels are lower compared to average Vietnamese yield levels (FAOSTAT, 2010) but are slightly higher than in the Thai model. Generally production conditions are unfavourable in the mountainous upland of Vietnam North Central Coast Region (World Bank, 2005). Production of upland rice is for home consumption. The sale of surplus production is practically non-existent due to limited market capacity for upland rice in the mountains and differences in consumption preferences of urban consumers in the lowlands. Often rice households in mountainous areas must supplement own rice production with the purchase of lowland rice to satisfy consumption needs (Pandey *et al.*, 2006). Mechanization is basically non-existent in mountainous areas, thus no fuel is required in crop production (see Table 7.2). However, labour-intensity is high. Chemical fertilizer and pesticides are used for spring rice and corn production.

No manure is applied, as livestock production is practised at low levels of intensity and in open pastures.

Figure 7.2 shows the changes in factor and product prices between 2007 and 2008 for Thailand and Vietnam respectively. For this purpose, these changes are based on price data from the complete set of households interviewed in the in-depth data collection among 64 households in Thailand and 60 households in Vietnam. The complete dataset has

Table 7.2 Production technology and input intensity of major crops (per hectare and year)

	Thailand				Vietnam				
	Jasmine rice	Glutinous rice	Vegetable	Cassava	Spring rice	Autumn rice	Cassava	Corn	Banana
Yield (kg)	1958.1	1527.0	1599.8	6250.0	2478.6	2934.8	7250.0	1120.2	330.6
Input use									
Seeds (kg)[a]	66.0	37.5	10.0	4890.5	120.0	120.0	516.7	40.0	0.0
Fertilizer (kg)									
Chemical	95.0	123.6	0.0	250.0	550.0	0.0	0.0	750.0	0.0
Organic	178.8	276.9	50.0	468.8	0.0	0.0	0.0	0.0	0.0
Manure	245.0	491.0	313.0	0.0	0.0	0.0	0.0	0.0	0.0
Pesticide (litre)	0.0	0.0	0.0	0.0	26.3	0.0	0.0	13.3	0.0
Herbicide (bags)	0.0	0.0	0.0	0.0	0.0	6.7	0.0	0.0	0.0
Fuel (litre)	15.6	15.4	0.0	20.3	0.0	0.0	0.0	0.0	0.0
Family Labour (person days)					510.9	256.1	816.0	543.0	338.5
Hard labour	24.5	26.5	87.5	3.1					
Light labour	67	69.6	212.9	99.6					

Crop type

[a] Unit of seeds for cassava is piece.

Source: In-depth survey Ubon Ratchathani and Thua Thien Hue provinces.

been used in order to overcome a potential bias that could be generated if using only the relatively small number of households which form the model households. It is assumed that market integration is similar across all households in the study area. Over a one-year period, the wholesale market price of jasmine rice in Thailand increased by 38 per cent, which is transferred to a 30 per cent increase in the farm gate price. While cassava experienced a decrease in the farm gate price of almost 15 per cent, the wholesale price had increased by 20 per cent. At the same time, prices of fuel, chemical and organic fertilizer increased by 43 per cent, 31 per cent and 13 per cent respectively. The net effect of the price therefore depends on the relative prices perceived by decision makers at the time when input decisions are made.

In Vietnam, results show that the retail price of rice increased sharply, indicating that the transmission of the price hike of the rice world market was effective there. For the model, the retail price of rice was relevant as no market for selling upland rice exists and households are net-buyers of rice. For cassava, corn, and banana where markets exist, as shown in Figure 7.2, the respective increase in farm gate prices was comparatively small, ranging from almost zero per cent (cassava) to up to ten per cent (corn). On the input side, chemical fertilizer prices

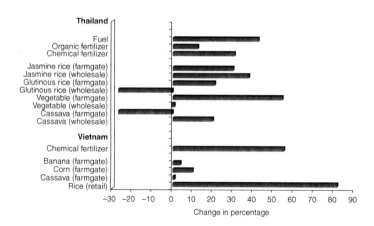

Figure 7.2 Price changes of output and input, 2007–8 in Thailand and Vietnam

Source: Thailand: (i) Farm gate prices: In-depth survey Ubon Ratchathani province; (ii) Wholesale prices: Office of Agricultural Economics and Department of Internal Trade, Vietnam: in-depth survey Thua Thien Hue province, n = 64 (Thailand) and n = 60 (Vietnam)

increased about 50 per cent, suggesting a possible negative effect on household welfare.

Table 7.3 summarizes the activity gross margins under different states of weather-related shocks for the 2007 and the 2008 prices. Gross margin is defined here as cash income from market sales and the imputed value of self-consumption based on farm gate prices. Results show that weather-related shocks can lead to negative gross margins, and the changes in relative prices from 2007 to 2008 generally augment such losses. In Vietnam, corn shows a negative gross margin even in the zero shock state, which suggests that objectives other than profit maximization, such as consumption preferences, are relevant.

In Figure 7.3, the individual risk coefficients of the households that underpin the representative households on which the models are based upon are presented. Results underline the assumption of risk-averse behaviour as captured in the Target MOTAD model. The data in Figure 7.3 is derived from the respondents' self-assessment of their attitude

Table 7.3 Activity gross margins across states of weather-related shocks

	Thailand				
	2007 prices				
	Gross margin per hectare per year (PPP$)				Probability of occurrence
Scenario	Jasmine rice	Glutinous rice	Vegetable	Cassava	
No shock	856	484	777	584	0.43
Drought	25	–91	136	–226	0.21
Flooding of agricultural land	185	19	259	–70	0.24
Both shocks	–137	–204	11	–384	0.12
Expected value	400	168	425	140	
Variance	32221	12312	23422	20802	
Standard deviation	180	111	153	82	

Continued

Table 7.3 Continued

Thailand

2008 prices

	Gross margin per hectare per year (PPP$)				Probability of occurrence
Scenario	Jasmine rice	Glutinous rice	Vegetable	Cassava	
No shock	1121	577	1206	330	0.43
Drought	39	–121	216	–361	0.21
Flooding of agricultural land	247	13	407	–228	0.24
Both shocks	–173	–257	23	–496	0.12
Expected value	527	194	663	–49	
Variance	55043	17739	56285	10572	
Standard deviation	235	133	237	67	

Vietnam

2007 prices

	Gross margin per hectare per year (PPP$)					Probability of occurrence
Scenario	Spring rice	Autumn rice	Cassava	Corn	Banana	
No shock	816	1633	988	–272	1482	0.51
Cold shock	196	1633	988	–1130	613	0.09
Drought shock	–59	1633	988	–1130	1482	0.11
Flood/rain/ storm shock	816	679	0	–272	0	0.19
Cold + Drought shock	–615	1633	988	–1130	613	0.02
Cold + Flood/ rain/storm shock	196	679	0	–1130	0	0.03

Continued

Table 7.3   Continued

Vietnam

2007 prices

| Scenario | Gross margin per hectare per year (PPP$) | | | | | Probability of occurrence |
	Spring rice	Autumn rice	Cassava	Corn	Banana	
Drought + Flood/rain/ storm shock	−59	679	0	−1130	0	0.04
All shocks	−615	679	0	−1130	0	0.01
Expected value	567	1371	716	−532	980	
Variance	157684	181393	194619	155262	434090	
Standard deviation	397	426	441	394	659	

2008 prices

| Scenario | Gross margin per hectare per year (PPP$) | | | | | Probability of occurrence |
	Spring rice	Autumn rice	Cassava	Corn	Banana	
No shock	1448	2746	997	−725	1540	0.51
Cold shock	414	2746	997	−1598	637	0.09
Drought shock	−10	2746	997	−1598	1540	0.11
Flood/rain/ storm shock	1448	1155	0	−725	0	0.19
Cold + Drought shock	−938	2746	997	−1598	637	0.02
Cold + Flood/rain/ storm shock	414	1155	0	−1598	0	0.03
Drought + Flood/rain/ storm shock	−10	1155	0	−1598	0	0.04
All shocks	−938	1155	0	−1598	0	0.01

Continued

Table 7.3 Continued

	Vietnam				
	2008 prices				
	Gross margin per hectare per year (PPP$)				**Probability of occurrence**
Scenario	**Spring rice**	**Autumn rice**	**Cassava**	**Corn**	**Banana**	
Expected value	1034	2308	723	−989	1018	
Variance	438727	504693	198022	161184	468854	
Standard deviation	662	710	445	401	685	

Source: In-depth survey Ubon Ratchathani and Thua Thien Hue provinces.

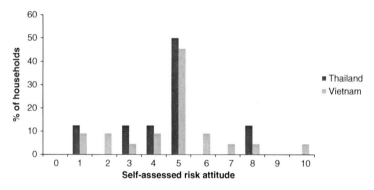

Figure 7.3 Self-assessment of risk attitude among households in Ubon Ratchathani (Thailand) and Thua Thien Hue (Vietnam) provinces

Source: DFGFOR756 base survey

Note: n = 8 for Thailand, n = 22 for Vietnam. Self-assessment ranges from zero (= unwilling to take risk) to ten (fully prepared to take risk).

towards risk, using a scale from zero (unwilling to take risk) to ten (fully prepared to take risk). Results show that households in Thailand and Vietnam represented in the two models generally are averse to risk, but the degree of risk aversion varies, with extreme risk aversion rather being the exception.

7.4   Results

Using the assumptions described in the previous sections first, a base solution for the two MOTAD models representing a specific type of agricultural household in Thailand and Vietnam was established for the situation of the 2007 prices.

In the Thailand case, varying the degree of risk aversion does not affect household resource allocation. Based on 2007 prices, under a high level of risk aversion ($\lambda = 0$), the optimal production portfolio is similar as under lower levels of risk aversion ($\lambda = 250, 300, 450$ and 600). Results are different, however, for the Vietnam model. Assuming high levels of risk aversion, that is not allowing any shortfall from the required consumption levels ($\lambda = 0$), leads to an infeasible model solution. This result indicates that our "typical Vietnamese rural farm household" must accept income falling below a defined minimum level or must generate additional income from other sources. Under the conditions postulated for the Vietnam case, this can only come from natural resources, which invariably means logging activities, some of which are illegal. In Table 7.4, time allocation for forest extraction is always at maximum capacity level.[8] This confirms the finding of a study that analysed households' response to health and weather-related shocks (Völker and Waibel, 2010). However, for households who are willing to accept a higher level of shortfall, that is lowering the degree of risk aversion, feasible model solutions exist which suggest that illegal logging activities may not be a general mode of behaviour.

In Table 7.4, the impact of the 2008 price shocks on the optimal crop portfolio of the typical households in Thailand and Vietnam is presented. Model output provides the expected household income, the standard deviation of income and the allocation of the household's resources over the different income-generating activities for different degrees of risk.

In the Thailand case, the price change from 2007 to 2008 lowered the expected income and prompted households to adjust by diversifying out of farming and reducing the area allocated to cassava and jasmine rice, the two commercial crops. Glutinous rice as a subsistence crop remained. This effect was particularly strong at high degrees of risk aversion (see Table 7.4). Results suggest that an agricultural household in Thailand as portrayed by our model did not benefit from the 2008 price hike. Reasons for this could be several. First, the immediate increase in input prices led to cash constraints for the purchase of inputs; this is concurrent with anecdotal evidence from the study area.

Table 7.4 Optimal farm household activity portfolios across price scenarios

	Thailand					
	Activity level					
	2007 prices			**2008 prices**		
Activity	λ = 0	λ = 250	λ = 600	λ = 0	λ = 250	λ = 600
Jasmine rice (ha)	1.236	1.769	1.769	1.069	1.436	1.436
Glutinous rice (ha)	0.735	0.735	0.735	0.735	0.735	0.735
Vegetable (ha)	—	0.053	0.080	—	0.080	0.080
Cassava (ha)	0.501	1.074	1.076	0.334	0.700	0.700
Off-farm employment (person days)	605	482	473	638	542	542
Feasible?	Yes	Yes	Yes	Yes	Yes	Yes
Total farm household income (PPP$)						
Expected value	7118.1	7560.9	7568.6	6893.7	7298.3	7298.3
Variance	3081098.4	7786115.0	8169386.7	2907562.4	6056191.4	6056191.4
Standard deviation	1755.3	2790.4	2858.2	1705.2	2460.9	2460.9

Continued

Table 7.4 Continued

	Vietnam					
			Activity level			
	2007 prices				2008 prices	
Activity	λ = 0	λ = 100	λ = 600	λ = 0	λ = 100	λ = 600
Spring rice (ha)	—	0.034	0.034	—	—	—
Autumn rice (ha)	—	0.034	0.034	—	—	—
Corn (ha)	—	0.011	0.011	—	—	0.011
Banana (ha)	—	0.113	0.113	—	—	0.146
Forest extraction (person days)	—	166.680	166.680	—	—	166.680
Feasible?	No	Yes	Yes	No	No	Yes
Total farm household income (PPP$)						
Expected value		1708.4	1708.4			1624.4
Variance		18463.6	18463.6			10410.5
Standard deviation		135.9	135.9			102.0

Note: Inconsistencies are due to rounding errors. Spring and autumn rice are rotated on the same land area in Vietnam. In case no feasible solution is possible, an optimal portfolio is produced by the model but interpretation is not possible. λ = maximum shortfall from target income allowed.

Source: Authors' calculation.

Such effects did not occur, however, for the larger commercial farmers in Central Thailand, where a positive supply response was observed. Second, since the price increase occurred suddenly, farmers did not trust in the persistence of these prices for future harvest times. Third, the changes in the agricultural input output price relationships from 2007 to 2008 decreased the marginal returns to labour in agriculture relative to non-farm wages. Fourth, the general uncertainty, inflicted especially by input price shocks such as fuel and fertilizer, augmented the tendency to opt for further off-farm opportunities. This seems plausible for the typical part-time agricultural households, which are now quite common for the lower-potential agricultural areas in Thailand. In Vietnam, results show that a large substitution effect used to take place, and it still does. The Vietnamese households specified in the model tend to substitute spring and autumn rice by banana to a significant degree. This is well in line with the price changes observed from Figure 7.2. An agricultural household producing under remote upland conditions does not benefit from higher producer prices of rice, due to a lack of marketing opportunities and especially higher input prices of chemical fertilizer. In the period of the study, the latter limited the increase in net revenue of rice production, thus both the marginal costs of rice production and the purchase costs of rice increased. The only crop in the portfolio that was, and still is, unaffected by higher input prices and that experienced slightly higher output prices is banana. Hence, the economically optimal adjustment, taking risk into account, is the expansion of banana production. However, since banana is a perennial crop, in this regard the model results need to be interpreted as a medium-term response to price increase. Taking into account the degree of risk aversion shows that the price increase induces stronger pressure on natural resources. This is shown by the infeasibility of the solution even if the extreme risk aversion coefficient is relaxed ($\lambda = 100$).

Figure 7.4 shows the effect of the price shock on vulnerability to poverty. The cumulative distribution functions of household income across different states of weather shock occurrence show the probability of falling below the defined level of minimum income (rural/provincial poverty line).

In both countries, our typical households were already vulnerable prior to the 2008 price shock. Furthermore, for some shock scenarios a considerable poverty gap existed, and continues to do so. The 2008 price shock has a different impact on household income in the two countries.

In Thailand, the increase in agricultural prices has lowered income variance (see Table 7.4), leading to a reduction in the probability of falling

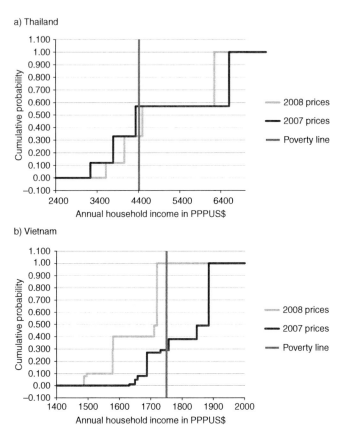

Figure 7.4 Discrete cumulative distribution functions of household income among and across price scenarios (Target deviation ≤ 600)

Source: Own calculations.

below the minimum income from 57 per cent to 33 per cent. However, the food price crisis has definitely made our typical farm household in Vietnam more vulnerable to poverty, mainly due to the remoteness which brings about a lack of market access. Households located in the mountainous areas are net-buyers of lowland rice and, due to poor land quality, are constrained in their ability to expand upland rice production. While the vulnerability level was at 29 per cent in the before-crisis price situation, the hike in food prices made such households 100 per cent vulnerable to poverty.

7.6 Summary and conclusions

In this chapter, the impact of the 2008 food price shocks on the vulnerability to poverty of poor rural households in Thailand and Vietnam is assessed using an MP approach. The objectives were threefold, namely: first to develop and test additional methodologies to measure vulnerability to poverty; second to assess vulnerability to poverty for a particular group of farm households in Thailand and Vietnam; and third to analyse the impact of the 2008 food price shocks by means of an MP model. A Target MOTAD model was developed for a specified household type in both countries to assess the response to the 2008 price increases considering other endogenous risks. The models also provide information on the agricultural production pattern and the implications of household resource constraints. Households portrayed in the models were defined as being typical of the poorer segment of rural households living in remote areas of the study provinces. The data established in the model assumptions were collected through complementary in-depth surveys in the province of Ubon Ratchathani (Thailand) and Thua Thien Hue (Vietnam), derived from the general data base of the DFG project (see chapter 3). The selected households were based on criteria such as: (i) household income below the poverty line, (ii) households engaged in own agricultural production, (iii) households with shock experience, and (iv) typical of the respective province with regard to income-generating activities (which refers to integrated crop-livestock farms with off-farm and/or non-farm employment for Thailand, and purely agricultural households for Vietnam).

As regards the first objective, it can be stated that MP models can be a useful tool for simultaneously considering different shocks such as economic and weather-related shocks in a theoretically consistent, albeit normative, framework. Although one might question the behavioural assumptions entered in the model, for instance regarding minimum consumption requirements, the Target MOTAD approach allows a plausible representation of the households' risk aversion. Furthermore the flexibility of constructing typical households based on the in-depth database which has been established in the project provides a direct way of calculating individual vulnerability measures for subsets of household types. In this way, conclusions can be drawn for poverty reduction policies of smaller administrative units, which would be more difficult to perform with positive econometric methods due to the problem of small sample size.

For the second objective, model results show that the typical farm households are vulnerable to poverty, with a 57 per cent and 29 per cent probability of being poor in a normal year before the price shock in Thailand and Vietnam respectively. In comparison to the cross-section based method of vulnerability computations (Chaudhuri *et al.*, 2002) the calculated vulnerability measure can be considered to be more situation-specific. The baseline solution of the model can be used as a benchmark for impact assessment of different types of policy interventions and external shocks such as the food price hikes analysed here.

The third objective was to assess the impacts of the 2008 food and input price shock in both countries. In Thailand, results from a 2007/2008 scenario comparison show that farm households tended to respond to the price shocks by reducing on-farm activity while shifting more labour towards off-farm employment. Economically optimal adaptation led to a reduction in the cropping area for cassava and jasmine rice, the two commercial crops, while glutinous rice c ultivation remained unchanged for subsistence consumption. This is possibly due to cash constraints for input purchase at the beginning of the planting period and the risk of falling prices at the time of harvest. Optimal adjustment led to a reduction in the variance of household income, reducing vulnerability to poverty from 57 per cent to 33 per cent.

In Vietnam, results are consistent with the findings of other research (for example Tung and Waibel, 2010) which found that although the food price hike of 2008 has reduced the overall national poverty level it has made the very poor people, such as remote agricultural households, poorer. The research shows that rural households of that type have also become much more vulnerable. Agricultural households in the mountain areas of Vietnam are among the losers from higher food prices. From a methodological point of view, the result of this modelling exercise supports the findings of other household studies in developing countries (for example Kuroda and Yotopoulos, 1978; Singh *et al.* 1986; Dyer *et al.*, 2006) that household consumption requirements can reverse a positive price effect due to market imperfections.

In conclusion, this chapter on the impact of the 2008 food price crisis using a case study approach provides a good starting point for further analysis on the differentiation of rural households (for example, commercially oriented farms or different locations with different natural environments). The methodology can also be used to test the impact of policy interventions and the introduction of new technologies on vulnerability to poverty.

It is important to note that the response to price shocks is primarily constrained by the availability of land, labour and capital in order to expand the production of cash crop. This finding is in line with the economic theory that the supply price elasticity is lower in the short run than in the long run due to rigidity of input availability, as outputs are influenced not only by prices but also by production factors, especially capital, labour and land, which are fixed in the short term (for example Binswanger, 1989). Furthermore, recognition of the household's objective of ensuring food security over cash-income maximization, substitution between cash crops and non-cash crops needs a substantial price incentive in addition to an alternative secure food source.

Concerning policy implications, this chapter discloses several possible constraints faced by rural farm households in their agricultural production in the short run. In Thailand, these constraints include limited land and labour endowment as well as high dependency on mechanization and purchased inputs. As a response to agricultural production contraction, options to generate income such as engagement in off-farm wage labour and non-farm self-employment provide an effective transitory strategy to cope with shocks. In Vietnam, households are constrained to limited endowment with agricultural land and have limited access to inputs. They also lack good alternatives to illegal forest extraction in order to generate income such as other crop or livestock products or engagement in off-farm wage labour and non-farm self-employment. Further investigation is needed to better understand underlying causes of such entry barriers to a more effective risk management strategy.

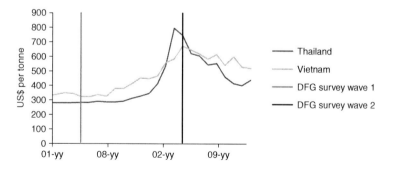

Figure 7.A.1 Monthly rice prices in Thailand and Vietnam 2007–9

Sources: http://www.bot.or.th/ (Bank Of Thailand) and http://agro.gov.vn/news/defaultE. asp (Agroinfo) via http://www.fao.org/giews/pricetool/ (FAO), Date of access: 28.3.2011.

Note: Thailand, Bangkok, Rice (25 per cent broken), Wholesale price; Vietnam, Hanoi, Rice, Retail price

Notes

1. Monthly income per capita poverty line in 2007 is equal to THB 1,316 or approximately PPP US$76.59 in Northeastern Thailand (National Economic and Social Development Board) and VND 200,000 or approximately PPP US$36.24 in rural Vietnam (General Statistics Office).
2. For Vietnam, the food poverty line used has been imputed based on data from the Vietnam Living Standards Survey (VLSS) 1998 and the Vietnam Health and Living Standards Survey (VHLSS) 2008.
3. Because non-agricultural lands, that is mainly forest areas, are included.
4. Thailand: (i) Annual hard labour capacity = 216 person days (male adult member) + 144 person days (female adult spouse) = 360 person days. (ii) Monthly light labour capacity during school time (January–March, June–September) = 8 person days (male adult member) + 12 person days (female adult spouse) + 10 person days (adolescent member) + 5 person days (child) + 10 person days (elder member) = 45 person days. (iii) Monthly light labour capacity during school break (April–May, October–December) = 8 person days (male adult member) + 12 person days (female adult spouse) + 20 person days (adolescent member) + 10 person days (child) + 10 person days (elder member) = 60 person days.
5. Vietnam: Annual hard labour capacity = 300 man days (male adult member) + 200 man days (female adult member) = 500 man days. Annual light labour capacity = 150 man days (adolescent member).
6. http://faostat.fao.org
7. The substitution ratio between manure and chemical fertilizer is assumed at 4:1 kg.
8. In the model, the natural resource access constraint has been defined in terms of time, which means that only during a period of four months per year households are allowed to extract timber from the commune's forest pool.

References

Balmann, A. (1997): "Farm-Based Modelling of Regional Structural Change: A Cellular Automata Approach", *European Review of Agricultural Economics*, 24(1–2): 85–108.

Berger, T. (2001): "Agent-Based Spatial Models Applied to Agriculture: A Simulation Tool for Technology Diffusion, Resource Use Changes and Policy Analysis", *Agricultural Economics*, 25: 245–60.

Binswanger, H. P. (1989): "The Policy Response of Agriculture", in: S. Fisher and D. de Tray (eds), *Proceedings of the World Bank Annual Conference on Development Economics*, 1989, World Bank, Washington DC: 231–56.

Brooks, J., G. Dyer and E. Taylor (2008): "Modelling Agricultural Trade and Policy Impacts in Less Developed Countries", *OECD Food, Agriculture and Fisheries Working Papers*, No. 11, OECD publishing, OECD, doi:10.1787/228626403505.

Chaudhuri, S., J. Jalan and A. Suryahadi (2002): "Assessing Household Vulnerability to Poverty: a Methodology and Estimates for Indonesia", *Department of Economics Discussion Paper*, No. 0102–52, Columbia University, New York.

Dyer, G. A., S. Boucher and J. E. Taylor (2006): "Subsistence Response to Market Shocks", *American Journal of Agricultural Economics*, 88(2): 279–91.

FAOSTAT (2010): "Yield per Hectare by Crop Type in Vietnam 2008". Available online at: http://faostat.fao.org. Accessed: 3 September 2010.

Freund, R. J. (1956): "The Introduction of Risk into a Programming Model", *Econometrica*, 24(3), 253–63.

Hazell, P. B. R. (1971): "A Linear Alternative to Quadratic and Semivariance Programming for Farm Planning under Uncertainty", *American Journal of Agricultural Economics*, 53(1): 53–62.

Hazell, P. B. R. and R. D. Norton (1986): *Mathematical Programming for Economic Analysis in Agriculture*, Macmillan, New York.

Hemme, T. (2000): "Ein Konzept zur international vergleichenden Analyse von Politik- und Technikfolgen in der Landwirtschaft", *Federal Agricultural Research Centre* (FAL), Landbauforschung Völkerode, Special Issue 215, Braunschweig.

Isvilanonda S. and W. Kongrith (2008): "Thai Household's Rice Consumption and Its Demand Elasticity", *ASEAN Economic Bulletin*, 25(3): 271–82.

Kuroda Y. and P. Yotopoulos (1978): "A Microeconomic Analysis of Production Behavior of the Farm Household in Japan: a Profit Function Approach", *Economic Review*, 29: 116–29.

Markowitz, H. (1952): "Portfolio Selection", *Journal of Finance*, 7(1): 77–91.

Mausch, K., D. Mithöfer, S. Asfaw and H. Waibel (2009): "Export Vegetable Production in Kenya: Is Large More Beautiful Than Small", *Journal of Food Distribution Research*, 40(3): 115–29.

McCarl, B. A., & Spreen, T. H. (1996): *Applied mathematical programming using algebraic systems* College Station, Texas: Texas A&M University, Department of Agricultural Economics. 466 pp. Available online at: www.agecon.tamu.edu/faculty/mccarl/books.htm. Accessed: November 2008.

National Economic and Social Development Board (NESDB) (2008): *Thailand Poverty Indicators 1988–2007*, National Economic and Social Development Board, Bangkok.

Office of Agricultrual Economics (2010): *Agricultural Statsitics of Thailand 2009*. http://www.oae.go.th./main.php (in Thai). Accessed: November 2010.

Pandey, S., N. T. Khiem, H. Waibel and T. C. Thien (2006): *Household Food Security and Commercialization of Agriculture in Uplands of Vietnam: A Micro-Economic Analysis*, The International Rice Research Institute, Los Banos, Philippines, 106 pp.

Singh, I., L. Squire, J. Strauss and World Bank (1986): *Agricultural Household Models: Extensions, Applications, and Policy*, Inderjit Singh, Lyn Squire, John Strauss (eds), Johns Hopkins University Press, Baltimore.

Tauer, L. W. (1983): "Target MOTAD", *American Journal of Agricultural Economics*, 65(3): 606–10.

Taylor, J. E. and I. Adelman (2003): "Agricultural Household Models: Genesis, Evolution, and Extensions", *Review of the Economics of the Household*, 1: 33–58.

Tongruksawattana, S., E. Schmidt and H. Waibel (2008): "Understanding Vulnerability to Poverty of Rural Agricultural Households in Northeastern Thailand", *mimeo*, paper presented at Deutscher Tropentag, 7–9 October, Hohenheim, Germany.

Tung Phung, D. and H. Waibel (2010): "Food Price Crisis, Poverty and Welfare in Vietnam: An Ex-post Decomposition Analysis", paper presented at International Conference organized by SFB 564, "Sustainable Land Use and Rural Development in Mountainous Regions of Southeast Asia", July, Hanoi, Vietnam.

Valero-Gil, J. N. (2008): "The Effects of Rising Food Prices on Poverty in Mexico", *mimeo*, working paper, Munich Personal RePEc Archive.

Völker, M., and H. Waibel (2010): "Do Rural Households Extract More Forest Products in Times of Crisis? Evidence from the Mountainous Uplands of Vietnam", *Forest Policy and Economics*, 12(6): 407–14.

Völker, M., E. Schmidt and H. Waibel (2008): "Approaches to Modelling Vulnerability to Poverty in Rural Households in Thua Thien Hue Province, Viet Nam", paper presented at Deutscher Tropentag, 7–9 October, Hohenheim, Germany.

World Bank (2005): *Accelerating Vietnam's rural development: growth, equity and diversification* – Volume IV: *Agricultural Diversification in Vietnam*, Hanoi: East Asia and Pacific Region Rural Development and Natural Resources Sector Unit, World Bank.

World Bank (2008): "Rising Food and Fuel Prices: Addressing the Risks to Future Generations", *Human Development Network and Poverty Reduction and Economics Management Network*, World Bank, Washington DC. Policy Research Working Paper No. 4682.

8

Agricultural Diversification and Vulnerability to Poverty: A Comparison between Vietnam and Thailand

Suwanna Praneetvatakul, Tung Duc Phung and Hermann Waibel

8.1 Introduction

Thailand and Vietnam are two emerging market economies where agriculture still plays an important role even though its contribution to their GDP has been reduced from 16 per cent and 40 per cent in 1985 to around 12 per cent and 22 per cent in 2008, respectively.[1] In the rural areas, however, agriculture is still the major source of income and employment. Agriculture in Thailand and Vietnam has differences as well as similarities. One of the main differences relates to the historical perspective. In Vietnam, prior to the introduction of the *doi moi* policy, performance of the agricultural sector was strongly influenced by the centrally planned economic system; the policy change towards a market-based pricing system of agricultural commodities can be seen as a starting point for a period of sustained growth in output and productivity. Today, Vietnam has become a major player in world food markets, and the country now ranks third among the world's leading rice exporters. However, Vietnam's economic policy reform has also introduced risks into the agricultural sector and the rural areas. The process of liberalization and rapid integration into the world economy with less trade protection and reduced subsidies has exposed the domestic markets to the fluctuations of the international markets. In contrast, such risks are not so severe in Thailand, as the agricultural sector has benefited from a long history of commercialization and market orientation. Thailand is now the top exporter for a number of agricultural raw materials and processed food products. The country has a well developed agribusiness sector, with some large multinational co-operations.

In terms of the natural conditions for agricultural production, Thailand is more favoured than Vietnam. High weather risks such as storms, floods and droughts are typical threats for a large part of Vietnam's agricultural areas. Drought is often recorded in the Central Highlands, while floods, typhoons, and storms are very frequent in the North Central Coast (Chaudhry and Ruysschaert, 2007). In recent years, Vietnam has also been strongly affected by livestock diseases such as avian flu and foot and mouth disease. Rural households are mostly affected by these threats, with strong implications for the economy considering that the agricultural sector accounts for almost half of total household income and absorbs 64 per cent of the labour force in rural areas in Vietnam (GSO, 2007). The likelihood of disasters is also increasing as a result of global climate change. A recent study by Dasgupta *et al.* (2007) on the potential impacts of sea level rise in 84 coastal developing countries showed that a 1-metre rise in sea level would affect about 7 per cent of agricultural land and 11 per cent of the population, which could reduce the agriculture sector's GDP by 10 per cent. The highly diverse geographic and geomorphologic conditions in Vietnam lead to considerable heterogeneity of agricultural systems including highly diversified subsistence agriculture in the marginal, mostly mountainous, areas and specialized farming in the more favoured regions.

While drought and flooding also affect parts of agricultural land in Thailand, the magnitude of such shocks are generally less severe than in Vietnam because Thailand has better infrastructure, especially in terms of irrigation and transportation. There is also a difference in the structural conditions and the organization of agriculture. For example, while in Vietnam farm size is small and labour intensity is high, in Thailand the level of mechanization in planting and harvesting is much more advanced.

However, while there are many differences between the agriculture of Thailand and Vietnam there are also similarities between the two. In both countries, agriculture has expanded to the marginal areas, which are marked by remoteness, poor infrastructure, and unstable job prospects as a result of high rates of rural–urban migration and traditional village institutions that are often dysfunctional.

Although even in these areas poverty has declined, households remain vulnerable to poverty due to the risky environment in which they live. Because of the absence or imperfection of formal insurance and credit markets, households in such areas often employ self-insurance strategies (Besley, 1994), in which activity diversification is a major measure.

This paper compares diversification strategies in the six provinces in Thailand and Vietnam included in the project.[2] Such country comparisons are necessary to better understand the success and failure of self-insurance mechanisms in agriculture in emerging market economies, which can provide important lessons to policymakers. The chapter is organized as follows. Sections 8.2 and 8.3 provide the methodology and data used for measuring diversification and its impact on the well-being of rural households and their degree of vulnerability to poverty. The empirical results are presented in Section 8.4. The last section presents some conclusions for policy and further research.

8.2 Diversification and vulnerability

The main objectives of this chapter are to measure diversification strategies of rural households in Thailand and Vietnam and to assess the effect of diversification strategies on household consumption. In addition, the chapter also explores the impact of diversification on vulnerability to poverty of rural households in both countries. Some theoretical consideration is given in the first part of this section. Thereafter, the quantitative measures of diversification are defined.

Reducing income risk by selecting a mixture of activities whose net returns have a low or negative correlation is a major strategy of self-insurance-based risk management (for example, Di Falco *et al.*, 2007; Just and Pope, 2003; Dunn, 1997; Reardon *et al.*, 1992). Diversification through combining activities with low positive covariance and income-skewing effects is a measure traditionally employed by risk-averse small-scale farmers in developing countries. To date, most studies related to diversification have investigated the impact on expected mean and variance of income (for example, Lanjouw *et al.*, 2001; Ersado, 2006). These analyses have mostly ignored the role that the environmental and economic shocks play when poor farmers decide to diversify. However, when developing a strategy to reduce vulnerability to poverty, an assessment of the role of activity diversification should be considered (see CGIAR, 2005; Slater *et al.*, 2007; IFAD, 2008; Tingem and Rivington, 2009). While most previous studies have shown that agricultural diversification can help to reduce income risk and thus it has been concluded that such a strategy can be effective in reducing poverty (Barghouti *et al.*, 2002; Ahmad and Isvilanonda, 2003; Pingali, 2004), it is less clear as to what extent diversification is also an effective strategy to reduce vulnerability to poverty in the rural areas of emerging market economies like Thailand and Vietnam.

To analyse diversification decisions of rural households and their effect on reducing vulnerability, it is necessary to incorporate covariate and idiosyncratic shocks in the respective models (Dercon, 1999).

Generally, poor households living in high-risk environments have developed rather sophisticated (ex-ante) risk-management and (ex-post) risk-coping strategies. For example, Menon (2009) in a study in Nepal found that households used occupational choice as a strategy to cope with rainfall uncertainty. When examining the response to covariate flood and idiosyncratic health shocks among peasant households in the Amazonian tropical forests, Takasaki *et al.* (2002) found that coping strategies include various diversification activities such as collection of food from natural resources, upland cropping and labour adjustment.

The methodology for comparing diversification strategies of rural households in six provinces in Thailand and Vietnam utilizes two steps. First, diversification is analysed as a function of village and household characteristics, shock events experienced by the household and the perceived future risks. In the second step, diversification is used to assess the impact on vulnerability to poverty.[3] In developing a model suitable to explain diversification decisions, Ersado (2006) has listed some important variables: (a) missing or imperfect insurance and credit markets that persuade households to take up self-insurance measures, (b) incomplete input and output markets resulting in the inability to specialize and promote diversification in consumption, (c) ability of ex-post coping actions, (d) complementarities and positive interactions between activities, and (e) returns to assets which can vary across assets, time and space.

When comparing diversification strategies of rural households between two countries, it is useful to base the comparison on aggregate measures such as land and labour allocation decisions. For land, households may select agricultural enterprises where the correlation between price and yield is low or by adjusting the crop portfolio to the specific characteristics of their land, for example growing different crops on different parcels of land in order to minimize the effect of biotic or abiotic stresses. The second option for households is to reallocate their labour into non-farm activities since it can be assumed that wage income is largely uncorrelated with agricultural income. In addition, non-farm income can help to accumulate assets in a good agricultural year, which increases the household's capacity to smooth consumption in the years when shocks affect agriculture.

Based on the analysis of some of the features of agriculture in Thailand and Vietnam and this brief review of the literature, it can be hypothesized that generally activity diversification could be an important strategy for rural households in emerging market economies as well. Secondly, it can be expected that the diversification strategy will depend on the socio-economic and institutional conditions in the two countries.

There are several methods to measure the diversification, as discussed by Culas and Mahendrarajah (2005) and Minot *et al.* (2006). In this study, two diversification indices, namely the Simpson Index of Diversity (SID) and the Shannon-Weaver Index (SW), are used. These were calculated for both land and labour as the two major resources of rural households. The SID gives more weight to the dominant activities of the household portfolio allocation; this is not the case with the SW index, which underscores the dominant activities within the portfolio. The SID is defined as:

$$SID = 1 - \sum_i P_i^2 \qquad (8.1)$$

where, P_i is the proportion of household portfolio allocated to activity *i*. The index ranges from 0 to 1, with 0 if a household devotes all resources to one activity and approaches 1 with rising number of activities in the portfolio.

The SW is defined as:

$$SW = -\sum_i P_i Ln\ (P_i) \qquad (8.2)$$

P_i is again the proportion of activity *i* in the portfolio.

The diversification indices for labour allocation were based on the main occupations of the household members aged from 10 to 60. Hence, P_i is the proportion of household labour devoted to each of the three main occupations, for example agriculture, wage employment and non-farm self-employment. The SID and the SW for agricultural land were based on the area that households allocated to each crop during the crop year 2006/07. Thus, P_i is the share of the total agricultural land allocated to crop *i*. In Thailand 23 crops were included, and in Vietnam a total of 26 crops were considered.

8.3 Data and methodology

8.3.1 Data

The data used for this analysis are from the two waves of a household survey conducted in three provinces, both in Vietnam (Dak Lak, Hue, Ha Tinh) and Thailand (Buriram, Ubon Ratchathani, Nakhon Phanom). The data for this analysis was taken from a comprehensive questionnaire of a total of almost 4400 households, and 440 village questionnaires. The sample was distributed proportionately to the population size of each district. There were some adjustments to over-sampling in the remote areas in Vietnam where the population is small and thus the number of households would have been insufficient for the estimation.[4] Hence, a weighting procedure was used to adjust for over-sampling in remote areas. Two questionnaires were used in this survey, one for the household and the other one for the village. In both waves, the household questionnaire was administered to collect information about various aspects of the socio-economic conditions of the household. It includes demographic conditions, migration, education, health, agriculture, off-farm and non-farm employment, borrowing and lending, remittance, insurance, consumption and assets. There is a special section that collects information about the different types of shocks that the household has experienced since 2002 and the different types of future risks that the household perceives to exist in the next five years. It includes the common (flood, drought, storm, avian flu) and the idiosyncratic (sickness, death, accident, loss of job, bankruptcy) shocks and risks. For each type of shock and risk, the respondent was asked to evaluate the impacts on his/her household as well as the coping strategies that the household used to cope with the shock. In the agriculture section, data was collected on agricultural land, the type of crops, grown area, and cost and output of each crop that a household has grown in the past 12 months. In addition, household members were asked to report about type of jobs, the duration, income and cost, for each type of occupation. This information can be used to calculate the SID and SW indices for each household.

The village questionnaire contains information about the infrastructure and basic public goods that could affect the livelihoods of the households and the decision of the households to cope with shocks and risks.[5]

8.3.2   Model to explain diversification

A linear regression model was used to measure the effect of shocks and risks on the portfolio and income diversification of the household.

$$Y_{ij} = \beta_0 + \sum_{k=1}^{K} \beta_k X_{ijk} + \sum_{n}^{N} \gamma_n X_{ijn} + \sum_{m}^{M} \varphi_m X_{ijm} + \varepsilon_{ij} \qquad (8.3)$$

Where Y_{ij} are the two measures of diversification for labour and land of the household i in village j, the number of income sources and the number of crops grown by household i in village j.

X_{ijk} are variables reflecting the various household and village characteristics believed to influence the diversification decision of a household.

A variable S_{ijn} for agricultural and economic shocks was included, while social and demographic shocks were excluded as these are not expected to have any impact on the diversification decision of the household. S_{ijn} was defined as dummy variable to capture the number of shocks of the household i in village j. R_{ijm} was included as risk variable. These reflect the likelihood of different types of events that the respondent, representing the household, would expect to take place in the next five years, and the impacts of these events on the household. R_{ijm} has the same variable labels as S_{ijn}. Thus, R_{ijm} reflects the risk management strategy of the household while S_{ijn} refers to the risk-coping strategy.

8.3.3 The effect of diversification on household consumption

Diversification of a household portfolio is expected to contribute to income stability and smoothness of consumption, and to reduce the vulnerability of the household to poverty. In this section, we investigate the impact of labour and land diversification on household consumption. This relationship is the pre-condition to establish a linkage between diversification and vulnerability; the latter defined as expected consumption to fall below a defined benchmark (poverty line). As pointed out by Deaton (1992), the main factors hypothesized to explain future consumption of a household are its current income and wealth, expected income and its variance, and the ability to smooth consumption in case of income shocks. These factors depend on household characteristics and external factors. The reduced form of the general consumption function could be expressed as:

$$C_{it} = C(X_i, \beta_t, S_{it}, \delta_{it}, e_{it}) \tag{8.4}$$

Where C_{it} is the consumption of the household i at the time t, X_i is a bundle of the household characteristics, S_{it} is the shock faced by household i at time t, β_t and δ_{it} are the corresponding regression coefficients, and e_{it} is the error term.

The measurement of the impact of diversification on consumption or income requires panel data because reallocation of resources may not be immediately measurable. For instance, changes in livestock along with allocation of land towards feed crops may lead to a higher production only in the following season or year. Also, moving labour from agriculture to non-farm activities may require other farm or household adjustments whose impacts in terms of income or consumption can only be measured later. The model developed here follows the models applied by Glewwe and Hall (1995), Dercon and Krishnan

(2000), Ersado (2006) and Isik-Dikmelik (2006). However, the model used here benefits from the panel nature of the data and thus allows land and labour allocation decisions in the previous period to be related with household consumption in the current period. This is formalized in the following equation:

$$Lnc_{it+1} = \alpha_i + \theta_t D_{it} + \beta_t X_{it} + \gamma_t \Delta X_i + \delta_{it+1} S_{it+1} + \varepsilon_{it+1} \tag{8.5}$$

Where Lnc_{it+1} is the log of household consumption of the household i in 2008, D_{it} is the land or labour diversification of the household in 2007, X_{it} are household characteristics in the year 2007, ΔX_i is the change in household characteristics between 2007 and 2008, and S_{it+1} are shocks that the household faced in 2008.

Deaton (1992) showed that consumption is dependent on income. Since in our models land and labour diversification are correlated with household income, they are also correlated with the error term of Equation (8.4). Hence an OLS regression could give a biased estimate. To overcome this problem, an instrumental variable approach was applied as recommended by Davidson and Mackinnon (1993). The first stage of a two-stage least squares (2SLS) procedure is defined as:

$$D_{it} = \omega_i + \varphi_t X_{it} + \pi_{it} Z_{it} + u_{it} \tag{8.6}$$

Where X_{it} is a vector of explanatory variables for both Equation (8.6) and Equation (8.4), and Z_{it} are instrumental variables that affect land or labour diversification D_{it}. These variables affect consumption only indirectly. As instrumental variables, the number of land plots a household is using for cropping and the share of households with one or more migrants are used. Wald tests of endogeneity are used to assess the validity of these assumptions.

8.3.4   Measuring the impact of diversification on vulnerability to poverty

The last hypothesis to be assessed is to what extent diversification as a self-insurance strategy is effective in reducing vulnerability to poverty. In defining the latter, we refer to the most common method of vulnerability, namely the probability of falling below the poverty line in the future (Chaudhuri 2003; Christiaensen and Boisvert 2000; Prichett *et al.* 2000). Due to the lack of the panel data, most current papers have used cross-sectional data to estimate the vulnerability to poverty of a household. We propose a probit model to estimate the chance of household consumption observed in the year *t+1* (2008) using the household characteristics and household land and labour diversification decision in 2007. In addition, we add the shocks that occurred in 2008. Thus, the following equation is developed:

$$V_{it} = P_i(\ln c_{it+1} < \ln z) = \alpha_i + \theta_t D_{it} + \beta_t X_{it} + \delta_{it+1} S_{it+1} + \varepsilon_{it+1} \tag{8.7}$$

In order to capture the endogeneity problem as described under 3.3, a 2SLS estimation procedure with the same instrumental variables as specified in Equation (8.4) is used.

8.4 Results

In this section, the results of the models outlined above are presented. First, a comparison is made between the factors that determine diversification of land and labour in both countries using the two diversification indices defined above. Next, the results of the consumption function are presented, and finally the relationship between diversification and vulnerability to poverty is established which allows some policy conclusions relevant to both countries to be drawn.

8.4.1 Diversification

Figures 8.1(a) and Figure 8.1(b) show the distribution of land (1a) and labour (1b) diversification measured by the SID. The two graphs underline the differences between the provinces of the two countries especially in land diversification. Clearly, in the three Thai provinces a large share of crop production is monoculture, consisting mainly of rice, cassava and rubber in areas with better agricultural conditions. In Vietnam, while there is practically no fully specialized farm-level crop production, farms are more diversified than in Thailand, the majority of households having an SID of more than 50 per cent. The difference in labour diversification, however, is less pronounced, although it is higher in Thailand.

Overall, the pattern of land and labour diversification is a good reflection of the differences in the socio-economic and institutional conditions of agriculture in the two countries. Agriculture in Thailand is marked by a kind of dualistic pattern, with on the one hand specialized farms, and on the other the existence of part-time farms with a high share of household members working on off-farm activities. In Vietnam, farming is still more subsistence oriented, and wage employment opportunities are still less developed. Hence, mixed cropping is a typical land use system in Vietnam, especially in the more remote areas.

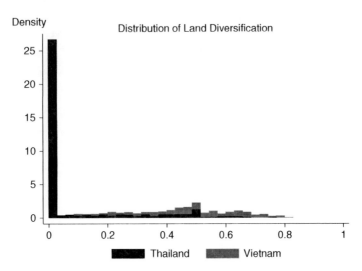

Figure 8.1(a)   Frequency distribution of land of Simpson Index of Diversification

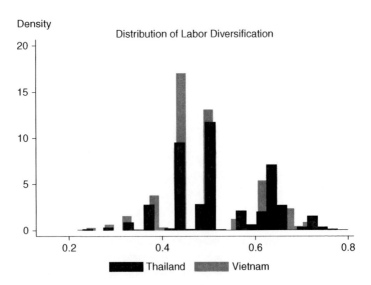

Figure 8.1(b) Frequency distribution of labour of Simpson Index of Diversification

Table 8.1 presents the variables included in all subsequent models, namely (i) diversification model, (ii) consumption model and (iii) vulnerability model. The mean and standard deviations show the major differences between rural households in the two countries, comparing the diversification indices between the two countries, the shocks experienced and the risks perceived by the respondents.

Table 8.1 Descriptive statistics of diversification models, Thailand and Vietnam, 2007

Variable code	Variables	Thailand		Vietnam	
		Mean	Std. Dev	Mean	Std. Dev
SID_land	Diversification of land based on SID	0.07	0.15	0.27	0.25
SW_land	Diversification of land based on SW	0.13	0.26	0.46	0.44
SID_labour	Diversification of labour based on SID	0.43	0.22	0.35	0.24
SW_labour	Diversification of labour based on SW	0.66	0.38	0.53	0.38
Log_cons08	Log of consumption per capita in 2008 (PPP US$)	7.20	0.65	6.90	0.59
Poor08	Poor household in 2008 (1 = yes, 0 = otherwise, using PPP U$2 per day)	0.16	0.36	0.29	0.45
S1	HH has experienced at least one shock in the past 5 years (1 = yes, 0 = no)	0.35	0.48	0.41	0.49
S2	HH has experienced at least two shocks in the past 5 years (1 = yes, 0 = no)	0.05	0.23	0.16	0.37
S3	HH has experienced 3 or more shocks in the past 5 years (1 = yes, 0 = no)	0.02	0.13	0.03	0.18
R1	HH expected at least one risk in the next 5 years (1 = yes, 0 = no)	0.10	0.30	0.15	0.35
R2	HH expected at least two risks in the next 5 years (1 = yes, 0 = no)	0.15	0.36	0.21	0.40

Continued

Table 8.1   Continued

Variable code	Variables	Thailand		Vietnam	
		Mean	Std. Dev	Mean	Std. Dev
R3	HH expected 3 or more risks in the next 5 years (1 = yes, 0 = no)	0.67	0.47	0.50	0.50
Aloss	Total asset lost due to shocks in the past 5 years (VND million or 1000 bath)	15.19	78.66	4.17	10.61
Borr	Household is currently borrowing (1 = yes, 0 = no)	0.80	0.40	0.66	0.47
SxBorr	Interaction between shock and current borrowing	0.49	0.50	0.55	0.50
Agri_asset	Total asset value for crop production (VND million or 1000 bath)	59.32	143.96	6.80	18.08
Labour	Total household member aged from 10 to 60	3.71	1.75	3.68	1.91
Ethnic	Ethnicity of the household (1 = Kinh & Hoa, 0 = other)	0.93	0.25	0.79	0.40
Age_hh	Age of the household head	54.75	13.25	47.94	13.86
Sage_hh	Square age of the household head	3172.91	1521.17	2490.37	1465.98
School_hh	Number of years in school of the household head	4.89	3.05	6.63	4.02
Sex_hh	Sex of the household head (1 = male, 0 = female)	0.74	0.44	0.84	0.36
D_ratio	Dependency ratio (year 2008)	0.42	0.50	0.48	0.53
Land	Total land area owned by household (hectare)	2.50	3.53	0.79	1.73
Land_LUC	Share of the household land area having Land Use Certificate (LUC)	0.90	0.28	0.64	0.45
Land_irri	Share of the irrigated land of the household	0.10	0.29	0.46	0.45
Land_plot	Number of agriculture land plots	2.61	1.20	3.42	1.71

Continued

Table 8.1 Continued

Variable code	Variables	Thailand		Vietnam	
		Mean	Std. Dev	Mean	Std. Dev
Migrant	Percentage of household in village has migrated person (%)	52.47	18.79	35.87	19.70
Distance	Distance from village to district town (km)	13.45	8.18	13.64	10.32
Shock08	Household experienced at least one shock in 2008	0.59	0.49	0.70	0.46
Hhsize07	Household size 2007	4.89	2.00	4.86	1.81
Tot_asset07	Total asset value in 2007 (VND million or 1000 bath)	59.93	144.17	7.34	19.28
Diff_hhsize	Difference in household size	0.27	0.88	0.13	0.51
Diff_tot_asset	Difference in total asset (VND million or 1000 bath)	−41.37	128.68	1.28	17.37
Diff_D_ratio	Difference in dependency ratio	0.03	0.33	0.02	0.29
School_adult	Average number of years in school of household member aged 10 to 60	0.44	2.27	7.52	3.21
Mtransport	Main transportation of the village (1 = motorbike, bus, 0 = walk, bicycle, ox cart)	0.96	0.19	0.50	0.50
Coastal_Area	Household is living in coastal area (1 = yes, 0 = otherwise)	n/a	n/a	0.27	0.45
Lowland_Area	Household is living in lowland rice area (1 = yes, 0 = otherwise)	n/a	n/a	0.32	0.47
Buri	Household is living in Buriram province (1 = yes, 0 = otherwise)	0.37	0.48	n/a	n/a
Ubon	Household is living in Ubon Ratchathani (1 = yes, 0 = otherwise)	0.44	0.50	n/a	n/a

Source: DFG FOR 756 household panel survey 2007 and 2008.

The data show that in Thailand consumption is higher and in Vietnam poverty, based on head-count ratio, is more severe. In both countries, however, poverty thus defined is above the national average.

As discussed in Section 8.1, Vietnam is more affected by climate-related risks, which is reflected in the difference in number of shocks (Table 8.1). The difference in shock experience, however, is not really reflected in the risk expectation. For example, 67 per cent of the households in Thailand expected three or more risky events to occur in the next five years, in contrast to only 50 per cent of households in Vietnam. On average, land endowment in Thailand is several times higher in Vietnam, whereas land security through titling is more advanced in Thailand. Labour capacity, measured by the number of household members aged from 10 to 60, is similar in both countries. On the other hand, formal education measured by number of years in school is higher in Vietnam than in Thailand. Access to irrigation in Vietnam is four times that of Thailand, while urban–rural migration can be observed in both countries.

The first model explains the labour diversification and allows a comparison between the two countries. The results are shown in Table 8.2. By and large, the factors that explain diversification of labour, measured by SID and SW, differ between Thailand and Vietnam. We find that some of the shocks are significant in the Thailand model, which suggests that households use reallocation of labour as an ex-post coping strategy. However, this strategy seems less feasible in Vietnam due to lower off- and non-farm opportunities. In both countries, however, expected risks lead to labour diversification, which suggests that rural households who anticipate a riskier future tend to place their labour outside agriculture as an ex-ante coping measure. Several of the significant variables underline similar structures in both countries; for instance, households' labour capacity and the number of land plots show a significantly positive effect.

Among the variables that show a significant negative effect on diversification is the age of the household head. Households with older people often have a lower propensity to migrate, or they may have returned home from urban migration. Also, the negative effect of the land size variable in both countries suggests that larger farms are less likely to be engaged in off- or non-farm work. Likewise, in Vietnam a longer distance to the village from the nearest district town reduces the household's ability to diversify labour. Furthermore, the significant interaction between borrowing and shocks in Vietnam shows that access to credit can be important to enable households to

Table 8.2 Results of model to explain labour diversification

Independent variables	Thailand		Vietnam	
	SID	SW	SID	SW
S1	0.034**	0.054**	−0.004	−0.014
	(0.013)	(0.022)	(0.013)	(0.021)
S2	0.029	0.051	−0.018	−0.032
	(0.020)	(0.035)	(0.018)	(0.029)
S3	0.012	0.022	−0.028	−0.056
	(0.036)	(0.060)	(0.033)	(0.051)
R1	0.022	0.030	0.018	0.030
	(0.023)	(0.037)	(0.020)	(0.030)
R2	0.045**	0.067*	0.024	0.041
	(0.022)	(0.036)	(0.019)	(0.029)
R3	0.058***	0.087***	0.033**	0.048*
	(0.020)	(0.033)	(0.017)	(0.026)
Aloss	0.000	0.000	−0.001	−0.001
	(0.000)	(0.000)	(0.000)	(0.001)
Borr	0.012	0.018	−0.034*	−0.060**
	(0.016)	(0.026)	(0.019)	(0.030)
SxBorr	-0.002	−0.002	0.063***	0.106***
	(0.016)	(0.027)	(0.019)	(0.030)
Agri_asset	0.000**	0.000**	−0.000	-0.000
	(0.000)	(0.000)	(0.000)	(0.000)
Labour	0.039***	0.074***	0.028***	0.050***
	(0.003)	(0.005)	(0.003)	(0.005)
Ethnic	n/a	n/a	0.019	0.040
	n/a	n/a	(0.018)	(0.028)
Age_hh	−0.001***	−0.001**	−0.001***	−0.002***
	(0.000)	(0.001)	(0.000)	(0.001)
School_hh	0.001	0.001	0.002	0.004
	(0.002)	(0.003)	(0.002)	(0.002)

Continued

Table 8.2 Continued

Independent variables	Thailand		Vietnam	
	SID	SW	SID	SW
Sex_hh	0.005	0.010	−0.014	−0.025
	(0.012)	(0.019)	(0.016)	(0.025)
Land	−0.005***	−0.009***	−0.008*	−0.012**
	(0.002)	(0.003)	(0.004)	(0.006)
Land_LUC	−0.027	−0.041	−0.019	−0.029
	(0.019)	(0.033)	(0.012)	(0.019)
Land_irri	0.026	0.037	0.041***	0.062***
	(0.016)	(0.027)	(0.012)	(0.019)
Land_plot	0.019***	0.032***	0.010***	0.018***
	(0.004)	(0.007)	(0.003)	(0.006)
Migrant	0.001***	0.002***	0.001**	0.001***
	(0.000)	(0.000)	(0.000)	(0.000)
Distance	−0.001*	−0.003**	−0.001**	−0.002*
	(0.001)	(0.001)	(0.001)	(0.001)
Number of observations	1,984	1,984	2,091	2,091
Adjusted R2	0.161	0.180	0.100	0.112

Note: Constant not reported. Robust standard errors in parentheses. The symbols *, ** and *** indicate that the coefficient is statistically significant at the 10, 5 and 1 per cent levels respectively.

Source: Authors' calculations.

smooth consumption in response to shocks through the diversification of labour.[6] When comparing the two diversification measurements, the models show quite consistent results. Therefore, in the subsequent analysis we limit the analysis to a single measure of diversification, namely the SID.

In conclusion, households in Thailand seem to be in a better position to move labour quickly out of agriculture into both the formal and informal labour markets, whereas this possibility is more limited in Vietnam. However, in both countries, expectation of high risk is a force driving the reallocation of labour into different sectors.

The land diversification model can provide information about the ability of rural households to use land diversification as a self-insurance measure in response to agricultural shocks in particular. Table 8.3 shows that shock and risk variables have a significant positive impact on the land allocation in Vietnam but are insignificant for the

Table 8.3 Results of model to explain land diversification

Independent variables	Thailand		Vietnam	
	SID	SW	SID	SW
S1	−0.011	−0.019	0.026**	0.039*
	(0.011)	(0.018)	(0.013)	(0.022)
S2	−0.009	−0.015	0.072***	0.116***
	(0.019)	(0.031)	(0.018)	(0.031)
S3	−0.008	−0.001	0.107***	0.175***
	(0.037)	(0.062)	(0.033)	(0.056)
R1	0.005	0.002	0.046**	0.059*
	(0.022)	(0.034)	(0.019)	(0.031)
R2	−0.002	−0.003	0.048***	0.076***
	(0.020)	(0.030)	(0.017)	(0.029)
R3	0.003	0.007	0.039**	0.062**
	(0.020)	(0.031)	(0.015)	(0.026)
Aloss	0.000	0.000	−0.000	-0.000
	(0.000)	(0.000)	(0.001)	(0.001)
Borr	0.027**	0.040**	0.045**	0.068**
	(0.012)	(0.018)	(0.019)	(0.031)
SxBorr	0.005	0.013	−0.026	−0.037
	(0.013)	(0.020)	(0.019)	(0.032)
Agri_asset	−0.000	−0.000	−0.001	−0.001
	(0.000)	(0.000)	(0.000)	(0.001)
Labour	−0.000	−0.001	−0.001	0.002
	(0.003)	(0.004)	(0.003)	(0.006)
Ethnic	n/a	n/a	−0.010	−0.011
	n/a	n/a	(0.017)	(0.025)

Continued

Table 8.3   Continued

Independent variables	Thailand		Vietnam	
	SID	SW	SID	SW
Age_hh	−0.001	−0.002	0.007**	0.010**
	(0.002)	(0.003)	(0.003)	(0.005)
Sage_hh	0.000	0.000	−0.000**	−0.000*
	(0.000)	(0.000)	(0.000)	(0.000)
School_hh	0.000	0.001	0.005***	0.010***
	(0.002)	(0.003)	(0.001)	(0.002)
Sex_hh	0.009	0.017	−0.032**	−0.045*
	(0.010)	(0.014)	(0.016)	(0.026)
Land	0.003**	0.005**	−0.001	−0.002
	(0.001)	(0.002)	(0.003)	(0.005)
Land_LUC	−0.009	−0.011	0.001	−0.004
	(0.017)	(0.025)	(0.012)	(0.020)
Land_irri	0.033**	0.047**	−0.182***	−0.300***
	(0.014)	(0.021)	(0.013)	(0.021)
Land_plot	0.046***	0.076***	0.058***	0.114***
	(0.006)	(0.010)	(0.004)	(0.007)
Migrant	−0.000	−0.000	−0.000	−0.008
	(0.000)	(0.001)	(0.000)	(0.020)
Distance	0.000	0.000	−0.001	−0.001
	(0.001)	(0.001)	(0.001)	(0.001)
Number of observations	1,702	1,702	1,890	1,890
Adjusted R2	0.146	0.160	0.292	0.325

Note: Constant not reported. Robust standard errors in parentheses. The symbols *, **, and *** indicate that the coefficient is statistically significant at the 10, 5 and 1 per cent levels respectively.
Source: Authors' calculations.

Thailand sample. One reason could be that the higher share of non-farm activities in the total household income of the Thai households and the more advanced process of rural–urban migration has a profound effect on their portfolio of agricultural activities. On average, households in the three provinces in Thailand have only 1.38 crops, compared to 2.22 in Vietnam; the part-time nature of farming in many of the remote, low potential agricultural areas in rural Thailand puts more limits on land diversification as a coping strategy than is the case in Vietnam.

Contrary results can also be observed for farm size and the share of irrigated land. In Thailand these two variables are significantly positively related to diversification while the opposite is the case in Vietnam. Larger farms with good infrastructure in Thailand tend to have a highly commercialized agriculture and thus diversify their agricultural portfolio. In Vietnam, farm size is smaller, and when irrigation infrastructure exists this is more likely to stimulate intensive rice production. Furthermore, in Vietnam older household heads tend to have a more diversified crop portfolio, possibly due to their knowledge, their attitude to risk and their greater experience of shocks.

In both countries, households with good access to credit and a higher number of agricultural plots tend to have a more diversified crop portfolio. However, in Vietnam the interaction between shocks and credit access is significant only for the SID index. Generally, the results are consistent with the results of the two country models. In conclusion, shocks and risks are really influential for land allocation decisions made by the households in Vietnam, while in Thailand for full-time farms other driving forces, such as existing and upcoming commercial opportunities, make households adopt a wider agricultural portfolio.

8.4.2   Effect of diversification on household consumption

In this section, the effects of land and labour diversification decisions in 2007 on household consumption in 2008[7] are investigated. Table 8.4 presents the regression results of 2SLS models.[8] The results confirm the difference in structure and the organization of agriculture between the two countries; in Thailand, it is labour diversification that has a positive effect on household consumption, while in Vietnam it is diversification of land. The equations generally give results consistent with the expected signs of the regression coefficients. Age, education of the household head, overall education level of household members

Table 8.4 Effect of diversification on consumption

Independent variables	Thailand		Vietnam	
	Coefficient	Standard error	Coefficient	Standard error
SID_land	0.001	0.003	0.003**	0.001
SID_labour	0.020***	0.006	0.003	0.008
Ethnic	n/a	n/a	0.312***	0.036
Age_hh	0.006***	0.002	0.004**	0.002
School_hh	0.038***	0.006	0.007**	0.004
Hhsize07	−0.141***	0.019	−0.103***	0.017
School_adult	0.007	0.006	0.033***	0.013
Tot_asset07	0.005***	0.001	0.023***	0.002
Mtransport	0.120	0.084	0.143***	0.025
D_ratio	−0.046	0.067	−0.159***	0.034
Diff_hhsize	−0.035*	0.019	−0.036	0.022
Diff_tot_asset	0.004***	0.001	0.020***	0.002
Diff_D_ratio	−0.084	0.057	−0.033	0.073
Shock08	0.018	0.031	−0.044*	0.025
Coastal_Area	n/a	n/a	−0.022	0.049
Lowland_Area	n/a	n/a	0.067	0.050
Buri	0.269***	0.047	n/a	n/a
Ubon	0.146***	0.046	n/a	n/a
_cons	6.127***	0.257	6.318***	0.193
Number of observations	1,986		1,855	

Note: Cluster at commune level. The symbols *, ** and *** indicate that the coefficient is statistically significant at the 10, 5 and 1 per cent levels respectively; n/a means "not available"

Instrument variables: Number of Land Plots and Percentage of Household have migrant people in the village.

Tests of endogeneity: H_0: variables are exogenous.

Vietnam: Robust score chi2(2) = 9.77 p = 0.0076); Robust regression F(2,1736) = 5.198 (p = 0.0056).

Thailand: Robust score chi2(2) = 19.08 (p = 0.0001); Robust regression F(2,1968) = 9.75 (p = 0.0001).

Source: Authors' calculations.

engaging in productive activity and value of productive assets have significant and positive coefficients. Household size and dependency ratio are significant, but they affect consumption negatively. The panel nature of our data provides additional explanatory variables, for example, the change in productive assets between the two survey years has a positive effect on consumption. Our model results support the notion of expanding the productive capacity in agriculture in response to rising food prices in 2008, which in turn leads to higher consumption for net sellers of food. We found that per capita consumption of households who invested more in productive assets in 2008 had increased significantly in both countries. However, the effect is more pronounced in Vietnam than in Thailand. In addition, the increase in household size between the two years has a negative effect on consumption in the three Thai provinces. This could be a result of the back migration of household members due to the economic downturn in 2008.

Reducing consumption to cope with shocks is one of the major coping strategies of the household. However, in Vietnam shocks were found to be significant for household consumption. It suggests that consumption smoothing to cope with shocks is limited in Vietnam compared to households in Thailand. Other interesting differences between the two countries are shown in transportation infrastructure; households living in the village with poor means of transportation (bicycle or ox cart) show lower levels of consumption.

This is different in Thailand, where motorized transportation is highly dominant. Another differentiating factor is ethnicity; this matters a lot in Vietnam, where ethnic minority households (H'mong, Tay, Nung, Dao and so on) have considerably lower levels of consumption.

In conclusion, our consumption models largely confirm the results found when comparing diversification strategies between the two countries. The different problems experienced in the agriculture of remote rural areas suggests different policy needs. For example, while in Thailand social protection may deserve more attention, in Vietnam infrastructure investments should be a main priority, and the government should pay more attention to the development needs of ethnic minority households.

8.4.3 Impact of diversification on vulnerability to poverty

Table 8.5 shows the results of probit models to assess the possibility of the households in our sample falling below the poverty line

Table 8.5   Effect of diversification on vulnerability to poverty

Independent variables	Thailand		Vietnam	
	coefficient	standard error	coefficient	standard errors
SID_land	−0.006	0.010	−0.009**	0.005
SID_labour	−0.043**	0.017	0.029	0.033
Ethnic	n/a	n/a	−1.019***	0.145
Age_hh	−0.008*	0.004	−0.002	0.007
School_hh	−0.051**	0.020	−0.008	0.014
Hhsize07	0.297***	0.053	0.193***	0.065
School_adult	−0.015	0.020	−0.121**	0.049
Tot_asset07	−0.036***	0.005	−0.095***	0.009
Mtransport	−0.066	0.203	−0.372***	0.099
D_ratio	−0.172	0.187	0.467***	0.132
Diff_hhsize	0.156***	0.049	0.248**	0.097
Diff_tot_asset	−0.035***	0.005	−0.074***	0.009
Diff_D_ratio	0.080	0.145	0.229	0.274
Shock08	−0.034	0.088	0.209*	0.110
Coastal_Area	n/a	n/a	−0.012	0.191
Lowland_Area	n/a	n/a	−0.223	0.197
Buri	−0.677***	0.123	n/a	n/a
Ubon	−0.419***	0.117	n/a	n/a
_cons	0.913	0.716	6.318***	0.193
Number of observations	1986		1,855	

Note: Cluster at commune level. The symbols *, **, and *** indicate that the coefficient is statistically significant at the 10, 5 and 1 percent levels respectively; n/a means "not available".
Instrument variables: Number of Land Plots and Percentage of Household has migrant people in the village.
Wald test of exogeneity for Vietnam: chi2(2) = 9.62 Prob > chi2 = 0.0081

in 2008. We use the same explanatory variables as in the consumption models. Results largely confirm the findings of the previous models. Land diversification in Vietnam is an effective strategy to reduce future poverty, and the same is true of labour diversification in Thailand. In both countries, households with more assets are less vulnerable; the variable which measures change in assets between two periods underlines this effect. Likewise, the direction of influence of transportation, ethnicity, dependency ratio, shocks and province differences in the Thailand variables are consistent. The opposite is, however, the case for the larger households; the effects of back migration as a result of economic slowdown may show up in this result. While in the consumption model (Table 8.4), change in household size is significant only in Thailand, in the vulnerability model this is also the case for Vietnam. This suggests that poor households in Vietnam engaged in often unstable non-farm employment are more vulnerable to falling into poverty.

Education of the household head, which is generally lower in Thailand (Table 8.1), is an important factor, as it reduces the vulnerability of the poor households. The same can be said for the education of household workers in Vietnam. Likewise, older people in Thailand are likely to be poorer than those in Vietnam. Overall, the models strongly suggest that diversification is effective in reducing future poverty. On the other hand, there are a number of factors based on the control of rural households that can make them fall into poverty.

8.5 Conclusion

This chapter shows that rural households in Thailand and Vietnam used diversification as self-insurance mechanism for ex-post and ex-ante coping. However, the diversification strategy differs in accordance with socio-economic conditions. We found that the rural households in Vietnam who are confronted with more weather-related shocks and who expect more agricultural risks tend to grow a higher diversity of crops, and so have a higher future consumption and a lower chance to be poor in the future. Thai households using labour diversification as a coping strategy, and households with higher levels of labour diversification, are less likely to be poor in the future. The results also partly reflect the differences in economic and institutional conditions in these countries. Households in Thailand are blessed with better non-farm job opportunities on the one hand, and have bigger farm sizes as compared to Vietnamese households on the other hand.

Improving the infrastructure and the access to credit for the households in Vietnam could reduce the negative impact of shocks. In Thailand, however, credit does not seem to be a strong limiting factor for the choice of shock-coping strategies. In both countries, land reconsolidation policies could increase the specialization process and the efficiency of resource use.

The findings from this chapter confirm the initial hypothesis that in both countries diversification is an important strategy to reduce vulnerability to poverty of rural households. One of the policy implications of these results is that there is a need for better infrastructure in the areas of transportation and irrigation as well as a need for some institutional innovations in the field of microfinance. Undoubtedly, better access to credit could help the farmers in Vietnam to specialize and thereby reduce their vulnerability to poverty. In addition, poverty reduction programmes in Vietnam should give more emphasis to ethnic minorities. In Thailand, providing more stable job opportunities, as well as improving education and skills of the rural population, can help reduce vulnerability to poverty, since better education will further increase options for labour diversification.

Notes

1. http://data.worldbank.org/indicator/NV.AGR.TOTL.ZS
2. DFG Research Unit 756, see Chapter 1.
3. The data used for this analysis comes from a panel household survey carried out under the auspices of the DFG research project "Impact of Shocks on the Vulnerability to Poverty: Consequences for Development of Emerging Southeast Asian Economies".
4. Detailed information about sample design of this survey is discussed in Hardeweg *et al.* (2007).
5. For details of data collection see Chapter 3.
6. When using a fixed effects model and omitting the village variables the overall fit of the model gets reduced, suggesting that location factors are influential of labour diversification.
7. As mentioned in Section 8.2, the Simpson Index of Diversification (SID) has a value in the range from 0 to 1. A household is considered as not being diversified if its SID index has the value 0 and vice versa when it has value 1. For interpretation, we have changed the value of SID land and labour of the household into a percentage; for instance, if the SID land index has a value of 0.35, it will have a value of 35 in our models.

8. The test of endogeneity shows that we can reject H_0 that land and labour diversification are exogenous variables for both countries.

References

Ahmad, A. and S. Isvilanonda (2003): "Rural Poverty and Agricultural Diversification in Thailand", *mimeo*, Paper presented at the Second Annual Swedish School of Advanced Asia and Pacific Studies (SSAAP), 24–26 October, Lund, Sweden.

Barghouti, S., Kane. S., Sorby, K. and M. Ali (2004): "Agricultural Diversification for the Poor: Guidelines for Practitioners", Agriculture and Rural Development Department, World Bank; http://www.google.com/url?sa=t&rct=j&q=&esrc=s &source=web&cd=1&ved=0CFoQFjAA&url=http%3A%2F%2Fwww.ruta.org %3A8180%2Fxmlui%2Fbitstream%2Fhandle%2F123456789%2F480%2FRN2 1.pdf%3Fsequence%3D1&ei=iAApUN_uAcySiQf1h4HYDg&usg=AFQjCNGn4 7bjvZorqBDPVd8xI1v8-nmSag

Besley, T. (1994): "Savings, Credit and Insurance", in *The Handbook of Development Economics*, vol. IIIA (ed. J. Behrman and T.N. Srinivasan). Amsterdam. North-Holland Press.

CGIAR (2005): *System Priorities for CGIAR Research 2005–2015*, Science Council Secretariat, Rome.

Chaudhuri, S. (2003): "Assessing Vulnerability to Poverty: Concepts, Empirical Methods and Illustrative Examples", *mimeo*.

Chaudhry, P. and G. Ruysschaert (2007): "Climate Change and Human Development in Vietnam: A Case Study", *Human Development Report 2007/2008 Occasional Paper*, UNDP.

Christiaensen, L. J. and R. N. Boisvert (2000): "Measuring Household Vulnerability: Case Evidence from Northern Mali", *Cornell University Working Paper*, No. 05, Ithaca, NY.

Culas, R. and M. Mahendrarajah (2005): "Causes of Diversification in Agriculture over Time: Evidence from Norwegian Farming Sector", *mimeo*, Paper provided by European Association of Agricultural Economists (EAAE), 23–27 August, Copenhagen.

Dasgupta, S. *et al.* (2007): "The Impact of Sea Level Rise on Developing Countries: A Comparative Analysis", *World Bank Policy Research Working Paper*, No. 4136, Washington DC.

Davidson, R. and J. G. MacKinnon (1993): *Estimation and Inference in Econometrics*, Oxford University Press, New York.

Deaton, S. (1992): *Understanding Consumption*, Clarendon Press, Oxford.

Dercon S. (1999): "Income Risk, Coping Strategies and Safety Nets", *World Bank Research Observer*, 17(2): 141–66.

Dercon, S. and P. Kishnan (2000): "Vulnerability, Seasonality and Poverty in Ethiopia", *Journal of Development Studies*, 36(6): 25–53.

Di Falco, S. and J-P. Chavas (2009): "On Crop Biodiversity, Risk Exposure, and Food Security in the Highlands of Ethiopia", *American Journal of Agricultural Economics*, 91(3): 599–611.

Di Falco, S., J.-P., Chavas and M. Smale, (2007), "Farmer Management of Production Risk on Degraded Lands: Wheat Diversity in Tigray Region, Ethiopia", *Agricultural Economics*, 36: 147–156.

Dunn E. (1997): *Diversification in the Household Economic Portfolio*, AIMS Project Report, Management Systems International, Washington DC.

Ersado, L. (2006): "Income Diversification in Zimbabwe: Welfare Implications from Urban and Rural Areas", *World Bank Policy Research Working Paper*, No. 3964, Washington DC.

General Statistics Office of Vietnam (GSO) (2007): *Result of the Vietnam Household Living Standards Survey (VHLSS) 2006*, Statistical Publishing House, Hanoi.

Glewwe, P. and G. Hall (1995): "Are Some Groups More Vulnerable to Macroeconomic Shocks than Others? Hypothesis Tests Based on Panel Data from Peru", *Journal of Development Economics*, 56(1): 181–206.

Hardeweg, B., H. Waibel, S. Praneetvatakul and P. D. Tung (2007): "Sampling for Vulnerability to Poverty: Cost Effectiveness Versus Precision", in Tielkes, E. (ed.), *Tropentag 2007*, Centre for International Rural Development, University of Kassel, Witzenhausen.

Isik-Dikmelik, A. (2006): "Trade Reforms and Welfare: An Ex-Post Decomposition of Income in Vietnam", *World Bank Policy Research Working Paper*, No. 4049, Washington DC.

Just, R. E. and R. D. Pope (2003): "Agricultural Risk Analysis: Adequacy of Models, Data, and Issues", *American Journal of Agricultural Economics*, 85(5): 1249–56.

Lanjouw, P., J., Quizon and R. Sparrow, (2001), "Non-Agricultural Earnings in Peri-Urban Areas of Tanzania: Evidence from Household Survey Data", *Food Policy* 26(4): 385-403;

Menon, N. (2009): "The Effect of Rainfall Uncertainty on Occupational Choice in Rural Nepal", *Journal of Development Studies*, 45(6): 864–88.

Minot, N., Epprecht, M., Anh, T.T.T. and L.Q. Trung (2006): "Income Diversification and Poverty in the Northern Uplands of Vietnam", *IFPRI Research Report*, No. 145, International Food Policy Research Institute.

Pingali, P. (2004): "Agricultural Diversification: Opportunities and Constraints", *mimeo*, FAO Rice Conference, 12–13 February, Rome.

Reardon, T., C. Delgado and P. Matlon (1992): "Determinants and Effects of Income Diversification amongst Farm Households in Burkina Faso", *Journal of Development Studies*, 28 (1): 264–96.

Skoufias, E. (2003): "Economic Crises and Natural Disasters: Coping Strategies and Policy Implications", *World Development*, 31(7): 1087–102.

Slater, R., Peskett, L., Ludi, D. and D. Brown (2007): *Climate Change, Agricultural Policy and Poverty Reduction – How Much Do We Know?* ODI Natural Resource Perspectives 109.

Takasaki, Y., B. L. Barham and O. T. Coomes (2002): "Risk Coping Strategies in Tropical Forests: Flood, Health, Asset Poverty, and Natural Resource Extraction", *mimeo*, Paper prepared for the 2nd World Congress of Environmental and Resource Economists, 23–27 June, Monterey.

Tingem, M. and M. Rivington (2009): "Adaptation for Crop Agriculture to Climate Change in Cameroon: Turning on the Heat", *Mitigation and Adaptation Strategies for Global Change*, 14(2): 153–68.

World Bank (1998): *Vietnam: Advancing Rural Development from Vision to Action. A report for Consultative Group Meeting for Vietnam*, World Bank in collaboration with the Government of Vietnam, ADB, UNDE, FAO, and CIDA and in consultation with international donors and NGOs.

9
Ex-Post Coping Strategies of Rural Households in Thailand and Vietnam

*Songporne Tongruksawattana, Vera Junge, Hermann Waibel,
Javier Revilla Diez and Erich Schmidt*

9.1 Introduction

Understanding shocks and their consequences is essential for the design of effective poverty alleviation strategies in poor countries and in emerging market economies. Information about existing coping strategies of poor households is especially needed in order to design effective public support schemes to mitigate negative shocks. Also, a better understanding of the effectiveness of self-insurance measures is important, as this may provide some hints on chances and constraints to establish private insurance markets and public risk management schemes. The literature on vulnerability to poverty suggests that shock-coping activities are not independent of shock type and household characteristics (for example Berloffa and Modena, 2009; Dercon, 2007; Hoddinott, 2006; Rashid *et al.*, 2006). However, there is a need to further explore this interaction on strong empirical grounds, which is only possible with a comprehensive empirical dataset.

To better understand the effects of shocks and choices of coping activities, four broad categories of shocks are defined in this study, namely agricultural, economic, health and social shocks (Klasen *et al.*, 2010). Agricultural shocks[1] refer to shocks caused by adverse weather conditions and other events of nature such as flooding, landslides, storms, drought, crop pests and livestock diseases. Economic shocks include price shocks,[2] job loss and collapse of own business, credit problems and termination of remittances from absent family members, relatives or friends. Illness or accidents of household members as well as death and birth are categorized under health shocks. Lastly, social obligation such as money spent on ceremony, theft, conflicts with neighbours, divorce or imprisonment of household members fall into the category of social shocks.

In the context of this research project, panel data were collected in six provinces in Northeastern Thailand and the Central Highlands of Vietnam (see Chapter 1 and Chapter 3). The survey instrument which has been administered to a sample of over 4000 rural households provides information that can help to answer the following four questions, dealt with in this paper:

1. What are the major shocks that rural households face in both countries?
2. What ex-post coping measures are used, and do they differ between the two countries?
3. What are the reasons that some households undertake coping actions in response to shocks while others do not?
4. Which factors determine the choice of a specific coping activity?

Below, Section 9.2 briefly reviews the literature on factors that are believed to influence the coping actions and presents the selected variables used in the subsequent analyses. Section 9.3 addresses research questions 1 and 2 above by discussing major shocks and the corresponding coping responses of rural households in the six provinces from the two panel waves. Following these descriptive analyses, Section 9.4 introduces two analytical models. The first model helps to explain the reasons why some households do undertake coping actions while others do not (see research question 3). The second model is used to explain the choice of specific coping actions (see research question 4). Section 9.5 summarizes the empirical findings and offers some policy conclusions.

9.2   Determinants of coping decisions

Shock events can be individual household-specific (idiosyncratic) such as illness and death of a household member, or they can have an impact on a larger group of population in the same area at the same time (covariate) such as adverse weather conditions and market fluctuation (Dercon, 2002). Effects of shocks are translated into income loss, which can put financial constraints on households and can lead to asset loss that may decrease future earning possibilities and savings. Since the majority of rural households engage in agricultural production, they are particularly prone to agricultural shocks, for example drought and flooding, which cause damage on yield and value of agricultural output and in turn reduce household income (Tongruksawattana *et al.* 2008; Asiimwe and Mpuga, 2007; Pandey *et al.*, 2007). The adverse effect of shocks is generally more severe for the poor who are less ex-ante insured against shocks and are therefore more likely to reduce consumption than wealthier households (Jalan and Ravallion, 1997). At the same time, poor rural households are also more likely to experience health shocks such as illness and death of a household member than are wealthier households (Heltberg and Lund, 2009; Tongruksawattana *et al.*, 2008). In some circumstances, these households are even more fragile to health shocks than to agricultural shocks (Kochar, 1995).

Concerning responses to shocks, existing studies show that households do not randomly select coping activities but follow a structured method that takes types of shocks and household resources into account (for example Frankenberger, 1992; Cutler, 1986; Watts, 1983 and 1988). In general, households who face sudden income or asset loss try to compensate for the loss, and attempt to earn additional income and/or reduce savings. As found by Rashid *et al.* (2006), the choice of coping actions of rural households in Bangladesh depends on the type of shocks as well as household characteristics, assets, and the diversity and stability of household income sources. Other authors (for example Newhouse, 2005; Kochar, 1999) found that when households face agricultural income loss, they try to compensate through off-farm or non-farm employment, asset sales and borrowing. However, poor households have to rely more on agricultural casual wage labour than on employment with regular salaries (Kijima *et al.*, 2006). Another study on flood and health shocks of households in Amazonian tropical areas observed that coping responses are influenced by local environmental endowments and household asset holdings (Takasaki *et al.*, 2002). For example, in coping with flood, a dominant coping activity was intensification of fishing efforts (Takasaki *et al.*, 2010). Recent studies also found that disposition of savings and assets, and income diversification, especially from off-farm employment and informal credit, help households cope with income shortfalls as a consequence of shocks (Heltberg and Lund, 2009; Dercon, 2007). While households with higher levels of assets tend to use savings or take up additional loans to cope with income loss, poor households are more likely to work off-farm (Berloffa and Modena, 2009; Hoddinott, 2006). Carter and Maluccio (2002) pointed out the role of social capital as an important element of coping mechanisms. The coping possibility of a household for any shock is limited in a community where many households suffer from covariate shocks, since mutual support from social network is restrained (Alderman and Paxson, 1992).

Based on the literature, we decided to distinguish three groups of influential determinants when it comes to responses to shocks: (i) household characteristics, (ii) type of shock and shock severity, and (iii) location factors.

First, among household characteristics, five variables were selected as potentially influential, namely income, wealth, education, occupation and number of migrant members. For example, households with higher income and wealth status generally find it easier to compensate the losses from shocks and their recovery time is shorter (for example Cutter *et al.*, 2003; Glewwe and Gillette, 1989). Beyene (2008) showed that higher education levels enable access to more qualified jobs in the non-farm economy and better access to information about the possibilities of mitigating shocks, such as the availability of public support programs. The demographic situation of a household, such as the share of household members engaged in agriculture and the number of migrant household members, is important for the coping capacity for shocks. Migration affects the age structure of a household, with younger and older people left behind which can reduce their coping capability. On the other hand, migration is generally associated with remittances, which can reduce the negative effect of shocks.

Type and severity of shocks are the second major determinants of coping actions. Type is classified in the four categories, agriculture, economic, health and social, as explained in Section 9.1. Severity was measured as respondents' assessment of income or asset loss caused by a shock, converted to per capita data. This is reasonable because households are confronted with direct damage costs as well as mitigation costs and, in some cases, costs of ex-ante risk management and prevention in order to reduce the impact of future risks.

The third group of determinants includes location factors such as travelling distance between the village and the provincial capital, and access to market and financial institutions measured by travelling time. These conditions can enhance a household's ability to cope. For example, if a provincial capital is easily reachable, then a larger labour market may facilitate access to non-farm jobs. At the same time a nearby town can possibly provide easier access to a market and borrowing in order to compensate for the smaller size or the lack of own village market and banking institutions (Beyene, 2008). However, regional characteristics can also hamper households' abilities to cope, that is if a region is heavily dependent on just one economic sector, opportunities can turn into constraints in the case of economic crisis (Cutter *et al.*, 2003).

9.3 Shock incidences and coping responses

This section provides insight into the general importance of shocks, shock types and the corresponding responses to shocks of rural households in the six provinces in Thailand and Vietnam. For the purpose of this study, all shocks with at least low subjective severity[3] that occurred during the first survey period in 2007 as well as during the second period in 2008 are considered. The results are generated from a comparative static analysis of the two data sets. This is the first step required to obtain a broader picture of shock situations and coping behaviour.

The overall situation of households with external shocks in both periods can be described by the proportion of households who reported at least one shock experience. Our data reveals that the share of shock-affected households is higher in Vietnam than in Thailand in both periods. In the second survey period, there are more households affected by shocks in both countries (see Table 9.1). Within each country the shock situation is quite different in the provinces, indicating that local factors play an important role and have to be taken into account in the models estimated in Section 4.

Moreover, looking at the number of shocks reported, our data clearly shows that many households are affected by more than one shock in either of the periods, and the number of shocks per household significantly increased in the second period in all provinces except Dak Lak (see Table 9.1, column "no. of shocks per household").

Based on these findings, we focused our descriptive analysis on households who experienced shocks in the respective periods. We identified the relative importance of the four groups of shocks defined in Section 1, measured in terms of frequencies. Figure 9.1 illustrates the type of shock incidences as percentage of affected households in the six provinces in both survey periods. Clearly agricultural shocks, especially flooding and drought, are the most common in both countries. This observation shows the same pattern as that found in weather-related disaster surveys (for example, World Bank, 2005). At the overall country level, agricultural shocks are more frequent in Vietnamese households (42 per cent in the first wave, 60 per cent in the second wave) than in Thai households (18 per cent in the first wave, 38 per cent in the second wave), and the strong increase from the first to the second period illustrates the high volatility of weather conditions over time and the associated acute sensitivity of rural households to agriculture-related incidences. In Thua Thien Hue and Ha Tinh in particular, the majority of households are affected by this type of shock. Both provinces are on the coastline of the South China Sea with a high exposition to storms which can lead to flooding. Dak Lak and the Thai provinces are more inland and therefore are less exposed to storms but generally are more at risk from drought.

Table 9.1 Number of households and shock incidences

Province/Country	1st wave (2007)			2nd wave (2008)		
	No. of surveyed households[1]	No. and % of households with shock experience [2]	No. of shocks per household	No. of surveyed households[1]	No. and % of households with shock experience [2]	No. of shocks per household
Thailand						
Buriram	796	180 (23)	1.14	788	443 (56)	1.64
Ubon Ratchathani	928	355 (38)	1.34	939	606 (65)	2.00
Nakhon Phanom	389	149 (38)	1.27	383	231 (60)	1.96
Total	2113	684 (32)	1.27	2110	1280 (61)	1.87
Vietnam						
Ha Tinh	677	317 (47)	1.38	709	637 (90)	2.23
Thua Thien Hue	697	487 (70)	1.45	691	485 (70)	1.72
Dak Lak	743	468 (63)	1.43	733	403 (55)	1.36
Total	2117	1272 (60)	1.42	2133	1525 (71)	1.84
Both countries	4230	1956 (46)	1.37	4243	2805 (66)	1.85

[1] In both survey periods some households were removed from the analysis due to incomplete data.
[2] Percentages are shown in parentheses.
Source: DFG survey

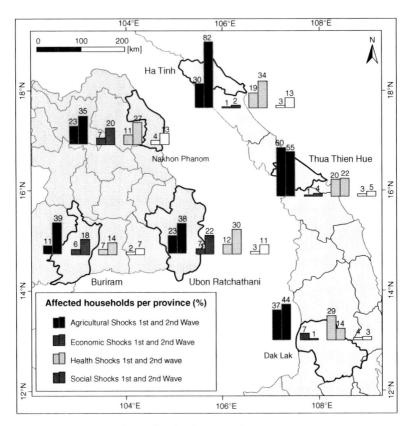

Figure 9.1   Shock incidences by shock type and province
Source: DFG survey.

Health shocks, especially illness of a household member, represent
the second most common shock type experienced by households in
both countries. In Thailand, the proportion of affected households
increased from 10 per cent in the first wave to 24 per cent in the
second wave, distributed among the provinces fairly similarly, although
somewhat less frequent in Buriram. In Vietnam, a constant proportion
of the households in the three provinces are affected by health shocks
(national average of 23 per cent in both survey years). However, in the
second survey period households in Ha Tinh and Thua Thien Hue
reported an increase in health shock incidences, while the opposite is
found in Dak Lak.

In contrast to the identical ordering of agricultural and health
shocks, the third most frequent shock type differs in the two countries.

In Thailand, economic shocks represent the third most common shock type for households in all provinces to a similar degree, with a considerable increase from 6 per cent on average in the first wave to 20 per cent on average in the second wave. In Vietnam, however, this type of shock is the least frequent (3 per cent in the first wave, 2 per cent in the second). Within the group of economic shocks, price shocks dominate in both countries, although Thai households are apparently more prone to price shocks than are Vietnamese households. Lastly, social shocks, mainly social obligation such as spending money for a ceremony, form the least frequent shock type in Thailand (3 per cent in the first wave, 10 per cent in the second wave). This type of shock, however, is found to be the third most frequent in Vietnam (4 per cent in the first wave, 7 per cent in the second wave).

In a third step, we characterize households that experienced shocks by means of the variables that are most likely to influence shock-coping strategies. The selected variables are grouped according to the three general determinants (household, shock, and village characteristics) derived in Section 2, and the national averages of the variables for the two countries and the two surveys are summarized in Table 9.2. In order to assure exogeneity, income per capita was defined as income before shocks, and wealth per capita was similarly defined as the sum of all productive and consumption assets including value of the house, own land, value of livestock and financial savings before shocks. Similarly, migration as coping strategy was explicitly specified as reaction to shocks.

As shown in Table 9.2, household income per capita on average is higher in Thailand than Vietnam in both periods, although the income increase from the first to the second period was significantly higher in Vietnam (+44 per cent) than in Thailand (+4 per cent). The same applies for household wealth per capita, which in Thailand is more than double that in Vietnam. In contrast to household income, household wealth has declined considerably in Thailand, but only slightly in Vietnam, from the first to the second survey period (see Table 9.2). Education, measured by school years of the household member with the highest education level, is higher in Vietnam, but the share of household members whose primary or secondary occupation is agriculture is 50 per cent in both countries. On the other hand, the number of migrants in Thailand during the first period is almost double that of Vietnam. However, in the second period migration increased relatively more strongly in Vietnam despite the relatively higher increase in shocks in Thailand.

With regard to location factors, there are marked differences between the two countries (Table 9.2). Although the distances to the provincial capital are about 20 per cent longer in Thailand than in Vietnam,

Table 9.2 Shock-affected household characteristics

Explanatory variables			Thailand						Vietnam					
			1st wave		2nd wave				1st wave		2nd wave			
			N = 684		N = 1280				N = 1272		N = 1525			
Variable description	Variable code	Unit	Mean	Std. Dev	Mean	Std. Dev			Mean	Std. Dev	Mean	Std. Dev		
Household characteristics														
Income per capita before shock	INC	100 US$ PPP[a]	21.6	24.0	22.5	38.1			13.4	18.9	19.3	29.2		
Wealth per capita before shock	WTH	100 US$ PPP[a]	156.1	227.1	39.3	173.7			64.5	138.4	64.2	98.0		
Maximum years of schooling	EDU	Years	8.4	3.6	8.8	3.7			9.0	3.4	9.3	3.4		
Ratio of household members engaged in agriculture	AGM	%	0.5	0.3	0.5	0.3			0.5	0.3	0.5	0.3		
Number of migrant member	MGM	Persons	0.9	1.3	1.1	1.5			0.5	0.9	0.7	1.0		
Shock characteristics														
Income loss per capita														
Agricultural shock	INCL_AG	100 US$ PPP[a]	1.5	3.0	1.8	5.4			1.8	6.9	3.3	9.0		

Economic shock	INCL_EC	100 US$ PPP[a]	0.8	3.6	0.8	8.1	0.3	3.5	0.2	3.0
Health shock	INCL_HL	100 US$ PPP[a]	0.8	4.1	0.4	2.6	0.8	3.6	0.3	1.8
Social shock	INCL_SC	100 US$ PPP[a]	0.1	0.9	0.2	1.8	0.1	1.0	0.1	0.6
All shock	INCL_ALL	100 US$ PPP[a]	3.2	6.0	3.1	10.6	3.1	8.5	3.9	10.0
Asset loss per capita										
Agricultural shock	ASSL_AG	100 US$ PPP[a]	0.5	3.1	0.3	1.8	0.9	3.0	0.6	1.9
Economic shock	ASSL_EC	100 US$ PPP[a]	0.9	5.3	0.1	1.4	0.1	1.3	0.01	0.1
Health shock	ASSL_HL	100 US$ PPP[a]	1.0	5.0	0.3	2.9	0.5	2.3	0.1	0.7
Social shock	ASSL_SC	100 US$ PPP[a]	0.5	3.2	0.2	2.3	0.1	1.1	0.1	0.7
All shock	ASSL_ALL	100 US$ PPP[a]	2.9	8.5	0.8	4.7	1.6	3.9	0.8	2.4
Village characteristics										
Distance from village to provincial capital	CAP	Kilometre	57.3	33.3	57.6	33.3	47.6	53.6	42.4	30.6
Travelling time to the next market	MKT	Minutes	14.1	14.3	15.2	14.1	17.0	11.4	0.18	12.1
Travelling time to the next bank	BANK	Minutes	23.0	13.6	22.8	12.8	30.5	25.6	30.9	25.3

[a] Measured in *PPP US$ (2005)* with conversion factor for Thai Baht (capital B) of 0.0600 (1st wave) and 0.0582 (2nd wave); for 1,000 Vietnamese Dong (capital D) of 0.1976 (1st wave) and 0.1812 (2nd wave)
Note: Standard deviations are shown in brackets.
Source: DFG survey.

travelling to the nearest market and bank in Thailand is less time consuming, due to its better infrastructure.

Although the average income loss per capita in absolute terms was at comparable levels in both countries during the first period, the income loss proportional to the households' initial income was markedly higher in Vietnam (–23 per cent) than in Thailand (–15 per cent).[4,5] In the second period, the income loss in Vietnam increased in absolute terms; however, the proportional loss decreased slightly – to 20 per cent, due to the important increase in real income (+38 per cent, from PPP US$1340 to PPP US$1930).

In contrast, in Thailand income level and income loss in absolute terms remained almost constant, and hence relative income loss also changed by only a marginal –15 per and –14 per cent in the first and second waves respectively). This indicates a higher vulnerability to poverty for households in Vietnam than in Thailand. On the other hand, the average asset loss per capita in absolute terms in the first period was significantly higher in Thailand, and the average loss decreased in both countries to almost the same PPP US$80. But again, the loss of assets relative to the wealth before shocks draws a quite different picture. Despite a large asset loss reduction (–72 per cent) from period 1 to period 2 in Thailand, there was a noteworthy increase of the proportional asset loss to household wealth before shocks, from –1.8 per cent to –4.1 per cent. This is due to a sharp decrease in the wealth level of affected households from period 1 to period 2 (–11 per cent). However, the proportional average asset loss per capita in Vietnam decreased from –2.5 per cent to –1.2 per cent due to the almost constant wealth level of affected households in Vietnam in both periods. Comparing the effects of the four different types of shocks, agricultural (that is, weather-related) shocks cause the highest average income loss per capita, accounting for roughly half of the income loss of all shocks in both countries. Referring to the asset loss, however, agricultural shocks are clearly dominant in Vietnam alone in both survey periods. However, in Thailand health shocks cause the highest asset loss in the first period whereas agriculture and health shocks are of equal importance in the second period.

In the next step, coping behaviour as a response to different types of shocks in both countries and periods is analysed. As summarized in Table 9.3, the majority of shock incidences in both countries was treated with at least one coping action, although more shock incidences were left uncoped with during the second period (Thailand 70 per cent and 51 per cent, Vietnam 79 per cent and 65 per cent in the first and second waves respectively). Non-coping may result from, for example, no specific action being available, or the perception, when acting, of low shock implications relative to the net benefits involved. In some cases, no special action may appear to be necessary, for example in the case of health problems in which a household may decide that there is no need to see a doctor, or no opportunity to do so. The phenomenon of coping or refraining from coping is more specifically addressed in Section 4, Model 1.

Concerning coping actions by shock type, observations in both periods show that health shocks often received more coping actions than other shock types (see Table 9.3).

Health shocks aside, Thai households are more responsive to economic and social shocks than to agricultural shocks even though agricultural shock was the most frequent and severe type of shock (as previously shown in Table 9.2). On the other hand, in Vietnam more coping actions were applied to deal with agricultural and economic shocks than with social shocks.

In order to generate information on the coping behaviour of households and to identify interrelations between shock types and specific coping actions, only shock-affected households who applied a coping action are considered in the following. In this context, a coping action is defined as an explicit and active undertaking to counteract the negative shock effect as reported by the households. On the other hand,

Table 9.3 Percentage of shocks where coping action is taken

	Coping action (%)			
	Thailand		Vietnam	
	1st wave	2nd wave	1st wave	2nd wave
Type of shock	N = 868	N = 2390	N = 1809	N = 2805
Agricultural	58	31	74	62
Economic	80	62	72	57
Health	86	70	91	79
Social	68	63	61	53
Total	70	51	79	65

Note: N is the number of shock incidences (see Table 9.1).
Source: DFG survey.

households were categorized as "do not cope" if they did nothing to deal with any of the shocks due to various reasons mentioned above.

The majority of households who undertook a coping action selected only one activity to cope with a shock although some households reported multiple measures taken simultaneously or consecutively. The coping activities reported by the households are categorized into four groups:

(i)   "Remittances and transfers", that is taking up transfers and grants from public support schemes and asking for (additional) remittances from migrant members, relatives, friends and neighbours.

(ii) "Resource reallocation", which is reallocating household resources for additional income generation, such as realigning labour including off-farm/non-farm employment and temporary or permanent migration. In some cases, children are taken out of school to work. Under this coping measure, household agricultural resources can be further adjusted by means of crop substitution and reduction of production inputs.

(iii) "Borrowing", that is taking loans from formal and informal sources. In general, common institutions for formal lending are commercial banks, the Bank for Agriculture and Agricultural Cooperatives (BAAC), village banks and cooperative banks in Thailand, and the Vietnam Bank for Social Policy (VBSP) and the Vietnam Bank for Agriculture and Rural Development (VBARD) in Vietnam. Informal borrowing sources include relatives, friends, neighbours, private money lenders and village funds.

(iv)"Use savings and sell assets", that is households can draw on savings or sell their assets such as land or livestock in exchange for a prompt and large amount of cash.

Table 9.4 and Table 9.5 summarize the relations between coping actions and the shock types in the two periods. The distribution of coping activities is presented as a percentage of all coping actions reported.[6] The calculated shares show some similarities as well as differences regarding coping behaviour between the two countries and survey periods. In the first wave, borrowing is the most frequent type of coping action in both countries, accounting for 33 per cent (Thailand) and 44 per cent (Vietnam) of all coping actions applied. The importance of borrowing remained high in the second wave (22 per cent and 34 per cent in Thailand and Vietnam respectively). However, in the second wave, the coping action most often applied in Thailand is the liquidation of

Table 9.4 Distribution of coping actions in percentage of all coping actions[1] taken per type of shock, Thailand

Type of shock	Survey period	No. of households who took coping action	Remittances and transfer	Resource reallocation	Borrowing	Use savings and sell assets
				(%)		
Agriculture	1st wave	309	33	26	25	16
	2nd wave	356	24	29	16	31
Economic	1st wave	138	4	30	48	18
	2nd wave	343	8	46	22	24
Health	1st wave	248	24	4	32	40
	2nd wave	494	24	4	24	48
Social	1st wave	53	9	8	49	34
	2nd wave	182	24	8	28	40
Total[2]	1st wave	748	23	18	33	26
	2nd wave	1375	20	22	22	36

[1] Coping actions always added up to 100%.
[2] For one household, multiple types of shocks and multiple coping actions per shock are possible.
Source: DFG survey.

Table 9.5 Distribution of coping actions[1] taken per type of shock, Vietnam

Type of shock	Survey period	No. of households who took coping action	Remittances and transfer	Resource reallocation	Borrowing	Use savings and sell assets
			(%)			
Agriculture	1st wave	1026	9	37	37	17
	2nd wave	1412	10	50	30	10
Economic	1st wave	60	–	20	53	27
	2nd wave	33	–	39	39	22
Health	1st wave	660	9	11	52	28
	2nd wave	542	21	14	43	22
Social	1st wave	58	7	10	50	33
	2nd wave	93	18	18	33	31
Total[2]	1st wave	1804	9	26	44	21
	2nd wave	2080	13	39	34	14

[1] Coping actions always added up to 100%.
[2] For one household, multiple types of shocks and multiple coping actions per shock are possible.
Source: DFG survey.

savings and selling of assets (36 per cent), whereas Vietnamese households most often referred to re-allocation of resources (39 per cent). This high share of borrowing emphasizes the importance of access to credit to cope with shocks. The coping action less frequently applied is the taking up of remittances from migrant household members, relatives, friends and neighbours as well as drawing on transfers from public programmes. In this respect, however, there is a considerable difference between Thailand and Vietnam, with much lower relative frequencies across all four types of shocks in Vietnam.

With respect to shock types, agricultural shocks in Vietnam generally cause the same actions as other shock situations. In the first period, borrowing and resource reallocation are the measures most frequently used (37 per cent), but in Period 2, resource reallocation went up to 50 per cent while borrowing and liquidation of savings went down. Economic setbacks are most often counteracted by borrowing in both countries in the first survey year (Thailand 48 per cent and Vietnam 53 per cent), while in the second year, frequency of borrowing to cope with economic shocks in Thailand decreased to 22 per cent and resource allocation increased (see Table 9.4). On the other hand, borrowing in Vietnam was down to 39 per cent in Period 2, and resource allocation increased to the same level (see Table 9.5).

Furthermore, remittances and public transfers were not used at all to cope with economic shocks in Vietnam in both periods. Finally, health and social shocks in Vietnam were most frequently counteracted by means of borrowing, while Thai households preferred borrowing and savings, with varying importance between the two periods.

In the next section, the methodology will be outlined and results will be presented that should provide an answer to the remaining research questions: 1) What is the difference in household and other characteristics between households who decide to undertake any coping action and those who do not? and 2) what is the precise relationship between household, shock and village characteristics and choice of coping activity?

9.4 Modelling coping decisions and choice of coping activity

9.4.1 Methodology

Assessing the choice of households to take or refrain from coping actions can be illustrated by means of a neoclassical random utility model for discrete choice decision-making (Greene, 2003; Manski, 1977; Fishburn, 1970).

When facing a shock, a household has two mutually exclusive choices: either to actively cope in order to minimize the damage or loss, or not to cope, that is to passively bear the consequences of the shock (see Section 9.3). Each of the alternatives is associated with advantages (utilities). The value of the utility associated with coping (U_1) and the utility associated with not coping (U_0) are intended to be index functions of deterministic variables (x') and stochastic elements (ε_0 and ε_1). β_0 and β_1 are parameters measuring the signs and magnitudes of the deterministic variables

$$\text{Utility from coping:} \quad U_1 = x'\beta_1 + \varepsilon_1 \tag{9.1}$$

$$\text{Utility from not coping:} \quad U_0 = x'\beta_0 + \varepsilon_0 \tag{9.2}$$

Keeping all other factors constant, a household will maximize utility constrained by their ability to cope, captured by the variable vector **x**. The utility is unobservable, so that straightforward application of the economic model is impossible. However, assuming utility maximization, the choice is observable and reveals which of the alternatives provides a higher utility. Hence, the observed choice (y) to be explained is binary, taking the value 1 for a coping action and 0 for non-coping, and we assume that a given set of explanatory variables (**x**) disposes the individual to cope with or to refrain from coping with a certain probability. The probability of choosing a coping action (observation $Y=1$) reflects the probability that utility from coping (U_1) is higher than utility from not coping (U_0) and for no coping action the opposite is observed (observation($Y = 0$)):

$$\text{Probability to cope:} \quad \Pr[Y = 1 \mid x] = \Pr[U_1 > U_0] \tag{9.3}$$

$$\text{Probability not to cope:} \quad \Pr[Y = 0 \mid x] = \Pr[U_1 > U_0] \tag{9.4}$$

The utility from taking a coping action can be captured as the benefit from undertaking measures that compensate for income and asset losses caused by shocks.

To estimate the relationship between coping action and explanatory variables, we applied a discrete choice decision-making model developed by Nelson and Maddala (Nelson, 1974; Maddala, 1999). The dependent variable in this model is an indicator of a discrete binary choice that is unobservable (Y_i^*), and is assumed to be a function of some household characteristics (X_i) and an error term ε_i for all households i up to n.

$$Y_i^* = X_i\beta + \epsilon_i; \quad i = 1,\dots,n \tag{9.5}$$

The result of the decision Y_i – in our case the chosen coping action – is observed, and takes the value 1 if a coping action is taken and 0 otherwise. The model can be expanded to any given number of coping activities $j=1,2,...,J$. The response probability that a coping action is chosen depends on the values of X_i and the parameters β which describe the impact of changes in X_i on the probability and the covariance of error terms (Greene, 2003; Pindyck and Rubinfeld, 1998).

$$Y_{ij} = \begin{cases} 1 \text{ (cope)} & \text{if } Y_i^* = X_i\beta + \varepsilon_i > 0 \\ 0 \text{ (do not cope)} & \text{if } Y_i^* \leq 0 \end{cases} \quad ; j = 1,...J \tag{6}$$

Theoretically, our research questions address two stages of decision making. In the first step, households decide between coping and non-coping action. To solve this problem the univariate binary response model can be applied (see Model 1 below). In the second step, the household will decide on the type of coping action. For this step the expanded model that allows for the coexistence of several strategies for one type of shock is needed. For this purpose, a multivariate probit regression with a standard normal distribution is suitable because it permits non-exclusiveness and non-exhaustiveness of the dependent choices, and it relaxes the assumption of the independence of the irrelevant options assumed by a logit model (Greene, 2003). The use of probit regression is becoming widely accepted in similar literature which explores the correlation between shocks and coping activities, and multivariate probit is appropriate for making different choices at a point in time where the dependent choice variables are binary (for example Rashid *et al.*, 2006, Takasaki *et al.*, 2002).

The functional form of a probit model assumes a cumulative normal distribution of the error term:

$$\Pr(Y_{ij} = 1 \mid X_i) = \Phi(\beta'X_i) \tag{9.7}$$

Estimation of a univariate binary probit model is based on the maximum likelihood method, and the log-likelihood function for a sample of n observations is:

$$\log L = \sum_{y_i=0}^{n} \log[1 - \Phi(\beta'X_i)] + \sum_{y_i=1}^{n} \log \Phi(\beta'X_i) \tag{9.8}$$

for observation $i = 1,...,n$.

The multivariate probit model takes the form of the equation (9.6) with an extension of the error term ε_i which now has multivariate normal distribution, each with a zero mean and variance-covariance matrix V, where V has values of 1 on the leading diagonal and correlations $\rho_{jk} = \rho_{kj}$ as off-diagonal elements to allow for correlation with each other (Cappellari and Jenkins, 2003):

$$Y_{i1} = \begin{cases} 1 \text{ (coping activity 1)} & \text{if } Y_{i1}^* = \beta_1 X_{i1} + \varepsilon_{i1} > 0 \\ 0 \text{ (otherwise)} & \text{if } Y_{i1}^* \leq 0 \end{cases} \tag{9.9}$$

$$Y_{i2} = \begin{cases} 1 \text{ (coping activity 2)} & \text{if } Y_{i2}^* = \beta_2 X_{i2} + \varepsilon_{i2} > 0 \\ 0 \text{ (otherwise)} & \text{if } Y_{i2}^* \leq 0 \end{cases} \tag{9.10}$$

$$Y_{ij} = \begin{cases} 1 \text{ (coping activity J)} & \text{if } Y_{ij}^* = \beta_J X_{ij} + \varepsilon_{ij} > 0 \\ 0 \text{ (otherwise)} & \text{if } Y_{ij}^* \leq 0 \end{cases} \tag{9.11}$$

Based on the simulated maximum likelihood method, estimation of the multivariate probit model applies the Geweke-Hajivassiliou-Keane smooth recursive conditioning simulator, which draws upon the product of sequentially conditioned univariate normal distribution functions with joint probability.

In the following, the empirical analysis presents the results along the theoretical concept of a two-step procedure from above. Firstly, the general decision to cope or refrain from coping is determined by a univariate probit model. Secondly, the selection of a specific type from the four coping actions set out in Section 9.3 is analysed by a multivariate probit regression which uses the same explaining variables as the univariate model of the first step.

9.4.2   Determinants of coping actions

The models set up to reproduce the discrete binary choice relate the reported outcome of the decision to cope or not to cope to the variables derived in the descriptive section as most likely to influence the decision-making process (see Section 9.3). The estimation results for the two countries and the two survey periods are presented in Table 9.6. Although the economic significance in terms of the magnitudes of the estimated coefficients are scale-sensitive and reflect only minor impacts on the decision-making process, the statistical significance is quite good and generally reflects plausible and significant directions (signs) of the influences on the probability to cope or to refrain from coping. Among the three types of determinants (household characteristics, shock characteristics and village characteristics), shock characteristics in terms of income and asset losses (INCL and ASSL) are statistically of highest importance for all types of shocks (agricultural, economic, health and social), and the signs are positive with only one exception (income loss due to agricultural shocks in Thailand for the first period, see Table 9.6). The results confirm the expectation that the probability to cope increases with the level of income and asset losses in both countries. The consistent positive significant coefficients of income and health shocks in all models suggest that health shocks receive the utmost attention by households, regardless of socio-economic conditions. In contrast, the variables representing household characteristics show unexpected low conformity and changing significance between the countries and periods. The same is true for location factors that show varying significance among the provinces within a country and between the survey periods.[7]

In both countries, the variable household wealth (WTH) as defined in Section 9.3 was found to be significant, although not consistently in the two survey years. It seems that wealthier households are less likely to take a coping action, though perhaps they did not report a coping action as their economic situation might have provided an adequate ex-ante cushion against shocks. Hence there is no need for such households to search for additional off-farm occupation, for example, or to take children out of school. The income variable shows the same direction of influence in all four models, although the coefficient was found to be significant only in the second wave in Vietnam.

Furthermore, in Thailand a positive influence for the variable number of migrant members (MGM) was found in the second year. This is plausible, as migrants represent an important source of complementary household income. The ratio of household members engaged in agriculture (AGM) had a negative significant effect in Thailand but was not significant in Vietnam. This is a reflection of the fact that off-farm and non-farm employment is more pronounced among rural Thai households than in Vietnam, where the rural population rely more on own agriculture as a main source of income. Perhaps the lower likelihood of coping by Thai households is related to the type of shocks and their stronger reliance on off-farm income sources. Since a majority of Vietnamese households rely primarily on agriculture as a major source of income, a sudden reduction in yield or damage to agricultural land caused by flooding, drought, crop pest and storms drive households to cope more than Thai households, who also earn from off-farm and non-farm occupations in addition to agricultural income.

Village variables show different implications of infrastructure between two countries. In rural areas in particular, the market place is

Table 9.6 Univariate probit results of coping action

| | Thailand | | | | Vietnam | | | |
| | 1st wave | | 2nd wave | | 1st wave | | 2nd wave | |
Explanatory variables	Coefficient	z–value	Coefficient	z–value	Coefficient	z–value	Coefficient	z–value
Household characteristics								
INC	-0.0011	-0.33	0.0016	1.08	-0.0038	-1.27	-0.0040 *	-1.79
WTH	-0.0007 **	-2.31	-0.0002	-0.53	-0.0004	-1.16	-0.0015 **	-2.54
EDU	-0.0089	-0.56	-0.0027	-0.25	0.0151	1.11	0.0054	0.44
AGM	0.0741	0.36	-0.4413 ***	-3.15	0.0344	0.2	-0.0233	-0.15
MGM	0.0297	0.67	0.0514 *	1.92	0.0236	0.44	-0.0520	-1.27
Shock characteristics								
Income loss per capita								
INCL_AG	0.0204	0.98	-0.0155 *	-1.73	0.0179	1.4	0.0191 ***	2.72
INCL_EC	0.0389 *	1.94	0.0576 **	2.33	0.0161	0.79	0.0086	0.57
INCL_HL	0.0639 *	1.76	0.0892 *	1.86	0.0367 *	1.73	0.1128 **	2.19
INCL_SC	0.7845 **	2.04	0.0509	1.21	0.1089	1.13	0.0622	0.75
Asset loss per capita								
ASSL_AG	0.0497	1.58	0.1707 ***	2.92	0.0765 **	2.56	0.0640 ***	2.68
ASSL_EC	0.0356	1.38	54.9989 ***	5.6	0.0196	0.41	–[1]	–[1]
ASSL_HL	0.1955 **	2.47	1.0394 ***	2.81	0.0999 **	2.32	0.2162 *	1.73

ASSL_SC	0.0151	0.72	0.0285	1.56	0.0489	0.74	-0.0647	-0.97

ASSL_SC	0.0151	0.72	0.0285	1.56	0.0489	0.74	-0.0647	-0.97
Village characteristics								
CAP	0.0006	0.36	-0.0001	-0.08	-0.0014 *	-1.90	0.0035 **	2.15
MKT	-0.0023	-0.5	-0.0075 **	-2.4	-0.0033	-0.73	-0.0054	-1.47
BANK	[2]		[2]		0.0006	0.28	0.0027	1.55
Province dummy:								
1=Buriram (TH)	0.0360	0.24	-0.5029 ***	-5.02	0.1525	1.18		
1= Ha Tinh (VN)							-0.0746	-0.68
Province dummy:								
1=Nakhon Panom (TH)	0.3201 *	2.13	-0.2224 **	-2.04	0.1831	1.59		
1 = Dak Lak (VN)							-0.3009 ***	-2.63
Constant	0.5076 *	2.2000	0.7695	4.6400	0.8505 ***	4.8900	0.7518 ***	4.7100
Observed probability	0.7510		0.6372		0.8616		0.7569	
Predicted probability	0.8178		1.0000		0.8748		0.7717	
Number of observations	684		1280		1272		1509	
Wald chi2 (19)	29.29		148.05		37.38		59.29	
Prob > chi2	0.0302		0.0000		0.0041		0.0000	
Pseudo R2	0.078		0.1006		0.0369		0.0472	
Log pseudolikelihood	-198618.84		-422698.74		-492.43		-275449.94	

* significant at the 10% level, ** significant at the 5% level and *** significant at the 1% level.

[1] Variable was removed due to insufficient cases.

[2] In Thailand, banks usually locate in the same area as market. Therefore, to avoid collinearity concern, travelling time to the next market was considered to represent travelling time to the next bank.

Source: Authors' calculation.

the platform for informal information exchange and social networking; hence being far from a market place reduces the ability to cope. This is shown in the negative significant coefficient (MKT) for the second year in Thailand. In Vietnam, distance to provincial capitals (CAP) is significant, albeit with different signs; this is possible because the sample is not identical between the two waves. In the next section, the choices of coping action are analysed in more depth.

9.4.3   Choice of coping strategy

Our multivariate probit models have been set up in order to detect specific relationships between a particular coping activity and the type of shock. The models use the same set of exogenous variables and allow for multiple counteractions to cope with a single shock. To facilitate interpretation, in Tables 9.7 (Thailand) and Table 9.8 (Vietnam) we concentrate solely on the direction of influence and the significance of the regression coefficients due to the scale sensitivity and the relative low impact of the magnitudes.[8] In general, the results reveal that rural households resort to any of four major coping measures: 1) asking for public transfers and remittances, 2) reallocating household resource, 3) borrowing, and 4) using savings and selling assets.

The results generally confirm the findings from the univariate model that households with higher income and wealth status are more likely to use savings and sell assets. Moreover, wealthier households are less likely to take up additional off-farm and non-farm employment or seek to borrow in order to cope with shocks.

Education shows different effects in the two countries. In Thailand the education variable is significant in the second-wave dataset for the coping action of resource allocation, meaning that better education increases the likelihood of reallocating resources. It can be assumed that such households find it easier to take up additional employment and, especially, to diversify labour. The result is in line with the hypothesis pointed out in the previous section, that education often means better access to information. However, in Vietnam education level is significantly negative to the coping measure "asking for more remittances and apply for public transfers", which seems to contradict the information hypothesis.

Thai households with more reliance on agriculture as a main source of income tend to avoid using savings and selling assets. This seems plausible, as sale of assets in particular could hamper their future productive capacity. This seems to be different from Vietnam where agricultural-oriented households respond to shocks with reallocation of household resources. The model does not, however, allow a conclusion as to which resources are reallocated, but Chapter 8 of this volume suggests that land allocation may be dominant.

The migration variable in the Thai model shows that households with migrant members are likely to ask for more remittances to cope with shocks, whereas in Vietnam the model for the second-wave data suggests that migration increases the likelihood of borrowing and reduces resource allocation. While the Thailand results seem quite plausible, the interpretation for Vietnam is less clear.

The shock variables, except for social shocks, are most often significantly related to specific coping activities. When comparing the two countries, the direction of influence of the independent variables is generally consistent. For example, for agricultural shocks which lead to income loss, households would turn to borrowing as shown by the positive and significant sign, while use of savings and asset sales is significantly negative in most models. Interestingly no significant relationship was found between asking for more remittances and public support programmes to cope with this shock type. This may include the fact that the practical implementation of existing government emergency programs may be rather poor. Especially in Thailand, households must go through a long application and approval procedure, and payment may be delayed for up to several months after the event.

On the other hand results for asset loss from agricultural shocks are less consistent. Whereas households in Thailand tend to apply for public transfers or ask for remittances from migrant members, relatives and friends (significant coefficient for the second wave, Table 9.6) households in Vietnam seem to be restricted to borrowing as their only choice (Table 9.7).

Results are more compatible for economic shocks that lead to income loss where borrowing is the dominant reaction. The positive coefficients are significant in all models. A similar relationship is found for resource reallocation in the first wave in Thailand and in the second wave in Vietnam. At the same time, savings and selling assets as well as asking for more remittances and public transfers are negatively related in most cases. This shows on the one hand that economic shocks affect migrants and natal households at the same time, and on the other hand that public programmes for such events may be largely non-existent. This is different for agricultural shocks, where public programmes are widespread. Similar to asset losses from agriculture, results are less conclusive for asset loss from economic shocks.

For health shocks, borrowing is the dominant coping action in both countries, although in Vietnam asking for remittances or applying for

Table 9.7 Multivariate probit results of coping activity, Thailand

| | Coefficient – Thailand | | | | | | | |
| | Remittance and transfer | | Resource reallocation | | Borrowing | | Use savings and sell assets | |
Explanatory variables	1st wave	2nd wave	1st wave	2nd wave	1st wave	2nd wave	1st wave	2nd wave
Household characteristics								
INC	+	+	–	–	–	–	–	+
WTH	–	–	–	– ***	–	– ***	+	+ ***
EDU	–	–	+	+ ***	–	–	+	–
AGM	–	–	–	+	+	+	+	– **
MGM	+	+ *	–	+	+	+	+	–
Shock characteristics								
INCL_AG	+	–	+ ***	+ **	–	+ ***	– **	–
INCL_EC	– ***	–	+ *	+	+ *	+ *	–	– *
INCL_HL	+	+	–	+	+	+ **	+	+
INCL_SC	+	+	+ **	+	+	+	–	–
ASSL_AG	+	+ **	–	+	+	+	–	–
ASSL_EC	– **	–	+	–	+	–	+	+

		1st wave			2nd wave			1st wave		2nd wave	
ASSL_HL	+	−		+	+		+	−		+	**	+
ASSL_SC	−	−	*	+	+		+	+	***	+	***	+
Village characteristics												
CAP	+	−		+	+	−	+	−		+	+	*
MKT	−	+	+	−	+	+	−	+	**	+	+	
Buriram (TH)	−	+	**	−	**	−	+	−	**	−	−	
Nakhon Panom (TH)	−	+	***	−	−	+	+	+	***	+	−	

	1st wave	2nd wave			1st wave	2nd wave
atrho21	−***	−***		rho21	−***	−***
atrho31	−***	−***		rho31	−***	−***
atrho41	−***	−***		rho41	−***	−***
atrho32	−***	−***		rho32	−***	−***
atrho42	−***	−***		rho42	−***	−***
atrho43	−***	−***		rho43	−***	−***

* significant at the 10% level, ** significant at the 5% level and *** significant at the 1% level.

1st wave: Number of obs = 514; Wald chi2(19) = 203.44; Prob > chi2 = 0.0000; Log pseudolikelihood = −60757.72; SML, # draws = 24
Likelihood ratio test of rho21 = rho31 = rho41 = rho32 = rho42 = rho43 = 0: chi2(6) = 1.2e+06 Prob > chi2 = 0.0000

2nd wave: Number of obs = 814; Wald chi2(19) = 186.07; Prob > chi2 = 0.0000; Log pseudolikelihood = −103705.1; SML, # draws = 30
Likelihood ratio test of rho21 = rho31 = rho41 = rho32 = rho42 = rho43 = 0: chi2(6) = 2.1e+06 Prob > chi2 = 0.0000

Source: Authors' calculation.

Table 9.8 Multivariate probit results of coping activity, Vietnam

| | Coefficient – Vietnam | | | | | | | |
| | Remittance and transfer | | Resource reallocation | | Borrowing | | Use savings and sell assets | |
Explanatory variables	1st wave	2nd wave	1st wave	2nd wave	1st wave	2nd wave	1st wave	2nd wave
Household characteristics								
INC	+	+	+	- ***	-	-	+	+ ***
WTH	- ***	-	- ***	-	***	- ***	+ ***	+ **
EDU	-	- **	- *	+ **	+	-	+	+
AGM	-	-	+ *	+ ***	-	-	+	+
MGM	-	+	-	- *	+	+ **	-	+
Shock characteristics								
INCL_AG	-	-	-	+	+ ***	+ ***	-	-
INCL_EC	- ***	- **	-	+ ***	+ *	+ **	+	-
INCL_HL	+ ***	+	-	-	+ ***	+ ***	-	-
INCL_SC	+	+	- **	-	+	+	+	-
ASSL_AG	+	-	+	-	+ ***	+	-	+
ASSL_EC	-	-	- **	-	+ **	-	+	-
ASSL_HL	+ **	+	- *	-	+	+	+	+

ASSL_SC	1st wave				2nd wave			
Village characteristics								
CAP	−	+	+	−	−	**	+	+
MKT	−	+	+	−	−	+	+	+
BANK	+	+	+	+	+	+	+	+
Ha Tinh (VN)	−	***	+	**	+	***	+	*
Dak Lak (VN)	−	***	+	***	+	***	**	+

	1st wave	2nd wave		1st wave	2nd wave
atrho21	− ***	− ***	rho21	− ***	− ***
atrho31	− ***	− ***	rho31	− ***	− ***
atrho41	− ***	+ ***	rho41	− ***	+ ***
atrho32	− ***	− ***	rho32	− ***	− ***
atrho42	− ***	− ***	rho42	− ***	− ***
atrho43	− ***	− ***	rho43	− ***	− ***

*significant at the 10% level, ** significant at the 5% level and *** significant at the 1% level

1st wave: Number of obs = 1096; Wald chi2(72) = 982.62; Prob > chi2 = 0.0000; Log pseudolikelihood = −704893.94; SML, # draws = 34
Likelihood ratio test of rho21 = rho31 = rho41 = rho32 = rho42 = rho43 = 0: chi2(6) = 1.4e+06 Prob > chi2 = 0.0000

2nd wave: Number of obs = 1153; Wald chi2(19) = 254.01; Prob > chi2 = 0.0000; Log pseudolikelihood = −843809.03; SML, # draws = 34
Likelihood ratio test of rho21 = rho31 = rho41 = rho32 = rho42 = rho43 = 0: chi2(6) = 1.4e+06 Prob > chi2 = 0.0000

Source: Authors' calculation.

public transfers is positive and significant in one case. The results are less consistent for the health shocks that lead to asset loss. In the case of Vietnam, a negative influence of "resource reallocation" and a positive influence of "remittances and public transfers" have been calculated, while in Thailand "use up savings/sales of assets" show a positive coefficient which is significant for the first wave.

For social shocks, the coping actions between the two countries are completely different; in Thailand, resource reallocation is positively related to social shocks that result in income loss, and for asset loss the variables "use of savings" is positive, and "borrowing" is significantly negative related, whereas the opposite effects were found for Vietnam.

Results of the village characteristics variables differ between the two survey years and the two countries. In general, the models show that travelling distance and access to markets and financial institutions influence the choice of coping method. This is shown by the differences between the provinces in both countries. In addition, in Thailand, households closer to the provincial capital are more likely to reallocate resources. Meanwhile, households living further away are more likely to use savings or sell assets, while the distance to the nearest market is positively related to borrowing, which is mostly from informal credit sources. This is different in Vietnam, where the likelihood of borrowing declines with increasing distance, perhaps due to a less developed system incorporating private moneylenders.

In summary, the results of the multivariate choice models for coping with shocks indicate that there is a significant relationship between shock types and the choice of coping. In addition, other variables, namely household characteristics, economic and demographic conditions, location factors and shock severity, are influential in making a household choose a particular coping activity. Wealthier households, especially those in more remote areas, tend to use savings and sell assets in response to shocks.

Overall borrowing is a dominant coping measure for different kinds of shocks provided the corresponding financial infrastructure is accessible in terms of location. Asking for remittances and public transfers are strongly associated with high losses from agricultural shocks in Thailand and with health shocks in Vietnam. On the other hand, reallocation of household resources is a strategy frequently used to cope with economic and social shocks in both countries.

However, despite the noticeable similarities model results differ between the two survey years and between the two countries in detail. This suggests that the environmental and macroeconomic conditions on the one hand and the policy and institutional condition on the other may have quite a strong effect on the choice of coping. Hence, this lends some support to the need to develop situation- and country-specific responses to assist rural households to cope with shocks more effectively.

9.5 Summary and conclusion

Understanding shocks and their consequences is an essential precondition for the design of effective poverty alleviation strategies not only in poor countries but also in emerging market economies such as Thailand and Vietnam. Information about existing coping strategies of poor households is needed in order to design effective public support schemes. Also, a better understanding of the effectiveness of self-insurance measures is important as essential information on constraints for the establishment of private insurance markets and the implementation of public risk management policies. The analyses presented here are based on two surveys carried out in 2007 and 2008 among 4000 households in Thailand and Vietnam. As a starting point, we computed tables to describe the broad shock-coping action structure in the two countries, including summarizing household characteristics and location factors. The aggregation criteria applied in order to categorize the variables, especially shocks and coping actions, are mostly taken from the literature, and they are based on plausible considerations. To find out why some households cope while others do not, a univariate probit model was developed. The analysis is then refined by use of a multivariate probit approach in order to assign special coping measures to the four different shock categories.

At the onset we had asked four questions to be dealt with in this chapter, namely:

1. What are the major shocks that rural households face in both countries?
2. What ex-post coping measures are used, and do they differ between the two countries?
3. What are the reasons that some households undertake coping actions in response to shocks while others do not?
4. Which factors determine the choice of a specific coping activity?

As regards the first three questions, the analysis of the two panel surveys shows that rural households experienced shocks in the periods April to March 2006/2007 and April to March 2007/2008, with more shock events in the second survey period. The most frequent type of shock in both countries is weather-related events which are especially significant for agriculture, and in this regard more Vietnamese than Thai households were affected in both periods. On the other hand, shock types in Thailand are more evenly distributed among the four categories. It is striking that in both countries many households who experienced shocks did not take any coping action and, most remarkably, coping in both countries is more likely to take place for health-related events as compared to other shock types, especially shocks related to agricultural or social relationships. Although it is difficult to provide a straightforward explanation for this, these shocks may in many cases be below the household's individual action threshold. This explanation is supported by the fact that Thai households take no action more often than households in Vietnam; one might argue that Thai households have less "need to cope" due to higher income and wealth which lowers their action threshold.

For the last question, the modelling of coping choices of rural households has revealed that significant relationships exist between shock types and their severity and the choice of coping measures. Household characteristics, economic and demographic circumstances and location conditions are additional factors. Borrowing emerges as one of the most important coping measures regardless of the event which households face. Asking for remittances and public transfers is a popular coping action as well, although the coefficients in the probit models are not always consistent between the two countries. Additionally, self-insurance measures such as the reallocation of household resources plays a prominent role.

In summary, it must be acknowledged that while the multivariate probit models showed a pattern of relationships, the results also carry a fair degree of variation, not only between the two countries but also between the two survey years. This is perhaps not surprising considering that environmental and macroeconomic conditions vary over time, and that policy and institutional settings are country-specific. Of course, in the absence of an analysis assessing the effectiveness and efficiency of the households' own coping measures, one must be careful to derive policy recommendations. Nevertheless, the analysis of the two-year data from the six provinces in Thailand and Vietnam indicates that in the design of social protection policies for remote rural areas, situation- and location-specific considerations are needed. These must take into account the extent of infrastructure in rural areas and the demographic pattern of village populations as well as the livelihood strategies and the resource base of the rural households. The results presented here are only a first step towards a better understanding of the role of shocks, coping choices and the vulnerability of rural households in Thailand and Vietnam. Further analyses using models which can address more specific aspects of the shock-coping structure and using a longer panel will provide further insights for deriving more concrete policy recommendations.

Notes

1. The term "agricultural shock" has been commonly used in the literature. Generally, these are weather-related shocks which, however, can also affect non-agricultural households, for example when houses are damaged by storm or flood.
2. This includes prices of agricultural commodities and prices of inputs.
3. In the shock section of the questionnaire, respondents were asked first whether there was any event causing a big problem (shock) affecting the household, followed by a subjectively estimate of the severity, that is high, medium, low or no impact. Subsequently, they were asked to estimate the associated income and asset loss.
4. Figures calculated from Table 9.2.
5. However, income and wealth level of households might be influenced by shock incidences prior to the respective survey period, and shock-affected households might differ between first and second period.
6. The figures are calculated in terms of coping activities, which is different from the perspective up to now. As already pointed out, several households experienced more than one shock (see Table 9.1), and although the majority of households took only a single activity to cope with one shock, some households applied more than one coping action.
7. To generate more detailed information on the shock-coping behaviour, the analysis has to be refined, especially with respect to the model specification, for example by selecting other or additional explaining variables and by setting up separate models for different shock types or provinces.
8. Comprehensive numerical estimates are given in the appendices, to allow for more detailed explanation.

References

Alderman, H. and C. Paxson (2003): *Do the Poor Insure? A Synthesis of the Literature on Risk and Consumption in Developing Countries*. World Bank Policy Research Paper No. 1008. Washington, DC.

Asiimwe, J. B. and P. Mpuga (2007): "Implications of Rainfall Shocks for Household Income and Consumption in Uganda", *AERC Research Paper*, 168, African Economic Research Consortium, Nairobi.

Berloffa, G. and F. Modena (2009): "Income Shocks, Coping Strategies, and Consumption Smoothing, An Application to Indonesian Data", *Department of Economics Working Papers*, 0901, Department of Economics, University of Trento, Italia.

Beyene, A. D. (2008): "Determinants of Off-Farm Participation Decision of Farm Households in Ethiopia", *Agrekon*, 47(1): 140–61.

Cappellari, L. and S. P. Jenkins (2003): "Multivariate Probit Regression Using Simulated Maximum Likelihood", *Stata Journal*, 3(3): 278–94.

Carter, M. R. and J. A. Maluccio (2002): "Social Capital and Coping with Economic Shocks", *FCND Discussion Papers*, 142, International Food Policy Research Institute.

Chaudhry, P. and G. Ruysschaert (2007): "Climate Change & Human Development in Vietnam: A Case Study", *Human Development Report 2007/2008*.

Cutler, P. (1986): "The Response to Drought of Beja Famine Refugees in Sudan", *Disasters*, 10(3): 181–8.

Cutter, S. L., B .J. Boruff and W. L. Shirley (2003): "Social Vulnerability to Environmental Hazards", *Social Science Quarterly*, 84: 242–61.

Dercon, S. (2002): "Income Risk, Coping Strategies, and Safety Nets", *World Bank Research Observer*, 17(2): 141–66.

Dercon S. (2007): "Fate and Fear: Risk and Its Consequences in Africa", *mimeo*, paper prepared for the African Economic Research Consortium, Oxford.

Fishburn, P. (1970): *Utility Theory for Decision Making*, Wiley and Son, New York.

Frankenberger, T. (1992): "Indicators and Data Collection Methods for Assessing Household Food Security", in: Maxwell, S. and T. Frankenberger (eds), *Household Food Security: Concepts, Indicators, Measurements, A Technical Review*, UNICEF and IFAD, New York and Rome.

Glewwe, P. and H. Gillette (1998): "Are Some Groups More Vulnerable to Macroeconomic Shocks Than Others? Hypothesis Tests Based on Panel Data from Peru", *Journal of Development Economics*, 56(1): 181–206.

Greene, W. H. (2003): *Econometric Analysis*, Prentice Hall International Editions.

Hoddinott, J. (2006): "Shocks and Their Consequences across and Within Households in Rural Zimbabwe", *Journal of Development Studies* 42(2): 301–21.

Jalan, J. and M. Ravallion (1997): "Are the Poor Less Well-Insured? Evidence on Vulnerability to Income Risk in Rural China", *Journal of Development Economics*, 58(1): 61–81.

Kijima, Y., T. Matsumoto and T. Yamano (2006): "Nonfarm Employment, Agricultural Shocks, and Poverty Dynamics: Evidence from Rural Uganda", *Agricultural Economics*, 35: 459–67.

Klasen, S., T. Lechtenfeld and F. Povel (2010): "What about the Women? Female Headship, Poverty and Vulnerability in Thailand and Vietnam", *mimeo*, No 43, Proceedings of the German Development Economics Conference, Hannover 2010, Verein für Socialpolitik, Research Committee Development Economics.

Kochar, A. (1995): "Explaining Household Vulnerability to Idiosyncratic Income Shocks", *American Economic Review*, 85(2): 159–64.

Kochar, A. (1999): "Smoothing Consumption by Smoothing Income: Hours-of-Work Responses to Idiosyncratic agricultural Shocks in Rural India", *Review of Economics and Statistics*, 81(1): 50–61.

Maddala, G. S. (1999): *Limited-Dependent and Qualitative Variables in Econometrics*, Cambridge University Press, New York.

Manski, C. F. (1977): "The Structure of Random Utility Models", *Theory and Decision*, 8(3): 229–54.

Nelson, F. D. (1974): "On a General Computer Algorithm for the Analysis of Models with Limited Dependent Variables", *NBER Working Paper*, No. 68.

Newhouse, D. L. (2005): "The Persistence of Income Shocks: Evidence from Rural Indonesia", *Review of Development Economics*, 9(3): 415–33.

Pandey, S, H. Bhandari, S. Ding, P. Prapertchob, R. Sharan, D. Naik, S. K. Taunk and A. Sastri (2007): "Coping with Drought in Rice Farming in Asia: Insights from a Cross-country Comparative Study", *Agricultural Economics*, 37(1): 213–24.

Pindyck, R. S. and D. L. Rubinfeld (1998): *Econometric Models and Economic Forecasts*, McGraw-Hill International Editions, New York.

Rashid, D. A., M. Langworthy and S. Aradhyula (2006): "Livelihood Shocks and Coping Strategies: An Empirical Study of Bangladesh Households", *mimeo*, paper prepared for presentation at the American Agricultural Economics Association Annual Meeting, 23–26 July, Long Beach, California.

Takasaki, Y., B. L. Barham and O. T. Coomes (2002): "Risk Coping Strategies in Tropical Forests: Flood, Health, Asset Poverty, and Natural Resource Extraction", *mimeo*, paper prepared for the 2nd World Congress of Environmental and Resource Economists, 23–27 June 2002, Monterey.

Takasaki, Y., B. L. Barham and O. T. Coomes (2010): "Smoothing Income against Crop Flood Losses in Amazonia: Rain Forest or Rivers as a Safety Net?" *Review of Development Economics*, 14(1): 48–63.

Tongruksawattana, T., E. Schmidt and H. Waibel (2008): "Understanding Vulnerability to Poverty of Rural Agricultural Households in Northeastern Thailand", *mimeo*, Tropentag, 07–09 October, Hohenheim.

Watts, M. (1983): *Silent Violence: Food, Famine and Peasantry in Northern Nigeria*, University of California Press, Berkeley.

Watts, M. (1988): "Coping with the Market: Uncertainty and Food Security Among Hausa Peasants", in: De Garine, I. and G.A. Harrison (eds), *Coping with Uncertainty in Food Supply*, Clarendon Press, Oxford: 260–90.

World Bank (2005): "Natural Disaster Hotspots: A Global Risk Analysis", *Disaster Risk Management Series*, No. 5, Washington DC.

Appendix 9.A.1 Multivariate probit results of coping activity (Thailand – 1st wave, 2007)

Number of obs = 514
Wald chi2(19) = 203.44
Prob > chi2 = 0.0000
Log pseudolikelihood = –604757.72
SML, # draws = 24

Thailand 1st wave (2007)	Remittance and transfer			Resource reallocation			Borrowing			Use saving and sell assets		
Explanatory variables	Coefficient	z-value	Marginal effect	Coefficient	z-value	Marginal effect	Coefficient	z-value	Marginal effect	Coefficient	z-value	Marginal effect
Household characteristics												
INC	0.0021	0.62	0.0007	-0.0025	-0.66	-0.0007	-0.0051	-1.28	-0.0019	-0.0034	-0.95	-0.0012
WTH	-0.0003	-0.91	-0.0001	-0.0007	-1.50	-0.0002	-0.0001	-0.22	0.0000	0.0004	1.26	0.0001
EDU	-0.0270	-1.50	-0.0086	0.0436 **	2.34	0.0121	-0.0058	-0.35	-0.0022	0.0196	1.20	0.0069
AGM	-0.2668	-1.24	-0.0848	-0.2721	-1.17	-0.0755	0.0926	0.46	0.0351	0.0087	0.04	0.0031
MGM	0.0244	0.50	0.0078	-0.0869	-1.58	-0.0241	0.0582	1.18	0.0221	0.0014	0.03	0.0005
Shock characteristics												
INCL_AG	0.0217	1.02	0.0069	0.1100 ***	3.61	0.0305	-0.0292	-1.30	-0.0111	-0.0516 **	-2.46	-0.0182
INCL_EC	-0.0870 ***	-3.42	-0.0276	0.0342 *	1.87	0.0095	0.0354 *	1.88	0.0134	-0.0024	-0.14	-0.0009
INCL_HL	0.0172	1.09	0.0055	-0.0222	-1.00	-0.0062	0.0010	0.08	0.0004	0.0341	1.63	0.0120

INCL_SC	0.0137	0.24	0.0043	0.1136 **	1.98	0.0315	0.0275	0.44	0.0104	-0.0467	-1.26	-0.0164
ASSL_AG	0.0001	0.01	0.0000	-0.0176	-1.03	-0.0049	0.0260	1.43	0.0099	-0.0037	-0.27	-0.0013
ASSL_EC	-0.0463 **	-2.03	-0.0147	0.0059	0.54	0.0016	0.0134	1.12	0.0051	0.0060	0.73	0.0021
ASSL_HL	0.0180	1.25	0.0057	-0.0494	-1.57	-0.0137	0.0094	0.79	0.0036	0.0325 **	2.53	0.0114
ASSL_SC	-0.0075	-0.31	-0.0024	-0.0434	-1.17	-0.0120	0.0152	0.69	0.0058	0.0471 ***	2.89	0.0166

Village
characteristics

CAP	0.0022	1.16	0.0007	-0.0030	-1.46	-0.0008	0.0022	1.28	0.0008	-0.0010	-0.55	-0.0004
MKT	-0.0043	-0.77	-0.0014	0.0016	0.33	0.0004	0.0000	0.00	0.0000	0.0030	0.65	0.0011
Buriram (TH)	-0.4361 **	-2.52	-0.1387	-0.2893 *	-1.70	-0.0803	0.2798 *	1.81	0.1061	-0.1757	-1.10	-0.0618
Nakhon Panom (TH)	-0.5802 ***	-3.58	-0.1845	-0.1757	-1.02	-0.0488	0.4278 ***	2.83	0.1623	0.2404	1.63	0.0846

atrho21	-0.2403 ***	-3.09	rho21	-0.2358 ***	-3.21
atrho31	-0.5335 ***	-6.91	rho31	-0.4881 ***	-8.30
atrho41	-0.2578 ***	-3.57	rho41	-0.2523 ***	-3.73
atrho32	-0.2525 ***	-3.37	rho32	-0.2473 ***	-3.52
atrho42	-0.2345 ***	-2.87	rho42	-0.2303 ***	-2.98
atrho43	-0.4097 ***	-5.71	rho43	-0.3882 ***	-6.37

Note: Likelihood ratio test of rho21 = rho31 = rho41 = rho32 = rho42 = rho43 = 0: chi2(6) = 1.2e+06 Prob > chi2 = 0.0000
*significant at the 10% level, ** significant at the 5% level and
*** significant at the 1% level
Source: Authors' calculation.

Appendix 9.A.2 Multivariate probit results of coping activity (Thailand – 2nd wave, 2008)

Number of obs = 814
Wald chi2(19) = 186.07
Prob > chi2 = 0.0000
Log pseudolikelihood = −1033705.1
SML, # draws = 30

Thailand 2nd wave (2008)	Remittance and transfer			Resource reallocation			Borrowing			Use saving and sell assets		
Explanatory variables	Coefficient	z-value	Marginal effect	Coefficient	z-value	Marginal effect	Coefficient	z-value	Marginal effect	Coefficient	z-value	Marginal effect
Household characteristics												
INC	0.0014	0.92	0.0005	−0.0009	−0.67	−0.0003	−0.0026	−1.60	−0.0009	0.0015	1.08	0.0006
WTH	−0.0004	−1.26	−0.0001	−0.0006	−1.60	−0.0002	−0.0015 ***	−3.30	−0.0005	0.0010 ***	3.20	0.0004
EDU	−0.0016	−0.12	−0.0005	0.0330 ***	2.64	0.0113	−0.0046	−0.34	−0.0015	−0.0089	−0.72	−0.0034
AGM	−0.1063	−0.59	−0.0347	0.2403	1.39	0.0821	0.1794	1.00	0.0598	−0.3225 **	−2.00	−0.1241
MGM	0.0540 *	1.68	0.0176	0.0142	0.46	0.0049	0.0153	0.48	0.0051	−0.0160	−0.58	−0.0062
Shock characteristics												
INCL_AG	−0.0028	−0.21	−0.0009	0.0305 **	2.28	0.0104	0.0420 ***	2.72	0.0140	−0.0121	−0.96	−0.0046
INCL_EC	−0.0119	−1.16	−0.0039	0.0029	0.76	0.0010	0.0191 *	1.82	0.0064	−0.0066 *	−1.88	−0.0025
INCL_HL	0.0114	0.63	0.0037	0.0072	0.50	0.0025	0.0482 **	2.40	0.0161	0.0163	1.04	0.0063
INCL_SC	0.0063	0.33	0.0020	0.0075	0.40	0.0026	0.0432	1.33	0.0144	−0.0241	−1.31	−0.0093

ASSL_AG	0.0504 **	2.42	0.0165	0.0088	0.31	0.0030	0.0151	0.58	0.0050	-0.0129	-0.46	-0.0049
ASSL_EC	-0.2458	-1.35	-0.0802	-0.0067	-0.32	-0.0023	-0.0893	-1.55	-0.0298	0.0755	0.90	0.0291
ASSL_HL	-0.0083	-0.59	-0.0027	0.0058	0.52	0.0020	-0.0034	-0.16	-0.0011	0.0019	0.16	0.0007
ASSL_SC	-0.1305 *	-1.85	-0.0426	0.0098	0.59	0.0033	0.0513 *	2.03	0.0171	0.0048	0.27	0.0018
Village characteristics												
CAP	-0.0006	-0.44	-0.0002	-0.0028 *	-1.89	-0.0009	-0.0018	-1.23	-0.0006	0.0026 *	1.90	0.0010
MKT	-0.0064	-1.31	-0.0021	0.0000	0.01	0.0000	0.0093 **	2.30	0.0031	-0.0033	-0.79	-0.0013
Buriram (TH)	0.3294 **	2.35	0.1074	0.2388 *	1.80	0.0816	-0.3085 **	-2.34	-0.1029	-0.1608	-1.27	-0.0619
Nakhon Panom (TH)	-0.0179	-0.14	-0.0058	0.2429 *	1.85	0.0830	-0.0073	-0.06	-0.0024	-0.1286	-1.02	-0.0495
atrho21	-0.2992 ***	-5.20	rho21	-0.2906 ***	-5.52							
atrho31	-0.2470 ***	-4.21	rho31	-0.2421 ***	-4.38							
atrho41	-0.4051 ***	-6.66	rho41	-0.3843 ***	-7.41							
atrho32	-0.1875 ***	-3.22	rho32	-0.1853 ***	-3.30							
atrho42	-0.4249 ***	-7.31	rho42	-0.4011 ***	-8.22							
atrho43	-0.1903 ***	-3.32	rho43	-0.1880 ***	-3.40							

Note: Likelihood ratio test of rho21 = rho31 = rho41 = rho31 = rho32 = rho42 = rho43 = 0: chi2(6) = 2.1e+06 Prob > chi2 = 0.0000.
*significant at the 10% level, ** significant at the 5% level and *** significant at the 1% level.
Source: Authors' calculation.

Appendix 9.A.3 Multivariate probit results of coping activity (Vietnam – 1st wave, 2007)

Number of obs = 1096
Wald chi2(72) = 982.62
Prob > chi2 = 0.0000
Log pseudolikelihood = -704893.94
SML, # draws = 34

Vietnam 1st wave (2007)	Remittance and transfer			Resource reallocation			Borrowing			Use saving and sell assets		
Explanatory variables	Coefficient	z-value	Marginal effect	Coefficient	z-value	Marginal effect	Coefficient	z-value	Marginal effect	Coefficient	z-value	Marginal effect
Household characteristics												
INC	0.0035	1.04	0.0006	0.0019	0.49	0.0007	-0.0044	-1.01	-0.0016	0.0029	0.95	0.0010
WTH	-0.0004	-0.58	-0.0001	-0.0025 ***	-3.50	-0.0009	-0.0029 ***	-4.13	-0.0010	0.0034 ***	4.60	0.0012
EDU	-0.0545 ***	-2.79	-0.0092	-0.0246 *	-1.82	-0.0087	0.0152	1.09	0.0054	0.0169	1.23	0.0058
AGM	-0.2926	-1.29	-0.0493	0.2978 *	1.80	0.1048	-0.0809	-0.50	-0.0286	0.1003	0.61	0.0343
MGM	-0.0387	-0.61	-0.0065	-0.0444	-0.91	-0.0156	0.0774	1.63	0.0274	-0.0232	-0.48	-0.0079
Shock characteristics												
INCL_AG	-0.0128	-0.76	-0.0022	-0.0014	-0.26	-0.0005	0.0513 ***	3.08	0.0182	-0.0219	-1.62	-0.0075
INCL_EC	-14.7307 ***	-14.40	-2.4829	-0.0156	-0.85	-0.0055	0.0225 *	1.77	0.0080	0.0011	0.14	0.0004
INCL_HL	0.0455 ***	3.23	0.0077	-0.0202	-1.07	-0.0071	0.0881 ***	2.68	0.0312	-0.0066	-0.68	-0.0023

INCL_SC	0.0235	0.67	0.0040	-0.1836 **	-2.14	-0.0646	0.0375	0.82	0.0133	0.0273	0.79	0.0093
ASSL_AG	0.0246	1.30	0.0041	0.0040	0.28	0.0014	0.0652 ***	3.50	0.0231	-0.0270	-1.64	-0.0092
ASSL_EC	-0.0769	-1.11	-0.0130	-0.0704 **	-2.12	-0.0248	0.1804 **	2.40	0.0639	0.0010	0.04	0.0004
ASSL_HL	0.0379	2.04	0.0064	-0.0559 *	-1.93	-0.0197	0.0407	1.39	0.0144	0.0370	1.53	0.0127
ASSL_SC	-0.0050	-0.13	-0.0008	0.0086	0.30	0.0030	-0.0101	-0.35	-0.0036	0.0348	0.87	0.0119
Village characteristics												
CAP	-0.0025	-1.13	-0.0004	0.0012	1.40	0.0004	-0.0031 **	-2.57	-0.0011	-0.0009	-0.82	-0.0003
MKT	-0.0098	-1.31	-0.0017	-0.0012	-0.28	-0.0004	0.0009	0.21	0.0003	0.0040	0.89	0.0014
BANK	0.0003	0.09	0.0000	-0.0014	-0.74	-0.0002	0.0024	1.26	0.0004	-0.0011	-0.59	-0.0002
Ha Tinh (VN)	-0.4800 ***	-3.49	-0.0809	0.3826 ***	3.18	0.1347	0.1229	1.03	0.0435	-0.1543	-1.26	-0.0528
Dak Lak (VN)	-1.1324 ***	-6.39	-0.1909	-0.0472	-0.42	-0.0166	0.6305 ***	5.46	0.2233	-0.2611 **	-2.27	-0.0893
atrho21	-0.2367 ***	-3.82	rho21	-0.2323 ***	-3.96							
atrho31	-0.1832 ***	-2.75	rho31	-0.1812 ***	-2.81							
atrho41	-0.0156	-0.22	rho41	-0.0156	-0.22							
atrho32	-0.6075 ***	-9.52	rho32	-0.5424 ***	-12.05							
atrho42	-0.1987 ***	-3.58	rho42	-0.1962 ***	-3.67							
atrho43	-0.4859 ***	-7.88	rho43	-0.4509 ***	-9.18							

Note: Likelihood ratio test of rho21 = rho31 = rho41 = rho32 = rho42 = rho43 = 0: chi2(6) = 1.4e+06 Prob > chi2 = 0.0000.
*significant at the 10% level, ** significant at the 5% level and *** significant at the 1% level.
Source: Authors' calculation.

Appendix 9.A.4 Multivariate probit results of coping activity (Vietnam – 2nd wave, 2008)

Number of obs = 1153
Wald chi2(19) = 254.01
Prob > chi2 = 0.0000
Log pseudolikelihood = -843809.03
SML, # draws = 34

Vietnam 2nd wave (2008)	Remittance and transfer			Resource reallocation			Borrowing			Use saving and sell assets		
Explanatory variables	Coefficient	z-value	Marginal effect	Coefficient	z-value	Marginal effect	Coefficient	z-value	Marginal effect	Coefficient	z-value	Marginal effect
Household characteristics												
INC	0.0008	0.36	0.0002	-0.0072 ***	-2.68	-0.0027	-0.0023	-0.90	-0.0009	0.0089 ***	3.29	0.0024
WTH	-0.0002	-0.28	-0.0001	-0.0008	-1.09	-0.0003	-0.0026 ***	-3.52	-0.0010	0.0018 **	2.31	0.0005
EDU	-0.0379 **	-2.57	-0.0097	0.0298 **	2.33	0.0112	-0.0066	-0.52	-0.0025	0.0143	0.99	0.0039
AGM	-0.2161	-1.20	-0.0556	0.5830 ***	3.83	0.2199	-0.2094	-1.37	-0.0790	0.1382	0.83	0.0374
MGM	0.0257	0.50	0.0066	-0.0744	-1.76	-0.0281	0.0893 **	2.06	0.0337	0.0206	0.44	0.0056
Shock characteristics												
INCL_AG	-0.0141	-1.18	-0.0036	0.0028	0.49	0.0011	0.0505 ***	5.48	0.0190	-0.0212 ***	-3.06	-0.0057
INCL_EC	-0.1916 **	-2.17	-0.0493	0.0578 ***	2.99	0.0218	0.1327 **	2.44	0.0501	-0.0462 **	-2.39	-0.0125
INCL_HL	0.0245	1.22	0.0063	-0.0198	-0.72	-0.0075	0.1460 ***	3.35	0.0551	-0.0276	-1.19	-0.0075

	(1) Coef.	(1) t	(1)	(2) Coef.	(2) t	(2)	(3) Coef.	(3) t	(3)	(4) Coef.	(4) t	(4)
INCL_SC	0.1061	1.45	0.0273	−0.0746	−1.04	−0.0281	0.0483	0.56	0.0182	−0.0508	−0.77	−0.0137
ASSL_AG	−0.0044	−0.20	−0.0011	−0.0051	−0.23	−0.0019	0.0195	0.77	0.0074	0.0181	0.76	0.0049
ASSL_EC	−0.2301	−0.69	−0.0592	−0.0889	−0.33	−0.0335	−0.0518	−0.20	−0.0195	−0.2738	−1.13	−0.0742
ASSL_HL	0.0729	1.25	0.0187	−0.0374	−0.81	−0.0141	0.0825	1.45	0.0311	0.0934	1.54	0.0253
ASSL_SC	−0.0111	−0.17	−0.0028	0.2882 **	2.31	0.1087	−0.0918	−0.98	−0.0346	−0.0622	−1.01	−0.0169
Village characteristics												
CAP	0.0015	1.05	0.0004	−0.0001	−0.04	0.0000	−0.0003	−0.16	−0.0001	0.0013	1.05	0.0003
MKT	0.0034	0.86	0.0009	−0.0020	−0.54	−0.0007	−0.0058	−1.53	−0.0022	0.0017	0.44	0.0005
BANK	0.0004	0.20	0.0001	0.0003	0.20	0.0001	0.0010	0.65	0.0003	0.0019	1.07	0.0005
Ha Tinh (VN)	0.2742 **	2.26	0.0705	−0.2070 *	−1.93	−0.0781	0.1575	1.47	0.0594	0.2441 *	1.93	0.0661
Dak Lak (VN)	−0.6555 ***	−3.99	−0.1686	−0.3878 ***	−3.15	−0.1462	0.1351	1.09	0.0509	0.0786	0.54	0.0213
attrho21	−0.2695 ***	−4.81	rho21	−0.2631 ***	−5.05							
attrho31	−0.2343 ***	−4.20	rho31	−0.2301 ***	−4.35							
attrho41	0.1679 ***	2.72	rho41	0.1663 ***	2.77							
attrho32	−0.7536 ***	−12.12	rho32	−0.6373 ***	−17.26							
attrho42	−0.2301 ***	−4.18	rho42	−0.2262 ***	−4.33							
attrho43	−0.2110 ***	−3.92	rho43	−0.2080 ***	−4.04							

Note: Likelihood ratio test of rho21 = rho41 = rho31 = rho42 = rho32 = rho43 = 0: chi2(6) = 1.4e+06 Prob > chi2 = 0.0000.
*significant at the 10% level, ** significant at the 5% level and *** significant at the 1% level.
Source: Authors' calculation.

10
Financial Shock-Coping in Rural Thailand and Vietnam

Niels Kemper, Rainer Klump, Lukas Menkhoff and Ornsiri Rungruxsirivorn

10.1 Introduction

This research examines financial decision-making not from the perspective of the ordinary but from the extraordinary. Shocks are extraordinary. Events such as excessive rainfall or drought, illness or death of a household member have the potential to dramatically impair household income streams. Shocks to income are shocks to consumption unless households manage to mitigate or avoid the reduction in consumption through the choice of an appropriate smoothing mechanism. Affected households take such measures under the commonly employed assumption that households prefer smooth over fluctuating consumption (due to risk aversion). It is the purpose of this research to analyse household financial decision making after the occurrence of a shock.

The literature suggests a number of smoothing mechanisms through which households may attempt to stabilize their consumption streams in the face of fluctuating incomes. Deaton (1991) examines the use of assets (in quite a general sense) for smoothing purposes. Among many others, Rosenzweig and Wolpin (1993) analyse the use of livestock selling for consumption smoothing. Life-cycle models examine saving and dissaving (of monetary saving) for income smoothing (see Paxson, 1992, among others). Udry (1994) examines the use of state-contingent informal loans as an insurance substitute. Eswaran and Kotwal (1989) analyse the use of credit as insurance in agrarian economies.

But there are also common mechanisms outside the financial nexus. Kochar (1995) analyses the elasticity of labour supply to shocks. Further, Platteau (1997) argues that formally uninsured households engage in informal reciprocal insurance arrangements. Finally, Zimmerman and Carter (2003) suggest that poor households with a subsistence constraint attempt to smooth their productive assets rather than to stabilize their consumption streams.

These approaches resort to a partial analysis of particular smoothing mechanisms. That is, while analysing one particular mechanism, they do not account for the existence of others. In fact, however, households seem to use various smoothing mechanisms after the occurrence of shocks, as we see in our household survey from Thailand and Vietnam. Therefore, we suggest an integrated empirical approach to account for the whole variety of smoothing mechanisms households have at hand and to analytically explore the factors that motivate households to prefer one approach over the other.

Two fundamental assumptions guide the use of smoothing mechanisms in the models mentioned above: firstly, the presence or absence of credit constraints (presence: Rosenzweig and Wolpin, 1993; Kochar, 1995 and Zimmerman and Carter, 2003; absence: Eswaran and Kotwal, 1989; Paxson, 1992 and Udry, 1994). Secondly, the consideration that covariate shocks have the same effect or a different effect from idiosyncratic shocks (the same: Rosenzweig and Wolpin, 1993; Eswaran and Kotwal, 1989 and Udry, 1994; different: Paxson, 1992 and Zimmerman and Carter, 2003). We test whether these theoretical assumptions are related to the actual use of smoothing mechanisms in our samples.

In so doing, we estimate choice probabilities for the different smoothing mechanisms via a multinomial logit model. However, given the limitations from observational data and the absence of a suitable control group, we cannot estimate causal effects from the model. We rather interpret the findings as an empirical relationship (that is, there is an effect but the direction of the effect is unclear) between, say, credit rationing and the choice of a smoothing mechanism.

The chapter proceeds as follows: Section 10.2 reviews theoretical and empirical models on smoothing mechanisms with respect to their assumptions on credit constraint and types of shocks. Section 10.3 gives a description of the dataset; it also provides a number of descriptive statistics on the key variables employed in the analysis of household shock coping. Section 10.4 details the empirical approach and the estimation results. In Section 10.5 we discuss the empirical results in the country-specific setting in Thailand and Vietnam, and conclude.

10.2 Theoretical considerations

The underlying assumptions on (the absence of) binding credit constraints and the nature of shocks (covariate versus idiosyncratic) have far-reaching consequences as to why certain smoothing mechanisms are used. This is why we test for the empirical relationship between credit constraints, type of shock and the choice of a smoothing mechanism. Before we do so, we review seven models dealing with smoothing mechanisms such as livestock selling, use of savings, borrowing, increases in labour supply, reciprocal insurance, and remaining inactive for asset-smoothing purposes. It is the purpose of this section to examine how the underlying assumptions on (the absence of) binding credit constraints (Section 10.2.1) and the nature of shocks (Section 10.2.2) affect the choice of smoothing mechanisms.

10.2.1   Credit constraints and the choice of a smoothing mechanism

There are many reasons why poor households in developing countries have either no or only limited access to credit markets: remoteness, discrimination, financial illiteracy and, particularly, information asymmetries, enforcement problems and transaction costs. The last three reasons are those which economics research has predominantly focused on; information asymmetries, enforcement problems and transaction costs in credit markets might induce financial institutions to deny financial services to poor households. Transaction costs of small loans can render lending unprofitable. Even though borrowers might be judged creditworthy by financial institutions, they remain unbanked due to the proportionally high cost of small loan transactions (Johnston and Morduch, 2008). Financial institutions have helped overcome these obstacles through innovative lending technologies such as group lending and individual loans based on dynamic incentives. It is fair to say that the depth and outreach of financial services have improved over the last years, but financial exclusion of both households and enterprises still exists to a high degree (Beck and Demirgüc-Kunt, 2008).

The reasons for limited access to credit are manifold. However, the assumption of binding credit constraints is employed in some models but not in others. In the model of Rosenzweig and Wolpin (1993) the assumption of a binding credit constraint causes households to buy and sell bullocks to smooth consumption in an environment characterized by high income uncertainty. This implies that there should be a relationship between binding credit constraints and the selling of livestock as an ex-post smoothing mechanism.

Paxson (1992), on the other hand, assumes the absence of binding credit constraints in her empirical permanent and transitory income model. Households may save and dissave (that is, take credit) to smooth transitory income fluctuations. Consequently, credit constraint should not matter for the use of credit and savings as smoothing mechanisms.

Eswaran and Kotwal (1989) argue along these lines, adding the caveat that credit access to formal sources may be limited due to the lack of collateral. They model the use of credit as an insurance mechanism for consumption smoothing in agricultural societies (for example, poor farmers borrow from rich farmers). Thus there are no credit constraints in informal borrowing, while credit constraints may exist for formal borrowing.

In a theoretical model on informal credit markets in a village economy by Udry (1994), credit constraints are also non-binding. He argues that this is due to the relative unimportance of information asymmetries in rural credit markets when people know each other well, as is the case in small geographic and social units such as villages. Consequently credit constraints should not matter for informal borrowing.

Kochar (1995) argues that credit markets are typically incomplete. She states, however, that this should not be a problem, as well-functioning labour markets may compensate for limited credit markets. This implies that binding credit constraints cause households to increase or decrease labour supply as a smoothing mechanism.

Zimmerman and Carter (2003) assume credit market imperfections and binding liquidity constraints. Covariate shocks impair reciprocal arrangements and the selling of assets as smoothing mechanisms. Consequently households remain inactive in the choice of smoothing mechanisms when a covariate shock occurs (they do not consider increases in labour supply).

In addition to these models we also refer to the concept of balanced reciprocity as described by Platteau (1997). In these arrangements, people condition their participation on the expectation that net payments will more or less balance out over time. Although this theory contains the use of loans, we focus on transfers going back and forth between households in these reciprocal arrangements. The implications of the balanced reciprocity theory for credit constraints are not clear.

10.2.2 Idiosyncratic and covariate shocks and the choice of a smoothing mechanism

Depending on the model, the assumption on the nature of the shock has implications for the choice of a smoothing mechanism. For instance, selling assets may not be a good smoothing mechanism in times of a covariate shock; shock-induced distress selling of assets may result in collapsing asset prices. However, as Rosenzweig and Wolpin (1993) argue, bullocks, as opposed to other types of capital such as land, can be moved and are hence particularly valuable as buffer stock in the face of spatially covariate income shocks. They introduce income uncertainty through both farm-level (idiosyncratic) and village-level (covariate) shocks. Risk-averse utility-maximizing agents smooth the resulting income fluctuations through buying and selling of bullocks. Village-level and farm-level shocks are distributed independently from each other. This means that idiosyncratic and covariate shocks are treated alike in the model. This implies that shocks in general should not have an effect on livestock selling as a smoothing mechanism.

Paxson (1992) employs a permanent and transitory income framework to explain fluctuations in income. She empirically models transitory income (from rice farmers) as deviations from average values of regional rainfall. Hence her empirical analysis is concerned with covariate shocks. Idiosyncratic shocks are not explained. She makes the implicit assumption that the effects of these shocks net out on average. This implies for our empirical model that only covariate shocks matter for the choice of saving and dissaving as a smoothing mechanism (although Paxson states in her paper that she would have controlled for idiosyncratic shocks if there were no data limitations).

Eswaran and Kotwal (1989) do not explicitly model shocks in their model. They capture uncertainty by treating income realizations to be stochastic. Further, they assume that incomes across households are uncorrelated and that households borrow from each other (and elsewhere) to smooth consumption. This implies that shocks are independent. They do not distinguish between idiosyncratic and covariate shocks. Consequently, the type of shock should not matter for informal borrowing.

Udry (1994) considers both village-level and idiosyncratic variations in income in his model. He allows for arbitrary correlation between shocks to income of different households in a village. Sources of income variability can be observable or unobservable. Variation in income caused by observable shocks may be correlated across households, while unobserved shocks are assumed to be independent. The type of shock only matters for the price of credit (with credit being more expensive for covariate shocks) and not for the availability. Consequently, the type of shock should not matter for the use of informal borrowing as a smoothing mechanism.

Kochar (1985) focuses on idiosyncratic shocks only. The occurrence of idiosyncratic adverse shocks causes households to increase their labour supply. No statement on the relationship between covariate shocks and changes in labour supply as a smoothing mechanism is made.

Zimmerman and Carter (2003) consider both covariate and idiosyncratic shocks. They argue that reciprocal arrangements can deal with idiosyncratic shocks. They doubt, however, that these mechanisms work if shocks are covariate in nature. Covariate shocks also affect distress selling of assets, as asset prices are correlated. This implies that households use no smoothing mechanism at all when a covariate shock occurs. They rather cut consumption.

10.2.3 Hypotheses and sets of variables

We test the implications of these models for the choice of smoothing mechanisms in Thailand and Vietnam. The decision process is modelled as a multinomial logit. We are mostly interested in testing two null hypotheses in the empirical analysis in Section 10.4:

H_{01}: Credit rationing does not matter for the choice of a particular smoothing mechanism.

H_{02}: Covariate shocks do not matter for the choice of a particular smoothing mechanism.

The outcome variable of interest is a categorically distributed variable indicating which smoothing mechanism a household affected by a shock was choosing. To measure whether credit constraints bind, we use a binary variable that equals one if a household was credit rationed (from either formal or informal sources) and zero if it was not. The other main variable of interest is also a binary variable that equals one if a household was affected by a covariate shock and zero if it was affected by an idiosyncratic shock.

We also control for the estimated income loss due to the shock the household was exposed to. Further, we control for a number of variables implied by the theoretical and empirical models above such as savings, livestock and land ownership. In addition, we control for household expenditures, family size, the number of household members and the type of employment (wage employment, off-farm self-employment, and agricultural self-employment).

10.3 Data and descriptive statistics

10.3.1 Data collection

The data used in this study were collected as part of the research project "Impact of shocks on the vulnerability to poverty: consequences for development of emerging Southeast Asian economies" (DFG-FOR756). An initial cross-sectional survey was carried out in Thailand and Vietnam between April and June 2007. Within each country, three provinces were chosen. The six provinces are: Buri Ram, Ubon Ratchathani and Nakhon Phanom from the Northeastern region of Thailand, and in Vietnam Dak Lak from the Central Highlands and Thua Thien-Hue and Ha Tinh from the North Central Coast.

Within each country, households were selected following a three-stage stratified sampling procedure where provinces are constituted strata, and the primary sampling units (PSU) are sub-districts (communes in Vietnam). Altogether, a total of 2,186 households from 220 villages in Thailand and 2,195 households from 220 villages in Vietnam were interviewed in this initial cross-sectional survey. Further details on the sampling procedure and questionnaire design are reported in Hardeweg *et al.* (2007).

The survey contains rich information on household demographics, occupation, health status, educational attainment, agricultural activities, off-farm employment activities, household businesses, income, expenditures, assets, borrowing, and transfers in the one-year period from May 2006 to April 2007. Retrospective questions were also included, to capture information about shock events in the previous five years and the corresponding coping strategies. Respondents were asked whether their household had experienced a shock event in the past five years, to name up to three major shock events, the type of shocks, the year that shocks occurred, and what measures were taken in response to the shocks.

10.3.2   Profile of sample households

Appendix 10.A.1 summarizes the basic characteristics of rural households in Thailand and Vietnam as derived from the survey. The average family size is 4 persons in Thailand and 4.3 persons in Vietnam. The majority of households are male-headed, but female-headed households are not uncommon; nearly 25 per cent of the Thai households are female-headed, whereas it is about 16 per cent in Vietnam. The average year of schooling for the head of household is 5 years in Thailand and 7.4 years in Vietnam. Although not shown in this table, we find that less than 15 per cent of the adult Thai population completed the present level of primary education (6th grade), whereas nearly 70 per cent of the Vietnamese attained that level.

We classify household occupations into six groups according to the main occupation of the head of household. These groups are farm households, wage-earners in the informal sector,[1] wage earners in the formal sector,[2] government officials, business owners, and the "economically inactive" group. Agriculture is the most important sector in both countries, providing employment for more than 60 per cent of the households. The dominant crop in both countries is rice, but coffee is also important in the Dak Lak province of Vietnam. After agriculture, the next in importance is the "economically inactive" group. A large proportion of the population in this group is found to be elderly.

Household income and other monetary variables are measured at purchasing power parity (PPP) adjusted prices to make comparisons in real terms between the two countries possible. We note that annual household income is composed of net income from farming, net income from household business, wage labour income, and other non-labour income such as land rent, but excludes remittances and transfers. We exclude the latter two because we want to consider income before any coping strategy has been used. The annual household income is, on average, PPP US$5200 in Thailand and PPP US$4000 in Vietnam.

The annual consumption expenditure for the average household in Thailand is PPP US$4600 and about PPP US$4400 in Vietnam. Food accounts for the largest proportion of household expenditures. The share of household expenditures on food is 40 per cent in Thailand and nearly 60 per cent in Vietnam.

The average Thai household owns twice as many assets as the average Vietnamese household. As for the type of assets,[3] land is the dominant asset for rural households, accounting for about 70 per cent of the value of all assets. Next in importance to land are durable household assets, which include farm machinery and non-farm business equipment. Savings and agricultural assets, including livestock and stored crops, account for very small shares of total assets.

Turning to the indicators of household access to credit markets, about 10 per cent of the Thai households claim to be credit rationed whereas 17 per cent of the Vietnamese households report credit rationing. Of these credit-rationed households, about half report being fully denied access to the credit markets.[4] The repeat default rate is very low in both countries, as less than 3 per cent of the households report that they have ever defaulted on loans. The incidence of late repayment is relatively higher; as a ratio of total loans outstanding, the value of loans defaulted or repaid late is in the order of 6 to 8 per cent of total loans outstanding for the average household. When we consider only households who report loan defaults or late repayment, this ratio is about 60 per cent on average, and reaches 100 per cent for some households.[5]

10.3.3   Shocks and coping strategies

In this section we provide information about the shock events causing serious hardship to rural households in Thailand and Vietnam. The main coping strategies used by households are also examined. Appendix 10.A.2 shows the number of households reported to have been affected by shock events in the period from 2002 to 2007. Rural households in Thailand and Vietnam report a high incidence of shocks. A total of 1383 Thai households (63 per cent of the total sample) and 1847 Vietnamese households (84 per cent of the total sample) have experienced at least one shock event over the past five years. Risk is therefore a central part of life for rural households in both countries.

Most households experience one shock per year. Nearly 86 per cent of the Thai households reporting shocks in 2006 were hit by one shock that year. Only 11 per cent of the Thai households report having two shocks that year and 3 per cent report having three or more shocks. For those households who had experienced shocks over the previous five years, the average number of shock events per household per year was in the range from 1.0 to 1.2 for Thai households and from 1.0 to 1.23 for Vietnamese households. Our data also reveal that households who experienced shocks in a given year tend to be repeatedly hit by shocks in subsequent periods. For example, 25 per cent of Thai households experiencing shocks in 2005 also report being hit by shocks in 2006. The number is even higher for Vietnam; almost 50 per cent of the households experiencing shocks in 2005 were also hit by shocks in 2006. An implication of this finding is that there seem to be recurrent shocks for a number of households. The recurrent exposure to shocks may limit asset accumulation by households which, in turn, makes it more difficult for households to escape poverty.

There is evidence that the most recent shocks are more likely to be reported, as nearly half of all shock events occurred in the period from 2006 to April 2007. For this reason, and because we have information on household characteristics in the period from 2006 to 2007, in the following and in the empirical analysis we will focus on the shocks reported for the 2006/2007 period. For households reporting more than one shock in 2006/2007, we use only the worst shock in that year.

Shocks can have major impacts on households' well-being. Appendix 10.A.3 reports the severity of shocks, the estimated loss due to shocks, the consequences of shocks to households' consumption, and the number of years needed to recover from shocks. More than 95 per cent of the households reported a high occurrence of shocks. The estimated loss as a percentage of annual household income is, on average,

26 per cent for Thai households and 34 per cent for Vietnamese households. The duration of impact tends to be longer in Vietnam than in Thailand; nearly 85 per cent of the Vietnamese households still have to reduce consumption expenditure as a consequence of shocks whereas only 50 per cent of the Thai households report having to do so. Also there seems to be variation in terms of the share of households who are able to recover from shocks by the time of the interview. Close to 50 per cent of the households reporting shocks are able to recover from the shocks within one year, whereas 40 per cent of the households had not recovered at the time of the survey.

The incidence of the different types of shocks faced by households in 2006/2007 is reported in Appendix 10.A.4. The most common types of shocks are agricultural-related: weather shocks and pest infestations, which affect 46 per cent and 62 per cent of the households in Thailand and Vietnam respectively. Shocks to household demographics, such as illness or death of household members, are the next most frequent shock events, reported by 28 per cent and 30 per cent of the households in Thailand and Vietnam respectively. Other shocks, such as macroeconomic shocks and higher household expenditures, affect only a few households but are relatively more important in Thailand than in Vietnam.

Faced with shocks, households in Thailand and Vietnam rely on various measures as their main coping strategy. Appendix 10.A.5 reports the percentage of households that use different measures in response to shocks. Interestingly, about 28 per cent of the Thai households and 17 per cent of the Vietnamese households report taking no measures in response to shocks. There are two interpretations for this. The first interpretation is that resource-poor households with limited access to credit markets have no available measures to cope with shocks and thus have to accept a shortfall in consumption. The second interpretation is that the impact of a particular shock on a household might not be too severe, reducing the need for a coping strategy. Besides taking no measures, the primary coping strategy used by households in both countries is borrowing, with informal borrowing playing a more important role than formal borrowing. Other important responses are livestock selling, use of savings, and increasing labour supply.

10.4 Estimation procedure and results

The empirical section tests whether binding credit constraints and the nature of a shock as assumed by the theoretical and empirical models described above affect the choice of a smoothing mechanism in the Thai and Vietnamese contexts. In contrast to the partial analysis of the models above, we do not have to maintain the a priori assumption that households chose a smoothing mechanism with only a single model in mind. It is quite plausible to argue that households form expectations relating to a variety of models and prefer the smoothing mechanism that minimizes their utility loss. Accordingly, the decision-making process of the household may appear as follows.

We link the choice of a post-shock smoothing mechanism to the theoretical and empirical models discussed above (see Table 10.1). To be more specific, the model by Rosenzweig and Wolpin (1993) assumes that credit constraints matter for livestock selling, but the type of shock does not.

According to Paxson's model (1992), credit constraints are non-binding in the choice to use savings and credit as a smoothing mechanism. Covariate shocks affect savings and dissaving. Eswaran and Kotwal (1989) as well as Udry (1994) also assume non-binding credit constraints in the use of credit as a smoothing mechanism. The difference between idiosyncratic and covariate shocks is captured by price effects.

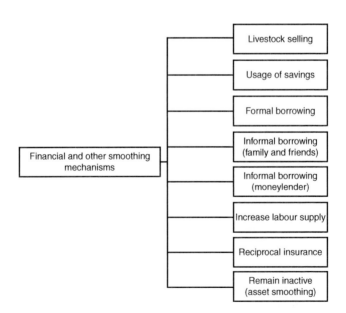

Figure 10.1   Household decision making of post-shock smoothing mechanism

Table 10.1 Credit constraints, type of shock and the empirical model

Model	Are credit constraints binding?	Does type of shock matter?	Smoothing mechanism in empirical analysis
Rosenzweig and Wolpin (1993)	Yes	No	Livestock selling
Paxson (1992)	No	Yes	Use of savings, taking credit
Eswaran and Kotwal (1989)	No	No	Taking credit (informal)
Udry (1994)	No	No	Taking credit (informal)
Kochar (1995)	Yes	?	Increase labour supply
Platteau (1997)	?	?	Reciprocal insurance
Zimmerman and Carter (2003)	Yes	Yes	Remain inactive (asset smoothing)

Kochar (1995) assumes that binding credit constraints cause households to increase their labour supply in the aftermath of an idiosyncratic shock.

Assuming that binding credit constraints and the nature of shock both matter, Zimmerman and Carter (2003) argue that households remain inactive after a covariate shock.

10.4.1 Sample division

As we want to determine the factors affecting the choice of smoothing mechanisms, we focus on the households that were affected by a shock during the survey period. Accordingly we split the random sample Z_{total} with N households into two subsamples, $Z_{noshock}$ and Z_{shock}, with K and $(N - K)$ households respectively. Let $s = 0$ denote the absence of a shock for a particular househod, and $s > 0$ denote its occurrence, then we split the sample according to the following selection rule: let household $i = 1 \ldots N$ be a member of subsample $Z_{noshock}$ if $s = 0$, and let household $j = 1 \ldots N$ be a member of Z_{shock} if $s > 0$ for $i \neq j$. Under the assumption that the selection rule is an exogenous variation in the data, the subsamples maintain their randomness property.

10.4.2 Estimation procedure

The choice probabilities for the choice of smoothing mechanism will be maximum-likelihood estimated from a multinomial logit model. Describing the model we follow Maddala (1983) and Greene (2002).

The utility of the choice of smoothing mechanism $j = 1 \ldots h \ldots J$ for household i is given by

$$U_{ij} = b'_i x_i + a'_i w_{ij} + e_{ij} \tag{10.1}$$

where x_i contains the household-specific characteristics and the w_{ij} attributes of the smoothing mechanism. The household chooses a particular smoothing mechanism h that maximizes its utility (or, to be more precise: minimizes its disutility). That is,

$$U_{ih} > U_{ij} \quad \text{for} \quad h \neq j \tag{10.2}$$

For the following analysis, we set $w_{ij} = 0$ and focus on the household-specific characteristics causing the choice of j (technically speaking, we estimate choice probabilities through a multinomial logit rather than a conditional logit model).

Let Y_i denote a random variable indicating the choice over J unordered smoothing mechanisms that are identically and independently distributed. Further, assuming the binary expression of probabilities, a logistic distribution and setting the coefficients $b_j = 0$ for any of the smoothing mechanisms implies that the probability for individual i to use smoothing mechanism j is given by

$$P(Y_i = j) = \frac{e^{b'_j x_i}}{1 + \sum_{j=1}^{J-1} e^{b'_j x_i}} \tag{10.3}$$

Given that $P(Y_i = J) = \dfrac{1}{1 + \sum_{j=1}^{J-1} e^{b'_j x_i}}$ it follows from the binary expression of probabilities in this model that after taking logs the log-odds ratio can be expressed as

$$\ln\left[\frac{P(Y_i = j)}{P(Y_i = J)} \right] = x_i \beta_j \tag{10.4}$$

where $\beta_j = (\beta_j - \beta_J)$ if smoothing mechanism $J = 0$. We assume that the ratios of the respective choices do not depend on the probabilities of other choices. For a causal interpretation of the estimated coefficients, the error terms must be assumed to be independent. The assumption of homoscedasticity must be made for valid inference.

10.4.3 Results

The decision-making process differentiates between the following smoothing mechanisms: livestock selling, use of saving, formal borrowing, informal borrowing from family and friends, informal borrowing from moneylender, increasing labour supply, engaging in reciprocal insurance, and doing nothing in response to a shock.

We want to examine how a set of variables implied by the theoretical models briefly reviewed above affects the choice of smoothing mechanisms. Given the role that (the absence of) borrowing constraints (as an assumption) take in these models, we pay special attention to it.

Given both the limitations from observational data and the absence of a suitable control group, we do not claim to estimate causal effects from the model. In particular, the fair degree of sophistication of the empirical model does not allow for an identification strategy to deal with unobservables and simultaneity. That is, the log-odd ratios measure the change in the use of smoothing mechanism $Y_i = j$ with respect to variable x_i relative to the restricted coefficient on the normalizing smoothing mechanism (in our case formal borrowing). But we cannot tell whether x_i (for example savings) actually causes $Y_i = j$ or if, for instance, forward-looking agents plan to use saving as a smoothing mechanism in the case of a shock. In this case, savings decisions are determined with $Y_i = j$. Furthermore, there might be unobserved characteristics related to x_i and $Y_i = j$ that we cannot control for and which therefore affect the marginal distribution of $Y_i = j$ conditional on x_i.

Please refer to Appendices 10.A.6 and 10.A.7 for the results for Thailand and Vietnam. As far as inference is concerned, we conclude that a significant relationship may or may not exist, but we cannot tell in what direction causality is running. Looking at Thailand first, we find that credit rationing (a binary variable taking the value 1 if a household was credit rationed and 0 if it was not) is significantly related to almost none of the smoothing mechanisms (relative to formal borrowing): livestock selling, use of saving, formal borrowing, informal borrowing from family and friends, informal borrowing from moneylender, increasing labour supply, and doing nothing in response to a shock. The only significant relationship is found between credit rationing and engaging in reciprocal insurance. However, the sign is negative and therefore opposite to the result expected.

In Vietnam the evidence is similar. We do not find a significant relationship between credit rationing and livestock selling, use of saving, formal borrowing, informal borrowing from family and friends, informal borrowing from moneylender, increasing labour supply, engaging in reciprocal insurance, and doing nothing in response to a shock (relative to formal borrowing). However, the p-value for the relationship between credit rationing and informal borrowing from moneylender is almost significant at the 10 per cent level, indicating that a number of households, if they are rationed in formal credit markets, resort to informal borrowing from moneylenders.

In summary, the empirical evidence in both countries points towards non-binding credit constraints. Although this might seem surprising, the reason for this, as we detail in Section 10.5, lies in government-sponsored financial institutions.

Besides credit rationing, the covariate and idiosyncratic nature of shocks is the other concern of this analysis. In Thailand, we find that covariate shocks are negatively related to livestock selling; this implies that households do not sell livestock when covariate shocks occur. Covariate shocks are also negatively related to the use of savings, informal borrowing, and reciprocal and they are positively related to the use of labour as a smoothing mechanism. Covariate shocks are positively related to choosing to remain inactive after a shock. However, we cannot identify whether this choice is actually in line with the model by Zimmerman and Carter (2003). We also see that lower income losses after a shock make it more likely for a household to remain inactive after a shock. Therefore, these households might simply be less affected and so remain inactive.

In Vietnam, covariate shocks matter little for the choice of smoothing mechanisms. It is neither related to livestock selling nor to informal borrowing and reciprocal insurance. There is a positive relationship between covariate shocks and the use of labour as a smoothing mechanism. Another positive relationship is found between covariate shocks and remaining inactive. Again, we cannot identify whether this is due to asset smoothing or to households being not so severely affected.

In summary, the nature of shocks may be more important for the choice of a smoothing mechanism than the (non-)existence of credit constraints. The relation between covariate shocks and smoothing behaviour is more pronounced in Thailand than in Vietnam.

10.5 Concluding remarks: interpreting the results in their country-specific setting

With respect to the empirical analysis it can be stated that credit restrictions are not very important for the choice of smoothing mechanisms in Thailand and Vietnam. This contradicts the assumption of a binding constraint in the models by Rosenzweig and Wolpin (1993), Kochar (1995), and Zimmerman and Carter (2003), but not Eswaran and Kotwal (1989), Paxson (1992), and Udry (1994). We presume that the reason for this lies in the financial institutions of the countries concerned.

According to Conning and Udry (2005), there are two types of rural credit markets in developing countries: those that are characterized by fragmented or absent credit markets and those that are characterized by government interventions in the provision of credit. Thailand and Vietnam belong to the latter. In both countries government-led credit institutions offer group-based or individual lending schemes to households (for example the Village Fund, the Vietnam Bank for Agriculture and Rural Development, and the Vietnam Bank for Social Policy). In addition to formal credit, the informal credit sector in both countries is still flourishing (although the share of informal credit has decreased over the last years). Loans from family and friends are particularly attractive, as they usually come at very low or zero interest. Moneylenders serve the informal credit sector too. These factors might explain why credit rationing in these two countries is not as severe as commonly presumed.

There is more evidence on this. Using the Vulnerability in South-East Asia database, we find by using a different approach that informal (versus formal) borrowing is used as a shock-absorbing mechanism in Thailand (Menkhoff and Rungruxsirivorn, 2011). For rural Vietnam, Kemper (2009) shows in a permanent and transitory income framework (based on the same dataset) that households actively use credit to smooth income fluctuations. Due to a land certification program, households in Vietnam are actually found to have good access to the formal credit sectors because land can be pledged as collateral to banks (Kemper *et al.*, 2011).

With respect to the role of covariate shocks in the choice of smoothing mechanisms, it can be stated that the nature of the shock is significantly related to every smoothing mechanism in Thailand and to two in Vietnam (increase in labour supply and remaining inactive). It does not fit the assumption by Kochar (1995), but it does fit the assumption made in Zimmerman and Carter (2003). However, we cannot conclude asset smoothing rather than consumption smoothing from this.

In Vietnam covariate shocks are negatively related to selling livestock. This is not in line with Rosenzweig and Wolpin (1993) who assume that livestock can be moved and is, therefore, still useful in the case of covariate shocks. The negative relationship between covariate shocks and use of savings and informal borrowing is not assumed by Paxson (1992) and Udry (1994).

Overall, our analysis provides mixed results: whereas the relationship between credit constraint and the choice of smoothing mechanism hardly matters in both countries, there is quite some variation in relations regarding the nature of shocks. These mixed results obviously support some theories and question others.

Notes

1. Wage earners in the informal sector include casual labour in non-agriculture, and off-farm labour in agriculture. However, the share of off-farm labour in agriculture in this group is very small.
2. Wage earners in the formal sector include permanently employed workers in non-agriculture, and employed workers in agriculture. A large proportion of the population in this group is found to be workers in the non-agricultural sector.
3. Household assets are broken down into the following categories: land and buildings, household durable goods including farm machinery and non-farm business equipment, agricultural assets such as livestock and stored rice, and savings and other financial assets.
4. In our questionnaire, households are asked to report whether they have ever applied for a loan, and if so whether their loan application was completely rejected or whether they obtained a certain amount but less than they applied for. Households whose loan applications were completely rejected are classified as fully credit rationed. Households who were given some credit but less than they asked for are classified as partially credit rationed.
5. These are households who have defaulted on all outstanding loans.

References

Beck, T. and A. Demirgüc-Kunt (2008): "Access to Finance: An Unfinished Agenda", *World Bank Economic Review*, 22(3): 383–96.
Conning, J. and C. Udry (2005): "Rural Financial Markets in Developing Countries", *Economic Growth Center Discussion Paper*, 914, Yale University.
Deaton, A. (1991): "Savings and Liquidity Constraints", *Econometrica*, 59: 1221–48.
Eswaran, M. and A. Kotwal (1989): "Credit as Insurance in Agrarian Economies", *Journal of Development Economics*, 37: 37–53.
Greene, William H. (2002): *Econometric Analysis*, 5th edn, Prentice Hall.
Hardeweg, B., H. Waibel, S. Praneetvatakul and T. D. Phung (2007): "Sampling for Vulnerability to Poverty: Cost Effectiveness Versus Precision", *mimeo*, 9–11 October, Tropentag, Witzenhausen, Germany.
Johnston, D. and J. Morduch (2008): "The Unbanked: Evidence from Indonesia", *World Bank Economic Review*, 22(3): 517–37.
Kemper, N. (2009): "Credit, Savings and Transitory Income Smoothing in Rural Vietnam", *mimeo*, Verein für Socialpolitik (Entwicklungsländerausschuß), 26–27 June, Frankfurt, Germany.
Kemper, N., R. Klump and H. Schumacher (2011): "Representation of Property Rights and Credit Market Outcomes: Evidence from a Land Reform in Vietnam", *mimeo*, 3 September, Verein für Socialpolitik, Frankfurt, Germany.
Kochar, A. (1995): "Explaining Household Vulnerability to Idiosyncratic Income Shocks", *AEA Papers and Proceedings*, 85(2): 159–64.
Maddala, G. (1983): "Limited-Dependent and Qualitative Variables in Econometrics", *Econometric Society Monograph*, Cambridge University Press, New York.

Menkhoff, L. and O. Rungruxsirivorn (2011): "Do Village Funds Improve Access to Finance? Evidence from Thailand", *World Development*, 39(1): 110–22.

Paxson, C. (1992): "Using Weather Variability to Estimate the Response of Savings to Transitory Income in Thailand", *American Economic Review*, 82(1): 15–33.

Platteau, J.-P. (1997): "Mutual Insurance as An Elusive Concept in Traditional Rural Communities", *Journal of Development Studies*, 33(6): 764–96.

Rosenzweig, M. and K. Wolpin (1993): "Credit Market Constraints, Consumption Smoothing, and the Accumulation of Durable Production Assets in Low-Income Countries: Investment in Bullocks in India", *Journal of Political Economy*, 101(2): 223–44.

Udry, C. (1994): "Risk and Insurance in a Rural Credit Market: An Empirical Investigation in Northern Nigeria", *Review of Economic Studies*, 61: 495–526.

Zimmerman, J. and M. Carter (2003): "Asset Smoothing, Consumption Smoothing and the Reproduction of Inequality Under Risk and Subsistence Constraints", *Journal of Development Economics*, 71: 233–60.

Appendix 10.A.1 Summary statistics of key variables of sample households

	Thailand		Vietnam	
	Mean or Fraction	Std. Dev	Mean or Fraction	Std. Dev
Demographic variables				
female head of household[1]	0.27	0.01	0.16	0.01
age of head	54.65	0.35	48.28	0.35
years of education	4.96	0.06	7.38	0.10
household size	3.98	0.04	4.30	0.05
number of adult males	1.26	0.02	1.22	0.02
number of adult females	1.42	0.02	1.35	0.02
number of children (<18 years old)	1.30	0.03	1.73	0.04
Occupational dummies[1]				
farmer	0.62	0.02	0.68	0.02
informal worker	0.09	0.01	0.06	0.01
formal worker	0.03	0.00	0.05	0.01
government official	0.04	0.00	0.04	0.00
business owner	0.08	0.01	0.07	0.01
economically inactive	0.15	0.01	0.10	0.01
Wealth variables[3]				
area of owned land[2]	2.01	0.09	0.73	0.05
income	5,185.74	333.86	3,913.77	196.57
consumption expenditures	4,581.58	144.90	4,400.25	126.12
food	1,674.80	50.79	2,319.62	58.31
non-food	2,906.78	109.48	2,080.62	81.13
total assets	61,800.00	2,696.77	29,583.33	1,775.71
savings and financial assets	1,168.72	106.09	881.64	291.31
livestock and stored crops	1,880.55	90.90	1,232.80	69.67
household durable goods	14,579.23	632.85	5,738.46	415.81
land and buildings	44,079.99	2,320.16	21,739.64	1,346.81

Continued

Appendix 10.A.1   Continued

	Thailand		Vietnam	
	Mean or Fraction	Std. Dev	Mean or Fraction	Std. Dev
Credit access variables				
dummy for credit rationing [1]	0.10	0.01	0.17	0.01
dummy for loan default [1]	0.03	0.00	0.01	0.00
dummy for late repayment on loan [1]	0.11	0.01	0.07	0.01
value of loan default as ratio of total loan outstanding	0.02	0.00	0.01	0.00
value of loan repaid late as ratio of total loan outstanding	0.06	0.00	0.05	0.00

[1] Number is expressed as fraction of total sample.
[2] Unit for land area is hectare.
[3] All variables in currency value are measured at PPP adjusted prices to make comparisons in real terms between the two countries possible. The unit of these variables is PPP US$ adjusted.

Appendix 10.A.2 Number of households reporting shock events in the period of 2002–7

	Thailand				Vietnam			
Year of shock	no. households	%[1]	no. shocks per household[2]	% of single shock[3]	no. households	%[1]	no. shocks per household[2]	% of single shock[3]
overall (2002–7)	1,383	63.27	1.45	67.25	1,847	84.15	1.93	38.60
2002	136	6.22	1.04	96.32	307	13.99	1.09	91.20
2003	177	8.10	1.02	97.74	295	13.44	1.05	95.25
2004	346	15.83	1.08	92.20	436	19.86	1.10	89.91
2005	407	18.62	1.08	92.87	563	25.65	1.12	90.23
2006	627	28.68	1.19	85.65	1088	49.57	1.23	78.40
2007 (Jan-April)	124	5.67	1.03	96.77	434	19.77	1.10	90.50
2006-April 2007	708	32.39	1.23	82.20	1316	59.95	1.38	68.16
Total	2,186				2,195			

[1]Number is expressed as percentage of total sample households.
[2]Number is the mean value of the number of shocks per household in each year that shock occurs.
[3]The number of households being hit by a single shock in each year as a percentage of households reporting shocks that year.

Appendix 10.A.3   Severity of the shock events in 2006–7

	Thailand		Vietnam	
	no. households	%	no. households	%
impact of shock event				
no impact	2	0.28	3	0.23
low impact	34	4.80	39	2.96
medium impact	219	30.93	317	24.09
high impact	453	63.98	957	72.72
still have to lower consumption?	372	52.54	1,096	83.28
years taken to recover from shock				
less than 1 year	278	39.27	305	23.18
1 year	136	19.21	272	20.67
more than 1 year	50	7.06	156	11.85
not yet recovered	235	33.19	559	42.48

	Thailand		Vietnam	
	Mean	Std. Dev	Mean	Std. Dev
estimated loss due to shock (PPP US$)	1,800.99	2,755.79	1,572.92	3,204.89
estimated loss as % of household income	26		34	
Total	708		1,316	

Appendix 10.A.4   Incidence of different types of shocks in 2006–7

	Thailand		Vietnam	
Type of shock	no. households	%	no. households	%
shock to household demographics[1]	200	28.25	407	30.93
social shock[2]	45	6.36	31	2.36
agro-climatic shock and pests[3]	330	46.61	810	61.55

Continued

Appendix 10.A.4   Continued

Type of shock	Thailand		Vietnam	
	no. households	%	no. households	%
higher household expenditures[4]	28	3.95	20	1.52
cannot pay back loan	53	7.49	4	0.30
macroeconomic shock[5]	50	7.06	33	2.51
others	2	0.28	11	0.84
Total	708		1,316	

[1]Shocks to household demographics include illness and death of household member, marriage into the household.
[2]Social shocks include theft, criminal offense, disputes, and conflict with neighbours.
[3]Agricultural shocks include floods, drought, pests, and livestock diseases.
[4]"Higher household expenditures" includes higher educational expense, higher ceremonial expense.
[5]Macroeconomic shocks include job loss, mass lay-offs, business closure, higher input prices, and lower output prices.

Appendix 10.A.5   Main smoothing mechanisms used by households in 2006–7

Smoothing mechanisms	Thailand		Vietnam	
	no. households	%	no. households	%
Selling livestock	29	4.10	85	6.56
Use of savings	95	13.42	132	10.03
Formal borrowing	37	5.22	114	8.67
Informal borrowing (1)	77	10.88	235	17.86
Informal borrowing (2)	26	3.67	117	8.89
Increase labour supply	72	10.17	212	16.11
Reciprocal insurance	48	6.78	36	2.73
Remain inactive	199	28.11	228	17.32
Other/Missing	125	17.65	157	11.83
Total	708	100	1316	100

Note: (1) Demographics include taking children out of school, migration to look for job. (2) Changing production includes substituting crops, diversifying agricultural portfolio, reducing production inputs. Informal borrowing (1) and Informal borrowing (2) stand for borrowing from family and friends or a moneylender respectively.

Appendix 10.A.6 Estimation results for Thailand

Variables	Selling livestock	Use of savings	Formal borrowing	Informal borrowing (1)	Informal borrowing (2)	Increase labour supply	Reciprocal insurance	Remain inactive
	Mean (s.d.)	Mean (s.d.)		Mean (s.d.)	Mean (s.d.)	Mean (s.d.)	Mean (s.d.)	Mean (s.d.)
rationed	-1.01 (0.77)	-0.61 (0.58)		-0.49 (0.55)	-0.21 (0.70)	-0.21 (0.57)	-1.44 (0.77)*	-0.84 (0.53)
hh size	0.19 (0.18)	0.06 (0.15)		0.21 (0.15)	0.09 (0.19)	0.02 (0.16)	0.17 (0.17)	0.09 (0.14)
wage	-0.09 (0.15)**	-0.04 (0.07)		0.00 (0.02)	-0.02 (0.06)	-0.04 (0.05)	0.01 (0.02)	-0.01 (0.02)
off-farm	-0.02 (0.01)	-0.01 (0.01)		-0.01 (0.00)*	-0.01 (0.01)	-0.01 (0.01)	-0.01 (0.01)	-0.01 (0.00)*
agri-self	-0.23 (0.24)	-0.09 (0.20)		-0.28 (0.20)	-0.17 (0.25)	-0.36 (0.22)*	-0.32 (0.24)	-0.37 (0.19)*
expendit	-0.00 (0.00)	0.00 (0.00)		-0.00 (0.00)	0.00 (0.00)	0.00 (0.00)	-0.00 (0.00)	0.00 (0.00)
covariate	-1.23 (0.61)**	-1.36 (0.51)**		-1.04 (0.48)**	-2.82 (1.09)**	0.93 (0.49)*	-1.33 (0.59)**	0.87 (0.44)**
savings	0.00 (0.00)	0.00 (0.00)		0.00 (0.00)	0.00 (0.00)	0.00 (0.00)	0.00 (0.00)	0.00 (0.00)
livestock	-0.00 (0.00)	-0.00 (0.00)**		-0.00 (0.00)**	-0.00 (0.00)	-0.00 (0.00)	-0.00 (0.00)**	-0.00 (0.00)*
land	-0.21 (0.12)*	0.09 (0.12)		0.17 (0.11)	0.03 (0.14)	0.08 (0.12)	0.14 (0.13)	0.12 (0.11)
shock loss	-0.00 (0.00)	-0.00 (0.00)**		-0.00 (0.00)	-0.00 (0.00)	-0.00 (0.00)	0.00 (0.00)	-0.00 (0.00)**
constant	0.52 (0.77)	1.80 (0.67)**		1.84 (0.65)**	0.56 (0.79)	0.92 (0.72)	1.70 (0.74)**	2.11 (0.64)**

Normalizing smoothing mechanism

Note: The estimation includes 549 households affected by shocks. The Pseudo R-squared value is 0.10, the log likelihood -925.55. The model is jointly significant at the 1 per cent level (Chi-square test). Informal borrowing (1) and Informal borrowing (2) stand for borrowing from family and friends or a moneylender respectively.

Appendix 10.A.7 Estimation results for Vietnam

Variables	Selling livestock	Use of savings	Formal borrowing	Informal borrowing (1)	Informal borrowing (2)	Increase labour supply	Reciprocal insurance	Remain inactive
	Mean (s.d.)	Mean (s.d.)		Mean (s.d.)	Mean (s.d.)	Mean (s.d.)	Mean (s.d.)	Mean (s.d.)
rationed	0.16 (0.35)	-0.47 (0.35)		0.09 (0.28)	0.49 (0.31)	-0.02 (0.29)	0.19 (0.49)	-0.33 (0.30)
hh size	-0.22 (0.10)**	-0.66 (0.09)		0.03 (0.07)	-0.01 (0.09)	0.07 (0.08)	-0.41 (0.17)**	0.05 (0.08)
wage	-0.19 (0.16)	0.13 (0.14)		0.02 (0.12)	0.17 (0.12)	0.21 (0.11)*	-0.20 (0.24)	-0.06 (0.13)
off-farm	-0.09 (0.26)	0.23 (0.20)		-0.03 (0.19)	-0.12 (0.24)	-0.21 (0.21)	0.09 (0.38)	-0.07 (0.20)
agri-self	0.26 (0.14)*	-0.29 (0.14)**		-0.00 (0.11)	0.20 (0.12)	-0.12 (0.11)	-0.45 (0.26)	-0.12 (0.12)
expendit	-0.00 (0.00)	0.00 (0.00)		-0.00 (0.00)**	-0.00 (0.00)**	-0.00 (0.00)*	-0.00 (0.00)**	-0.00 (0.00)**
covariate	0.59 (0.33)	-0.09 (0.27)		-0.09 (0.27)	0.23 (0.30)	1.17 (0.27)**	0.19 (0.45)	0.67 (0.27)**
savings	-0.00 (0.00)	0.00 (0.00)**		0.00 (0.00)	0.00 (0.00)	0.00 (0.00)	0.00 (0.00)	0.00 (0.00)**
livestock	0.00 (0.00)	0.00 (0.00)		0.00 (0.00)	-0.00 (0.00)**	0.00 (0.00)	-0.00 (0.00)*	-0.00 (0.00)
land	-0.02 (0.8)	0.07 (0.07)		-0.47 (0.14)**	-0.03 (0.11)	0.00 (0.07)	0.14 (0.11)	-0.17 (0.10)
shock loss	-0.00 (0.00)	0.00 (0.00)		-0.00 (0.00)	-0.00 (0.00)	-0.00 (0.00)**	-0.00 (0.00)	-0.00 (0.00)
constant	0.71 (0.48)	0.64 (0.44)		1.48 (0.39)**	-0.01 (0.45)	0.52 (0.41)	2.76 (0.59)**	1.30 (0.40)**

Normalizing smoothing mechanism

Note: The estimation includes 1123 households affected by shocks. The Pseudo R-squared value is 0.08, the log likelihood -2024.91. The model is jointly significant at the 1 per cent level (Chi-square test). Informal borrowing (1) and Informal borrowing (2) stand for borrowing from family and friends or a moneylender respectively.

11
The Village Fund Loan Programme: Who Gets It, Keeps It and Loses It?

Carmen Kislat and Lukas Menkhoff

11.1 Introduction

The Village Fund (VF) programme in Thailand is one of the largest microfinance programmes in the world. It aims at improving access to finance and income in rural areas. These are worthwhile objectives for policy as finance is often limited in rural areas and incomes are low. In this sense, the introduction of a programme that sets up an additional fund of one million baht, roughly US$28,000, per village leading to a significant increase of loanable funds is welcome. Indeed, the rural population seems to be highly sympathetic to the 2001 government's decision to start the village fund programme, as election results continuously show.

However, at the same time there are several concerns with a programme such as this one. First, it is a matter of record that many large state-sponsored lending programmes have failed in the past, as documented for example in Krahnen and Schmidt (1994). All of them were started with high ambitions, but in the end the money was too often lost and diverted into dubious purposes. Second, and related to the first concern, political economy models suggest that governments may use gifts of this type to win political support in upcoming elections. Third, there are simple practical concerns about how such a huge programme could be successfully implemented given that it is virtually impossible to rely on finding experienced bankers.

As this programme has been operational for some time now, there are a few analyses available studying the outcomes of the VF programme. Two studies indicate that, as intended, it increases income (Boonperm *et al.*, 2009; Kaboski and Townsend, 2009). Moreover, a study shows that VFs helped to improve access to finance (Menkhoff and Rungruxsirivorn, 2011). However, considering the size and relevance of the VF programme, the available evidence is surprisingly thin. It would be most interesting for policy making in Thailand, and possibly for decision makers in other countries as well, to learn more about the functioning of VFs in order to make informed policy decisions.

We contribute to the issue of access to finance by extending the cross-sectional evidence in Menkhoff and Rungruxsirivorn (2011) by incorporating a time dimension. In effect, we rely on two waves of the large household survey conducted in three provinces of Northeastern Thailand in the years 2007 and 2008. It is this time dimension – even though consisting of only two consecutive years – that helps us understand how changes in the provision of VF credit may be related to household characteristics: which kinds of households get a VF loan, which ones keep it, and which ones lose it?

We find that VF borrowers are indeed somewhat different from other households and that these differences are consistent across the two periods. VF borrowers are characterized by a lower economic status, and the loss of a VF loan seems to worsen their economic situation. Also, VF borrowers are more often business owners. Finally, we cannot identify any significant substitution between VF loans and other loans, indicating that the VF loans are rarely used for longer-lasting credit-financed projects and thus that they have only a slight impact on permanent behaviour at household level.

We proceed in this study as follows. Section 11.2 briefly reports the findings of earlier studies in order to motivate our own research. The data basis is described in Section 11.3, characterizing borrowing households and the rural credit market. In Section 11.4 we analyse borrowers of the VFs regarding the four types of households who get it, keep it, lose it and do not use it. Section 11.5 concludes.

11.2   Expectations on the Thai village fund programme

Expectations and motivations about the VF programme are shaped by debates about microfinance in general and in Thailand. We briefly refer to these discussions before we discuss the specific research on the Thai VF programme.

In the last decades a lot of research has been conducted on the functionality of microfinance concepts and programmes. An early overview of different lending institutions in rural credit markets is given by Bell (1990). For an empirical impact study of microfinance on poverty reduction, see Khandker (2005). Separating lenders within rural credit markets into informal, formal and semiformal lenders, Pham and Lensink (2007) focus on different lending practices of those types of institutions. Policy-induced microfinance programmes especially were subjected to closer scrutiny, as they are expensive programmes whose impacts are not easy to assess. Most researchers agree that microfinance institutions can enhance the living conditions of poor people in developing countries. In particular, these institutions can contribute to reducing poverty; they allow farmers to borrow, especially when harvests are bad, and so give them the opportunity to smooth their consumption even if current production possibilities are scarce. In addition, they allow entrepreneurs to set up businesses, and permit a diversification of income generation and the establishment of a more sustainable sector based on non-agricultural business and innovation (World Bank, 2008). So the overall assessment of many microfinance programmes tends to be positive.

With respect to Thailand, an early benchmark study by Siamwalla *et al.* (1990) analyses the Thai rural credit market. Although the interventions of the Thai government into the rural credit market date back to the beginning of the 20th century, the establishment of the state-owned Bank for Agriculture and Agricultural Cooperatives (BAAC) in 1966 was the major intervention in recent decades. Aiming at an improved access to finance for rural farmers, the BAAC has customers that are mainly people in the rural areas. Another intervention, in the 1970s, was the requirement that commercial banks had to spread their business into the rural areas of the country. These measures were undertaken to ease the dependency of rural households on informal lenders.

The introduction of the VFs in each of the Thai villages is another step to improve access to finance in rural Thailand. But despite the efforts to establish formal and semi-formal institutions in the rural areas, informal lenders still play an important role. The segmented rural credit market, its institutions and their impact on the poor are therefore an interesting target for researchers (for a general discussion, see Hermes and Lensink, 2007).

Coleman (1999) examines the impact of group lending in Thailand, using a panel dataset with two waves. In a quasi-experimental setting he studies the effect of group lending on the welfare of borrowers. He finds that group lending procedures of so-called village banks (another microfinance concept introduced prior to the VF in Thailand) which are based on the idea of the Grameen Bank, are limited in thir ability to enhance the living conditions of borrowers. Focusing on the rural small-scale entrepreneurs and especially on women, the author does not find any significant impact on physical assets, enhanced spending or even education. But the data Coleman is using reveals many inter-dependencies and substitution effects among the different sources of credit. It seems that some households borrow to pay back other loans, and some even borrow to lend the money out at higher interest rates. Therefore it will be interesting to know which category the current VF loans can be assigned to.

In a later study, Coleman (2006) evaluates the impact of two microfinance institutions, namely the Rural Friends Association (RFA) and the Foundation for Integrated Agricultural Management (FIAM) which are operating in Northeastern Thailand. According to Coleman, the impact evaluation of policy-induced programmes suffers from two biases: first, self-selection of members and non-members, and second, programme placement in certain villages based on unobserved characteristics of the villages chosen. Only households which are better able to use credit funds and therefore realize higher returns will self-select into the pro-grammes; these might be placed in villages that are more appropriate for funding due to unobservable characteristics like high entrepreneur-ial skills and good organization. Both biases lead to an overestimation of programme impacts. Fortunately, in the case of VFs, the second bias does not occur because the fund is established in all Thai villages, mak-ing placement selection impossible. Coleman finds that the wealthier households are more likely to borrow from those programmes, and by controlling for the selection biases he discovers larger positive effects of finance on the welfare of programme committee members than on the welfare of "rank-and-file" members.

Schaaf (2010) examines the effect of community groups with micro-finance components on the well-being of poor village people. Using data from a single village in Northeastern Thailand, her focus lies on the assessment of improvements in living conditions through micro-finance institutions. Extending a model of Chen (1997), she uses a multidimensional framework to measure people's well-being with the following dimensions: material, cognitive, perceptual and relational. She finds that the VFs, together with community banks, have the high-est number of members compared to other microfinance institutions, though women are not specially targeted. But compared to other com-munity groups such as product groups, the VFs concentrate on finance, and they are therefore restricted to improving primarily the material dimension of people's well-being.

Kaboski and Townsend (2005) evaluate microfinance programmes also using data from Thailand (before the VF programme was implemented) and find that microfinance promotes asset growth, helps to smooth consumption, eases occupational mobility and is able to decrease moneylender reliance.

In a later study, Kaboski and Townsend (2009) analyse the impact of VF credits on rural households. They use a panel dataset which captures data on 960 households in 64 villages over a seven-year time period. Their most striking findings are that the introduction of VFs enhances consumption, short-term credit, investment in agriculture, income growth and wages in the labour market and for businesses. Asset endowment of households, however, decreased. The authors rely on two theories to explain these patterns. The buffer stock model suggests that formerly credit-constrained households increase their consumption if the credit constraints have eased due to the availability of VF credits. The second model relies on the assumption that more available credit will lead to more business start-ups. As a consequence, higher wages in the labour market can be expected; indeed, the study finds higher wages but no more new businesses.

Furthermore, this study finds that the overall credit amount increases if VF loans are available. The authors take this as evidence that VFs do not crowd out other sources of credit. This assumption is amplified by the observation of no lower interest rates, indicating still some scarcity of capital in the rural markets. The injection of capital via VFs does not reveal an additional effect, as one unit of injected capital does not lead to more than a single unit of further credit. Our study confirms this finding by and large, however, by choosing another perspective; we focus on household characteristics distinguishing between households who receive such loans successively and those who receive a VF loan only once.

Boonperm *et al.* (2009) address in their analysis the effect of VF loans on income, expenditure and the endowment with assets. Using the Thailand Socioeconomic Surveys of 2002 and 2004, with an overall sample of 35,000 households in each survey, they assess the extent of VF impact. By applying a propensity score-matching method, they compare borrowing households with households which have similar characteristics but do not borrow from VFs. They find an effect for VF borrowers of 1.9 per cent more income, 3.3 per cent more expenditures and 5 per cent higher endowment with durable assets compared to the control group. In combination with loans from the BAAC, the effect on income is even higher. Furthermore, the effects seem to be larger for households with lower expenditures, indicating a good targeting of poor households. But VF loans are not used by everyone; about 24 per cent of the households in the sample did not want to borrow from VFs because they had no need for credit, and another 25 per cent did not want to go into debt. A majority of VF borrowers, according to their own statements, profited from the access to finance but most of them are not satisfied with the current form of the programme. For example, they want the loans to be larger and the duration of the loans to be longer. This has to be expected due to the favourable terms of VF loans, and is consistent with our own interview experiences in the field.

Menkhoff and Rungruxsirivorn (2011) examine whether VFs are indeed improving access to finance and whether they are working in the intended way, i.e. targeting the relatively poor more than already existing institutions. Using a multinomial logit model to describe what determines borrowing from a certain institution, the authors find that the VFs serve especially those households which are in an intermediate state regarding income and wealth and are more prone to borrow from informal lending institutions. Although it remains unclear whether the VF programme is more efficient than other lending institutions, VF loans are reaching their aim in targeting the poor and reducing credit constraints, and therefore improve access to finance. We extend this work by stretching the analysis over two waves of the household survey.

Thus there are some encouraging findings on the impact of the VF programme. At the same time, however, some scepticism seems to be appropriate, as Morduch (1999: 1571) warns about new microfinance institutions in general: "Most of those funds are being mobilized and channelled to new, untested institutions, and existing resources are being reallocated from traditional poverty alleviation programmes to microfinance. With donor funding pouring in, practitioners have limited incentives to step back and question exactly how and where monies will be best spent."

11.3 Our data

In this section we briefly describe our data, from general to specific. The data is part of a larger household survey study from which we consider here only those households which get a loan. We characterize (a) the survey, (b) the borrowing households, (c) the lending institutions in general and (d) the VF in more detail.

(a) The data emanates from a research project funded by the German Research Foundation analysing vulnerability to poverty of rural households. For this project, representative household surveys were conducted from April to June in 2007 and in 2008 respectively, in three provinces in Northeastern Thailand (namely Buriram, Nhakon Phanom and Ubon Ratchathani). Households were chosen in a three-stage random sampling procedure being representative for the rural population in the three provinces (see Menkhoff and Rungruxsirivorn, 2011, see Chapter 3).

(b) From the total of almost 2200 households we consider a subset which fulfils three requirements: First, households must be covered by both waves of the survey; second, households must take at least one new loan during one period; and, third, we do not consider outliers, defined as values beyond the median plus or minus eight times the standard deviation. Due to these requirements we get a sample of 1575 households. This sample, covering about 74 per cent of the representative survey sample, is characterized as can be seen in Table 11.1.

Table 11.1 Borrower characteristics

Household characteristics	2007			2008		
	mean	std. dev	Obs	mean	std. dev	Obs
Age of household head	53.9	(12.932)	1570	54.7	(13.043)	1569
Proportion of female-headed household	25.1%	(0.434)	1570	25.2%	(0.434)	1569
Number of adults per household	2.7	(1.179)	1570	2.7	(1.216)	1569
Number of children per household	1.3	(1.090)	1570	1.4	(1.083)	1569
Household occupation (%)						
Farm household	64.1%	(0.478)	1570	62.5%	(0.484)	1569
Informal worker	9.7%	(0.297)	1570	11.7%	(0.322)	1569
Formal worker	7.2%	(0.259)	1570	7.0%	(0.256)	1569
Business owner	7.8%	(0.269)	1570	7.6%	(0.266)	1569
Inactive	11.1%	(0.315)	1570	10.8%	(0.311)	1569
Years of education	4.6	(2.684)	1396	4.6	(2.810)	1402
Income (1000 THB)	112	(134)	1546	122	(155)	1568
Assets (1000 THB)	219	(317)	1570	202	(395)	1569
Area of owned land (hectare)	2.1	(3.184)	1570	1.9	(3.022)	1568

Household heads are usually male and on average 54 years old. Their education reflects their age, that is schooling happened decades ago and according to the compulsory schooling years at that time it was only four to five years long. Almost two thirds work as farmers, and their own land is as small as two hectares. Household size is about four persons. Household assets are worth above 200,000 baht, which is roughly US$5600, and their annual income is above 110,000 baht, which is roughly US$3100. Changes between 2007 and 2008 are largely negligible for our purposes. Overall, most of these household members live in modest living conditions, as one might expect for the relatively poor Northeastern region of Thailand.

(c) Finally, we briefly characterize the lending institutions operating in rural Thailand. The rural credit market in Thailand is somewhat segmented, with many players granting loans. Whereas some authors follow the classification of formal versus informal lending institutions, our approach divides all lending institutions into seven groups. In order of tentatively decreasing formality these are (1) commercial banks (CB), (2) the Bank for Agriculture and Agricultural Cooperatives (BAAC), (3) village funds (VF), (4) credit and savings groups and cooperatives (CRED), (5) policy funds (POLICY), (6) private moneylender (ML), and (7) relatives and friends (RELA). This approach is also used by Menkhoff and Rungruxsirivorn (2011), and is applied here, too, to make the results of this research compatible with their results.

CBs are normal commercial banks, including some government institutions such as the Government Savings Bank. The BAAC is a state-owned bank that was founded in the 1960s to support the rural population and, especially, to provide financial access to farmers. The VFs are policy-induced funds that are organized at the village level; they exist in every one of the 77,000 Thai villages, and have operated since 2001. CREDs are mainly community based, and include a variety of slightly different institutions, for example rice banks. POLICYs include all policy loans that have been given for the purpose of alleviating poverty and supporting the poor. MLs are private moneylenders and pawnshops who are often the only source of credit and therefore usually charge a high interest rate. The most informal source of credit are RELAs, who lend money very informally and often short-handedly, without charging interest in many cases. Table 11.2 provides an overview of the importance of these seven lending "institutions" with respect to volume and number of loans in 2007 and 2008. Please note that we do not cover all outstanding loans but only newly granted loans which are outstanding. In this respect, the BAAC is the largest institution regarding volume of

Table 11.2 Share of different lending institutions on overall volume and credit contracts

	CB	BAAC	VF	CRED	POLICY	ML	RELA
2007							
average loan size (1000 THB)	92	51	16	39	14	44	30
volume of credit (1000 THB)	3,900	25,900	15,800	10,800	1,500	5,900	4,200
average volume per hh (1000 THB)	98	57	18	45	14	48	34
share on volume	5.7%	38.1%	23.2%	15.9%	2.2%	8.7%	6.2%
number of loan contracts	42	512	974	275	107	134	140
share on loan contracts	1.9%	23.4%	44.6%	12.6%	4.9%	6.1%	6.5%
number of borrowing households	40	457	879	240	106	122	124
2008							
average loan size (1000 THB)	71	50	16	42	9	58	27
volume of credit (1000 THB)	1,600	26,700	15,600	12,000	900	3,500	4,100
average volume per hh (1000 THB)	76	57	18	47	10	64	33
share on volume	2.5%	41.4%	24.2%	18.6%	1.4%	5.5%	6.4%
number of loan contracts	23	536	964	285	100	60	149
share on loan contracts	1.1%	25.3%	45.5%	13.5%	4.7%	2.8%	7.0%
number of borrowing households	21	471	862	253	95	55	124

loans, while the VF is the largest regarding the number of loans. More than 44 per cent of all new loans granted in our sample stem from the VF, but due to their smaller size – about 16,000 baht each – they add up to a volume of market share of only about 24 per cent. Still, this makes the VF the second largest lending institution behind the BAAC, following this criterion (share of new loans by volume).

Any changes between 2007 and 2008 are small with two notable exceptions, namely the decreasing number of loans granted by CBs and MLs. As we observe only two periods and the absolute numbers are small, we are not sure whether these decreases reflect systematic changes. If so, the origins of these changes are unclear; possibly, they are a consequence of the financial crisis, in that more market-oriented institutions (in contrast to state-run institutions) react to the crisis by a more rigid lending policy.

(d) Based on the idea of microfinance institutions – as established all over the world – the Thai government started the VF programme in 2001. Within a very short time, self-governed vehicles – the so-called VFs – were introduced in every one of the 77,000 Thai villages. Each fund was equipped with 1 million baht of initial capital. The overall costs of 77 billion baht, or US$1.8 billion, which is 1.5 per cent of the Thai GDP in the same year, makes the VF programme one of the largest in the world (Kaboski and Townsend, 2009).

VFs are run by the village members themselves, who have to form a VF committee and have to open a bank account at the BAAC or another state bank or savings cooperation via which the money transfer is provided. The borrowers have to open an account at the same credit institution to receive the loan. Only members of the VF can apply for a loan, and to solve moral hazard and adverse selection problems they have to provide personal guarantors from among other members of the fund.

11.4   Borrowers of the village fund

Our research is focused on the borrowers of the VF and whether and how they change over time. We analyse these issues in three sections: in Section 11.4.1 we differentiate all borrowers into four groups, depending on whether they borrowed from the VF in either 2007 or 2008, or in both years or never. This describes the outreach of the VF. Section 11.4.2 examines characteristics of these groups, allowing comparisons across groups and tentatively over time. Section 11.4.3 describes in detail all new loans granted in 2007 and 2008 for the four groups of interest, which allows a first impression on which direction the loss or gain regarding a VF loan may have influenced the household behaviour. This also indicates possible substitution effects between the VF and alternative sources of credit.

11.4.1 Characteristics of four groups of borrowers

We divded our sample into four categories of households according to their borrowing from the VF. We distinguish borrowing from the VF in two periods, namely the 12 months up to the respective survey waves in 2007 and 2008: (1) The first group of borrowing households borrowed from VFs only in the first year but not in the second year. (2) The second group borrowed from the VF only in the second year, (3) the third group borrowed from the VF in both years, and (4) the fourth group never borrowed from the VF at all.

Table 11.3 briefly gives some characteristics of these four groups. Interestingly, the largest group by far is Group 3, that is those households who received a loan from the VF in 2007 and 2008. Of the total of 1575 households in our sample, the "permanent" VF borrowers make up about 40 per cent. The second largest group is Group 4, that is households which never borrowed from the VF. Interesting for our purposes are also those households which either lost a VF loan or got one for the first time, that is Groups 1 and 2 respectively.

Analysing the descriptive statistics documented in Table 11.3, Group 4 seems to be better off in economic terms compared to the other three groups in both survey waves, as these households have slightly longer education, higher income, more assets and more land at their disposal. This is consistent with the finding in Menkhoff and Rungruxsirivorn (2011), covering the 2007 wave only, that the VF reaches households with slightly lower socio-economic status. It also indicates that the VF works differently from the microfinance institutions analysed by Coleman (2006).

Regarding changes between the two waves, it seems interesting that despite a certain increase in income, other wealth indicators – such as assets and the area of owned land – drop. In this latter respect, it is Group 1 in particular which has to face a problematic situation, as the loss of the VF loan in 2008 coincides with the worst economic status of the four groups and the most significant losses in assets and land; it is a topic for speculation that the somewhat higher income in 2008 could have been caused by sales of assets. For Group 2, income increases in the second wave where the VF loans have been received, but the loans seem to stabilize the economic conditions rather than leading to an overall improvement of the economic conditions. Group 3 relies on VF loans in both waves; obviously, those households are economically

Table 11.3 Borrower characteristics for lending groups and the weighted average over all groups

Household characteristics	group 1	group 2	group 3	group 4	average
2007					
Age of household head	54.30	56.02	52.58	54.72	53.94
	(13.050)	(13.475)	(12.733)	(12.742)	(12.932)
Proportion of female- headed household	29.3%	29.3%	23.9%	23.2%	25.1%
	(0.456)	(0.456)	(0.427)	(0.422)	(0.434)
Household size	4.20	4.06	4.09	4.02	4.08
	(1.769)	(1.859)	(1.684)	(1.620)	(1.698)
Household occupation (%)					
Farm household	58.6%	62.0%	65.6%	65.2%	64.1%
	(0.494)	(0.487)	(0.475)	(0.477)	(0.480)
Informal worker	11.3%	9.3%	8.2%	11.3%	9.4%
	(0.317)	(0.291)	(0.2749)	(0.317)	(0.297)
Formal worker	5.9%	8.8%	6.2%	8.4%	7.2%
	(0.235)	(0.284)	(0.242)	(0.278)	(0.259)
Business owner	12.2%	5.9%	10.0%	4.0%	7.8%
	(0.3276)	(0.235)	(0.300)	(0.198)	(0.269)
Years of education	4.48	4.41	4.61	4.61	4.57
	(2.892)	(2.841)	(2.487)	(2.783)	(2.684)
Income (1000 THB)	100	109	115	115	112
	(118)	(108)	(152)	(126)	(134)
Assets (1000 THB)	204	208	216	236	219
	(293)	(300)	(283)	(374)	(317)
Area of owned land (hectare)	1.74	1.92	2.10	2.25	2.07
	(2.653)	(2.791)	(2.913)	(3.844)	(3.184)

Continued

Table 11.3 Continued

Household characteristics	group 1	group 2	group 3	group 4	average
2008					
Age of household head	55.04	56.84	53.44	55.32	54.71
	(12.89)	(13.283)	(12.780)	(13.188)	(13.043)
Proportion of female-headed household	29.3%	28.3%	24.5%	22.9%	25.2%
	(0.456)	(0.452)	(0.430)	(0.420)	(0.434)
Household size	4.05	4.15	4.15	4.02	4.1
	(1.762)	(1.829)	(1.742)	(1.649)	(1.730)
Household occupation (%)					
Farm household	55.0%	58.0%	64.5%	64.7%	62.3%
	(0.499)	(0.495)	(0.479)	(0.478)	(0.484)
Informal worker	14.4%	14.1%	9.3%	12.7%	11.7%
	(0.352)	(0.349)	(0.290)	(0.333)	(0.322)
Formal worker	6.3%	8.8%	6.2%	7.6%	7.0%
	(0.244)	(0.284)	(0.242)	(0.265)	(0.255)
Business owner	12.2%	5.4%	8.5%	5.7%	7.6%
	(0.328)	(0.226)	(0.279)	(0.232)	(0.266)
Years of education	4.71	4.43	4.54	4.59	4.56
	(3.310)	(3.080)	(2.537)	(2.820)	(2.811)
Income (1000 THB)	112	130	116	130	122
	(128)	(181)	(136)	(176)	(155)
Assets (1000 THB)	161	200	193	233	202
	(227)	(389)	(342)	(506)	(395)
Area of owned land (hectare)	1.45	1.70	1.93	1.96	1.85
	(2.379)	(2.794)	(2.662)	(3.725)	(3.022)

Note: Standard errors in parentheses. Group 1 are households who received VF loans only in the first wave; Group 2 are households who received VF loans only. In the second wave, Group 3 received VF loans in both waves, and Group 4 never borrowed from VF, but did borrow from other institutions.

better off than one-time recipients and worse off than Group 4 house-holds. Furthermore, the economic situation of the Group 3 households can be described as fluctuating less over time than the households of all other groups. There are at least two explanations for this: first, these households do not really want to improve their economic situation, or, second, they are simply unable to change it. On closer inspection, we see that their situation gets worse in 2008, so the second explanation may be more satisfactory. According to this interpretation, VF loans help stabilize the situation at a medium level, but households are unable to improve their situation further.

11.4.2   Characteristics of village fund borrowers

Table 11.4 shows what kinds of households in general do receive VF loans, using a multivariate panel probit model. Indeed, VF borrowers and non-VF borrowers are systematically different. Starting with the household-related characteristics, VF borrowers are likely to be large households (in terms of both number of adults and number of children) with a young household head who is less educated. Another interesting finding is the occupation of VF borrowers. We know from Table 11.3 that VF borrowers are frequently "business owners", which does not necessarily imply a comfortable economic situation; having any of the occupations listed in Table 11.4 leads to a lower probability of having a VF loan. This has to be interpreted in relation to the omitted base category, which is "business owner". Being a business owner therefore increases the probability of receiving a VF loan.

Turning to the economic status variables, these do not give a clear pattern. Whereas income is negatively related to VF loans, asset endow-ment and the area of owned land is not. Thus none of these variables is significant, which makes any conclusions at this point problematic.

Another interesting finding is the size of the villages the borrowers come from. Every VF received the same amount of initial capital – one million baht – regardless of village size. As a result, loan applicants from small villages are more likely to be successful with their application. This pattern is confirmed by Table 11.4, showing that an increasing vil-lage size leads to a lower probability of receiving a VF loan.

In order to hone our analysis more finely, we compare the characteris-tics of VF borrowers (belonging to Groups 1 to 3) to Group 4 households (which never borrowed from the VF). We choose a multinomial logit as our estimation approach because we do not want to impose any struc-ture on Groups 1 to 3. This analysis is conducted by taking the average of the observed values of both waves for each variable and for each

Table 11.4 Panel probit model predicting VF loans

Independent variables	vf loan	independent variables	vf loan
household characteristics		occupation dummies	
number of children	0.0867*	farmer	-0.325*
	(0.0497)		(0.173)
number of adults	0.101**	informal	-0.483**
	(0.0440)		(0.207)
female household head	-0.0712	formal	-0.476*
	(0.131)		(0.253)
age of household head	-0.0237***	inactive	-0.244
	(0.00517)		(0.2237)
income per household	-2.71e-07	village size	-0.00253***
	(2.16e-07)		(0.000558)
education	-0.0389*		
	(0.0202)		
assets	5.37e-08		
	(8.79e-08)		
area of landholding	0.00816		
	(0.0167)		
		Constant	1.309***
			(0.370)
		Observations	3767
		Number of households	1953

Note: Standard errors in parentheses; *** $p < 0.01$, ** $p < 0.05$, * $p < 0.1$.

household. This approach allows the time dimension problem of the data structure to be solved; however, we lose information about changes over time. To control for individual effects, we use cluster robust standard errors at household level. Results can be seen in Table 11.5, where relative-risk ratios are presented.

A relative-risk ratio of 0.579 for the dummy variable "farmer" for Group 1 households shows the relative probability of belonging to Group 1 relative to the reference category (Group 4) if the dummy changes from 0 to 1. In other words, the probability that a household

Table 11.5 Multinomial logit predicting being in different groups

Independent variables	hhtype 1	hhtype 2	hhtype 3
household characteristics			
number of children	1.023	0.919	0.986
	(0.0863)	(0.0845)	(0.0628)
number of adults	1.125	1.145	1.133*
	(0.0994)	(0.111)	(0.0757)
female household head	1.292	1.227	1.196
	(0.267)	(0.272)	(0.195)
age of household head	0.995	1.004	0.982***
	(0.00794)	(0.00874)	(0.00594)
ln income per household	0.741**	0.970	0.853
	(0.0972)	(0.121)	(0.0826)
education	1.004	0.984	0.980
	(0.0371)	(0.0401)	(0.0247)
ln assets	1.104	1.060	1.105
	(0.118)	(0.115)	(0.0894)
area of landholding	0.949	0.945	0.987
	(0.0387)	(0.0415)	(0.0207)
dummy variables			
farmer	0.579**	0.779	0.823
	(0.125)	(0.181)	(0.134)
small village	1.672***	1.552**	1.480***
	(0.308)	(0.295)	(0.207)
Constant	5.003	0.211	5.322
	(7.315)	(0.315)	(5.882)
Observations	1389	1389	1389

Note: The table shows relative risk ratios, clustered standard errors are in parentheses. Logarithmic transformations of income and asset variables are used. *** $p < 0.01$, ** $p < 0.05$, * $p < 0.1$.
hhtype1: households who only received VF loans in first wave
hhtype2: households who only received VF loans in second wave
hhtype3: households who received VF loans in both waves
The regression is run on average values of first and second wave.

will fall into Group 1 is about 58 per cent if the probability of belonging to the reference category is 100 per cent.

The household size measured as number of adults is still important, even if it is significant for Group 3 only. Having a young household head increases the probability of being in Group 3 but not Group 2. Group 2 and Group 3 households are more likely to be less well educated, but this is not true for Group 1. Higher-income households are less likely to be assigned to Groups 1, 2 and 3, although this effect is only significant for Group 1 households. For all groups, being a farmer decreases the probability of being a VF borrower, but this is statistically significant only for Group 1. Living in a small village increases the probability of being a VF borrower, which is consistent with Table 11.4.

VF borrowers of Groups 1 or 2 either are occasional borrowers by choice or are able to receive VF loans only once in a while. To address this issue, we take a closer look at the differences between the groups. Table 11.3 suggests that Group 1 has lower income than Group 3, but Group 2, after receiving the VF loan, has higher income than Group 3. In terms of education, income and assets, Group 3 seems to be in a central category, between Groups 1 and 2. The better educated Group 1 may receive VF loans only because of their relatively high education compared to Group 2 households, which indicates lower risk (Beck and Demirgüç-Kunt, 2008). Group 2, which is richer in terms of assets, can pledge more collateral and can be considered as more creditworthy than Group 1 households. Even though the VFs usually do not require tangible collateral, it may still be an indicator for lower risk. Either way, the loss or the receipt of a VF loan generates changes in the economic situation of both groups, as can be seen in Table 11.3: Losing a VF loan downgrades the economic situation (see Group 1), and receiving a VF loan improves the economic situation (see Group 2). For those households who permanently rely on VF loans, namely Group 3, the loans seem to have no observable impact on income and assets over the two-year period considered.

11.4.3   Changes in new loans

As a last step in our analysis, we document the number and volume of new loans in both periods. From this, we can see whether the loss or gain of a VF loan in Groups 1 and 2 respectively leads to noticeably different behaviour.

Interestingly, Group 1 indicates that households losing a VF loan, that is after a VF loan in 2007 with a one-year duration and no new VF loan in 2008, do not seem to apply for (or receive) new loans from other lenders (see Table 11.6). In fact, neither the number nor the volume of loans from the six other sources increases much in 2008 compared to 2007. Consequently, the VF loan is a limited event for these households– it is available for a certain limited period only. This is consistent with the hypothesis that the purpose for borrowing, too, is limited, and is fulfilled on termination of the loan. Another interpretation may be that VF loans are seen as windfall profits which come and go but do not affect behaviour much.

The surprisingly unrelated role of VF loans can also be seen for Group 2. Even though the newly gained VF loans are important for these households, they do not change their behaviour much regarding other lenders: the number of loans from lenders other than the VF, and the volume that households receive from these loans, are hardly affected by the many newly received VF loans. This is a different finding compared to Coleman (1999) who observes much substitution between loans.

The overall stability in households' borrowing behaviour is also shown by the results for Groups 3 and 4 in Table 11.6, where number and volume of loans remain quite stable across the two periods. Thus it appears that the VF loans do not crowd out other lending programmes, but are rather seen as a supplementary lending source, presumably due to their attractive conditions.

11.5   Conclusions

This article examines the role of VFs in the rural credit market of Thailand. In order to better understand the role of VFs, we form four groups of borrowers, namely (1) borrowers who lose their VF loan in the second period, (2) borrowers who get a new VF loan in the second period, (3) those who have a VF loan in both periods and (4) those who have never had a VF loan.

Based on the two-wave panel on the borrowing of northeastern households, we contribute three findings to the literature on VFs in Thailand: First, despite the widespread use of VF loans, there is some structure across households, as VF borrowers seem to have a worse economic status than non-borrowers, which is underlined by the fact that households losing a VF loan report lower wealth than other households. Second, the regression approach indicates that VF borrowers are characterized not only by a lower economic status but also by having more adults in their household and more often being business owners. In combination with their lower economic status – less often owning land and less often being a farmer – this tentatively indicates underemployment of the workforce. Third, the examination of new loans across the two periods indicates

Table 11.6 New loans (loans per household in 1000 THB and shares on overall loan volume)

Household category	2007			2008		
	number of borrowing households	volume per household	share on overall loan volume (%)	number of borrowing households	volume per household	share on overall loan volume (%)
Group 1						
CB	6	148	9.2	2	20	0.9
BAAC	58	55	33.3	56	62	76.2
VF	222	17	40.0	17	31	11.8
CRED	28	41	11.9	10	5	1.1
POLICY	17	5	0.9	8	35	6.2
ML	11	24	2.7	11	16	3.8
RELA	15	12	1.9			
Total	357	43.1	100.0	104	28.2	100.0
Group 2						
CB	5	88	8.8	6	77	5.6
BAAC	36	78	55.8	51	55	34.0
VF	23	25	11.5	205	17	41.1
CRED	7	18	2.5	30	30	11.0
POLICY	14	55	15.4	9	5	0.6
ML	8	38	6.0	8	38	3.6
RELA				11	30	4.0
Total	93	50.3	100.0	320	36.0	100.0

Continued

Table 11.6 Continued

Household category	2007			2008		
	number of borrowing households	volume per household	share on overall loan volume (%)	number of borrowing households	volume per household	share on overall loan volume (%)
Group 3						
CB	10	80	2.3	5	39	0.6
BAAC	199	54	31.6	194	57	34.9
VF	657	18	35.1	657	19	38.7
CRED	120	41	14.5	130	32	13.0
POLICY	48	18	2.6	45	7	1.0
ML	41	65	7.9	13	143	5.8
RELA	43	46	5.9	45	43	6.0
Total	1118	46.0	100.0	1089	48.6	100.0
Group 4						
CB	19	92	8.9	8	118	4.7
BAAC	164	56	47.3	170	55	46.8
VF						
CRED	69	60	21.4	76	85	32.3
POLICY	34	12	2.0	31	17	2.6
ML	56	40	11.4	26	39	5.1
RELA	58	30	8.8	57	29	8.4
Total	400	48.3	100.0	368	57.2	100.0

that VF loans do not seem to have a permanent impact on borrowing behaviour at household level. Otherwise, one would expect either that VF loans partially substitute other loans or that they are partially substituted by other loans – but we cannot observe any such behaviour.

Obviously, this raises new questions regarding the targeting of lending and the behaviour of borrowers. In subsequent work, we plan to analyse households in more detail in order to find out which circumstances may lead to a deterioration of the economic situation after losing the VF loan. Furthermore, we would like to learn about a possible impact of VF loans on small-scale businesses. Finally, we plan to extend the loans considered in order to come close to a full loan portfolio which may provide new insights into loan substitution. In any case, the VF deserves more thorough investigation.

References

Beck, T. and A. Demirgüc-Kunt (2008): "Access to Finance: An Unfinished Agenda", *World Bank Economic Review*, 22(3): 383–96.

Bell, C. (1990): "Interactions between Institutional and Informal Credit Agencies in Rural India", *World Bank Economic Review*, 4(3): 297–327.

Boonperm, J. *et al.* (2009): "Does the Village Fund Matter in Thailand?" *World Bank Policy Research Working Paper*, No. 5011.

Chen, M. A. (1997): *A Guide for Assessing the Impact of Microenterprise services at the individual level*, Management Systems International, http://www2.ids.ac.uk/impact/files/strategy/chen_impact_individual_level.pdf

Coleman, B. E. (1999): "The Impact of Group Lending in Northeast Thailand", *Journal of Development Economics*, 60(1): 105–42.

Coleman, B. E. (2006): "Microfinance in Northeast Thailand: Who Benefits and How Much?" *World Development*, 34(9): 1612–38.

Hermes, N. and R. Lensink (2007): "The Empirics of Microfinance: What Do We Know?", *Economic Journal*, 117(517): F1–F10.

Kaboski, J. P. and R. M. Townsend (2005): "Policies and Impact: An Analysis of Village-Level Microfinance Institutions", *Journal of the European Economic Association*, 3: 1–50.

Kaboski, J. P. and R. M. Townsend (2009): "The Impacts of Credit on Village Economies", *Working Paper*, University of Chicago.

Khandker, S. R. (2005): "Microfinance and Poverty: Evidence Using Panel Data from Bangladesh", *World Bank Economic Review*, 19(2): 263–86.

Krahnen, J. P. and R. H. Schmidt (1994): *Development Finance as Institution Building: A New Approach to Poverty-Oriented Banking*, Westview Press, Boulder, CO.

Menkhoff, L. and O. Rungruxsirivorn (2011): "Do Village Funds Improve Access to Finance? Evidence from Thailand", *World Development*, 39(1): 110–23.

Morduch, J. (1999): "The Microfinance Promise", *Journal of Economic Literature*, 37(4): 1569–614.

Pham, T. T. T. and R. Lensink (2007): "Lending Policies of Informal, Formal and Semiformal Lenders", *Economics of Transition*, 15(2): 181–209.

Schaaf, R. (2010): "Financial Efficiency or Relational Harmony? Microfinance through Community Groups in Northeast Thailand", *Progress in Development Studies*, 10(2): 115–29.

Siamwalla, A. *et al.* (1990): "The Thai Rural Credit System: Public Subsidies, Private Information, and Segmented Markets", *World Bank Economic Review*, 4(3): 271–95.

World Bank (2008): "Finance for all? Policies and Pitfalls in Expanding Access", *World Bank Policy Research Report*, http://siteresources. world bank. org/ INTFINFORALL/Resources/ 4099583–1194373512632/FFA_book.pdf

12
Participation in Different Regional Non-Farm Wage Activities: Evidence from Thailand and Vietnam

Jürgen Brünjes, Dominik Schmid, Javier Revilla Diez and Ingo Liefner

12.1 Introduction

The times when the rural population in developing countries and emerging economies generated virtually all their income from agriculture are long gone. Research has shown that a significant percentage of earnings nowadays are derived from non-farm activities, with Asia in general being the forerunner in this process (Haggblade *et al.*, 2007: 4). Non-farm employment can be applied to at least two contemporary concepts in development research: the discourse on vulnerability to poverty and the sustainable livelihoods framework. In both concepts, non-farm income diversification is regarded to be one amongst a wide range of options for the rural population to earn their living and to reduce risks and uncertainty (Ellis, 2000: 30). The term "non-farm employment" in this sense may include a broad range of activities and sources of income: permanent or temporary work in a large city, and employment outside the agricultural sector within the rural area. In this article, we limit ourselves to the latter, and focus on regional non-farm wage employment in six study areas in Thailand and Vietnam.

Our chapter addresses two key questions. First, not every non-farm employment offers the same opportunity to reduce vulnerability to income poverty. Its effectiveness as buffer against income losses arising from agricultural shocks may depend on several characteristics, such as the sector of employment, the wage level or the average duration of employment. By differentiating between high- and low-income activities as well as permanent and temporary employment, we aim at identifying those occupations which are best suited to reduce vulnerability. Our second main goal is to find out about factors influencing access to these different forms of non-farm employment. A special emphasis is laid on location characteristics, such as the distance to regional centres or the status of local roads. In addition to these, the relevance of selected other indicators including education is tested.

This chapter is structured as follows: Section 12.2 outlines the relevance of non-farm employment in the two above-mentioned theoretical concepts of vulnerability and livelihood, introduces the classifications and definitions of regional non-farm wage employment and gives a short overview on the data used in this article. Section 12.3 briefly presents the study areas, which comprise Buriram, Nakhon Phanom and Ubon Ratchathani provinces in Thailand's northeast, and Ha Tinh, Thua Thien-Hue and Dak Lak provinces in Vietnam. We then turn to our main empirical analysis, using descriptive and analytical statistics. The last section concludes.

12.2   Conceptual ideas and classifications

In general, non-farm employment is regarded as one possibility for households to smooth income to "reduce the risk in the income process" (Dercon, 2002: 15). In this case, a household voluntarily diversifies its income portfolio to include activities which are not prone to the same risks. Whereas agricultural income is subject to climate-related shocks, diseases and fluctuating world market prices, non-farm employment is generally influenced to a much lesser extent by such events, even if this premise may not apply in extreme cases (Fafchamps *et al.*, 1998). Other (but not necessarily fewer) risks are more relevant for non-farm employment and the associated income, including job losses or wage cuts due to macroeconomic shocks and collapsing demand, declining competitiveness of industrial sectors, increasing mechanization and so on. Especially if non-farm businesses are linked to global value chains, trends in the national and international economy may have strong impacts on the risk situation of rural households that are employed in these businesses.

Given these circumstances, it becomes clear that diversifying into non-farm activities as a risk mitigation strategy is usually well suited to reducing the risks associated with agricultural income. But at the same time, it introduces new risks, whose significance will largely depend on the characteristics of the non-farm activities taken up. In sum, diversification does not automatically lead to an overall improvement of the household's risk situation. In contrast, it might even be a sign of distress: as a result of shocks, households may be pushed into poorly paid jobs in the non-farm economy when no other income options remain. In that case, non-farm employment serves as a coping mechanism (Möllers and Buchenrieder, 2005: 24). The importance of a differentiated analysis of the various forms that non-farm employment can take is therefore evident. Once we accept that some non-farm jobs are better suited to reducing vulnerability than others, it is of course interesting to know what influences the ability of poor households to enter any such desirable employment.

This leads to our second conceptual framework, the sustainable livelihoods approach where income diversification as a means to reduce risks and vulnerability also plays an important role. Supplementing the vulnerability perspective, it offers a framework which integrates most of the important factors for rural non-farm activities. The approach has gained popularity in rural development thinking since the 1990s and can be described as holistic and bottom up (Ellis and Biggs, 2001). To a certain extent, the approach deals with aspects that have already been covered under the notion of Geographical Risk Research in the German-speaking world (Bohle, 2001; Geipel, 1992). Some of the most important contributions to the sustainable livelihoods framework have been published by Chambers and Conway (1991), Scoones (1998), Bebbington (1999), Ellis (2000) Bohle (2001) and Carney (2002). Ellis (2000) defines the term livelihood as follows: "A livelihood comprises the assets, the activities, and the access to these that together determine the living gained by the individual or the household". The livelihood process thus incorporates how individuals or households with a different composition of assets pick up a certain strategy which involves one or more activities in order to sustain their livelihood. This process is embedded in, and influenced by, a wider natural and socio-economic context. Regional non-farm wage activities can therefore be seen as one set of strategies within the livelihood process. There is disagreement in the literature about what the relevant asset categories in a sustainable livelihoods framework are (Ellis, 2000: 8); one popular arrangement comes from Scoones and comprises the following asset categories: natural, physical, human, financial, and social capital (Scoones, 1998: 7 et seq.). Natural capital refers to all natural resources that can be utilized (for example land), physical capital refers to capital that can be used in the economic production process (for example machinery), human capital refers to the education and health status, financial capital refers to monetary stocks that can be used for purchasing production or consumption goods (for example cash, savings or access to credit), and social capital refers to social networks and communities that constitute support.

Related to participation and income level in non-farm wage labour, the sustainable livelihoods approach draws attention to several relationships. First, assets can influence what kind of activity a household or an individual picks up. For example, a person with a university diploma and thus a high endowment of human capital can more easily get a job in the public administration, while a farmer without primary school education might be more likely to participate in the construction sector. Second, this activity choice also depends on a number of context conditions that are often location-specific. Any observation of regional activity participation should therefore consider locational characteristics. For example, the participation in regional non-farm wage employment depends on the availability and accessibility of regional jobs, which in turn depend on the larger socio-economic conditions and trends in the region. This assumption has been confirmed in previous empirical studies by Isgut (2004) and Deichmann *et al.* (2009). Third, as a result of the first two relationships, the asset endowment and the locational context together indirectly determine the livelihood strategy and thus affect the vulnerability of the respective household.

When studying non-farm diversification, one needs to be clear about the definitions used (Barrett *et al.*, 2001b). In this study, we define regional non-farm wage activities as being non-agricultural wage activities that are exercised by members of rural households and do not require migration. In order to exclude migrant activities, we only consider those jobs that are reached by commuting, which means that the worker has to return to the rural household on a regular basis (daily). In terms of location, regional non-farm activities can thus be in the same village or in the local countryside (rural), in a nearby town or in the provincial capital (urban). We do not exclude urban jobs, because many scholars have emphasized the importance of rural towns and agglomerations as an important part or supplement of the rural non-farm economy. In addition, our definition allows a single household or individual to have multiple activities; to consider only primary activities would mean understating the importance of rural non-farm activities (Haggblade *et al.*, 2007). For example, a farmer could be primarily self-employed in agriculture but may also have a job in the construction sector (secondary sector) and a small food stall operation (tertiary sector). This also has important implications for the statistical methodology one may apply (for example, multinominal probit or logit models can only be used for primary activities).

We classify these non-farm wage activities in three ways. First, we broadly distinguish activities in different sectors (industry, construction, private and public services). A sectoral distinction is important because from a regional development perspective, economic policies eventually need to be sector-specific. Second, because this chapter is broadly dealing with non-farm labour as a vulnerability or risk-reducing strategy, it is important to classify activities according to their income level and according to their permanence. This is because some non-farm activities are expected to do little to raise the expected income or to reduce risk exposure (Barrett *et al.*, 2001b). Many non-farm jobs even earn lower returns than the median wage in agriculture. Because of that, we apply a classification that distinguishes low-return activities that earn less than the median wage in agriculture from high-return activities that earn more than the median wage in agriculture, and we differentiate between permanent activities that are carried out throughout the whole year (12 months) from temporary activities that are carried out only seasonally or temporarily (less than 12 months).[1]

12.3 Study regions and sampling

The two countries analysed in this chapter, Thailand and Vietnam, feature significant differences in their socio-economic history. Thailand, one of the few Southeast Asian nations that have never been under colonial rule in modern times, relied to a great extent on the market economy and foreign trade during its development process after 1960 (Lohmann, 2009: 119). In contrast, Vietnam initiated profound changes to the state-directed economy only after 1986 with the *doi moi* reforms, which improved property rights, opened the economy to foreign trade and laid emphasis on fostering the private sector (Dang, 2009).

While both of these countries have made impressive progress in poverty reduction and economic growth in recent years, huge disparities between growth centres and less favoured regions persist. In this project, data was collected in three provinces in Thailand and three in Vietnam. All six provinces considered here mostly belong to those regions where incomes have risen considerably slower, and poverty rates still remain comparatively high. This is especially the case in Thailand. Buriram, Nakhon Phanom and Ubon Ratchathani provinces belong to the Northeastern region, bordering Cambodia and Laos; poverty headcount ratios in these provinces vary from 2 to 30 per cent, compared with the nationwide average of slightly less than 10 per cent (Lohmann, 2009: 146). Despite some moderately successful efforts to establish growth poles, such as the Eastern Seaboard region, outside the capital, Bangkok, the economic activity in Thailand especially in manufacturing remains very concentrated in the Central and Southeastern regions. While the average share of agricultural employment in the overall workforce is around 38 per cent on the national level (NSO, 2009: 1), all three of the Thai study provinces feature agricultural employment shares of up to 61 or 68 per cent (depending on the season), thus underlining the rural character of these areas (Lohmann, 2009: 146). To a lesser extent, this is mirrored in the share of agriculture in total GDP, which ranges from 16 per cent in Ubon Ratchathani to 21 per cent in Buriram and 22 per cent in Nakhon Phanom, compared with only 9 per cent for the national average (NESDB, 2008). Major agricultural activities include rain-fed rice as well as sugar cane and cassava cultivation. However, in contrast to other major rice-growing regions in central Thailand, the Northeast offers less favourable conditions for agriculture. Drought or floods are not uncommon (NESDB and World Bank, 2005: 149), and the water supply in general is much less stable than in the central regions, where major streams provide enough water for wetland rice cultivation. Given these natural and economic conditions, the three study provinces seem well suited to exploration of the risk management strategies pursued by the local population.

This also applies to the three study areas in Vietnam, which are slightly more heterogeneous regarding their economic conditions and natural environment. This reflects the profound regional disparities that developed in Vietnam since the shift to a more market-oriented system (Revilla Diez, 1999). The study provinces thus differ regarding infrastructure, development potential and their agro-ecological conditions. Nevertheless, they have in common a low average per capita income and high poverty rates, and a high dependence on agriculture, and are subject to special risk factors such as a peripheral location and poor infrastructure. Ha Tinh lies in the northern part of the central region of Vietnam and is the most rural of all three provinces. 88.5 per cent of the population lives in rural areas, and agriculture makes up 43.5 per cent of the regional GDP, with rice and cattle being the main agricultural products. Despite the dominance of agriculture, GDP growth between 2002 and 2006 reached 9.1 per cent on average. The growth occurred mainly in the industry and construction sector, which increased its share of GDP by more than six percentage points to 22.8 per cent (Hatinh Statistical Office, 2007: 8). Thua Thien-Hue lies in the central region of Vietnam around the city of Hue. Compared to the other two provinces, Thua Thien-Hue is relatively urban and industrialized, and experienced the highest growth rates from 2002 to 2006. In Thua Thien-Hue, 68.5 per cent of the population lives in rural areas while agriculture contributes only 20.1 per cent to the regional GDP. The secondary sector makes up 36.1 per cent of the GDP, with food processing, construction, textiles and the production of non-metal goods being the most important branches (Thua Thien Hue Statistical Office, 2007: 19, 69). The last province, Dak Lak, lies in the Central Highlands of Vietnam, close to the border of Laos. It is largely rural and dominated by agriculture; 77.6 per cent of the population lives in rural areas and agriculture makes up 53.9 per cent of GDP and 75.7 per cent of the employment. Most of the production is geared towards world markets. Main products are coffee, cashew nuts, rubber, vegetables, rice, corn and cassava. Despite the importance of agriculture, this sector is receding; the share of agriculture in GDP declined by 4 per cent, while the shares of industry and construction have increased by similar amounts (Dak Lak Statistical Office, 2007: 39).

The household data used in this chapter were collected in these provinces in the context of a research project funded by the German Research Foundation in summer 2007 (see Chapter 3). The sampling for the household survey was designed for an absolute number of 2200 households per country, according to the guidelines of the UN Department of Economic and Social Affairs. It was arranged in a three-stage procedure in which sub-districts and villages were selected with respect to size, and households were selected randomly with equal probability from household lists. In Vietnam, the first stage additionally had to be designed with respect to different agro-ecological zones (coastal, mountain, and rice plain areas) in order to not to get insufficient sample sizes in some of these zones. In Thailand, this was not necessary because the provinces in Thailand could be assumed to be sufficiently homogeneous (Hardeweg *et al.*, 2007). In order to reflect the oversampling in some areas, a weighting procedure was used in some of the analysis in this chapter.

In our sample, people are considered as household members if they were identified as such by the household head. Using this rather wide household definition, we were able to capture a good variety of non-farm activities by collecting household, household member, and job level data. Eventually, detailed information about the activities of 15,766 individuals above the age of 15 that live in households was made available. These people engaged in 1,636 regional non-farm wage activities during May 2006 and April 2007. The advantage of collecting detailed data for each of these activities is that it reveals detailed information not just about primary activities but about every non-farm activity the households were engaged in during the last year. The composition and structure of the wage labour markets in Thailand and in Vietnam are outlined in the next section.

12.4   Non-farm labour markets in Thailand and in Vietnam

The non-farm wage labour markets in the research provinces of the two countries differ with respect to their size and composition. First of all, regional non-farm wage employment is more common among rural households in Thailand than it is in Vietnam, as shown in Table 12.1. While about 24 per cent of all rural households in Vietnam participate in regional non-farm wage employment, more than 31 per cent do this in Thailand. Two general points need to be made regarding differences in the sectoral composition of the regional non-farm labour markets. While construction work is among the most important non-farm activities in both countries, private services and industry wage employment is more common for Thai rural households than for their Vietnamese counterparts. This reflects the better established private sector in rural Thailand, where the market economy has been around for a considerably longer time period.

In Vietnam, jobs in private companies have become more widespread since the shift to a more market-orientated economic system in the 1980s and 1990s, but the Vietnamese provinces have not yet reached the same level as the Thai provinces. Second, in the rural areas of both countries, the state retains an important role as an employer, because many regional non-farm jobs can be found in the public local administration or in public organizations.

Besides the sectoral classification, Table 12.1 also contains participation shares for our classification of non-farm wage activities according to their income level and permanence. It is evident that high-return permanent wage activities are about twice as common among households in Thailand than in Vietnam. Also high-return temporary activities are more widespread, demonstrating that non-farm jobs that pay more than the provincial median agricultural wage are more frequent in Thailand than in Vietnam. The picture changes for low-return permanent and temporary jobs, which have relatively low shares in both countries. These low shares are generally a good sign for the non-farm economies in both countries, as they show its potential for reducing poverty and vulnerability for rural households and for being an alternative to agricultural wage labour.

The composition of the different non-farm wage employment types is shown in Table 12.2. A large part of high-return permanent

Table 12.1 Household level participation shares in different types of regional non-farm wage employment

	Thailand	Vietnam	Design-based F-Test
Any regional non-farm wage employment	31.65%	24.39%	12.85**
Classification by sector:			
Industry	6.09%	3.90%	6.61*
Construction	11.03%	9.24%	2.78
Private services	11.55%	5.30%	33.12**
Public services	7.93%	8.03%	0.01
High-return permanent employment	12.70%	5.60%	37.66 **
High-return temporary employment	13.51%	10.43%	5.92*
Low-return permanent employment	4.81%	4.49%	0.19
Low-return temporary employment	5.54%	6.23%	0.73
N	2,186	2,195	

Note: Shares are adjusted by sampling weights. Stars denote significance of the design based F-test, a modification of the Person chi-square test that accounts for the sampling design: * $p < 0.05$, ** $p < 0.01$. Research provinces: Buriram, Ubon Ratchathani and Nakhon Phanom in Thailand and Ha Tinh, Thua Thien-Hue and Dak Lak in Vietnam.

activities consist of work in public services in both countries although to a larger degree in Vietnam. Besides jobs in public schools and hospitals, a relatively high share of these worthwhile public local jobs is provided by the local government in Thailand (village headmen, members of the administration) and by the districts' and communes' peoples committees as well as by different community unions (for example the war veterans, women or the farmers union) in Vietnam.

In addition, private service jobs (for example vendor, driver, cleaner or mechanic) and industry jobs (predominantly in textiles and apparel) also make up high shares of the high-return permanent activities. High-return temporary activities in turn are dominated by construction jobs

Table 12.2 Sectoral composition by type of regional non-farm wage employment

	High-return permanent		High-return temporary		Low-return permanent		Low-return temporary	
	TH	VN	TH	VN	TH	VN	TH	VN
Industry	17.9%	15.5%	12.1%	7.2%	23.3%	20.4%	28.6%	25.10%
Construction	8.8%	11.2%	60.2%	51.1%	7.70%	7.4%	25.7%	38.8%
Private services	35.2%	17.9%	20.6%	16.4%	39.7%	18.8%	40.7%	25.9%
Public services	38.1%	55.4%	7.0%	25.4%	29.3%	53.4%	5.0%	10.2%
Total	100.0%	100.0%	100.0%	100.0%	100.0%	100.0%	100.0%	100.0%
Design-based F-Test	4.66**		15.26**		4.22**		3.37*	
N	341	156	355	260	116	118	140	149

Note: Shares are adjusted by sampling weights. Stars denote significance of the design based F-test, a modification of the Person chi-square test that accounts for the sampling design: * $p < 0.05$, ** $p < 0.01$. Research provinces: Buriram, Ubon Ratchathani and Nakhon Phanom in Thailand and Ha Tinh, Thua Thien-Hue and Dak Lak in Vietnam.

in both countries, followed again by public service jobs (predominantly teacher) in Vietnam and by private service jobs (for example carpenter, vendor and tailor) in Thailand.

Low-return permanent activities consist again mostly of public services in Vietnam. This indicates that some of the staff that work in the commune administration or for commune unions earn lower wages than the median agricultural wage. In Thailand, low-return permanent activities are mostly private services such as watchman, vendor, or housemaid. The most common type of non-farm wage employment in both countries, namely low-return temporary activities, takes up a good share of construction activities in Vietnam, while this type of activity makes up a large part of private service activities in Thailand. In addition, both kinds of temporary non-farm activities consitute about 25 to 30 per cent of industrial jobs in Thailand and in Vietnam, mainly textiles and apparel, food processing and wood products. It can be expected that the sectoral shares among all kinds of activities will transform during the process of development and structural change; for example, while jobs in the public service sector have high shares among high-return permanent activities at the moment, this might change once the private sector develops more strongly in the rural regions.

12.5   Non-farm wage employment and household risks

It can be expected that participation in these different types of non-farm activities has a significant effect on the household's risk situation. But which activities have the highest potential in functioning as an ex-ante risk-mitigating strategy?

First, we expect that high-return activities have a risk-reducing character, because households that engage in these kinds of activities are more easily able to cope with income shocks through consumption smoothing, which could decrease the impact of the shock. Low-return activities, however, do little to improve the risk situation of the household, because with the small amount of income earned in this activity consumption smoothing cannot be applied for a long enough time. Second, we assume that permanent activities have a higher potential to reduce risks than temporary activities, because they provide a stable source of income throughout the year. Although many temporary activities are taken up over several consecutive years by rural households, there is no guarantee of future employment; while in some years firms might readily hire new labour, they may be reluctant to do so in other years due to the overall economic situation or strategic decisions.

As shown above, many temporary jobs in Thailand as well as in Vietnam form a large share of construction work activities. This sector is known to be highly sensitive to general regional economic trends, thus future employment may strongly depend on overall economic development in the region. Also, other economic sectors may change in their capacity to hire new workers, due to regional, national or global trends. For example, the local food processing industry, especially prominent in the Thai provinces, can be affected by covariate natural shocks such as drought or flooding and at same time relies on global prices for its products. Only the public sector may be less affected by global economic and natural trends (although the absolute number of jobs in this sector can be expected to remain limited). For any employer, it is usually easier to refrain from employing new temporary workers than to fire permanent employees. Therefore we can assume that the temporary workers are subject to higher risks.

A household's risk situation of course does not simply depend on those risks that persist in the non-farm economy, but is instead closely linked to very different shocks that may or may not happen in the future. Household shocks can be either covariate (community shocks like economic crisis, natural catastrophes or pandemics) or idiosyncratic (household-level shocks like death, injury or job loss). Finding an appropriate measure for the risk situation of a household is tricky because it requires the forecasting of future events. This is very difficult, as rural households find themselves in very local, complex, diverse and multidimensional realities (Chambers, 1995). Because these realities and circumstances are both very dynamic, it is not appropriate to simply rely on the evaluation of past shocks; we cannot assume that those events that happened in the past will happen to the same extent in the future and will have the same influence on the household. In addition, to observe only past events would disregard all those expected negative events that just did not occur but nevertheless influenced the decision making of the household. Another way of looking at the risk situation would be to rely on secondary data sources (for example climatic data, aerial photographs or other household surveys). However, these may not accurately reflect the complex context the individual household lives in, or may simply not be available. And even if they were, researchers would probably come to perceptions different from those of the local farmer himself (de Weerdt, 2005).

The problems of measuring a household risk situation can be tackled by asking the households directly about the shocks they expect to happen in the future (Barrett *et al.*, 2001a; de Weerdt, 2005;

Povel, 2009). The respondent may be best at capturing his or her own complex risk and vulnerability situation, and could thus be a good predictor of future shocks. In our survey, the household head was therefore confronted with several negative events and asked whether he or she expected them to happen within the next five years.[2] An event only constitutes a shock (that influences vulnerability to poverty) if it has a negative effect on the income of the household.[3] Because of that, the household head was also prompted to rate how the impact of the event on the household's income would be if it occurred in the next year.[4] Using this data, we constructed two indicators that can function as proxies for the perceived risk situation of the household. For the first indicator, we summed up the all expected shocks ES_i for each household i by only counting those events that were expected to happen within the next five years and that would have a high impact on the household income. For a second indicator, we calculated a perceived risk index PR_i that weights all events by their probability and their severity. It was calculated for each household i according to the following formula

$$PR_i = \sum_{k=1}^{n} p_{i,k} \times s_{i,k} \qquad (12.1)$$

In this formula, the probability value for an event p could have the values of 1 (will happen), 0 (will not happen) or 0.5 (don't know). The severity s in turn could have the values 0 (no impact), 1 (low impact), 2 (moderate impact) or 3 (high impact). The results were then normalized on a range from 0 to 1 using the Min–Max normalization method in each country (OECD, 2008). Both indicators display the perceived risk situation of rural households; the first indicator reveals those events that will happen with high probability and that will have a high impact on the household, while the second indicator more accurately displays the overall risk situation of a household by acknowledging that events that are uneasy to predict or that would have only a low or a moderate impact may also influence the risk situation of a household (although to a lower degree).

Although the use of such subjective measures has important advantages, as outlined above, caution is required in assessing the probabilities of uncertain events, because systematic errors can occur (Tversky and Kahneman, 1974). In our case, several key points need to be considered when interpreting the prediction of future shocks by rural households. First, a shock may be easier to imagine if it has already occurred to the same household in the past or if a respondent has heard of this shock through other sources, for example from neighbouring households or from the media. Second, households might expect that the past order of shocks influences their future order. Third, the respondents may be influenced by any values that are suggested during the process of the interview. While the last point can be addressed by good training of the interviewers and by the design of the questionnaire, the first two points show that care is needed when analysing subjective data, as respondents may be biased by occurrences and patterns of past shocks.

The most common expected types of shocks in our sample were illness of a household member, drought, flooding, unusually heavy rainfall, crop pests and livestock disease in Vietnam, and drought, illness of a household member, strong increase of output price, strong decrease of input price, flooding and job loss in Thailand. The dominance of expected shocks that involve agricultural production is not surprising, as most households in rural Thailand as well as in rural Vietnam base their income to a certain extent on agricultural activities. However, it is evident that expected shocks that are related to non-farm employment are clearly more visible in Thailand. The negative event "job loss" that directly relates to non-farm employment accounts for 8.24 per cent of all expected shocks in Thailand but for only 2.67 per cent in Vietnam, which to a certain extent reflects the higher shares of non-farm wage employment in Thailand or the more stable employment opportunities in the state sector in Vietnam. Using our database, it was also possible to calculate the total number of different types of expected shock for each household. This number is meaningful because a household that diversifies out of agriculture and participates in non-farm wage labour might be subject to fewer risks related to agricultural production and marketing of agricultural products, but could find themselves facing new risks that relate to the non-farm activity (for example job loss). Therefore, in order to have a positive impact on a household's risk and vulnerability situation, it is important to have a low number of total shocks and not just a low number of agricultural shocks.

To test our assumptions about the impact of different types of non-farm wage employment on the risk situation of rural households, we utilized standard multivariate regression models. We present here two linear regression analyses for each country. In the first regression, the dependent variable is the number of expected shocks (*ES*) and the independent variables are dummies for participation in high-return permanent wage activities, participation in high-return temporary wage activities, participation in low-return permanent wage activities, and participation in low-return temporary wage activities. It should be noted that participation in one type of employment does not rule out participation in another activity. Thus, the reference category is participation in no non-farm wage activity. In the second regression, we use the same independent variables but predict their effect on the perceived risk index (*PR*). We do not include other household or village level variables in the models, because these are often strongly correlated with participation in some of the different non-farm wage activities and we want to avoid problems of multicollinearity and mixed causality. Furthermore, it is not the aim here to fully explain perceived risk in this chapter, but rather to estimate the effect of non-farm wage employment on the perceived risk situation of a household. The effect of other household characteristics as well as of village characteristics on participation in these different non-farm activities will be shown in the next section.

The results of the regression models are shown in Table 12.3. In general, one should take into consideration the coefficients of determination being relatively low. Thus we can confirm that participation in non-farm wage employment types only explains a fraction of the risk situation that rural households face – there are sure to be some other explanatory factors that contribute to the risk environment of the household.

However, the outcomes do reveal some highly significant results that fully support our assumptions regarding the impact of high-return permanent wage activities on the risk situation of rural households. In both countries, households that participate in high-return permanent activities expect on average around 0.8 fewer shocks than households that do not participate in non-farm wage activities.

Also, the effect of such activities on the perceived risk index is highly significant in both countries. The result is due to the fact that these households expect fewer, or less precarious, risks that are related to agricultural production but also face fewer or less precarious economic risks such as job loss because their activities are generally safer and more permanent.[5]

The results for high-return temporary and low-return permanent wage employment in turn reveal no statistically significant values in any of the regressions – thus an effect of these jobs on the household's total risk situation could not be shown in any of the two countries. This indicates that the additional risks that emerge due to the non-farm wage employment outweigh the mitigated risks in other activities that the households engage in. However, it should be noted that especially the absolute numbers of households that participate in low-return permanent activities are relatively low, so that this could also lead to lower levels of significance.

Table 12.3 Impact of participation in non-farm wage activities on risk indicators

Dependent variable:	Expected Shocks (ES)		Perceived Risk index (PR)	
	TH	VN	TH	VN
Household is engaged in...				
...high-return permanent wage labour (yes = 1)	−0.76619** (−3.82)	−0.82864** (−4.44)	−0.04939** (−4.37)	−0.05588** (−3.79)
...high-return temporary wage labour (yes = 1)	−0.10785 (−0.55)	−0.27619 (−1.83)	0.00455 (0.44)	−0.01509 (−1.34)
...low-return permanent wage labour (yes = 1)	0.37139 (1.13)	0.07136 (0.30)	0.02350 (1.34)	0.01101 (0.71)
...low-return temporary wage labour (yes = 1)	0.33405 (1.21)	0.66829** (2.82)	0.00862 (0.58)	0.04198* (2.56)
Constant term	4.27305** (52.79)	2.34374** (41.93)	0.36894** (82.62)	0.28687** (70.20)
N	2186	2186	2186	2186
R^2	0.008	0.014	0.010	0.011
adj. R^2	0.006	0.012	0.008	0.009

Note: t statistics in parentheses, robust standard errors, adjusted using sampling weights
* $p < 0.05$, ** $p < 0.01$.

Participation in low-return temporary wage activities is also not significant in Thailand in both models. In Vietnam on the contrary, the results for low-return temporary activities are clearer as they have a positive and significant effect on the number of expected shock types and on the perceived risk index. We can therefore conclude that these activities expose the households to more shocks instead of improving the overall risk situation in Vietnam. However, it should be noted that this result could also be due to a reverse causality; households that live in uncertain environments and that have experienced shocks in the past may be more likely to take up low-return temporary jobs as ex-post coping strategies. In addition, as stated above, these households may perceive that they live in a more risky environment simply because of their past experiences.

To sum up, the data reveals two results. First, it shows that high-return permanent activities generally have a positive effect on the perceived risk situation of a household. Second, it shows that low-return temporary wage labour may even have a negative effect in Vietnam, although there are some serious doubts about the causality in this case. A high-return activity thus only has a significant risk-reducing effect if it is also of permanent character, and a low-return activity may only have a significant risk-increasing effect if it is temporary. In turn, permanent activities only have a positive effect when the returns for this activity are not lower than the agricultural wage, while temporary activities only have a negative effect on the risk situation if the income in this activity is relatively low. Those activities that are permanent and low return or temporary and high return eventually have no significant effect on the risk situation of a household; in these activities either the positive effect of the permanent activity is superimposed by a low income or the positive effect of having a high income is minimized by the temporary character of the job. The outcome thus fully supports the idea that non-farm wage employment is not necessarily a positive thing for rural households – it very much depends on the kind of work the household engages in. This of course is often not a free choice for the household and depends on a number of different factors that may be internal and external to the household. Thus, determinants of participation in the different non-farm wage activities are studied in the next section.

12.6 Determinants of household participation

The previous results indicate that high-return permanent activities have the highest potential to improve a household's risk situation in both countries. But what drives households to participate in these and in the other kinds of non-farm wage activities? Sustainable livelihoods frameworks, as presented in our section on conceptual issues, outline that it is the individual's and the household's assets, along with the complex contextual setting, that determine a household's livelihood strategy (Ellis, 2000; Scoones, 1998). Thus a number of studies have analysed the impact of these different assets and contextual settings on activity participation (for a good overview see Winters *et al.*, 2009). In these studies, there are a few key assets that have proven to be closely linked to participation in non-agricultural activities across very different countries and contextual settings. Land ownership is usually negatively associated with non-agricultural activities, because households that own land usually focus on different types of agricultural production. In contrast, households with higher levels of education usually enjoy better access to non-farm employment and, accordingly, increased participation rates. Infrastructure and urban proximity can also have a positive effect on non-agricultural activities, although the empirical results for this are mixed. Finally, demographics, wealth, social capital and other factors are also likely to influence the household's decision to participate in non-agricultural activities (Winters *et al.*, 2009). In our analysis, we investigate to what extent some of these key features determine participation in high-return permanent activities and in the other three types of non-farm employment in our study provinces in Thailand and Vietnam. For this purpose we used probit regression models to estimate the effects on the participation in regional high-return permanent wage activities. Independent variables in the models are gender, age, ethnicity and membership in socio-political organizations of the household head, the average number of years of schooling of the household members above the age of 15, the size of the household, the size of the household's land, the road infrastructure of the village, the size of the village and the location of the village in relation to the respective provincial capital.

The results of the regression models are shown in Table 12.4. We will focus in our interpretation on some of the key findings. First, households with an older household head are less likely to participate in most non-farm activities. At the same time, if the household head is member of a socio-economic organization the whole household is more likely to participate in high-return and low-return permanent activities in both countries. If the household head is a member of such an organization, this is an important social capital for all household members because it enables them to find well-paid permanent wage labour. In some cases, though, when the household head him- or herself is working in the non-farm wage job, the order of events might be the other way around; in this case, the household head may have become a member of an organization after getting the high-return permanent employment. For example, in Vietnam party membership is often a precondition for working in public administration; however, some people become party members directly after they have attained their job through other channels. To sum up, especially with respect to the high share of public sector activities within the permanent activities, the importance of socio-economic organizations in the rural economies comes as no surprise.

Table 12.4 Household participation in different regional non-farm wage jobs

Probit model Dependent variable: household participation in respective activity	Thailand				Vietnam			
	High-return permanent	High-return temporary	Low-return permanent	Low-return temporary	High-return permanent	High-return temporary	Low-return permanent	Low-return temporary
Household head								
Female (yes=1)	-0.00808 (-0.56)	0.00262 (0.16)	-0.01433 (-1.60)	0.01534 (1.31)	0.00177 (0.15)	0.00092 (0.05)	-0.00566 (-0.50)	0.01839 (1.11)
Age (years)	-0.00162** (-3.14)	-0.00307** (-5.12)	0.00004 (0.13)	-0.00161** (-4.10)	-0.00122** (-3.21)	-0.00208** (-3.90)	-0.00100** (-2.63)	-0.00140** (-3.42)
Member of socioeconomic organisation (yes=1)	0.06997** (2.66)	0.03070 (1.25)	0.06817** (3.25)	0.02108 (1.27)	0.02414** (2.87)	0.00707 (0.50)	0.02758** (3.57)	0.00299 (0.27)
Minority (yes=1)	-0.03003 (-1.41)	-0.03989 (-1.62)	-0.00941 (-0.61)	-0.01107 (-0.67)	-0.01191 (-1.05)	-0.04296* (-2.55)	0.01650 (1.12)	-0.03348** (-2.95)
Household								
Average schooling (years)[1]	0.02357** (8.96)	-0.00047 (-0.16)	0.00172 (1.09)	-0.00318 (-1.51)	0.01092** (6.96)	0.01086** (4.24)	0.00410** (2.74)	-0.00031 (-0.16)
Size (number)[1]	0.00802* (2.04)	0.01927** (4.33)	0.00381 (1.53)	0.00844** (2.78)	0.00074 (0.25)	-0.00638 (-1.42)	0.00379 (1.35)	0.00978** (2.80)
Land (ha)	-0.01228 (-0.80)	-0.00007 (-0.01)	-0.02012* (-1.99)	-0.00933 (-0.83)	-0.00807 (-0.37)	0.02552 (0.73)	0.02862 (1.90)	-0.20198* (-2.02)

Continued

Table 12.4 Continued

Probit model Dependent variable: household participation in respective activity	Thailand				Vietnam			
	High-return permanent	High-return temporary	Low-return permanent	Low-return temporary	High-return permanent	High-return temporary	Low-return permanent	Low-return temporary
Village								
Paved road (yes=1)	0.01988 (1.18)	0.05765** (3.56)	0.01363 (1.31)	0.00526 (0.43)	0.00283 (0.33)	0.00103 (0.08)	-0.00659 (-0.75)	-0.00286 (-0.27)
Inhabitants (number)	0.00005* (2.39)	-0.00004 (-1.61)	-0.00002 (-1.03)	0.00000 (0.29)	0.00002** (2.78)	0.00003** (2.97)	0.00000 (0.62)	0.00001 (0.97)
Distance to prov. capital	-0.00156** (-6.82)	-0.00090** (-3.87)	-0.00023 (-1.57)	-0.00015 (-0.96)	0.00003 (0.15)	-0.00136** (-4.58)	-0.00001 (-0.03)	-0.00016 (-0.66)
N	2186	2186	2186	2186	2175	2175	2175	2175
observed probability	0.127	0.135	0.048	0.055	0.054	0.105	0.044	0.063
Log likelihood	-725.68	-830.48	-404.79	-454.72	-413.55	-681.64	-376.56	-494.12
Wald test (df: 10)	186.54	67.26	39.39	24.65	68.12	74.70	32.03	25.36
Pseudo R2	0.128	0.041	0.040	0.028	0.100	0.067	0.045	0.034

Note: Standard errors are adjusted by sampling weights. Reported are marginal effects to the mean; *t* statistics in parentheses. * $p < 0.05$, ** $p < 0.01$.
[1] Only household members above the age of 15 considered.

Second, membership of an ethnic minority has different consequences in Thailand than in Vietnam. In Thailand, the effects are not significant for any activity; in Vietnam, however, minority households are less likely to be engaged in high-return temporary activities and are also less likely to have a low-return temporary job. In our sample, most ethnic minorities could be found in the Central Highlands province of Dak Lak. However, it should be noted that the local road infrastructure, the size of the village and the relative location of the household within the province (distance to provincial capital) was included in the models. Thus our results support the idea that ethnic minorities are disadvantaged because they predominantly live in areas with poor infrastructure, less access to markets and therefore fewer opportunities for off-farm work, as concluded in studies that focus more directly on the issue of ethnicity in Vietnam (van de Walle and Gunewardena, 2001; Baulch *et al.*, 2004).

Third, the level of schooling seems to be one of the most important determinants for high-return permanent activities in both countries while it is also important for high-return temporary and low-return permanent activities in Vietnam. The better educated the household members are, the more likely they are to take part in these activities. On the other hand, education seems to play no role when it comes to low-return temporary activities; these jobs do not usually require any education.

Fourth, the amount of land a household owns has a negative effect on the probability to work in low-return permanent activities in Thailand and for low-return temporary activity in Vietnam. It seems that limited access to land pushes households into regional non-farm wage activities – however, not into those activities that really reduce the risk situation of the household but rather into unstable and low-paid jobs. In turn, households with more land may for preference work on their own farm rather than sending members out to work in low-paying non-farm jobs.

Fifth, improved infrastructure, meaning the presence of a made road (one or two lanes), does not have a significant effect on participation in most non-farm activities in both countries. Only in Thailand, households that live next to a solid road participate more often in high-return temporary activities. The roads may on the one hand stimulate the local non-farm economy and on the other hand make commuting to other places such as the provincial capital more convenient.

Sixth, the size of the village generally has a positive effect on participation in high-return regional non-farm employment. This effect is significant for all high-return permanent activities in Thailand and

Vietnam. The importance of spatial concentrations of demand and economic activity is thus not only evident when it comes to rural towns and cities but can already be observed on the village level. Larger villages have a higher capacity to generate well-paid non-farm employment than smaller villages, and at the same time may be the location of most public sector activities, such as schools and local administration.

Seventh, the effect of proximity to the provincial capital differs between the provinces in Thailand and Vietnam. In Thailand, households that live closer to the provincial capital are more likely to participate in high-return permanent and temporary activities reflecting the fact that in urban proximity households have better access to well-paid jobs. This effect has also been well documented in Lohmann (2009). In Vietnam, distance to the provincial capital does not significantly influence participation in high-return permanent, but only in high-return temporary, activities. This reflects the exceptionally high share of public sector activities among the high-return permanent activities in Vietnam. Jobs for civil servants are spread out relatively evenly and can be found in any commune, hamlet or village. High-return temporary activities in turn are more probable in proximity to the provincial capital, reflecting the increasing private wage labour opportunities in peri-urban areas.

12.7 Conclusion

This article has analysed the contribution of different non-farm wage activities to the risk situation of rural households in Thailand and Vietnam, and identified factors that determine participation in these activities.

The descriptive results from our study areas confirm the importance of non-farm wage employment for rural populations, a fact that has been repeatedly acknowledged by empirical investigations. There are, however, significant differences between Thailand and Vietnam regarding overall participation rates as well as the sectoral composition of the non-farm wage employment. Households in our Thai study areas feature a participation rate which is about eight percentage points above the respective value for the Vietnamese study provinces. In addition, private services and rural industries are by far more important in Thailand than in Vietnam, reflecting the fact that the market economy has been established in Thailand for a much longer time.

We can conclude that the rural non-farm economy will only contribute to the overall objective of poverty and vulnerability reduction if (at least) two necessary conditions are met. First, in order to achieve vulnerability-reducing non-farm growth, businesses and sectors need to develop that provide high-return and permanent activities, as these are most likely to contribute to the reduction of risks for rural households. This is confirmed by our empirical investigation of the relationship between type of non-farm employment and the perceived risk situation of the household. We measured the risk situation with two differently constructed measures. Standard multivariate regression models revealed that engagement in high-return permanent non-farm activities has a significantly risk-reducing effect on both of these measures. This can be explained by two effects: First, the number of expected agricultural risks is lower due to the diversification into the non-farm sector. And second, shocks related to this non-farm employment (for example job loss) are perceived to be less likely due to the stable character of well paid permanent jobs. Other forms of non-farm wage employment, in contrast, do not show any overall robust influence on a household risk situation. There is even evidence that temporary low-return employment correlates with an increase in the risk situation of rural households in Vietnam. This would suggest that risks associated with non-farm employment outweigh any reductions in expected agricultural risks in low-return temporary activities or that those households that live in very risky environments use temporary non-farm wage employment as ex-post coping strategies. In our data we find that the rural non-farm economy in our study areas is not yet able to provide large amounts of risk-reducing employment activities to rural households, and those jobs that exist are often in the public sector. However, there are some permanent jobs that provide an income above the provincial median agricultural wage and they are more widespread in Thailand than in Vietnam.

The second condition that should be met is that rural households are able to access these risk-reducing activities. We applied multivariate probit models in order to gain insights into the determinants of the different non-farm activities. Some factors stand out with regard to their importance for participation in different forms of non-farm employment. A higher level of education significantly increases the participation in high-return permanent jobs, as does the membership in a socio-economic organization. At the same time, location plays a role as well, with increased village size also increasing the likelihood of employment in high-return permanent jobs. Being close to the provincial capital has a positive effect in Thailand, while in Vietnam no such effect can be observed yet, due to the more equal distribution especially of high-return public service jobs. Proximity to the provincial capital is already significant for the privately dominated high-return temporary activities in both countries. Thus, it may become also observable for high-return temporary activities in Vietnam once the private sector develops.

Some open questions remain that are of crucial importance in order to derive fair policy conclusions. First, and maybe most importantly, it needs to be clarified which sectors have the highest potential to provide risk-reducing employment to rural households in the future. At the moment, public services account for the largest share of regional high-return permanent activities in both countries. However, state budgets are limited and further public sector jobs will only intensify state dependence in rural areas. Thus, while it can be reasonable to hold up the absolute number of public sector activities in rural areas, it may be desirable to increase the relative share of the private sector, which may have a higher growth potential on the long run. In Thailand, the private sector already makes up a larger share of the high-return permanent activities than in Vietnam. Here, it should be noted that in most industries that provide high-return permanent activities, such as the textile or the agrofood industry, most activities are low return or temporary while only a small amount is high return and permanent. Thus, even growth in manufacturing does not necessarily provide exclusively risk-reducing employment opportunities for rural household members; eventually, each region will have to find its own strategy in order to exploit its endogenous development potentials. Future research should be directed towards identifying these potentials for each particular region and at the same time carefully evaluating the impact of non-farm growth, in certain branches, on the risk situation of rural households.

The second open question is on how to enable rural households to access risk-reducing activities. We identified entry barriers for high-return permanent wage employment, such as the level of education and social capital along with locational opportunities. It is safe to assume that more public investment in education and vocational training can address at least the first of these above-mentioned barriers. It is more difficult – if not impossible – however, for external actors to influence social capital and locational issues. It thus remains a daunting challenge for policymakers in both countries to generate an environment that stimulates pro-poor non-farm development on the one side and that enables rural households to participate in these developments on the other.

Notes

1. The median wage in agricultural wage labour was PPP US$8.2 in Buriram, PPP US$8.0 in Ubon Ratchathani, PPP US$7.8 in Nakhon Phanom, PPP US$6.1 in Ha Tinh, PPP US$6.3 in Thua Thien-Hue, and PPP US$7.8 in Dak Lak (own calculations based on household survey).
2. Possible categories were "yes", "no" and "don't know".
3. Because our overall objective is to make statements about the vulnerability to poverty of the household, to look at risk exposure alone is not enough. As Calvo and Dercon (2005) note, the term "vulnerability" refers to a general defencelessness or helplessness of the affected people, and is thus not the same as risk exposure.
4. Possible categories were "high", "moderate", "low" and "no impact".
5. See Appendix 12.A.1 for models that predict the effect of non-farm wage labour on different kinds of expected shocks.

References

Barrett, C., K. Smith and P. Box (2001a): "Not Necessarily in the Same Boat: Heterogeneous Risk Assessment Among East African Pastoralists", *Journal of Development Studies*, 37: 1–30.

Barrett, C., T. Reardon and P. Webb (2001b): "Nonfarm Income Diversification and Household Livelihood Strategies in Rural Africa: Concepts, Dynamics, and Policy Implications", *Food Policy*, 26: 315–31.

Baulch, B., Chuyen, T. T. K., Haughton, D., and Haughton, J. (2004): "Ethnic Minority Development in Vietnam: A Socioeconomic Perspective", in: Paul Glewwe, N.A. and D. Dollar (eds): *Economic Growth, Poverty, and Household Welfare in Vietnam*, World Bank Publications, Washington DC.

Bebbington, A. (1999): "Capitals and Capabilities: A Framework for Analysing Peasant Viability, Rural Livelihoods and Poverty in the Andes", *World Development*, 27(4): 739–52.

Bohle, H.-G. (2001): "Neue Ansätze der geographischen Risikoforschung. Ein Analyserahmen zur Bestimmung nachhaltiger Lebenssicherung von Armutsgruppen", *Die Erde*, 132: 119–40.

Calvo, C. and S. Dercon (2005): "Measuring Individual Vulnerability", Economics Series Working Papers.

Carney, D. (2002): "Sustainable Livelihoods Approaches: Progress and Possibilities for Change", mimeo, Department for International Development, London.

Chambers, R. (1995): "Poverty and Livelihoods: Whose Reality Counts?" *Environment and Urbanization*, 7: 173–204.

Chambers, R. and G. Conway (1991): "Sustainable Rural Livelihoods: Practical Concepts for the 21st Century", IDS Discussion Paper.

Dak Lak Statistical Office (2007): *Statistical Yearbook 2006*, Thang.

Dang, H. L. (2009): Strukturwandel und außerlandwirtschaftliche Beschäftigung in Vietnam: Rahmenbedingungen, Potenziale und Hemmnisse der Unternehmensentwicklung, Dissertation, Naturwissenschaftlichen Fakultät der Leibniz Universität Hannover, Hannover.

De Weerdt, J. (2005): "Measuring Risk Perceptions: Why and How", SP Discussion Paper, No. 0533.

Deichmann, U., F. Shilpi and R. Vakis (2009): "Urban Proximity, Agricultural Potential and Rural Non-farm Employment: Evidence from Bangladesh", *World Development*, 37: 645–60.

Dercon, S. (2002): "Income Risk, Coping Strategies, and Safety Nets", *World Bank Research Observer*, 17: 141–66.

Ellis, F. (2000): *Rural Livelihoods and Diversity in Developing Countries*, Oxford University Press, New York.

Ellis, F. and S. Biggs (2001): "Evolving Themes in Rural Development 1950s-2000s", *Development Policy Review*, 19: 437–48.

Fafchamps, M., C. Udry and K. Czukas (1998): "Drought and Saving in West Africa: Are Livestock a Buffer Stock?" *Journal of Development Economics*, 55: 273–305.

Geipel, R. (1992): Naturrisiken. Katastrophenbewältigung im sozialen Umfeld, Darmstadt, Wiss. Buchges.

Haggblade, S., P. Hazell and T. Reardon (2007): "Introduction", in: Haggblade, S., P. Hazell and T. Reardon (eds), Transforming the Rural Nonfarm Economy – Opportunities and Threats in the Developing World, International Food Policy Research Institute (IFPRI).

Hardeweg, B., Praneetvatakul, S., Duc, T. P. and Waibel, H. (2007): "Sampling for Vulnerability to Poverty: Cost Effectiveness versus Precision", mimeo, Proceedings of Tropentag 2007 – Conference on International Agricultural Research for Development, University of Kassel-Witzenhausen.

Hatinh Statistical Office (2007): Statistical Yearbook 2006, Statistical Publishing House, o.A.

Isgut, A. E. (2004): "Non-Farm Income and Employment in Rural Honduras: Assessing the Role of Locational Factors", *Journal of Development Studies*, 40: 59–86.

Lohmann, C. (2009): Außerlandwirtschaftliche Beschäftigung im ländlichen Thailand. Ursachen, Auswirkungen und Zugangsfaktoren, Nomos, Baden-Baden.

Lohmann, C. and I. Liefner (2009): "Location, non-Agricultural Employment, and Vulnerability to Poverty in Rural Thailand", Erdkunde, 63: 141–60.

Möllers, J. and G. Buchenrieder (2005): "Theoretical Concepts for the Analysis of non-Farm Rural Employment", *Quarterly Journal of International Agriculture*, 44: 19–36.

NESDB (2008): "Gross Regional Product and Dross Provincial Product 2007", National Economic and Social Development Board, Bangkok.

NESDB and World Bank (2005): *Thailand Northeast Economic Development Report*, World Bank, Bangkok.

NSO (2009): "Labour Force Survey 2008 – Executive Summary", Bangkok.

OECD (2008): Handbook on Constructing Composite Indicators: Methodology and User Guide, OECD Publishing, Paris.

Povel, F. (2009): "Vulnerability to Downside Risk", mimeo, University of Göttingen.

Revilla Diez, J. (1999): "Vietnam – Addressing Profound Regional Disparities", Southeast Asian Affairs, 1999: 358–74.

Scoones, I. (1998): "Sustainable Rural Livelihoods: A Framework for Analysis", IDS Working Paper, 72.

Thua Thien Hue Statistical Office (2007): *Statistical Yearbook 2006*, Hue.

Tversky, A. and D. Kahneman (1974): "Judgment under Uncertainty: Heuristics and Biases", *Science*, New Series, 185: 1124–31.

Van de Walle, D. and D. Gunewardena (2001): "Sources of Ethnic Inequality in Viet Nam", *Journal of Development Economics*, 65: 177–207.

Winters, P., Davis, B., Carletto, G., Covarrubias, K., Quiñones, E. J., Zezza, A., Azzarri, C. and Stamoulis, K. (2009): "Assets, Activities and Rural Income Generation: Evidence from a Multicountry Analysis", *World Development*, 37: 1435–52.

Appendix 12.A.1 Impact of participation in non-farm activities on different expected shocks

	Expected Shocks (ES)							
	Demographic		Social		Agricultural		Economic	
	TH	VN	TH	VN	TH	VN	TH	VN
Household is engaged in...								
...high-return permanent (yes=1)	-0.12095* (-2.43)	-0.19088** (-2.82)	-0.04220 (-1.02)	-0.05447 (-1.89)	-0.22833** (-2.78)	-0.38179** (-4.18)	-0.37418** (-3.71)	-0.20149* (-2.37)
...high-return temporary (yes=1)	-0.06955 (-1.47)	-0.11337* (-2.24)	-0.10246** (-2.74)	-0.01076 (-0.41)	0.01315 (0.16)	-0.10905 (-1.24)	0.05154 (0.50)	-0.04302 (-0.66)
...low-return permanent (yes=1)	-0.07538 (-1.04)	0.00151 (0.02)	0.05705 (0.77)	-0.06296* (-2.08)	0.08496 (0.65)	0.00104 (0.01)	0.30524 (1.75)	0.13177 (1.19)
...low-return temporary (yes=1)	0.07941 (1.03)	0.13345 (1.87)	0.00408 (0.07)	0.07703 (1.94)	0.03479 (0.30)	0.25257* (2.03)	0.21620 (1.41)	0.20524 (1.91)
_cons	0.66681** (33.00)	0.57586** (28.51)	0.43655** (25.84)	0.15183** (16.02)	1.21455** (36.31)	1.08133** (36.08)	1.95448** (45.16)	0.53472** (20.45)
N	2186	2186	2186	2186	2186	2186	2186	2186
R^2	0.004	0.007	0.004	0.005	0.004	0.008	0.008	0.005
adj. R^2	0.002	0.005	0.002	0.003	0.002	0.006	0.006	0.003

Note: t statistics in parentheses, robust standard errors, adjusted using sampling weights * $p < 0.05$, ** $p < 0.01$.

Appendix 12.A.2   Sample summary statistics for linear regressions on risk indicators

Variable	Obs	Mean	Std.Dev	Min	Max
Thailand					
Expected Shocks (ES)	2186	4.20	3.18	0	18
Perceived Risk Index (PR)	2186	0.40	0.24	0	1
Household is engaged in...					
...high-return permanent wage labour (yes=1)	2186	0.13	0.33	0	1
...high-return temporary wage labour (yes=1)	2186	0.13	0.34	0	1
...low-return permanent wage labour (yes=1)	2186	0.05	0.21	0	1
...low-return temporary wage labour (yes=1)	2186	0.06	0.23	0	1
Vietnam					
Expected Shocks (*ES*)	2186	2.41	2.32	0	15
Perceived Risk Index (*PR*)	2186	0.15	0.17	0	1
Household is engaged in...					
...high-return permanent wage labour (yes=1)	2186	0.06	0.24	0	1
...high-return temporary wage labour (yes=1)	2186	0.11	0.31	0	1
...low-return permanent wage labour (yes=1)	2186	0.05	0.22	0	1
...low-return temporary wage labour (yes=1)	2186	0.06	0.24	0	1

Appendix 12.A.3   Sample summary statistics for probit models on participation in different non-farm jobs

Variable	Obs	Mean	Std. Dev	Min	Max
Thailand					
Household head					
Female (yes=1)	2186	0.27	0.44	0	1
Age (years)	2186	54.64	13.36	23	104
Member of socioeconomic organization (yes=1)	2186	0.11	0.31	0	1
Minority (yes=1)	2186	0.07	0.25	0	1
Household					
Average schooling (years)[1]	2186	5.25	2.43	0	17.33
Size (number)[1]	2186	3.75	1.60	1	16
Land (ha)	2186	0.48	0.57	0.0	9.9
Village					
Paved road (yes=1)	2186	0.83	0.37	0	1
Inhabitants (number)	2186	676.20	309.62	7	2200
Distance to prov. capital	2186	56.33	32.63	2	200
Vietnam					
Household head					
Female (yes=1)	2175	0.16	0.36	0	1
Age (years)	2175	47.82	13.94	17	99
Member of socioeconomic organization (yes=1)	2175	0.70	0.46	0	1
Minority (yes=1)	2175	0.21	0.41	0	1
Household					
Average schooling (years)[1]	2175	5.20	3.03	0	15.5
Size (number)[1]	2175	3.45	1.59	1	9
Land (ha)	2175	0.09	0.19	0	4.076
Village					
Paved road (yes=1)	2175	0.50	0.50	0	1
Inhabitants (number)	2175	812.60	650.05	153	4500
Distance to prov. capital	2175	42.09	27.42	4	130

[1] Only household members above the age of 15 considered.

Index

Printed and bound in Great Britain by
CPI Antony Rowe, Chippenham and Eastbourne